Beneath the Backbone
of the World

THE DAVID J. WEBER SERIES IN THE
NEW BORDERLANDS HISTORY

Andrew R. Graybill and Benjamin H. Johnson, editors

Editorial Board

Juliana Barr
Sarah Carter
Kelly Lytle Hernández
Cynthia Radding
Samuel Truett

The study of borderlands—places where different peoples meet and no one polity reigns supreme—is undergoing a renaissance. The David J. Weber Series in the New Borderlands History publishes works from both established and emerging scholars that examine borderlands from the precontact era to the present. The series explores contested boundaries and the intercultural dynamics surrounding them and includes projects covering a wide range of time and space within North America and beyond, including both Atlantic and Pacific worlds.

Published with support provided by the William P. Clements Center for Southwest Studies at Southern Methodist University in Dallas, Texas.

Beneath the Backbone
of the World

Blackfoot People and the
North American Borderlands,
1720–1877

Ryan Hall

The University of North Carolina Press CHAPEL HILL

*This book was published with the generous financial support of the
Colgate University Research Council.*

Set in Merope Basic by Westchester Publishing Services

The University of North Carolina Press has been a member of the
Green Press Initiative since 2003.

Library of Congress Cataloging-in-Publication Data
Names: Hall, Ryan, 1986– author.
Title: Beneath the Backbone of the World : Blackfoot People and the North
American Borderlands, 1720–1877 / Ryan Hall.
Other titles: David J. Weber series in the new borderlands history.
Description: Chapel Hill : The University of North Carolina Press, [2020] |
Series: The David J. Weber series in the new borderlands history | Includes
bibliographical references and index.
Identifiers: LCCN 2019041166 | ISBN 9781469655147 (cloth ; alk. paper) |
ISBN 9781469655154 (paperback ; alk. paper) | ISBN 9781469655161 (ebook)
Subjects: LCSH: Siksika Indians—History—18th century. | Siksika Indians—
History—19th century. | Siksika Indians—Foreign relations. | Kainah Indians—
History. | Piegan Indians—History. | Great Plains—Colonization—History. |
Canadian-American Border Region—History.
Classification: LCC E99.S54 H28 2020 | DDC 978.004/97352—dc23
LC record available at https://lccn.loc.gov/2019041166

Cover illustration: Karl Bodmer, "Great Camps of the Piekanns near Fort
McKenzie," from Maximilian Wied, *Travels in the Interiors of North America* (London:
Ackerman and Co., 1843). Courtesy of the Beinecke Rare Books and Manuscript
Library, Yale University.

For Becca

Contents

Illustrations and Maps

MAPS

Acknowledgments

The process of researching and writing this book has been more challenging and more rewarding than I ever could have imagined when I began. I could never have reached this point without immense support in both my professional and personal lives, and I owe many debts. Whatever strengths this book may have exist because other people lifted me up throughout this journey.

First, I must thank the brilliant collection of scholars who have taken the time to read the manuscript at various stages of its evolution. Sarah Carter, Michel Hogue, Andrew Graybill, John Mack Faragher, Ned Blackhawk, Joanne Freeman, Jay Gitlin, and Becca Loomis all read the entirety of the work at different points, and I am deeply grateful for their guidance and insights. Stephen Aron, Carolyn Podruchny, Boyd Cothran, Gerald and Joy Oetelaar, George Colpitts, Dave Petruccelli, Max Scholz, Andrew Offenburger, Ben Johnson, and Eric Meeks all read at least a chapter or provided invaluable feedback. I have also shared portions of my written work with several working groups, including the Yale Group for the Study of Native America, the Imagining and Inhabiting Northern Landscapes group at the University of Toronto, the History of Indigenous Peoples Network at York University, the Western History Workshop hosted by the University of Washington, and the Newberry Library's American Indian Studies Workshop. Thank you to everyone who took the time to read my work and who challenged me to do better.

I am also grateful for the guidance and advice I received from historical communities in Montana and Alberta, and in the Blackfoot nations themselves. Rosalyn LaPier has inspired me with her incisive and imaginative scholarship and her commitment to the Blackfeet community. As I was just beginning my research in 2010, I emailed Rosalyn and she generously invited me to a conference at the Blackfeet Reservation's Piegan Institute on the topic of dogs in Blackfoot history and culture. The experience impressed on me deeply the richness and complexity of the Blackfoot experience. In subsequent visits to Browning, I had edifying conversations with Carol Murray, Darrell Norman, Lea Whitford, Marvin Weatherwax, Ginny Weeks, Woody Kipp, and especially the late Darrell Robes Kipp. At the University of

Montana, Bill Farr and Kate Shanley took the time to meet with me and give me good advice. In Fort Benton, the guys at the Overholser Historical Research Center, especially the late Bob Doerk, pointed me toward sources on early Montana history. In Lethbridge, Ryan Heavy Head and Sheila McManus both gave me valuable guidance. Ted Binnema, Gerhard Ens, Alice Kehoe, Elizabeth Fenn, and Pekka Hämäläinen each helped to orient me early on and graciously shared their wealth of research experience on the northern plains, despite my being a newcomer to their field.

My career has taken me to several stops, each of which has shaped my perspective on this history. During my graduate studies at Yale University, I benefited from an extraordinary group of mentors and friends. Ned Blackhawk championed my research and pushed me to immerse myself in Indigenous studies and to strive for incisive argumentation. He also proved a spirited adversary on the basketball court most Friday mornings. John Mack Faragher has always given me sage advice and impressed upon me how to behave both as a scholar and as a colleague in this profession, and how to build arguments carefully from a deep foundation of empirical research. He has remained a trusted mentor and friend long after I graduated. Joanne Freeman, Jay Gitlin, Paul Sabin, Chuck Walton, George Miles, and many other members of the Yale community challenged me to hone my craft at every step. At the same time, I learned a great deal from the amazing friends I made in graduate school, including Dave Petruccelli, Max Scholz, Caitlyn Verboon, Chris Bonner, Andrew Offenburger, Taylor Spence, Tiffany Hale, Alice Baumgartner, and many others. I could say a great deal about each and every one of them and the many times they inspired me to grow and learn.

Living and working in Canada deepened my appreciation for northern history, beginning with my two years as a fellow at the University of Toronto's University College (U.C.). I am grateful to U.C. principal Donald Ainslie and vice-principal John Marshall for giving me the opportunity to start my career at an amazing institution and to truly immerse myself in Canadian history and culture. My office neighbors VK Preston and Scott Rayter made U.C. a fun place to spend my days. Boyd Cothran and Tanya Cothran introduced me to the city of Toronto, and Robert Bothwell and Tim Sayle reached out to welcome me from the University of Toronto History Department.

After leaving Toronto I spent one marvelous semester as a Fulbright Canada Research Chair at the University of Calgary (U of C), in the heart of traditional Blackfoot territory. The U of C History Department gave me the incredible opportunity to teach an original course on Blackfoot History and Culture, the first course of its kind in the department. I owe a great deal to my amazing students in that class, who challenged me in all the right ways and learned alongside me in a spirit of humility and respect. I also learned a great deal about Alberta's deep history from U of C archaeologists Gerald Oetelaar and Dale Walde, and had the pleasure of spending an afternoon with Hugh and Paulina Dempsey, the longtime pillars of Alberta's historical community. I am also grateful to all the great friends I made in Calgary, especially Shannon Murray and Ryan Blaney, Frank Towers and Jewel Spangler, Donald Smith, and Annette Timm and Scott Anderson (along with their daughter, Maddie, and cats Effis and Stella), who suffered me to live in their basement for a very reasonable rent.

For the last two years I have taught at Northern Arizona University in beautiful Flagstaff, Arizona. I am thankful to all of my colleagues in Flagstaff, including Eric Meeks (with whom I have spent many an afternoon discussing borderlands history over martinis at The Annex), Tom Finger, Ryan Kashanipour, Heather Martell, Jeremy LaBuff, Daniel Burton-Rose, Ana Varela-Lago, Leilah Danielson, Sanjay Joshi, Sanjam Ahluwalia, Linda Sargent Wood, Scott Reese, Christi Carlson, Paul Dutton, Mike Amundson, and my chair, Derek Heng. By the time this book is in print I will have begun a new position at Colgate University in Hamilton, New York. I thank my department chairs Rob Nemes and Heather Roller, as well as Carol Ann Lorenz, Chris Vecsey, and Antonio Barrera for welcoming me into this new community.

Finally, I thank my family. My mother, Bonnie Hall, and my late father, Daniel Hall, instilled in me a love of history and learning from a young age. I'm sorry my father couldn't have been here to see this project unfold and to explore the northwest plains with me. I am grateful for my sister, Lauren, and her husband, Chad, who have always been there for me and given me good advice. I am grateful for my indefatigable niece and nephew, Avery and Carter Little, for reminding me there is more to life than history books. I am grateful for my in-laws, Jim and Carol Loomis, who have supported me and welcomed me into the Loomis clan. Thanks to my sister-in-law, Kat (the BOAPSIL), and my brother-in-law, Rich, for being true friends and always buoying my mood. Lastly, I thank my wife, Becca Loomis, the smartest and funniest person I know. She has gone through a great deal during the writing of this book and has supported me in every imaginable way through many ups and downs. I can't imagine how I could have done it without her love, so I dedicate this book to her.

Introduction

Late in the summer of 1832, a Blackfoot chief named Stámiksoosak, or Bull Back Fat, and his wife Buffalo Stone Woman visited a fur trading post called Fort Union, situated at the confluence of the Missouri and Yellowstone Rivers in what is now North Dakota. The visit was cause for excitement for the traders there, since Bull Back Fat was one of the most powerful chiefs in the three Blackfoot nations, which made him one of the most powerful Indigenous people in all of North America. The chief touted a lifetime of war deeds and commanded respect across the northern Great Plains. As a leader, he carefully curated his appearance to radiate authority. He painted his face a brilliant vermilion red, a carefully trimmed lock of hair falling across the bridge of his nose. Intricate circular designs of porcupine quills—the product of countless hours of women's careful needlework—adorned the chest and shoulders of his shirt. Upon his collar hung more than a dozen locks of human hair.[1]

Like any good chief, he was also an accomplished diplomat who could inspire either fear or trust when it suited him. His greatest achievement had come just a year earlier, when he had helped broker a peace between the Blackfoot and Americans that ended decades of bitter and bloody conflicts. The chief thus met a warm reception from the grateful traders at Fort Union, who greeted him with gifts and salutes. True to form, Bull Back Fat made clear that he had not traveled several hundred miles just to exchange pleasantries and used the occasion to deliver a fearsome warning. He told the Americans that he was "anxious" to be friends with them, but only if they came to Blackfoot lands solely to trade. If the traders did as he wished, they "would be well treated" and would have nothing to fear. If they ignored his warnings and trapped furs themselves, however, he assured them that his warriors "would kill whenever they found them." The Americans promised to oblige.[2]

About a year later, Bull Back Fat undertook another journey, this time northwest across the broad undulating prairies of his homeland, to visit a British trading post more than five hundred miles away from Fort Union. There he met a friendly reception from the British Hudson's Bay Company men who, like the Americans, made every effort to flatter and woo the chief.

Bull Back Fat came to Fort Union in 1832 both to honor and to intimidate American traders, then sat for this portrait during his visit. The chief made a strong impression on his portraitist, who mused that the Blackfoot were "perhaps the most powerful tribe of Indians on the continent." (George Catlin, *Stu-mick-o-súcks, Buffalo Bull's Back Fat, Head Chief Blood Tribe*, 1832, Smithsonian American Art Museum, Gift of Mrs. Joseph Harrison Jr.)

They likely greeted him with a gun or cannon-fire salute, then offered him tobacco and presented him with rum and other gifts. Privately, however, the British grumbled that the chief had become a "vagabond," having made friends with the hated Americans despite decades of ties with the British.[3] By moving back and forth between American and British domains, Bull Back Fat made the British traders feel suspicious and powerless, but the chief felt perfectly comfortable inspiring these resentments. Such was the price of his friendship. The Blackfoot dominated the northwest plains precisely because of these journeys. Bull Back Fat knew that Blackfoot country sat at the crossroads of North America's two great empires but was beholden to neither, which allowed Blackfoot people like him to shape circumstances for their own needs.

This book is about Blackfoot people like Bull Back Fat and the world they created for themselves during the era of the fur trade. Beginning in the 1720s, Blackfoot people thought constantly about how to organize their relationships with strangers and outsiders, how to adapt to changing ecologies and economies, and how to preserve their vitality as a people. They drew from a deep well of experience. At the time of Bull Back Fat's visit to Fort Union, the people who came to constitute the three Blackfoot nations—the Kainai, Piikani, and Siksika—had already lived on the northwest plains for more than a millennium. They dominated a region nearly the size of Germany, stretching from the North Saskatchewan River in the north, past the Missouri River in the south, and extending east from the foot of the Rocky Mountains hundreds of miles onto the Great Plains. Knowledge of this region, its history, its natural features, and its religious connotations defined Blackfoot identity. Starting in the early decades of the eighteenth century, this ancient homeland became subject to extraordinary transformations. Until the signing of their final treaty with non-Native settlers in 1877, the essential challenge for Blackfoot people was to manage these changes while maintaining their own sovereignty, territory, and peace of mind. Between 1720 and 1877, the Blackfoot used the northwest plains' unique geography to create one of the most vibrant and lasting Indigenous homelands in North America.

The circumstances of Bull Back Fat's era are all the more remarkable when viewed within the long scope of Blackfoot history. Bull Back Fat's journey would have seemed almost unimaginable to his forebears, who lived very different lives from him. As late as the 1710s, Blackfoot people defined the limits of their world almost entirely by how far they could walk. They had little use for boats, since their rivers were shallow and winding, and they had nothing that could carry them across their homelands' huge expanses of prairie. Nevertheless, they moved often, hauling their possessions on their backs or attaching them to their dogs using travois. They went to war rarely, and when they did they carried wooden and stone weapons. These predecessors of Bull Back Fat likely may have been perturbed to see the twelve scalp locks fringing his chest, which flaunted a lifetime's worth of killing. They would have marveled at his steel weapons and envied his vermilion face paint. They would have been amazed at the relative ease of his five-hundred-mile journey between the Americans and the British. And of course, they would have been fascinated by the strangers he met.

The Blackfoot's traditional way of life forever changed around the 1720s, when horses and European manufactured goods first arrived on the northwest plains. Blackfoot people saw opportunity in these changes and embraced them. They became some of the most skilled raisers of horses on the continent despite the sometimes-deadly cold of their homelands. They mastered new forms of warfare. They used technologies to speed up their daily tasks and crafted relationships that gave them privileged access to trade goods. Women developed new artistic styles and found new ways to build status. To maintain access to these new advantages, the Blackfoot became savvy trade partners and sometimes forceful adversaries to the whites who began to populate the region in the 1780s, whom they called *náápiikoan*.[4] They exploited the strategically important location of their homelands, which neatly bridged two of the continent's major watersheds (those of the Saskatchewan River basin, whose waters drained into Hudson Bay, and the Missouri River, whose waters drained to the Gulf of Mexico), to play the outsiders against one another and to shape the diffusion of new technologies. The Blackfoot became masters at turning circumstances to their advantage and as a result became one of the most formidable Native polities in all of North America.

But this is not only a story of power; it is also a story of powerlessness, loss, and instability. During the era of the Blackfoot's ascendancy, waves of European disease swept across the land and killed much of their population. These repeated traumas changed Blackfoot relationships to one another and to the world around them. More insidious changes crept into their lives as well. Indigenous nations became locked in a bitter arms race for horses, guns, and captives, and the northwest plains became more violent than they had ever been. Warfare grew easier and more essential to young men, who became obsessed with proving their value through combat. Women became more vulnerable to captivity and abuse. Blackfoot people became dependent on trade with outsiders and participated in the gradual destruction of the northwest plains' ecology. Ultimately, as the fur trade waned and bison populations collapsed, the Blackfoot were forced to look to government treaties to ensure their survival. Their encounter with the náápiikoan brought extraordinary wealth, opportunity, and influence, but it ultimately robbed them of control over most of the northwest plains, and with it their own destiny as a people.

This book asserts that Blackfoot history offers unique and essential insights into North America's Indigenous past. From the late eighteenth through the mid-nineteenth century, the Blackfoot were among the most powerful, prosperous, and geographically expansive polities in all of North

America. The Blackfoot accomplished this in large part by recognizing and mastering the transnational dimensions of their homeland. They stifled and rerouted early Canadian, British, and American exploration, and controlled the flow of European technologies like guns and metal weaponry into the trans–Rocky Mountain West for more than a generation. Later, the Blackfoot negotiated the expansion of American fur companies onto the Upper Missouri River to spur competition with the British, thus creating a borderland—in this case, a contested space between rival colonial projects—where there had been none. Blackfoot history illuminates how Indigenous people creatively managed colonial geography to their own benefit, to great consequence. The Blackfoot ascendancy is therefore essential to understanding the history of the U.S. and Canadian West.[5]

The foundations of the Blackfoot ascendancy lay in their careful management of the disruptions brought on by Europeans' arrival in North America, many of which swept across their homelands long before actual European exploration or settlement on the northwest plains. Around the 1720s, Blackfoot people experienced the arrival both of horses and of European manufactured goods like steel weapons, tools, and textiles. These arrivals had a profound impact on Blackfoot life. By the middle of the eighteenth century, their homeland had become a tempest of competition and reorganization, as competing peoples vied for access to transformative new technologies and animals. Eventually, every corner of the continent would experience similar disruptions, and Native people everywhere had to rethink fundamental aspects of their lives as they became enmeshed in what historian James Merrell has called the "Indians' New World." Rarely, if ever, did these changes arrive in such quick succession and with such intensity as in Blackfoot country. The unique confluence of these phenomena, and Blackfoot people's creative response to it, makes their history an important study in colonial change far beyond the traditional settler "frontier."[6]

Blackfoot history therefore also forces us to expand our framework for "early" North America to include regions that have long been considered remote or peripheral. By the early eighteenth century, places like the northwestern Great Plains had already undergone changes that were no less dramatic or essential than those experienced in and around European settler colonies along the East Coast. Yet despite recognition of this reality, historians continue to define early North American history in terms of European settlement, and focus overwhelmingly on the East Coast, and to a lesser extent the Spanish Southwest.[7] These geographic limitations have obscured and marginalized the dramas playing out at the same time in the continent's interior, where the rippling impacts of European colonization re-shaped Indigenous life far in advance of European explorers and settlers. Our map of early North America needs to expand beyond its narrow confines and engage with the experiences of people like the Blackfoot; only then can historians truly reckon with the impact of "Old" World expansion upon "New" World societies.

The Blackfoot experience also uniquely demonstrates the transformative impact of the fur trade on the North American West. The fur trade has re-ceived scattered attention from historians in recent years, particularly the trade west of the Mississippi River. Historians have mostly plumbed fur trade history for ethnographic insights, including stories of intermarriage, family networks, and the formation of ethnic identities.[8] U.S. historians in partic-ular portray the fur trade era as an ephemeral and ultimately transitionary period that laid the foundation for the more important stories of settler co-lonialism and state expansion.[9] But the fur trade also played an essential role in the diplomatic and political history of the West. Far more than an exchange of pelts, what we call the fur trade involved a huge variety of Native and non-Native goods, and sometimes included humans themselves. These ex-changes changed daily life for generations of Indigenous people, especially women. They also created new incentives for Indigenous people to change their hunting, gathering, and farming practices, and incited new conflicts. The fur trade shaped how Blackfoot and other Indigenous people understood their relationships with outsiders, even after exchanges waned. Blackfoot history reveals the fur trade as an arena in which Indigenous people and whites reconceptualized, negotiated, and contested political power.

Blackfoot history is likewise essential because it forces us to look beyond national borders in both Indigenous and Western North American history. North Americans are accustomed to thinking of their histories along a hori-zontal axis: the United States and Canada both began as settler colonies along the East Coast and eventually expanded to the Pacific, so naturally the most important stories must proceed from east to west. This master narrative has an especially strong hold on American history with its fixation on an ever-expanding "frontier."[10] In this formulation, Indigenous history requires only a simple reversal of perspective, to "face east" from besieged homelands. Such an orientation, however, can obscure the more complex dynamics of Indigenous life. On the northwest plains, the most important connections ran north and south, between British-claimed lands that would eventually become Canada and American-claimed lands that would become part of the United States. Rather than bracing against a slowly expanding westward frontier, the Blackfoot positioned themselves between rival empires, traveling north and south as it suited them, and preserving their own homeland in the process.

This book therefore demonstrates connections between U.S. and Canadian history and offers grounds for transnational comparison. Because the U.S.-Canadian border eventually split Blackfoot country in half, Blackfoot history during this era has often been understood in the context of either of two separate national histories.[11] But Blackfoot history transcends modern borders. By placing Blackfoot people at the center of the story and looking outward, we can see key connections between these national histories and recognize how Indigenous people linked the United States and Canada in creative ways. We can also see the fundamental similarities between the western histories of the United States and Canada, whose people tend to see their expansionary origins as far more different than they actually were, for better or worse.

Emphasizing Indigenous people's "agency"—that is, their power to shape circumstances to their own ends—entails opportunities and pitfalls. This book, like others before it, shows Indigenous people as creative and not simply reactive, and demonstrates how they impacted colonial North American history in important ways. These insights reframe Indigenous North America as a place full of contingent possibilities instead of a doomed homeland fated to be colonized. At the same time, some scholars have pointed out that a focus on Indigenous nations' agency can itself marginalize historical actors by ascribing fixed identities and motivations upon them, thereby implicitly labeling other forms of adaptation, like diaspora, intermarriage, or ethnic reformation, as failures. A focus on agency also runs the risk of downplaying the very real traumas and losses that Indigenous people suffered as a result of European colonization.[12] This book takes these critiques seriously. Not all Blackfoot people followed the same path. Blackfoot power was always circumscribed; Blackfoot people were never all-powerful, and they suffered profound and irrevocable losses. But as political actors, they showed brilliant creativity in trying times, and shaped the circumstances of their own lives and those around them for generations.

Finally, Blackfoot history is illustrative in the connection it shows between geographical persistence and political resiliency. The most influential histories of Indigenous agency in the prereservation era have emphasized the role of geographic mobility to Indigenous power, be it the Comanches' move from the intermountain West onto the southern plains, the Lakota Sioux's dramatic expansion from midwestern woodlands onto the northeastern plains, or the political reformations of refugee groups in the "middle ground" of the Great Lakes region. The Blackfoot wrested considerable power and influence in their own right, at times rivaling even the Comanches' or Lakotas' in scope. But their history also differs in fundamental ways. Instead of using newfound mobility to conquer new lands or peoples, the Blackfoot used it to master the existing geography of their homeland. As a result, the geographical boundaries of Blackfoot country, with some fluctuation, remained remarkably stable during the fur trade era.

At its heart, this is a history of a people, a place, and the connection between them. The northwest plains, though long seen as barren, liminal, or divided by outsiders, had extraordinary coherence for the Blackfoot. Knowledge of this region's rivers, hills, plants, animals, and supernatural forces empowered and motivated them. Blackfoot identity could exist outside of the northwest plains, and Blackfoot people did—and do—build lives outside of them. But especially in the period discussed in this book, the northwest plains were essential to who the Blackfoot were as a people, and to what they accomplished.

This book unfolds chronologically over three parts. Part I, "Homelands," examines the period from around 1720 to 1806, when the Blackfoot adapted their traditional livelihoods, belief systems, and environmental practices to ecological and economic changes. Chapter 1 provides an overview of Blackfoot life on the northwest plains prior to the eighteenth century. Beginning in the 1720s, the arrival of horses and metal goods through Indigenous trade networks changed their traditional practices but also provided new opportunities that Blackfoot people embraced. Chapter 2 describes the period from 1782 until 1806. Following a devastating smallpox epidemic, the Blackfoot established direct trade with non-Native people for the first time. They carefully structured their relationships with newcomers, repurposing regional traditions of peaceful exchange for a new era. At the same time, they deliberately prevented the British and Canadians from expanding their trade into new regions, thus securing crucial advantages for themselves.

Part II, entitled "Boundaries," deals with the period between 1806 and 1848, a time when Blackfoot people confronted increasing colonial activity and competition in their homelands. Following the expeditions of Canadian David Thompson and the American Corps of Discovery in 1806, the Blackfoot adopted new strategies for managing outsiders that combined violent conflict and careful diplomacy. After rejecting an entire generation of American fur traders and trappers, Blackfoot leaders brokered a deal in 1831 that brought Americans onto the Missouri River and facilitated the creation of a contested borderland between British and American fur trade companies. As the midpoint of the nineteenth century approached, the Blackfoot had grown dependent on British and American markets and goods but were also at their most expansive, wealthy, and influential.

Part III, "Collisions," details the period from 1848 to 1870, a time defined by traumatic conflict and rapid change, as the extractive colonialism of the fur trade era gave way to state expansion and settler colonialism. South of the international border, U.S. government officials made ambitious plans to displace and marginalize the Blackfoot by the early 1850s. Chapter 5 focuses in particular on the 1855 Blackfeet Treaty, a crucial turning point in Blackfoot history. While U.S. treaty commissioners believed the treaty would facilitate rapid immigration and settlement, Blackfoot signers imagined that the treaty would strengthen their position in the region. Chapter 6 shows how by the late 1860s escalating tensions exploded into open conflict in what became Montana, culminating in the U.S. massacre of an entire Piikani band in 1870. By the 1870s, Blackfoot people in Montana faced little choice but to settle on reservations or flee to Canada. The epilogue examines treaty negotiations between Blackfoot leaders and Canadian officials in 1877, which formalized the colonial relationship that defines Blackfoot country today.

Reconstructing this history poses many challenges. As a non-Native person, I recognize that there are limits to my knowledge and my capacity to understand the nuances of Blackfoot culture. In this book, I have primarily used written sources to reconstruct key elements of Blackfoot historical actions, and I have therefore relied in large part on what might be called a "colonial archive": documents written or mediated by outsiders like myself.[13] Fur trade journals, including the bounteous records of the Hudson's Bay Company, form the most important source base for the early chapters. In later chapters, records from government officials, travelers, explorers, settlers, and journalists become essential. These sources' depictions of Blackfoot people reflect the biases of authors who sought to justify their own actions and reify their notions of superiority. However, these sources also provide an indispensable window into Blackfoot history when read carefully. I have tried whenever possible to locate and privilege sources written by Blackfoot people or that include Blackfoot voices. Blackfoot winter counts, interviews, memoirs, and reminiscences, as well as archaeological scholarship, have improved my understanding of this history immeasurably, as has groundbreaking work written by Blackfoot and other Indigenous scholars.[14]

In this book I have attempted to use language that is respectful and historically accurate, but also accessible to nonspecialist readers. The word "Indian," while considered unacceptable in Canada today, is still used widely in the United States and reflects the language used during the time period covered in this book. I have generally opted to use the adjectives "Indigenous" and "Native," and when I use the word "Indian" it is to refer to whites' perspectives. (Canadian terms like "First Nation" and "Aboriginal" are largely twentieth-century adoptions and have little purchase in the United States.) For the main subjects of this book, I have chosen to use the word "Blackfoot," since it is the most common word used by the modern-day Blackfoot nations to refer to themselves collectively, and in the region "Blackfeet" is generally used to refer specifically to residents of the Blackfeet Reservation in the United States. For the three historic Blackfoot nations, I have used names and spellings used by those nations today: Kainai, Piikani, and Siksika.[15] I have attempted to use specific band names whenever possible as well, but sources often make such identification difficult.

Terminology for the non-Native actors in this book is also complicated, particularly in the lands that became Canada. Most of this book occurs prior to Canada's 1867 confederation, and during this period "Canada" generally referred to the region formerly known as New France, surrounding the St. Lawrence River and eastern Great Lakes in what is now Quebec and Ontario. Prior to 1867, I use "Canadian" to refer to people and organizations based in this particular region, especially the Montreal-based North West Company. I use "British" to refer to people and organizations from or based in Great Britain and tied directly to the British Empire, especially the London-based Hudson's Bay Company. I use "American" to refer to people and organizations from the United States.

Between 1720 and 1877, these sets of actors met on the northwest plains to form an extraordinary and troubling history. As a result of the events of this era, Blackfoot nations today continue to occupy the same homelands they have trod for more than a millennium, but the borders and dynamics of power have changed. Blackfoot reservations and reserves are relatively new, but Blackfoot country is an ancient place. When profound changes began to unfold there three centuries ago, the Niitsitapi (Real People) responded with resolve and ingenuity. This is the story of how they survived, suffered, and prospered in that place.

PART I | Homelands,
1720–1806

CHAPTER ONE

Náápi's Place

> In our belief system this is where we were put. It provides. The
> water, the plants, the berries, the birds. It's all part and parcel.
> —NARCISSE BLOOD (Kainai), 2003

> We point out to our children various places where Napi slept,
> or walked, or hunted, and thus our children's minds become
> impressed.
> —BIG PLUME (Siksika), 1888

At the dawn of the twentieth century, elders in the windswept reservation town of Browning, Montana, welcomed a young Piikani researcher named David Duvall into their homes and explained to him where their people came from. In interview after interview, the elders explained that their history began many ages before 1877, the year of the last Blackfoot treaty when Duvall was born. It began in ancient times, when the Creator Sun had covered the world in a great flood of water, and the only land above the water was a tall mountaintop. On that dry island lived Náápi, or Old Man, surrounded by the different animals of the earth. After some time living on this island, Náápi grew curious about what lay below the water that surrounded him, so he asked his companions to dive in and investigate. One by one, they plunged deep into the water while Náápi watched and waited. The otter went first, but after a few moments he floated back up to the surface, drowned. Then the beaver went, but he drowned as well. The muskrat volunteered next, only to meet the same fate. Finally, the duck volunteered. As with the others, the duck drowned and floated to the surface, but Náápi noticed that its webbed feet were now packed with mud. Náápi took the mud in his hands, molded it, and blew into it. He then dipped it in the water three times and dropped it in. The submerged ball of earth grew and grew until it burst from the flooded depths. In time, rains came to make plants sprout from the fecund soil. This ball of earth became the world as we know it today.

Náápi and Kipitáaakii, or Old Woman, then traveled the surface of the land and crafted the landscape, the animals, the plants, and the people. Together they decided how the people would look and how their bodies would work. Náápi suggested that people's eyes should align vertically on their face,

13

but Kipitáaakii convinced him they should be set crosswise. Náápi thought people should have ten fingers on each hand, but Kipitáaakii said that was too many, and that they should have four fingers and a thumb. Most importantly, Kipitáaakii convinced Náápi that when people died, they should die forever, to ensure that they felt empathy for one another during life. After making the people, the creators showed them how to hunt, how to fight, how to collect roots and berries, and how to stay warm. In these early days the people had no language, so one day Náápi gathered them all together on top of Chief Mountain and gave them each cups of different colored water, then bade them to speak. When they opened their mouths, each person who drank a different color produced a distinct sound, and thus the different peoples of the world were divided. When the people who drank black water opened their mouths, the language that came out was Blackfoot. Their homes would be at the base of the great mountains where Náápi molded the world, where the languages were given, and where Náápi and Kipitáaakii would remain forever to watch over the people. The Blackfoot dubbed these peaks the "Backbone of the World."[1]

Archaeologists and anthropologists mostly tell a different story, but one that likewise emphasizes continuity with an ancient past. These scholars say that Blackfoot people and their ancestors have lived on the northwest plains of North America for at least one thousand years, and perhaps much longer. They speak an Algonquian language, meaning they share a historical lineage with an array of peoples whose homelands today lie mostly in eastern woodlands, including the Potawatomis, Crees, Foxes, Ojibwes, and Shawnees. Many Algonquian oral traditions place their distinctive cultural origins along the Atlantic coast, though some archaeologists have argued that these kindred nations originated in the vast forests and lake-lands ringing Hudson Bay, and that they fled south when a cooling climate shrunk the northern forests. Others have suggested that the Algonquian languages originated in the Great Lakes region. From there, some Algonquian groups broke off from the others and for reasons now lost to us, made their way to the western plains between 1,000 and 1,700 years ago. These westering Algonquian-speakers included those who became Blackfoot.[2]

Whatever their origins, the people who now know themselves as Blackfoot have lived on the northwest plains for a very long time. By the time of their first contact with Europeans in the eighteenth century, the Blackfoot-speaking people of the northwest plains had come to know themselves as the Niitsitapi, or Real People. The Niitsitapi consisted of three kindred nations: the Siksika, or Black Foot people, so named for a story of walking across a

Chief Mountain plays a central role in the Blackfoot origin story. The distinctive peak is now located in Glacier National Park, just west of the Blackfeet (South Piikani) Reservation in Montana. (Photo by author.)

burnt prairie; the Kainai, or Many Chiefs people, so named for an ancient custom of their members each introducing themselves as chiefs when visiting other nations; and the Piikani, or Scabby Robes people, so named for a time when some women did a poor job preparing bison robes. Only later, long after the first European visitors mistook the northernmost nation's name for that of the whole, did they begin to refer to themselves collectively as Blackfoot.[3]

Their arrival on the northwest plains represented the most important and transformative moment in Blackfoot history until around three hundred years ago, when their way of life once again underwent profound upheaval. During their first millennium-plus on the northwest plains, Blackfoot people fit their lives to the lands around them (and sometimes fit the land to their lives). They learned how to keep warm during the harsh winters; how to use plants for medicine, ceremony, and food; how to stalk, fool, and kill bison; how to make and transport fire; how to keep balance with animal life; how to maintain access to water; how to keep peace with their many human neighbors; how to build relationships with the supernatural world; and how to imbue their landscape with meaning. The Blackfoot taught themselves to thrive on the northwest plains through centuries of experience, and they had no reason to believe that future generations would live any differently than they had. But during the early years of the eighteenth century, the foundations of their world changed. Gigantic new animals appeared, intelligent and swift of foot, which could carry humans upon their backs. Fabulous new materials appeared that were shiny, sharp, and hard as rocks, which revolutionized daily tasks. A new device appeared that made deafening noise and killed with bewildering speed. Violent conflict became more common. These changes would test Blackfoot tradition and force them to reshape their ancient way of life.

BLACKFOOT PEOPLE MADE their homelands in the far northwest corner of the Great Plains, a massive swath of dry grasslands in the continent's interior that stretches from the Rio Grande River through the western United States and into Canada. Prone to capricious weather patterns, aridity, and drought, the northwestern sections of the Great Plains consist mostly of treeless shortgrass prairie, but key features punctuate the region's monotony. To the west, the prairies give way abruptly to the thickly wooded foothills of the Rocky Mountains, whose peaks create a jagged line of peaks across the sky that today include Banff and Glacier National Parks. Rivers like the Oldman, Bear (now known as Marias), and Belly carry melted snowpack from the peaks east onto the plains, carving deep valleys and providing shelter for lush groves of cottonwoods to line their banks. North of the Bow River (where the city of Calgary now stands), the prairies begin to transform into transitional partially wooded areas known as parklands, which then give way to dense sub-Arctic forests north of the North Saskatchewan River.

Blackfoot people traversed all parts of this vast and varied environment. Traditionally, the Rocky Mountains formed the western boundary of Blackfoot territory, while the North Saskatchewan River marked its northern edge. The eastern and southern boundaries were less easily fixed by environmental features. In the period after 1300 C.E., Blackfoot homelands generally extended east to the Eagle Hills in what is now Saskatchewan, and at least as far south as the Missouri River in what is now western Montana. At their most expansive, Blackfoot territories measured around three hundred miles from west to east, and five hundred miles from north to south—an area comparable in size to the present-day state of Montana or the country of Germany. Most of the Siksika bands lived in the northernmost portions of this territory, in the mixed parkland environment between the Battle and North

Saskatchewan Rivers. The Kainais and Piikanis ranged to their south, in territories composed mostly of undulating shortgrass prairies situated closer to the mountains. A landscape of huge skies and boundless horizons, the northwest plains likely sustained between ten and fifteen thousand Blackfoot people at the beginning of the eighteenth century.[4]

The northwest plains were more than just an environmental setting to the Blackfoot, for they also contained a rich archive of historical knowledge and supernatural power. Landmarks of Náápi's creation journeys affixed Blackfoot identity and history throughout the northwest plains. The Blackfoot saw such reminders wherever they went. For example, two large buttes north of the Teton River marked a spot where Náápi once stumbled and fell to his knees. Ancient man-shaped arrangements of stones on hillsides across the region marked the places where Náápi had lain down to rest. An oblong clearing containing several boulders near the sources of the eponymous Oldman River marked the place where Náápi had once stopped to play the hoop-and-arrow game, a popular Blackfoot pastime. Elsewhere, a massive split boulder reminded visitors of the time Náápi gave his robe to an exposed rock then took it back, prompting a frantic chase that ended with the angry boulder breaking apart. Northward near the Porcupine Hills stood a cliff used for bison hunting known as Old Women's Buffalo Jump, the site of the story of when a group of women scorned Náápi, prompting him to turn himself into a lone pine tree that watched over the site long after. According to many storytellers, Náápi and Kipitáaakii continued to dwell in the nearby mountains, making them an inescapable presence that forever loomed on the western horizon.[5]

Adults used Náápi stories to impart lessons to new generations of Blackfoot youth. As bands made their annual journeys across the prairies, they stopped at landmarks to tell stories, to sing, and to perform ceremonies. In 1888, a Siksika chief named Big Plume explained to a visitor, "We point out to our children various places where [Náápi] slept, or walked, or hunted, and thus our children's minds become impressed." Telling Náápi stories served several purposes. It taught new generations about the Blackfoot's ancient presence on the landscape and carried the implicit lesson that that connection was worth defending. It conveyed crucial life lessons and values. Prone to the human foibles of selfishness and impulsivity, Náápi's actions often provided lessons in how *not* to behave toward others, as in the case of Náápi taking his robe back from the boulder. Stories also carried ecological lessons. Spiritual sites were often located at important environmental locations, such as stands of trees, river crossings, or mountain passes. Mapping Blackfoot

Blackfoot elders taught that this massive boulder in the Alberta town of Okotoks (so named after the Blackfoot word for big rock) split in two after it chased Náápi across the prairies. Stopping to tell stories at familiar locales formed an important part of Blackfoot travels during the Opened season and imprinted Blackfoot history and identity on the landscape. (Photo by author.)

history onto these locations taught children about the reciprocal relationships between the Blackfoot and the environment that surrounded them. In effect, the landscape itself became a repository of Blackfoot history and knowledge, and the very act of traveling educated every generation anew. The presence of these historical places in the heart of Blackfoot territory marked the lands as sacred and essential. The northwest plains were the center of the Blackfoot world, and had been for countless generations.[6]

Blackfoot elders also took care to educate children about the supernatural realities that animated the lands around them. To Blackfoot people, the visible realm represented only a portion of reality, which in fact consisted of three distinct but interrelated dimensions. The Above world was home to celestial beings like the Creator Sun, the Moon, and the Morning Star, as well as visible beings like the raven. The Water world consisted of underwater beings like fish, otters, and beavers, as well as forceful spirits like Wind Maker, who lived in Saint Mary Lake in what is now Glacier National Park. (Eating creatures from the Water world was considered taboo, so fish rarely entered Blackfoot diets.) Finally, the Below world consisted of the human beings and other land creatures, as well as spirits like Cold Maker, who lived in the north. Knowledge of these three worlds was essential to Blackfoot identity, and Blackfoot people could gain special power by developing alliances with the supernatural beings that lived all around them, like the raven, the mouse, or the beaver. Blackfoot people could make supernatural allies by interacting with them in person or in dreams, or by purchasing the alliance from another person. Especially potent supernatural alliances gave some Blackfoot people the power to control the weather or to charm bison herds, but they employed these formidable powers only rarely. Alliances with the bear or the bald eagle, according to Kainai elder George First Rider, could give people the ability to heal the sick. Religion, and the supernatural knowledge it bestowed, profoundly shaped Blackfoot thinking and gave them the confidence to thrive in the plains environment.[7]

Practical knowledge likewise linked the people to the land, and through the generations Blackfoot people learned to find bounty in the prairie landscape. During the warmer months of the year, women collected more than forty-five different types of roots, berries, and other edible plants. The most important was the prairie turnip, which they ate raw, cooked, or pounded into flour to thicken soups. To unearth turnips and roots from the hard soil, women either invaded the underground burrows of small mammals or wore rawhide belts in order to lean their bodyweight onto heavy digging sticks. In the late summer they collected berries from mountain foothills and river valleys. To make these seasonal foods last year-round, women dried roots and berries in the sun, or combined the latter with bison fat to make a high-calorie food called pemmican. Wild plants grew in sufficient abundance that Blackfoot people cultivated no plants themselves besides a breed of tobacco they used for ceremonial purposes. Beyond food, foothills and river valleys also provided wood for burning, poles for lodges and travois, shafts for arrows and spears, pipe stems, and material for building seatbacks, drying racks, and children's toys. The ground itself provided clay that women used to create bowls and other receptacles. Although European and North American explorers on the Great Plains typically fixated on the perceived scarcity and monotony of what some called the "Great American Desert," the Great Plains were in fact a land of plenty for Blackfoot people.[8]

While women collected plants and prepared food, tradition obligated that men do the hunting. The northwest plains' vast herds of bison provided plenty of targets, but the animals' size and speed forced hunters to plan carefully. The most spectacular method involved stampeding entire herds over cliffs known as *pisskans*. Highly trained "runners" used a variety of tactics to move the herd in the desired direction. Sometimes they set small fires on

These Kainai women, pictured in 1924, display their knowledge of ancient technologies like dog travois and digging sticks. Behind them, their painted lodge covers tell complex stories based on the relationship between the Above, Below, and Water worlds. (Glenbow Archives, NA-3331-2.)

the prairie. Other times a designated runner donned a bison robe and approached a herd from downwind while mimicking the sounds and movements of a stranded calf, thereby engaging the herd's instinct to surround and protect him. When the herd approached, the runner backed away, eventually leading the herd in the direction of preplanned drive lines. Men and women then leapt up from behind stone piles as the herd trotted by, panicking them into a stampede that led directly over a cliff. As scores of bison tumbled to the earth, armed hunters stood ready to dispatch any survivors. (Their most heavily used site, known as Head-Smashed-In, recalled the unfortunate fate of a young man who became overeager to watch the spectacle from below—another story that elders used as a lesson for impressionable youth.) If no cliff was available, hunters lured small herds into "pounds," which were often circular constructions of covered brush that trapped panicked bison into confined areas for slaughter. Other times they simply surrounded bison on foot. When the hunt concluded, women and men together butchered the animals, whose meat, fat, and grease provided sustenance throughout the year; whose heavy woolen furs kept them warm during the winter months; and whose stretched hides literally provided the shelter over their heads. Bison formed the material foundation of Blackfoot life. As one chief cautioned his first ever British visitor in 1754, the Blackfoot "could not live without Buffalo flesh."[9]

Centuries of experience taught Blackfoot people to value the region's delicate ecological balance and the supernatural forces that helped maintain it. Relationships with beavers were especially vital. During the bison's late summer mating season, hunting on the plains became dangerous and unpredictable, so Blackfoot bands retreated to river valleys to hunt and pick berries. Unfortunately, this move often coincided with late-summer droughts that could desiccate those same valleys. Beaver dams solved this problem because they created reservoirs for water, thereby sustaining grasses and foliage and attracting diverse animal life. As an added benefit, beaver-felled trees and branches provided wood for Blackfoot fires. Beavers were also crucial supernatural allies for Blackfoot people. According to Blackfoot stories, sometime in the distant past a beaver named Kitaiksísskstaki, or the Not Real Beaver, gave his supernatural power and knowledge to a human visitor, and prominent Blackfoot families continued to maintain that power through their sacred collections of objects known as beaver bundles. Fittingly, beaver bundle owners earned the title *iiyaohkiimiiksi*, or "the ones that have water," because by maintaining the bundle they maintained a direct tie to the Water world of the beavers. These bundle keepers took on the obligation of maintaining the stories that accompanied the bundle's contents as well as the sacred alliance with the beaver. Although the rivers and streams in and around the northwest plains hosted significant beaver populations, Blackfoot people maintained an aversion to hunting or eating them because, as First Rider later explained, "We consider them holy."[10]

Beyond supernatural alliances, mastering the prairie landscape required knowledge, mobility, and cooperation, especially during the summer months the Blackfoot called the "Opened season." During the Opened season, bands moved camp around a dozen times to follow bison herds, collect berries and roots, and cut lodge poles. Blackfoot people traveled in independent bands numbering between 80 and 160 people, which took on distinctive names like the Hard Top Knots, the Black Patched Moccasins, and the Lone Eaters. Toward the end of summer, the bands of each of the three nations gathered together to hold religious ceremonies, which reaffirmed their collective bonds while providing opportunities to socialize with members of other bands. Frequent movement necessitated careful planning. When moving camp, women either carried lodges and possessions themselves or attached them to the backs of dogs using travois. Known as *imitáá*, or "spirits that travel with us," dogs were the Blackfoot's only domesticated animal and Blackfoot people valued them highly for their strength and loyalty. The Blackfoot's special relationship with dogs meant that they would only eat them when facing starvation. During the winter months, or the "Closed season," Blackfoot bands retreated to river valleys to shelter themselves from the bitter cold. Although Blackfoot people have often been referred to as "nomadic" by outsiders, they spent about six months of the year in one place and even their summer movements followed familiar routes. They knew the land well and rarely wandered.[11]

People made plenty of time for socializing during both the Opened and Closed seasons, which kept camps lively and vivacious. Children passed the time pretending to fight wars, hunting gophers by bow and arrow, cradling baby dolls, and playing husband and wife. Parents doted on their children and the community frowned on physical punishment. When children became old enough, perhaps six or seven, they began to help their parents with daily tasks. Girls learned to cook, gather food, and maintain the home, while boys learned to hunt and fight. Although labor was clearly divided along gender lines, not everyone conformed. Some biological males lived as women and as wives, and some females hunted and went to war. Women with assertive personalities who bucked traditional gender roles became known as "Manly-Hearted Women" and were held in high esteem. For most people, marriage occurred after adolescence, in the late teens for women and the mid-twenties for men. Families played a major role in matchmaking. Girls' parents often took the lead in identifying potential husbands for their daughters, interviewing a boy's parents and investigating his family background to ensure there were no close blood ties. Marriages typically took place during the summer religious ceremonies, close to the groom's family, but afterward couples generally stayed closer to the wife's family and husbands became members of their wife's band. This was not a fixed rule, however, and depending on living arrangements, couples could sometimes join the husband's band. Men sometimes married multiple wives, especially in communities where women outnumbered men.[12]

Blackfoot people depended on wise leadership to keep their families safe and healthy. Each band generally selected its own leader, or chief, who governed by building consensus among band members. Chiefs gained support by demonstrating generosity toward others and by exhibiting bravery and success in warfare. In times of conflict, bands sometimes chose a war chief in addition to their regular civil chief. Some chiefs held more power than others, and during summer encampments or communal hunts, conjoined bands often chose a "head chief" to lead them temporarily, but typically no band leader had the power to compel members of other bands to his will. Kainai, Siksika, and Piikani bands acted according to shared interests and based on a common cultural heritage but did not share any formal alliance or confederation. Politically diffuse but culturally united, Blackfoot people reaffirmed their distinct identity through shared language, cultural practices, ceremonies, and relations with outsiders. Although they shared no formal confederation, every Kainai, Piikani, and Siksika person understood herself or himself as part of the collective Niitsitapi, drinkers of Náápi's black water who were forever linked together and distinct from others.[13]

The Blackfoot drew physical and cultural boundaries, though they also mingled frequently with their neighbors. Although outsiders have often assumed that Native borders were less fixed than those of Europeans, the Blackfoot clearly marked their boundaries, often using painted and carved images on rocks and along well-known trails and mountain passes to clearly identify Blackfoot territory to travelers as a distinct and sovereign space. At the same time, Blackfoot people relied on exchange with outsiders and hosted frequent visitors. For thousands of years, trade networks funneled goods from throughout North America onto the northwest plains. Archaeological sites in Alberta have yielded copper from the Great Lakes, shells from the Gulf of Mexico, beads from the Pacific coast, and, most abundantly, flint from what is now North Dakota. Few if any Blackfoot individuals actually traversed these huge distances; instead, goods made their way to the northwest plains after passing through a series of regional trade centers and rendezvous. The margins of Blackfoot territory hosted several of these meeting places. Located at the junction of mountains, plains, and forest environments, Blackfoot territory often served as a meeting ground for peoples with radically different lifestyles and interests.[14]

Blackfoot people traded frequently with the diverse Native peoples in the mountains and foothills to their west. Kootenai, or Ktunaxa, people lived in the lands surrounding the Kootenai River drainage, just across the Rocky Mountains from the headwaters of the North Saskatchewan and Bow Rivers. The Kootenais shared many cultural similarities to plains groups, especially in their ceremonies and clothing, but most lived in the grassy plateaus west of the continental divide. Kootenai hunting parties frequently traveled east onto the plains to collect bison for pemmican, and at least one Kootenai band may have lived on the plains year-round. The Flathead people (today mostly known as Bitterroot Salish), as well as their close Pend d'Oreille relatives, lived in the valleys and plateaus to the Kootenais' south. Like the

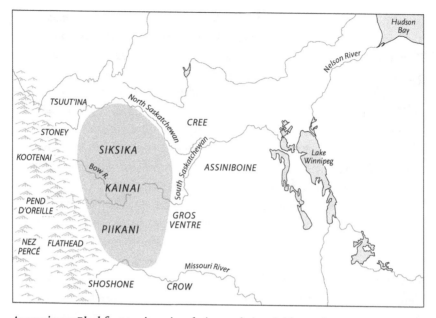

Approximate Blackfoot territory in relation to their neighbors, circa 1780.

Kootenais, Flathead and Pend d'Oreille bands made their homelands in the foothills and mountains, but frequently traveled to the plains between the Yellowstone and Missouri Rivers to hunt. The homelands of Nez Percé, or Nimiipuu, peoples were slightly farther west, and they likewise traveled frequently through mountain passes to chase bison, as did smaller nations like the Kalispell and Spokane. Pend d'Oreille and Flathead traders held regular trade rendezvous near the present-day city of Missoula, and also maintained trading routes that ran north along the Rocky Mountain foothills, through which traders brought woven baskets, stones and pipes, shells, and other goods to Blackfoot and Kootenai bands in return for robes, skins, and other goods.[15]

Trade also connected the Blackfoot to the powerful nations inhabiting the wooded regions to their north and east. Cree, or Nehiyaw, people spoke an Algonquian language distinct from Blackfoot and maintained a diverse presence through much of what is now Canada, from the Atlantic coast through the lands ringing Hudson Bay and into the forests surrounding the North Saskatchewan River. Some Cree bands likely moved west and established themselves in the parklands south of the North Saskatchewan River by at least the fifteenth century C.E., which placed them on the northern margins of Blackfoot territory. To the north and east of the Blackfoot lived Assiniboine, or Nakoda, people, Siouan speakers who like the Crees adapted to a mixed lifestyle in forests and parkland areas. Assiniboine territories followed the North Saskatchewan River system, extending from Lake Winnipeg west into what is now central Saskatchewan. Assiniboine and Cree bands maintained close ties to one another and occupied many of the same territories. The Stoneys, a smaller group closely related to the Assininiboines, lived in the woodlands and foothills to west of the Blackfoot. To the Blackfoot's northwest, in the parklands north of the North Saskatchewan River, lived the Tsuut'ina (sometimes called Sarcee) people, Athapascan speakers who had separated from the woodland-based Beaver people and moved south sometime around the seventeenth or eighteenth century. The Tsuut'inas numbered less than a thousand, and they maintained mostly positive relations with their more powerful Blackfoot neighbors. Woodland Crees maintained a series of rendezvous sites along the Saskatchewan River where these woodland and plains people socialized and exchanged goods.[16]

Finally, Blackfoot people kept close ties with other Indigenous nations of the plains. Gros Ventre, or A'aninin, people lived to the east, between the North and South Saskatchewan Rivers, a homeland that sometimes overlapped with the eastern portions of Blackfoot territory. Speakers of an Algonquian language, the Gros Ventres broke off from the Arapahoes of the central plains and made their way north at some point in the sixteenth or seventeenth century. Like the Tsuut'inas, the less populous Gros Ventres maintained mostly positive ties with the Blackfoot, especially after 1806. Crow people, or Absaalooké, lived on the plains beyond the Yellowstone River to the southeast. Crow history followed a similar trajectory to the Gros Ventres, in that they broke off from the horticultural Hidatsas of the central Missouri River valley sometime around the seventeenth century and developed an independent identity by moving north and west. And finally, Shoshone people lived to the Blackfoot's southwest, on the high prairies south of the Missouri River's headwaters. Ancestrally residents of the Great Basin, the eastern Shoshones moved onto the plains around the year 1500 by adopting a lifestyle based on bison hunting. In addition to trading directly with one another, members of these plains nations sometimes congregated at the trading center villages of the horticultural Mandan, Hidatsa, and Arikara peoples along the Missouri River in what is now North Dakota. Much of the Blackfoot's flint originated in these communities, likely making its way to the

Blackfoot through Cree and Assiniboine intermediaries who visited from the north, or through Crow, Arapaho, and Gros Ventre traders who came from the west.[17]

Trade intertwined communities in many ways. In addition to exchanging goods, different nations frequently intermingled socially and shared games and ceremonies. Intermarriage, captive-taking, and adoption were all common practices, and most communities had foreign-born guests or outsiders living among them. Visitors and foreign-born community members often translated during trade and could serve as key diplomats when unfamiliar peoples crossed paths. If such translators were unavailable, people communicated through a system of signs known today as Plains sign language, which was understood by peoples from the Gulf Coast to the Pacific Northwest. To identify oneself as Piikani, one would make a loose fist and move his or her knuckles in a circle against the lower jaw; a Kainai would draw two fingers along the length of his or her lips in horizontal motion; and a Siksika would move his or her hand in a small circle around the top of the foot. Sign language provided a basis for peaceful exchange in a region where speakers of Algonquian, Athapascan, Siouan, Uto-Aztecan, and other language groups frequently intermingled.[18]

When peaceful exchange broke down, the peoples of the northwest plains sometimes found themselves in conflict. Warfare before European contact was dangerous but probably infrequent. Surviving Blackfoot artwork from the era portrays warriors wielding large circular shields, spears, and clubs against enemies. A Piikani elder named Saahkómaapi, or Young Man, who came of age in the years before guns and horses arrived, later recounted pre-equestrian fighting in detail. Sometime during the early eighteenth century, Young Man and a party of Piikani and Cree warriors went to war against a Shoshone band armed with leather shields and bows and arrows, and exchanged volleys for several hours before parting ways with several wounded men but no fatalities. Warriors walked to and from these engagements, which likely limited their frequency. Pursuing enemies meant temporarily abandoning the search for bison and plants and could require traveling long distances on foot. Moreover, unlike in settled agricultural communities, warfare among mobile plains people offered limited material reward, since they owned few material goods. Capturing women or children could motivate attacks, and the forced adoption of captives fueled interethnic mixing throughout the region. In all likelihood, conflicts most often arose in times of scarcity, when bands ventured into new territories in search of people and resources. As in all human societies, violence and injustice grew worse in times of difficulty. So it had been for generations beyond memory.[19]

THE BLACKFOOT'S OLD WAY of life changed forever beginning in the first decades of the eighteenth century, when Cree and Assiniboine traders began to bring fantastic new items to their trade meetings with plains peoples. Blackfoot traders had long come to trade meetings expecting to see curiosities from far afield—fine, delicate shells from the coasts, for example, or shiny obsidian from the Yellowstone region—but the items that the Crees and Assiniboines now brought had no parallel. The new knives, axes, kettles, and arrowheads they offered were made from something altogether unfamiliar. They somehow felt as hard as rocks but lighter, and they had sharp edges and precise forms that were impossible to create with stone. The Crees and Assiniboines brought blankets and cloth as well, which felt and looked different from the hides or weavings they had known before. Though they had only just appeared, these new goods had the potential to revolutionize warfare, hunting, and domestic labor. Their application seemed endless. The items were wondrous, but also mysterious. Where had these strange items come from? Who made them? And was there more to come?

Their Cree and Assiniboine counterparts may have explained to the Blackfoot that these goods originated with an entirely unfamiliar group of people who lived far to the east. The Crees and Assiniboines had become key players in what we now refer to as the "fur trade," which itself had taken a circuitous path to the northwest plains. Europeans and Native people had been exchanging New World furs for Old World manufactured goods since even before European settlement on the East Coast, but it took centuries for the trade to penetrate fully into the western portions of the continent. That initiative came in the 1650s, when French traders Médard Chouart des Groseilliers and Pierre-Esprit Radisson began exploring Cree lands northwest of the Great Lakes. Finding that these lands abounded in furs and potential trade partners, the Frenchmen sought to establish a lasting presence there, but the governor of New France claimed they had gone west without permission and denied them a trading license. The pair then hatched a plan to bypass the governor's authority by approaching Cree territories from Hudson Bay instead of New France. Failing to secure French financial support for their northern venture, Groseilliers and Radisson brought their case directly to the court of Britain's King Charles II, where they enraptured officials with tales of copious furs and eager Indigenous trade partners accessible directly by sea. Their promises of vast beaver populations in the waterlogged northern interior piqued British interest, since the soft, durable, and waterproof beaver pelts fetched high prices in Europe for use in coats and hats. Convinced of its potential, the king placed his cousin Prince Rupert in charge of the project, and in 1670 he granted Rupert and his investors a royal charter that gave the newly minted "Hudson's Bay Company" (HBC) a monopoly over trade in all the lands that drained Hudson Bay, dubbed "Rupert's Land."[20]

Blackfoot people would first experience the fur trade through other Native people, not European traders. Unlike the intrepid *voyageurs* of New France, the British HBC traders felt content to work exclusively from fortified coastal outposts, where they provided metal goods, guns, textiles, tobacco, and rum to Native visitors in exchange for pelts and provisions. After the HBC built York Fort on the bay's western shore in 1684, Native traders began to travel from far inland to trade with the British, especially Crees and Assiniboines. By asserting control over the labyrinthine waterways west of Hudson Bay, Cree and Assiniboine trading brigades dominated exchange at the post, which enabled them to exchange their own products as well as those produced by Indigenous people to the west. The early ambitions of these Indigenous "middlemen" were temporarily hampered when poorly provisioned French traders seized control of the post between 1697 and 1714. After the British regained control of York Fort in 1714 and renamed it York Factory, the Crees and Assiniboines again expanded their trading networks westward, hoping to enrich themselves by incorporating new Indigenous nations into the fur trade.[21]

Blackfoot trade with Cree and Assiniboine middlemen became common sometime around the 1720s, when Blackfoot traders began exchanging wolf and fox pelts for metal goods like hatchets and kettles, as well as cloth and occasional bits of tobacco, alcohol, and beads. Guns attracted particular curiosity, but the need for regular access to gunpowder, ammunition, and maintenance limited Blackfoot buyers' ability to acquire them in significant numbers. Since they depended on the middlemen for access to European goods, Blackfoot traders had to pay high prices for whatever goods they provided, the majority of which the Crees and Assiniboines traded only after having used them themselves. British explorer Anthony Henday noticed as much when he accompanied a brigade of middlemen west in 1754, remarking that by the end of his journey "there [was] scare a Gun, Kettle, Hatchet or Knife amongst us, having traded them" to the Blackfoot. Typically, Blackfoot people collected and prepared furs during their communal hunts in the late fall and winter, then met with Cree and Assiniboine traders in the spring before the latter made their long summer journey by canoe to the HBC's York Factory. The trade likely became a yearly event, and Blackfoot traders planned carefully for the middlemen's visits.[22]

Though Blackfoot people accumulated them gradually over several decades, European goods soon impacted almost every facet of their lives. Women in particular appreciated the reduction in the time it took to perform traditional domestic labors. Iron kettles allowed them to prepare food without the onerous task of digging pits, lining them with pelts, then filling them with water and heated stones. Kettles also allowed them to abandon their heavy clay pottery, which broke easily during travel. By acquiring metal axes and hatchets, they could gather firewood and lodge poles much more easily, by simply chopping wood instead of using stone wedges or hanging on branches until they snapped. Fires heated with wood burned much hotter than fires heated with dried bison dung, and heated food without leaving a distinctive smell and taste. With steel blades, they could butcher animals much more quickly and easily and could scrape the meat off of hides for use in trade, clothing, and lodging. Iron awls and needles could easily puncture holes in leather and cloth. Women could also find new ways to express themselves artistically, using glass beads and dyes to paint lodge covers and adorn shirts, leggings, and moccasins. Since women owned the products of their labor, technologies like these enabled individual women to build up their own wealth and community status. The advent of European technologies brought bounty and opportunity for women, but at the same time, the market put pressure on women to produce more furs for trade. In a paradoxical cycle that would grow over time, the desire for labor-reducing trade goods also forced women to work harder.[23]

The incorporation of European technologies also reshaped Blackfoot hunting and warfare. When possible, Blackfoot hunters replaced many of their flint arrowheads with iron ones they purchased from the middlemen. Flint arrowheads chipped easily and required considerable effort to prepare. Iron arrowheads, on the other hand, were far more durable and could inflict greater damage. The Piikani warrior Young Man later recalled that when he went to war against the Shoshones, his flint-headed arrows broke upon his enemies' wooden shields but his iron arrows stuck into them — certain... up in the right direction. Iron arrowheads boosted archers' ... in warfare and in hunting, since archers could retrieve ... arrowheads if they missed. Blackfoot warriors attached ... ends of their lances and warriors brought metal knives ... hile historians have typically fixated on the impact of guns in Indigenous communities, basic metal weaponry proved more trans-formative at first, instantly improving the effectiveness of warriors and hunters.[24]

From the beginning, Blackfoot people anxiously guarded their access to European trade goods. For example, in August 1740, HBC traders learned that a large party of warriors from the western plains—probably Blackfoot, but perhaps Gros Ventres or Shoshones—had attacked and killed several Cree "trading Indians" while they trapped beavers the previous winter. The attack likely served as a warning to the frightened Crees, who kept more than two hundred of their most prominent warriors on full alert throughout the winter and spring. Because the Blackfoot relied exclusively upon the middle-men traders for European goods, the prospect of the Crees trapping furs themselves threatened to choke off demand for Blackfoot goods. The lesson stuck, for in subsequent years Cree and Assiniboine travelers carefully avoided trapping for furs in Blackfoot lands. In 1754, Henday's Cree guides told him that the Blackfoot would "kill them, if they trapped in their coun-try," but would be perfectly welcoming if they came to trade. Violence and intimidation formed effective tools for maintaining stability.[25]

Just around the time when the middleman trade began bringing European goods into Blackfoot communities in the 1720s, rumors began to circulate among the Blackfoot of even stranger developments: immense deer-like animals had been spotted in neighboring lands that could carry grown men upon their backs. According to Young Man, the Piikanis gained their first glimpse of this new creature after one was killed during a fight with Sho-shones. "Numbers of us went to see him, and we all admired him," Young Man recalled. "He put us in mind of a Stag that had lost his horns." Later generations credited a war chief named Shaved Head with first bringing live horses, known as *ponokáómitaa* or "elk dogs," to the Blackfoot. According to one story, Shaved Head led a war party to the plains south of the Milk River, where he discovered a small herd of horses brought by Indigenous people from west of the mountains. Shaved Head captured the animals and brought them home where, after much discussion among the community about what to do with the strange beasts, a woman attached a dog travois to one and climbed upon its back. Coinciding closely with the acquisition of European manufactured goods from the East, the adoption of horses forever ended the era Blackfoot elders later dubbed the "dog days."[26]

Curiously, the horses that Shaved Head discovered had an entirely differ-ent origin than the manufactured goods the Blackfoot had recently acquired. While European material goods came to Blackfoot country from the Northeast, horses came from the West and South, where they had descended from horses that Spanish settlers brought to New Mexico in the seventeenth century. In 1680, Pueblo and Apache forces temporarily expelled the Spanish from New Mexico and took control of the Spaniards' large horse herds. In subsequent decades, these New Mexican herds grew and spread through other Indigenous nations in the Southwest. Horses' path to the northwest plains most likely ran through Comanche and Shoshone bands in the Great Basin, then northward through Nez Percé, Flathead, and Pend d'Oreille bands in the intermountain West, or eastward through Shoshone bands on the western Great Plains. Sometime in the second quarter of the eighteenth century, horses appeared in Blackfoot country, where Shaved Head and others acquired them through peaceful trade and capture.[27]

In embracing horses as an opportunity for the Blackfoot, Shaved Head followed a path that countless other Indigenous people took before him. Across the North American West, and especially on the open expanses of the Great Plains, Indigenous people saw extraordinary potential in horses and quickly adapted their lives to them. Comanches and Apaches in the Southwest developed sophisticated raiding economies and expanded their reach onto the southern plains, while others like the Lakota Sioux moved onto the northeastern plains to reorient their lives around bison hunting. Horses offered an entirely new way of experiencing the world. "It must have been the realization of an ancient dream to be elevated, to be severed from the earth, cut free," Kiowa novelist N. Scott Momaday has mused. "What a sense of life that must have been, different from anything they'd ever known, [for] they had conquered their oldest enemy, which was distance." Indeed, Blackfoot people could explore the world around them and travel distances beyond what they had ever imagined. Journeys that used to take weeks could now be undertaken in a matter of days. They eagerly seized upon the exhilarating possibilities that horses offered.[28]

The Blackfoot mastered horsemanship in a remarkably short time, as they proudly displayed to Henday in 1754. The British visitor went hunting with two Blackfoot youths, and while he struggled to control his own horse, he watched in amazement as his guides turned their horses to a "hard gallop" directly toward a bison and killed it with just two arrows. The riders' demonstration showed how the advent of horses had changed the fundamental calculus of Blackfoot hunting: now, rather than relying on complex herding operations, hunters could actually give chase to their prey. No longer did they have to worry that one mistake might spook the entire herd and end the hunt before it began. Henday also observed the impact that horses had on the size of Blackfoot hunting encampments. In the pre-horse era, bands usually hunted separately due to the high difficulty of killing enough bison to feed them all together. Soon, mounted hunters grew confident in their ability to pursue and kill however many bison they needed. The size of individual bands grew, and joint encampments became more common both during communal hunts and during times of conflict with outsiders, when numbers provided strength.[29]

The advent of horses likewise transformed the experience of women, beginning with the traditionally feminine task of moving camp. Before horses arrived, women moved lodges and possessions by attaching them to dog travois or by carrying them on their own backs. By attaching their loads to horses, women relieved their physical burdens and allowed themselves to accumulate new possessions. Travois poles doubled as lodge poles, so building longer travois for horses also increased the height and size of Blackfoot tipis. Because women built the tipis, they also owned them. Women also owned the horses they used for riding or moving camp, though men owned the bands' large herds of unbroken horses and all horses used for hunting, racing, and warfare. The arrival of horses therefore significantly increased the wealth of individual women as well as men. Furthermore, having horses meant that children, the disabled, and the elderly could ride on horseback or sit on travois during travel. As camp movements became easier, they likely became more frequent as well, allowing Blackfoot bands to follow bison and adapt to changing circumstances more quickly. Horses even enabled bands to follow herds during the bison's late-summer mating season, when their movements became erratic. Horses changed the lives of everyone, not just the male warriors and hunters whom outsiders later romanticized.[30]

Horses became central to identity and power among Blackfoot people, and owners treasured them. Even men who accumulated large herds knew each of their horses individually and named them using physical descriptors like "Little-Gray-Horse" or "Flop Ears." Men who did not care properly for their horses earned scorn, so families made sure to look after their horses at all times, typically by deputizing young boys. Boys watched over the horses carefully, directing them to pasturage and water and hobbling lead mares at night to prevent the herd from straying. Horse owners also worked diligently to increase the size of their herds, which had become an essential marker of influence. For people accustomed to keeping only as many possessions as they and their dogs could carry, horses provided an unprecedented source

Blackfoot people adopted horses for use in hunting, warfare, and travel starting around the 1720s. This later image depicts a hunter using a gun, but until the 1870s mounted Blackfoot hunters preferred bows and arrows over their slow-loading trade guns. (Detail from Many Mules painting, ca. 1893–1896, courtesy of the Royal Alberta Museum, Indigenous Studies Program.)

of potential wealth. Some grew rich: by the beginning of the nineteenth century, some men had between forty and fifty horses, and one Piikani man reputedly owned a herd of three hundred. Others owned none and found themselves reliant on wealthy men for access to mounts. The unequal distribution of horse herds exacerbated inequality within Blackfoot communities and provided a challenge to traditional communal values. Sharing and lending horses to less-wealthy individuals became linked to power, and wealthy men used horses to curry favor and attract followers. The ability to acquire and manage horses became inextricably linked to men's position in society. As such, they grew keen to augment their herds by whatever means they could.[31]

Horses brought wealth, adventure, comfort, and power, but they also brought danger. Prior to the arrival of the horse, plains people fought but lack of transportation made protracted warfare difficult, especially over long distances. When groups did fight, wooden and leather shields provided protection against stone arrowheads and few people died in pitched battles. Horses drastically expanded people's capacity for war. Moving on horseback offered warriors the opportunity to travel farther faster, so going to or from enemy territory no longer meant abandoning one's community for extended periods of time. Warriors could also inflict damage and terror much more quickly. The Piikani warrior Young Man recalled how the first mounted Shoshones he met dashed at their pedestrian enemies "swift as the Deer," and crushed their heads with stone clubs. Attacking from horseback and swinging clubs, shooting arrows, or heaving lances downward at slower pedestrian adversaries gave warriors an enormous advantage. Plains communities without large numbers of horses suddenly found themselves in great danger.[32]

Blackfoot people learned firsthand how owning horses could change the balance of power on the Great Plains. Because horses first made their way to the northwest plains from the southwest, the Blackfoot's neighbors in that direction acquired horses earlier, and used them to their advantage. Eastern Shoshone people in particular wielded superior horse herds, which they acquired and augmented through their access to Comanche horse-trading markets to their south. The newly mounted Shoshones pushed northward during the early years of the eighteenth century, raiding Blackfoot, Gros Ventre, and even Cree and Assiniboine bands with impunity while also ranging freely over prime hunting grounds. Sometimes joined by their Crow allies, the Shoshones raided as far north as the South Saskatchewan River and perhaps beyond by the 1730s, well within Blackfoot territory. The Shoshones' expansion demonstrated how horses could confer extraordinary power to whoever mastered them, a lesson Blackfoot people took to heart.[33]

Faced with ongoing aggression by mounted enemies, Blackfoot people sought to augment their own horse herds however possible. Young warriors began to form parties with the exclusive goal of capturing horses, especially from horse-rich neighbors like the Shoshones, as well as the mountain-based Flatheads and Pend d'Oreilles. Raiding enemy encampments for horses became a way for Blackfoot men to demonstrate bravery while also enriching themselves personally. As these raids grew more frequent, Blackfoot herds grew and thus attracted the attention of their comparatively horse-poor neighbors to the north and east. Cree and Assiniboine people in particular targeted Blackfoot herds for raids, which, combined with their access to trade for European weaponry, enabled some Cree bands to adopt an increasingly plains-based lifestyle. The Blackfoot therefore experienced a growing imperative to make up for their own losses through raiding others. Ever-intensifying cycles of violent horse-raiding became a way of life on the northwest plains, as ambitious men (and very occasionally women) sought horse herds to gain both security and prestige.[34]

Horses likewise accelerated the circulation of people throughout the region, often against their will. Before horses, the capture of women and children had been a central feature of plains warfare. As horses increased the frequency and lethality of conflicts, so too did they increase the number of captives. On Henday's visit to the Blackfoot in 1754, he observed "many fine girls" and a few boys whom Blackfoot raiders had captured from other nations. Most likely, these children were to be adopted into Blackfoot families who had lost children to war or illness. Captive women likewise typically married into their captors' band and eventually became full members of the community. Incorporating captives in these ways helped to offset growing population losses sustained in warfare. Some Blackfoot people became captives themselves. While wintering with a Cree band in 1754–55, Henday met several women and children taken captive from the Crees' plains neighbors. Some of these captives even traveled with the middlemen as far as York Factory, where they shared intelligence about their western homelands with HBC traders. Like the Blackfoot, Cree and Assiniboine raiders adopted captives into their communities to offset the growing ravages of war.[35]

As horses expanded trade networks, it became more common for warriors to view captives as tradable commodities rather than potential wives or family members. Many Blackfoot people likely fell captive to invading Shoshones, who maintained strong connections to Spanish-Native slave-trading networks in the Great Basin and New Mexico. The Shoshones brought captive plains women and children south to barter with Utes and Comanches in return for horses and other goods. Conceivably, some Blackfoot women and children could have ultimately found themselves serving Spanish masters, either in New Mexico or even farther south. Although they lacked their own connections to southwestern markets, some Blackfoot people became involved in trading captives to buyers in the east. "Many female slaves are taken" from the plains, reported veteran HBC trader Edward Umfreville in 1790, "who are sold to the Canadian traders and taken down to Canada." The Blackfoot also used captives to serve diplomatic functions. For example, when Henday visited the Blackfoot in 1754, his hosts offered him and his guides a gift of two captive children. Although the "Indian slave trade" on the northwest plains never reached the proportions that it did elsewhere on the continent, like the Southwest borderlands or the American Southeast, it served similar functions and reflected similar dynamics. As colonial changes ripped across the land and incited ever greater conflict and exchange, some human beings were robbed of their own freedom. New dangers and possibilities lurked throughout the northwest plains.[36]

BY THE 1770S, Blackfoot people had reoriented their lives around new realities. Frequent conflict, expanding trade, new military and domestic technologies, and horses had transformed their day-to-day existence. Elsewhere on the continent, similarly momentous changes transpired as well. Along the Eastern Seaboard, British colonists agitated against increased taxes and limitations to expansion, sparking a war that would eventually cleave British North America in two. In Spanish New Mexico, officials implemented a series of reforms meant to improve relations with the expansive and unconquered Indigenous nations who plagued their frontiers, with limited success. In California, Fray Junípero Serra recruited and coerced thousands of Indigenous people into a new string of Catholic missions along the Pacific coast. In Alaska, coastal Aleut people waged a desperate and increasingly doomed resistance to Russian invaders. In the center of the continent, Lakota people accelerated their migration from the woodlands of what is now Minnesota onto the eastern Great Plains, reaching the Black Hills in 1776. Although developments on the northwest plains have attracted less historical attention than these other events, they were no less extraordinary. Legends later held that British soldiers sang a song called "The World Turned Upside Down" after their defeat at the Battle of Yorktown. The same phrase could apply to life on the other side of the continent.[37]

The people of the northwestern Great Plains experienced sweeping transformation during the eighteenth century, but this history has remained scarcely understood because it occurred beyond the view of European, American, or Canadian chroniclers. Each of the forces that reshaped Blackfoot life during this period—from the arrival of European trade goods in the 1720s to the advent of horses a short time later, to the explosion of intertribal warfare, to the expansion of the slave trade—moved independently from colonial planning. The northwest plains had become a tempest of change and reformation, but the traditional archival record leaves us with mere glimpses of this past, flashes of insight into a complex and confusing era. The northwest plains had become a "new world," and many of the old ways of living would be lost forever. Nevertheless, the Blackfoot's ancient ties to the northwest plains—the lands that Náápi created and shaped for their use—would provide continuity and purpose as they faced this new era.

CHAPTER TWO

Strangers on the Land

Very few escaped death by Small Pox.

—BULL PLUME (Piikani), 1910

Every movement of the Slave Indians is attended by
a parade of ceremonies.

—ALEXANDER HENRY THE YOUNGER (British), 1808

When the sun first crept over the prairie horizon on October 14, 1754, it shone a thin light onto more than two hundred lodges of slumbering Blackfoot people who had gathered together for their autumnal bison hunt. The dawn's rising light revealed a dazzling array of designs on each of the lodges' covers that told ancient stories of the Above, Below, and Water worlds. As the sun climbed, signs of life began to stir in the camp. Women emerged to tend to smoldering fires, and boys on the brink of manhood checked on hobbled horses grazing nearby, gladdened to find that none had disappeared overnight. As the sun rose still higher, the slow murmur of activity grew. Within hours, the community hummed with the sounds of life. Horses whinnied; dogs barked; children shouted and played; and more than a thousand women and men chatted, joked, gossiped, flirted, and laughed as they went about their daily tasks. The people appreciated the opportunity to socialize. The Opened season was ending, and before long the combined encampment would need to break up and each band would retreat to their Closed season homes in the river valleys, where people's social lives would shrink to familiar circles. People relished those times of the year when fresh faces entered their lives.

Though the morning of October fourteenth buzzed with a familiar energy, the events of the coming day would shape Blackfoot history forever. Two weeks earlier, scouts had brought back word that they had encountered a party of Assiniboines traveling in their direction, who brought along a trio of familiar Cree traders named Attickosish, Connawapa, and Cokamaniaki-sish. The timing of the visit was somewhat peculiar, since the middleman traders typically came to ply their wares in the spring. More peculiar was the news that the middlemen had brought a young náápiikoan with them—one of the Old Man People, those strangers with light skin and bearded faces who dwelled far to the east and purportedly provided the middlemen with the metal knives, glass beads, tobacco, and cloth that Blackfoot people enjoyed purchasing. The náápiikoan had presented the Blackfoot scouts with a knife, a fire steel, a string of beads, and some tobacco. The gifts signaled the stranger's peaceful intentions and his Cree guides vouched for his goodwill, but the stranger had left his reasons for visiting mysterious. What exactly did this man want from Blackfoot people that made him come so far to meet them? Keen to hear what the visitor had to say, the camp's civil chiefs prepared carefully to receive him. On the morning of the fourteenth, they sent four emissaries to meet the travelers and guide them into the camp. Meanwhile, twenty leading men gathered together in the towering lodge of the highest-ranking civil chief, who sat himself on a carefully folded white bison robe. There they awaited the visitors' arrival.

The stage was set for a consequential meeting. When Attickosish, Connawapa, Cokamaniakisish, and Anthony Henday finally entered the lodge, the ranking civil chief—whose name is lost to us—gestured with his right hand for them to sit. In silence, the Blackfoot hosts lit several pipes to share with the visitors and passed baskets of boiled bison meat to satisfy their hunger. They then presented gifts to the visitors, including ten bison tongues to Henday. Attickosish, who was familiar with the protocol, broke the long silence only after these steps were completed. The Cree then explained that the white man had been "sent by the Great Leader who lives down at the great waters," who wished for Blackfoot people to come "to see him and to bring with them Beaver skins, and Wolves skins: and they would get in return Powder, Shot, Guns, Cloth[,] Beads," and other goods.

So this was what the náápiikoan wanted: for the Blackfoot to paddle nearly a thousand miles east to trade directly with the whites, instead of relying on middlemen like Attickosish to do it for them. They had probably already guessed at Henday's purpose, because with little pause the leading chief politely declined, explaining that his young men did not possess the boats or the knowledge to navigate the labyrinthine waterways that separated Blackfoot country from Hudson Bay. He then turned to Attickosish to discuss more realistic matters. The council adjourned, but Henday returned the next day to press his case. The chief again calmly explained to him that not only did Blackfoot people lack canoes, they also did not eat fish, and he did not want young Blackfoot men to starve during the long and unnecessary journey east. To avoid bad feelings, he presented the disappointed Englishman with a bow and a quiver of arrows. To the Crees, he presented two captive girls and forty bison tongues. He then invited them all to leave.[1]

Combined Blackfoot encampments like this one buzzed with social energy and the sounds and smells of hundreds of dogs and horses. A similar scene would have greeted British envoy Anthony Henday during his visit in 1754. (Karl Bodmer, *Great Camps of the Piekanns near Fort McKenzie*, in Maximilian, *Travels in the Interior of North America*, 43, courtesy of the Beinecke Rare Book and Manuscript Library, Yale University.)

The 1754 meeting proved fruitless in the short term, but it foreshadowed major realignments in northern North America during the mid-eighteenth century that would soon crash upon Blackfoot country. Henday came west hoping to reshape a system of trade that already spanned much of the continent. His employer, the British Hudson's Bay Company (HBC), had begun operating in 1684 on the western shores of Hudson Bay, where employees lived year-round awaiting the visits of Indigenous "middlemen," who canoed hundreds of miles to barter furs from the interior in return for guns, iron tools, textiles, and other European goods. This system had sustained the HBC for decades, but beginning in the 1730s the British received reports that French traders had begun operating west of Hudson Bay, thereby intercepting the Native middlemen upon whom the HBC relied. To address the French threat, chief factor James Isham selected twenty-eight-year-old Henday to travel into the interior, gather intelligence, and convince uncontacted Indigenous people to bring their goods directly to the HBC's main post, called York Factory. To guide and translate, Isham engaged three trusted Cree traders, who likely agreed only because they knew that the scheme had little chance of success. For Indigenous peoples like the Crees, controlling access to Europeans had become the key to wealth and power.[2]

For the Blackfoot, their meeting with Henday demonstrated the judicious and assertive approach that would long define their relations with non-Native people. Over the following years, Blackfoot people would have to confront the presence of hundreds of such visitors, as British, French, and later Canadian traders came west to ply their wares. Eventually, in 1782 the Blackfoot finally cast aside middlemen like Attickosish, thus creating direct ties with the newcomers that would define the region's economy for nearly a century thereafter. At every step along the way, Blackfoot people carefully managed their new relationships. They employed traditional forms of diplomacy and gift-giving to ensure that their exchanges would be profitable, orderly, and personally advantageous. And when necessary, they put strict limitations on the newcomers' behaviors to ensure that they maintained privileged access to both trade and natural resources. That access fueled a remarkable ascendancy for the Blackfoot between 1782 and 1806, which often came at the expense of neighboring nations. Although this period would also bring times of enormous trauma and upheaval, Blackfoot people found in the arrival of the náápiikoan an opportunity to fortify their position and safeguard their livelihoods.

BLACKFOOT BANDS HAD reckoned with the presence of non-Native people for years prior to Henday's arrival. Henday was the first of the English-speaking náápiikoan, or Old Man People, to visit Blackfoot country, but the French-speaking *niitsáápiikoan*, or Original Old Man People, had appeared years earlier. The Frenchmen first came to the northern plains under the leadership of an explorer and entrepreneur named Pierre de La Vérendrye, who in 1730 received royal permission to build trading posts west of the Great Lakes. Despite limited financial support from France, Vérendrye ambitiously expanded into the homelands of the Crees and Assiniboines in what is now Manitoba and Saskatchewan. By the early 1740s, Vérendrye had built a string of trading posts between the Lake of the Woods and the lower Saskatchewan River, culminating in the establishment of Paskoyac, at the Saskatchewan River's junction with the Pasquia River, and Fort La Jonquière, near the juncture of the North and South Saskatchewan Rivers. Vérendrye chose these sites wisely, for they were already the locations of seasonal Cree trade rendezvous and religious ceremonies. He hoped that by positioning himself in key gathering places, he could intercept Native middleman traders before they journeyed to Hudson Bay. He succeeded with some, but because the posts were difficult for the French to access and therefore poorly provisioned, Vérendrye struggled to siphon the bulk of trade away from the HBC. Nevertheless, the French posts drew curiosity from far afield, including from Blackfoot people.[3]

Located along familiar trails within a few hundred miles of Blackfoot territory, the first French posts were close enough to be enticing, but Blackfoot traders quickly learned to associate the establishments with danger. In the autumn of 1751, an unspecified party of *ayahciyiniwaks*—a Cree word for strangers they typically applied to Blackfoot or Gros Ventre people—visited Fort La Jonquière. Some days later, an Assiniboine trading brigade also arrived. According to French observers, leaders of the two groups met and shared a ceremonial tobacco pipe in a show of diplomacy, and the ayahciyiniwaks remained at the post for several more days, assuming they had nothing to fear. The Assiniboines then sprung a surprise attack, massacred the entire ayahciyiniwak party, and spared only a few women and children as prisoners. French witnesses blamed the faraway British for inciting the Assiniboines "to make war on the nations who do not trade with them"; however, the HBC had no such power. More likely, the Assiniboines recognized the threat that direct trade between the French and the plains Indigenous people posed to their position as middlemen. Destroying the ayahciyiniwak party would send a powerful message across the northwest plains that the nearness of French traders on the northern plains did not release plains people from needing to go through Cree and Assiniboine intermediaries. If the Blackfoot wanted goods, they still had to go through the middlemen. When Henday visited Blackfoot lands three years later in 1754, this lesson surely lingered in Blackfoot people's minds.[4]

War between the British and French soon shifted the balance of trade on the northern plains. On July 3, 1754, less than a week after Henday set off from Hudson Bay and more than a thousand miles south, French and Native forces routed a British regiment under Lieutenant Colonel George Washington and forced him to abandon Fort Necessity in the Pennsylvania interior. In 1756, tensions between France and Great Britain exploded into a war that lasted seven years and ended with the French surrendering their imperial claims to continental North America. Indigenous people on the northwest plains soon felt the effects of the conflict, even though most of the fighting happened half a continent away. The British blockaded shipments into Montreal, which in turn choked off the supply of goods to the French posts on the Saskatchewan River, and beginning in 1757 French traders were forced to abandon Vérendrye's posts in the interior. Cree and

Assiniboine middlemen shifted their attentions back toward the British on Hudson Bay, where receipts for furs increased markedly. The French exodus was an unexpected but welcome surprise for the HBC, who now had little incentive to abandon their reliance on the middlemen. Blackfoot people surely heard the news of the niitsáápiikoans' hasty departure, though it made no major difference to them.[5]

To the surprise of the region's Indigenous people, traders returned to the Saskatchewan River a few years later, this time with even better goods to trade. After the Seven Years War ended in 1763, a new "Canadian" (meaning residents of the former New France) alliance composed of Montreal-based Scots and French-speaking *voyageurs* mobilized to reestablish trade relations in the Northwest by reoccupying the previously abandoned French trading posts on the Saskatchewan River. As subjects of the British Empire, these newly formed Canadian outfits had significant advantages over their French predecessors, especially access to British-manufactured goods and Brazilian tobacco, which Native buyers far preferred to French varieties. Cree and Assiniboine traders preferred visiting the convenient Canadian posts over paddling all the way to Hudson Bay, and as a result trade receipts at the HBC's York Factory plummeted by the end of the 1760s. The HBC's leadership finally conceded that the company needed to expand inland in order to survive, and in 1774 they built Cumberland House on the Saskatchewan River, about forty miles west of the old French post at Paskoyac. Hudson House followed a few years later, some two hundred miles upriver on the North Saskatchewan. Through the middlemen, Blackfoot people likely learned that the Original Old Man People and the Old Man People had begun to compete fiercely with one another for trade with the Crees and Assiniboines. As a result, European goods became less expensive and more plentiful than ever before.[6]

Blackfoot people used the suddenly vibrant Saskatchewan River trade to their advantage in the 1760s and 1770s, despite still relying on the middlemen. As before, Blackfoot traders bought knives, bayonets, axes, and iron for arrow tips from the Crees and Assiniboines, but they also purchased guns in significant numbers for the first time. They knew that European weapons gave them enormous advantages over their enemies to the west and south, who lacked trade ties with the middlemen and therefore had not acquired such goods. In a reminiscence taken in 1787, the Piikani elder Young Man described the boost that the new weapons gave Blackfoot warriors. When Young Man first went to war against Shoshone bands several decades earlier, the Piikanis had a few iron-tipped lances and arrows, but no guns. His pedestrian Shoshone adversaries used heavy wooden shields to defend themselves, and the battle ended inconclusively. Years later, Young Man's Piikanis again went to war against the Shoshones, this time armed with guns that they had acquired through trade. Young Man and his fellow warriors routed the Shoshones, whose shields failed to protect them from the Piikanis' bullets. "Our shots caused consternation and dismay along their whole line," Young Man recalled, and "the greater part of the enemy took flight." With growing supplies of guns and steel in the 1760s and 1770s, Piikani bands in particular grew more confident in fighting their longtime Shoshone adversaries, who years earlier had used horses to invade their homelands.[7]

The Piikanis' growing assertiveness after their embrace of the gun trade had tragic and unforeseen consequences. According to Young Man, one day in the summer of 1781 some Piikani scouts rode south and spotted a Shoshone encampment. They returned to their band and reported that although the Shoshones had substantial horse herds, strangely nobody seemed to be tending them, and herds of bison lingered near the camp unperturbed by Shoshone hunters. The Piikanis' leaders met in council and resolved to attack the Shoshones at once, lest their enemies attack first or summon more warriors to their defense. Young Man, despite now approaching old age, came along. The Piikanis attacked en masse at dawn, whooping loudly while ripping into the Shoshones' tipis with knives and daggers. "But our war whoop instantly stopt," Young Man recalled, and "our eyes were appalled with terror, [for] there was no one to fight with but the dead and dying, each a mass of curruption [sic]." The sores and pustules that covered the Shoshones indicated that they were suffering from smallpox, but the Piikanis had no way of knowing that, or of knowing that the disease was highly contagious and could sometimes travel through infected goods. The Piikani warriors plundered the Shoshones' lodges and horses before returning home. "We had no belief that one Man could give [the illness] to another, any more than a wounded Man could give his wound to another," Young Man later explained. The Piikanis rode north carrying the illness with them, and within a week or two they began to grow ill themselves. Nothing could prepare them for the horrors that lay ahead.[8]

Variola major—the virus that causes smallpox—already shaped American history for centuries before it reached Blackfoot country. In 1520, smallpox had devastated the Aztec capital of Tenochtitlán, weakening the continent's mightiest empire to the point that Spaniards dismantled it entirely within the year. It had a similar impact in the highlands of South America, where a smallpox epidemic caused a crisis in the leadership of the Incan empire that precipitated its collapse. But these are only the most famous examples, for smallpox impacted every Indigenous community in the Americas in similar ways. Millions died before the disease was finally eradicated in the twentieth century, making it the single greatest killer of Native people in history. One key to the disease's effectiveness was that it had an incubation period of between one and two weeks, during which infected people showed no symptoms. This made it extremely easy for unaware victims to transport it unwittingly from place to place. Once symptoms did arrive, there was no mistaking them. It began with a fever, headache, and severe muscle pain, often in the back. After a day, a rash appeared all over the body, which soon gave way to raised pustules. Most Indigenous people died within a week of their first symptoms. Blackfoot people most likely had been mercifully spared from the illness prior to 1781, due to their homeland's distance from colonial settlements and the long travel times needed to access the region. Their previous isolation from the disease meant they had no warning, no immunity, and no experience.[9]

Smallpox decimated Blackfoot bands during the late fall and winter of 1781. A number of factors made the outbreak particularly deadly. It was the disease's first appearance in the region, so Blackfoot people had no acquired immunity from previous outbreaks, nor did they have knowledge of how to treat it or prevent its spread. Some sufferers, especially men, unintentionally exacerbated the illness's effects by sitting in sweat lodges then immersing themselves in cold water. Some victims who may have otherwise survived died because they lost their would-be caretakers, as did infants and the elderly. Some people may have ended their own lives in fear or despair. Young Man recalled that the survivors' lodges shook with "tears, shrieks, and howlings of despair for those who would never return to us." By the time it ebbed in the winter of 1781–82, the devastation became clear. A Piikani winter count later described it as the year when "very few escaped death by smallpox," and one observer later estimated that the Piikani population declined from at least 350 lodges to 150 following the epidemic. It undoubtedly took a similar toll on the Kainais and Siksikas. Surviving the aftermath presented another challenge, since stores of food and provisions shrunk during the epidemic and because it interrupted the communal bison hunts of late fall. Survivors had difficulty locating bison to hunt, partly because so many experienced trackers and hunters had perished. Without access to meat, women's knowledge of plant life and food preservation became more essential than ever.[10]

The epidemic impacted Blackfoot survivors in profound and irreversible ways. Smallpox robbed bands of key political leaders, hunters, healers, and warriors, which forced some bands to merge together for protection and stability. The disease spurred spiritual crises as well. Some religious societies, which were responsible for maintaining traditional dances and ceremonies, ceased to exist entirely. Likewise, when religious bundle holders and their confidants died, communities lost the spiritual power, history, and organizing structure that the bundles provided. On an individual level, smallpox survivors bore deep psychological scars in addition to physical ones. For example, in 1786 a teenaged British trader named David Thompson observed a tall, withered white pine tree standing amidst a grove of aspens near the Red Deer River. He learned that as the only pine of its kind in the area, the tree had once held strong spiritual significance to Piikani people. When smallpox struck in 1781, a man from a nearby Piikani band made offerings to the tree hoping it would save his wives and children. When his family members died despite his pleas, the man climbed the tree and hacked off the top third, causing it to wither and die. (Memory of the pine, and the events that preceded its death, live on in the name of Lonepine Creek near Olds, Alberta.) Unimaginable grief and a sense of spiritual abandonment haunted many Blackfoot survivors, who had never experienced such devastation.[11]

The *Variola* virus quickly moved on to the Blackfoot's neighbors, thus demolishing the social and economic networks that structured the region. Traders at the HBC's westernmost post of Hudson House witnessed the devastation it wrought among the Cree and Assiniboine middlemen. Returning from his yearly visit to York Factory in the fall of 1781, trader Mitchell Oman encountered several infected Crees lying alongside the North Saskatchewan River to cool themselves. He discovered an encampment of tipis nearby, "in many of which they were all dead, and the stench was horrid." Eventually, survivors informed him that disease had almost entirely destroyed the Indigenous communities in the nearby forest. As the epidemic raged into the winter, HBC traders realized that as the Crees and Assiniboines died, so too did their trade connections. They complained to their superiors that they had no hope of discharging their wares while the middlemen lay "Dead about the Barren Ground like Rotten Sheep, their Tents left standing & the Wild beasts Devouring them." Oman estimated that three-fifths of the Crees and Assiniboines died in lands surrounding the North Saskatchewan River, and at York Factory traders noticed a marked decrease in Native visitors from the west. The epidemic had thrown the fur trade into disarray.[12]

Taking stock of the post-smallpox reality, Blackfoot survivors looked to the fur trade for stability and security. Survivors desperately needed to hunt and replace depleted food stores. They also needed to protect themselves from potential attack by neighboring nations. This meant that they needed to resume their trade for European goods like guns, arrowheads, blades, and tools. They may have sought tobacco or dyes and beads for religious ornamentation as well, in order to perform ceremonies or reaffirm their spiritual alliances. Because so many of the Cree and Assiniboine middlemen had perished, Blackfoot traders decided to visit the British and Canadian traders directly for the first time. In March 1782, a group of HBC traders near Hudson House encountered a party of fourteen Siksika men, whose scarring indicated they had "all recover'd of the Small Pox," on their way to trade at the nearby Canadian establishment. On August 18, 1782, the first Siksika traders visited the HBC's Hudson House, accompanying a small Assiniboine trading party. More followed. With their arrival, the middlemen's role in the northern plains fur trade ended forever, and a new era in Blackfoot history began.[13]

THE 1781 SMALLPOX EPIDEMIC cleared the way for dramatic changes to the fur trade. Prior to the epidemic, Cree and Assiniboine middlemen had opposed British and Canadian traders' attempts to build posts west of their territories, which would have enabled the companies to establish direct ties with the Blackfoot and other plains peoples, but the smallpox epidemic robbed the middlemen of the power to prevent expansion. At the same time as the middlemen lost their power to control the outsiders, competition between the British and Canadians over access to the interior's Native survivors accelerated. In 1779, sixteen Montreal-based Canadian traders, keen to break the HBC's dominance over the fur trade, joined together to form the North West Company (NWC). The Canadians had previously operated in small independent units, but their new partnership allowed them to share knowledge, resources, and transportation routes across the vast fur-trading regions of the Northwest. Their experience far surpassed that of their HBC competitors, who had only just begun to plumb the interior.[14]

The Canadian upstarts proved themselves formidable adversaries for the British, and the North Saskatchewan River and nearby Blackfoot homelands soon became a key economic battleground between the two companies. As the NWC grew and took on new partners over the following decade, its partners honed a strategy based on vigorous direct competition with the HBC and ambitious exploration of areas the British had yet to reach. In 1786, both

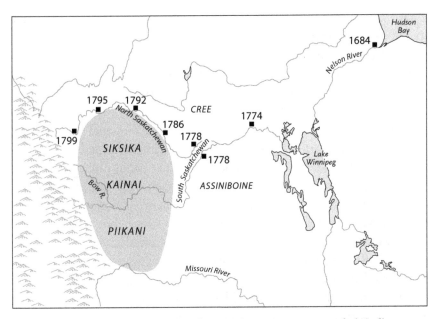

Fur trade expansion along the Saskatchewan River, 1684 to 1799. Labels indicate when the posts were first established, including the HBC's York Factory (1684), Cumberland House (1774), Upper and Lower Hudson House (1778), Manchester House/Pine Island Fort (1786), Buckingham House/Fort George (1792), Edmonton House/Fort Augustus (1795) and Acton House/Rocky Mountain House (1799).

companies pushed nearly two hundred miles upriver and built Manchester House (HBC) and Pine Island Fort (NWC) adjacent to one another. In 1792, they pushed farther west to build Buckingham House and Fort George, then Edmonton House and Fort Augustus in 1795, and finally Acton House and Rocky Mountain House in 1799. In the years immediately following the epidemic, British and Canadian fur companies pushed almost five hundred miles west, establishing themselves on the northern fringes of Blackfoot territory and within sight of the Rocky Mountains.[15]

At the new western posts, Blackfoot people gained access to a huge bounty of European goods. According to trade ledgers, Blackfoot traders most often sought guns, balls, gun flints, and powder but also traded frequently for textiles, art supplies like vermilion paint and beads, alcohol, tobacco, awls, scrapers, and axes. These goods came far more cheaply from the HBC and NWC without the previous markup imposed by the Cree and Assiniboine middlemen. For example, a used gun that had cost the equivalent of fifty beaver skins (an abstract fur trade standard known as "made beaver") from middlemen in 1766 cost just fourteen when purchased directly from the NWC in 1794. The quality of goods also improved. While the middlemen had often traded used and worn-out items to the Blackfoot, the companies offered newer, sharper, and better-maintained goods. Many posts employed blacksmiths and gunsmiths to repair Native people's weapons. Unsurprisingly, Blackfoot traders flocked to the new trading posts as they became more conveniently located. Visits usually occurred during the winter, or Closed season, which meant they did not disrupt bands' annual movements. Blackfoot trading parties varied in size, typically numbering between two and thirty male traders, though sometimes entire bands came as one unit. The leaders of trading parties were typically men with influence, though not necessarily chiefs. Taking advantage of their generation's newfound ability to travel long distances and carry heavy loads on horseback, traders from all three Blackfoot nations made the trek from their winter camps to the North Saskatchewan posts. Siksika elder Augustine Yellow Sun later explained that they called the trade "bush-buying," since it required a journey north into more heavily wooded areas like those surrounding the "Big House" of Edmonton.[16]

Blackfoot people crafted exchanges that allowed them to acquire European goods without violating their religious beliefs. Although the fur companies valued beaver pelts above all else, Blackfoot traders were reluctant to trap and kill beavers due to their ecological and spiritual relationship with the animal, and Blackfoot hunters instead chose to provide mostly wolf and fox pelts to the companies. Although canines fetched lower prices than beavers, Blackfoot hunters compensated through volume. HBC visitor William Pink first described their canine-hunting skills in January 1770. Pink's Siksika hosts began their hunt by constructing a circular pound in which they spent a week trapping and slaughtering small herds of bison. After collecting meat and hides for their own use, they left portions of bison carcasses strewn about in the center of the pound, then opened several gaps in the sides of the enclosure. They then waited patiently for scavenging wolves and foxes to enter the pound through the gaps, only to step into carefully placed snares. In addition to wolf and fox pelts, Blackfoot traders also brought in occasional pelts from muskrats, wolverines, lynxes, and bears, but bison robes were generally deemed too bulky and heavy for the companies to transport east by canoe. They sometimes brought beaver pelts, although many of these may have been captured during raids on other groups or acquired through secondary trade. They often traded horses to the fur companies as well, a necessary service since British and Canadian traders came west by canoe.[17]

The Blackfoot also became involved in the burgeoning "provisions" trade, which likewise allowed them to avoid trading beavers. Provisions consisted mostly of food, especially dried bison meat and fat, which Blackfoot women or company employees mashed together with berries to make pemmican. Easily transportable, long lasting, and packed with calories, pemmican became vital for British and Canadian fur traders, who expended enormous amounts of energy canoeing between trading posts. Companies transported much of the pemmican they acquired from the Saskatchewan River posts back east, then on to their more northern operations, where large edible game was scarce but where beaver pelts were more plentiful. Pemmican from the plains therefore literally fueled the fur trade, providing the calories necessary to expand British and Canadian operations deep into Arctic and sub-Arctic regions. Pemmican became increasingly important to both the HBC and NWC during the 1790s, as competition between the companies grew ever more heated. The pemmican-based system suited Blackfoot people well, and most Blackfoot trading parties brought in a combination of furs and provisions. In February 1788, for example, a Kainai trading party brought 550 wolf pelts, fifteen beaver pelts, ten fox pelts, and four hundred pounds of provisions to trade at Manchester House.[18]

How they traded mattered nearly as much as what they traded, and Blackfoot people carefully planned their visits to trading posts in order to maximize their advantage. Upon approaching, Blackfoot parties sent young men ahead as envoys to both NWC and HBC posts, which were almost always located nearby one another for safety and convenience. These scouts informed the companies' traders about the number of men coming to trade, when they would arrive, and what they would bring. They also collected information about trading conditions at the posts and gauged the companies' interest in their goods. The scouts then brought this information back to their fellow travelers, who used it in their negotiations. They rarely held loyalty to one company over another, and in the words of one HBC writer traded "indiscriminately, according as they are better or worse paid at our place than the other." Such gamesmanship frustrated white traders. In their official journals, HBC traders frequently expressed their "mortification" when Blackfoot traders brought their goods to their NWC competitors, either because the NWC had superior goods to trade or because they paid more. Blackfoot traders' canny use of competition compelled the companies to woo them using whatever means they could, and leaders often received extra gifts of clothing, alcohol, and tobacco in return for bringing their people to one

This image by an unnamed Indigenous (likely Blackfoot) artist depicts the arrival of a Native trader to a fur trading post. While one of the white traders—who are depicted here with their hands on their hips—waits inside, another exits the post to pay respect to the visitor. (Detail from painting by unknown artist, ca. 1846, Nicolas Point Fonds, The Archive of the Jesuits in Canada.)

company instead of the other. Blackfoot traders understood how to leverage competition to compel gifts and raise prices.[19]

Carefully choreographing their arrival at their chosen trading post assured Blackfoot traders that the ensuing exchanges would unfold on equitable terms. When Blackfoot trading parties arrived within view of a trading post, the men stopped, made a fire, and smoked the tobacco that the companies had given to the scouts the day before. The women meanwhile continued on to the shadow of the post to unpack the travois and erect the tipis. After smoking, the most prominent men often painted their faces and clad themselves in their finest clothing, and then the entire party formed a line behind their leader before proceeding onward. As they processed toward the post, the company's head trader exited the main gate and walked forward to meet them. "The further he [went] to meet them the greater the compliment," one NWC trader noted. Before they followed the head trader through the palisades and into the main hall, Blackfoot visitors often received a flag as a gift, or in later years were greeted with a cannon-fire salute. Each of these steps assured them of the friendly intentions of the company traders and affirmed the status of the Blackfoot leaders who visited.[20]

Ceremonies inside the fort served similar purposes. Inside the main hall, Blackfoot leaders sat together with the company traders and smoked. After smoking, the head trader presented the Native visitors with a gift of liquor (usually rum), amounting to a quart for each man in 1810. In large groups, the Blackfoot leader often reciprocated by giving the head trader a horse, which was sometimes loaded with gifts of skins or furs. Blackfoot leaders sometimes presented painted bison hides to the head trader as well, draping them over his shoulders while others looked on. When the day's ceremonies concluded, the Blackfoot traders returned to their encampment, where they spent the night drinking their alcohol. Trade typically began the next day (or the day after, depending on the night's revelry), and when the Blackfoot had finished trading their furs and provisions, the company traders presented them with more gifts of tobacco and ammunition. The visitors then packed up their lodges and left. Visits rarely lasted more than three days. The routine rarely varied: gifts always changed hands at multiple intervals, and the two groups always smoked tobacco together. Only after leaders had been honored and friendships affirmed could trade commence.[21]

The elaborate choreography of Blackfoot trade visits, which could seem tedious to outsiders, derived from long-standing diplomatic traditions on the plains. Blackfoot people used these exchanges to affirm peaceful ties with the náápiikoan just as they did with other neighbors in the region. Gift exchanges formed the backbone of diplomacy between plains peoples, who frequently used gifts to help settle conflicts and solidify peace. For example, in June 1792 Piikani leaders settled a short-lived peace with Shoshone bands by exchanging gifts, and in 1802 Siksika chiefs gave "large presents" to make peace with visiting Arapaho bands. Gift-giving helped to settle disputes within communities as well, and Blackfoot people frequently quashed perceived affronts or grievances by exchanging gifts, especially horses. The exchange of gifts between Blackfoot and white traders served a similar function, and reinforced peaceful ties with the Canadian and British visitors to the region. In previous generations, Cree and Assiniboine trading brigades had placed an almost identical emphasis on gifts and ceremony during their visits to York Factory, which underscored the ubiquitous connections between gifts and diplomacy throughout northern North America.[22]

Blackfoot people valued alcohol highly in their trade with whites. In this image by an unnamed (likely Blackfoot) artist, a representative of the Above world witnesses the exchange, which hints that intoxication may have included a religious significance for the Blackfoot. (Detail from painting by unknown artist, ca. 1846, Nicolas Point Fonds, The Archive of the Jesuits in Canada.)

Exchanging gifts with company employees likewise enhanced the status of Blackfoot traders within their bands. Within Blackfoot bands, giving gifts to the less fortunate demonstrated the generosity and empathy required to lead. Giving gifts to the strangers therefore established individuals' capacity for leadership. It could also be an opportunity for the giver to show the personal wealth he had accumulated. The ceremonial exchanges at the trading posts therefore offered a unique platform for Blackfoot men to demonstrate their worth. Receiving gifts in return was equally important to Blackfoot leaders, since it signaled the recipient's high status, as well his ability to command valuable goods from the outsiders. Such qualities inspired loyalty, and Blackfoot visitors were always careful to ensure that the companies acknowledge their status. One observer noted that the Blackfoot were "extremely punctilious in points of honour," and refused to trade when fur company employees neglected to present them with the proper gifts and ceremonies. To Blackfoot traders, ceremonies and gift exchanges could play just as important a role as the commerce itself.[23]

Giving and receiving clothing in particular became a marker of prestige for Blackfoot leaders. Wearing one's finest clothing, which traditionally consisted of elaborately beaded and painted leather shirts and leggings, demonstrated respect for one's counterpart, so Blackfoot leaders dressed carefully for councils. This tradition extended to the fur trade interactions, and Blackfoot traders expected whites to dress formally when they visited. (Indeed, sending envoys before their arrival helped to remind their counterparts to dress appropriately the following day.) Prominent Blackfoot visitors also expected the traders to provide formal clothing as gifts. These gifts became so important that large trading posts like Edmonton employed tailors who made clothing specifically for Native visitors. When companies' supplies of new clothing ran low, or when meetings occurred away from the trading posts, company traders sometimes gave Blackfoot leaders the clothes off their backs, and the Blackfoot leaders would reciprocate in turn. Exchanges in which two men exchanged their own clothing directly demonstrated the highest form of respect. For example, HBC trader John Harriott later recalled that during a moment of high tension at Edmonton when a Siksika party found Harriott in the company of some enemy Crees, he and a Siksika chief exchanged their outfits, thus performing "the greatest proof of friendship that an Indian knows" and diffusing the situation. Clothing had political and diplomatic meaning that far exceeded its physical value.[24]

To further facilitate trade, some Blackfoot people developed close personal ties with the whites. Beginning shortly after the 1781 smallpox epidemic, as many as a dozen Blackfoot families per year took HBC and NWC company traders into their lodges during the winter months. These winterers became like family for some. The HBC employee James Gaddy reported that his Piikani host treated him "as his own son" in 1786, and the NWC's Duncan M'Gillivray recalled that the Siksika chief Gros Blanc adopted him as "his little brother" in 1795. While company officials sent these men hoping that they would learn the Indians' language and encourage them to trade, influential Blackfoot families saw the visits as an opportunity to build lasting bonds with the trade companies. The creation of new family ties through adoption was a deep-rooted tradition among plains peoples, and Indigenous people considered these connections to be permanent and real. Adopting outsiders as sons or brothers created permanent personal relationships, which obligated both sides to behave as family members, to remain loyal and trustworthy, and to provide gifts when necessary. Adoption also reflected a common diplomatic practice, as Indigenous people sometimes took in wards from neighboring tribes to solidify peace accords.[25]

While Blackfoot men could formalize trade relationships through ceremony and arranging adoptions, some women formed more fleeting connections with the newcomers. Few if any Blackfoot women married whites during these early decades of exchange, but sexual liaisons with the traders were common. According to NWC trader Alexander Henry the Younger, Blackfoot men often took the lead in arranging connections, and would "intrude themselves, into every Room and Cabin [of Fort Augustus], followed by their Women," and would "insist upon [employees] doing them charity and accepting the company of at least one of their women for the night." At other times, Henry described the encounters as bluntly transactional, with Piikani men offering their wives to "customers" in return for "payment" in the form of trade goods. Despite Henry's assumptions, women may not always have been passive in these scenarios. Sex with the strangers provided access to trade, while also building a rapport that could lead to better trade terms in the future. Blackfoot couples may have seen such arrangements as a form of gift exchange or diplomacy, not prostitution or debasement. In any case, the use of sex demonstrated the high value Blackfoot people placed on trade, and on seeking out any advantage they could.[26]

Blackfoot people also used their knowledge of the region's ecology to gain leverage with the náápiikoan, and purposely made it difficult for British and Canadian hunters to locate wild game themselves. For example, during the abnormally warm winter of 1799–1800, bison herds did not approach the area around Edmonton as they usually did, and Blackfoot hunters deliberately drove off the few bison who ventured near the post using their traditional hunting techniques. In February, a party of HBC hunters complained that "twenty tents of Blackfeet have made a pound quite near the hunting tent and drove off every buffalo that our hunters are now quite at a loss where to go." Their only choice was to purchase provisions directly from Native suppliers. Blackfoot people sometimes set the plains ablaze to gain the upper hand as well. In 1794, a trader at the NWC's Fort George complained that "the Indians often make use of [fire] to frighten away the animals in order to enhance the value of their own provisions." Blackfoot people and their neighbors had long used fire as a tool to direct bison herds, to improve grasslands for grazing, and to improve conditions for prairie turnips and berries to grow. They used this ecological knowledge to shape the fur trade to their own benefit.[27]

While most Blackfoot people shared ambitions of profitable trade with whites, leaders sometimes disagreed on tactics. A significant divide formed among the Siksikas after the 1794 death of Old Swan, their most prominent civil chief. Old Swan had advocated peaceful relations with British and Canadian traders, who held him in high esteem for his accommodating and diplomatic nature. After his death, leadership among the Siksika bands split between two factions: one led by Old Swan's son, also named Old Swan, and the other led by an upstart named Big Man, the leader of the Cold band, whom M'Gillivray described as "a man of unbounded ambition and ferocity." While the younger Old Swan maintained his father's accommodating stance toward outsiders, Big Man applied a more aggressive approach. In 1793 and 1794, Big Swan's people joined Gros Ventre warriors in a series of raids on the NWC's Pine Island Fort and the HBC's neighboring Manchester House, taking several Cree women captive and seizing horses and material goods. Big Man reckoned that attacking these two posts would not damage his ability to trade at others, but after NWC traders confronted him about his behavior the following autumn, he decided direct raids were not in his long-term interest. He nevertheless maintained an often-bellicose posture toward outsiders, and his followers gained a reputation for aggressive begging and bartering.[28]

The divergence between Old Swan and Big Man showcased a central tension of Blackfoot relations with the newcomers: Blackfoot people needed to build and maintain relationships with the fur traders, but they also spent the vast majority of their time far from the trading posts and generally chose to keep the outsiders at arm's length. Unlike elsewhere on the continent, where fragmented Indigenous nations eagerly built alliances with Europeans, intermarried, and built hybrid cultures over the course of generations, Blackfoot people mostly avoided intermingling with whites for more than a few days at a time during the early decades of the fur trade. Indeed, Blackfoot people's independent mindset confounded observers like M'Gillivray, who complained that they wanted little to do with him besides acquiring goods. The NWC's Henry described the Blackfoot as "the most independent and happy people" he had encountered, whose true passions lay in hunting and raiding, not exchange. While they adopted some white traders into their own families, few if any Blackfoot people intermarried or joined the tiny communities springing up at Edmonton or Fort Augustus. Compared with groups like the Crees, Assiniboines, and Ojibways, the Blackfoot had very limited interactions with non-Native people. Visits to NWC or HBC posts rarely lasted more than a few days, at which time Blackfoot traders would return south to their normal seasonal routines. Blackfoot country never became a "middle ground." Instead of building a shared world, Blackfoot people allowed the newcomers to exist on the margins of *their* world, with all its rules and limitations. In fact, harnessing the fur trade enabled the Blackfoot to strengthen their own social and cultural autonomy.[29]

BUILDING A STABLE TRADE with the whites after 1781 provided Blackfoot people with the confidence and technological wherewithal to dominate their adversaries. Steady supplies of guns, ammunition, and metal blades gave Blackfoot warriors crucial advantages over neighbors who did not have such access, including the Shoshones to their south and the Flatheads to their west. Although these nations lacked European weaponry, they maintained huge horse herds due to their homelands' milder climates and their access to southern horse-trading markets. As such, they made perfect targets for heavily armed Blackfoot (and sometimes Gros Ventre) horse raiders, who victimized them with relative impunity. In the words of one observer, these communities "had nothing to oppose [Blackfoot raids] but arrows and their own undaunted bravery," and they frequently lost horses. The Piikanis, who occupied the southern and westernmost portions of Blackfoot territory, benefited the most from this imbalance, and Piikani herds soon far outnumbered those of the Kainais and Siksikas. Capturing new horses grew the wealth of individual Blackfoot men and ensured that Blackfoot bands would have more than enough horses to travel, hunt, conduct warfare, or trade directly to the whites for more weapons. Blackfoot power grew at the expense of their neighbors.[30]

In turn, raiding their horse-rich neighbors to the west and south also gave Blackfoot people an advantage over other nations to the north and east. Cold winter weather, heavy snows, and the scarcity of winter forage prevented northern plains and parkland peoples from growing their horse herds purely through breeding and husbandry in the way that southern plains peoples like the Comanches could. Following a blizzard in February 1802, for example, a party of famished Siksika traders reported that many of their horses had died, since they were not "able to scrape the snow away and maintain themselves." Even if horses did survive such winter hardships, by spring they could often be too weak to ride. Blackfoot raiders, especially Piikanis, were able to offset such losses by capturing mounts from the horse-rich nations to their west and south. The Crees and Assiniboines, who occupied even colder climes to the north and east of the Blackfoot, had no such luxury. Since winter weather frequently decimated their herds, they focused their attentions on raiding heavily armed Blackfoot and Gros Ventre bands. Such raids were dangerous and yielded fewer horses than did raids on unarmed groups. As a result, Cree and Assiniboine bands struggled to keep pace.[31]

Raids also provided the opportunity for Blackfoot bands to rebuild their human population, which had plummeted due to smallpox. The Piikani elder Young Man later recounted that after 1781, Blackfoot raiders emphasized capturing women and children for adoption in order to reconstitute their decimated communities. One such raid occurred about three years after the epidemic when, in response to a Shoshone attack, a Piikani war chief organized a large revenge party with the specific instructions that "the young women must all be saved, and if any has a babe at the breast, it must not be taken from her, nor hurt." Moreover, "all the Boys and Lads that have no weapons must not be killed, but brought to our camps, and be adopted amongst us, to be our people, and make us more numerous and stronger than we are." The Piikani war chief Kotonáyaapi, or Kootenai Old Man, played a central role in the captive-taking campaigns against the Shoshones. In 1787 he led a party of 250 warriors south, and the keeper of a winter count recorded it as the year when the Piikanis succeeded in taking "the Snake [Shoshone] Indian wives & children." Capturing women and children as captives served the dual purposes of rebuilding the Blackfoot population and weakening their adversaries. For the Piikanis in particular, who had been in constant conflict with the Shoshones for decades, acquiring captives bolstered their security in the precarious post-smallpox years.[32]

The growing aggressiveness of Blackfoot raids for horses and captives put other groups on the run, especially the Shoshones. Early in the eighteenth century, Shoshone bands had used their superior herds and riding skill to push deep into traditional Blackfoot territory, hunting and raiding as far north as the South Saskatchewan River by the 1730s. Blackfoot (and to a lesser extent Gros Ventre) bands used guns and horses to reverse this tide in the later decades of the century. James Gaddy, who wintered with a Piikani family in 1786, reported that all three Blackfoot nations went "constantly to war against the snake [Shoshone] indians," taking "numbers of Horses & mules." The raids took a toll on the Shoshones, who were themselves still recovering from the smallpox epidemic, and who had few European weapons with which to defend themselves. By 1800 the Shoshone bands were forced to withdraw from virtually all of their plains territories. The Shoshones retreated to mountain valleys west and south of the Missouri River and returned to the plains occasionally only to raid or hunt bison. When American explorers Meriwether Lewis and William Clark ascended the Missouri in 1805, outdated intelligence made them expect to find a vast "Snake" (Shoshone) nation controlling the plains south of the Missouri; instead, they encountered a reduced people dwelling in the mountains, desperate to be "relived [sic] from the fear" of their Black-foot enemies. The balance of power on the northwest plains had swung decidedly in favor of the Blackfoot.[33]

Emboldened by their superior weaponry, Blackfoot warriors forced other Native people to avoid the northwest plains entirely, including the mountain nations that had long frequented the plains to hunt bison. By 1800, Kootenai bands largely retreated from the western plains and foothills and chose to take refuge year-round in the Kootenay River region west of the mountains. The move ended a long Kootenai tradition of living and hunting on the plains for at least part of the year. Blackfoot raids had a similar impact farther south along the Rockies. As Blackfoot hunters and warriors asserted their control over the headwater regions of the Missouri River in the late 1700s, they increasingly clashed with nations that hunted bison along the western edge of the prairies, including the Flatheads, Nez Percés, Pend d'Oreilles, and others. Each of these groups regularly rode east through well-trodden mountain passes to hunt bison on the plains, sometimes for months at a time. The mountain nations' use of these passes had likely grown after they acquired horses, since horses made travel easier and bison populations may have declined west of the continental divide. By the late eighteenth century, these outsiders' hunting expeditions became frequent targets for increasingly well-armed Blackfoot warriors who raided them for horses and captives. Their access to the fur trade therefore allowed the Blackfoot to assert their control over key bison hunting grounds, and by the end of the century Black-foot raids had forced most of the mountain nations to abandon their hunting expeditions and retreat into the mountains year-round.[34]

Blackfoot leaders maintained their people's dominance over the Shosho-nes, Flatheads, and Kootenais and others by denying them access to the fur trade. Kootenai people in particular tried repeatedly to barter with the Black-foot for permission to visit the North Saskatchewan, and Kootenai chiefs visited the plains in both 1792 and 1795 to offer large gifts of horses to Black-foot leaders in exchange for access but were rebuffed both times. The Flat-heads and Shoshones, frustrated by their own inability to access the North Saskatchewan trading posts, resorted instead to trading with Crow peoples, who transported their horses and other goods nearly seven hundred miles east to the Mandan and Hidatsa trading centers on the Missouri River. The Crows charged a heavy price for moving goods over this distance, which yielded mountain groups far fewer European items than the Blackfoot could acquire by trading directly with whites on the North Saskatchewan. Relying on Crow intermediaries also meant that the Blackfoot's neighbors had no access to gunsmiths for repairs and could not build direct relationships with traders. Blackfoot people knew that without regular and direct access to trading posts, the Shoshones, Flatheads, and others could not keep pace with them.[35]

Blocking their neighbors' access to trade yielded ancillary benefits as well, and some Blackfoot people profited by shuttling goods between the North Saskatchewan and the Rocky Mountains at a substantial markup. The HBC's Peter Fidler remarked that the Piikanis in particular made "vast profits" by purchasing furs from the mountain nations and reselling them to the HBC for ten to twelve times as much. More than other mountain nations to the south, the nearby Kootenais relied entirely on Blackfoot middlemen for European goods, and the NWC's David Thompson remarked that the Piikanis held them in "dependence" through trade. Positioning themselves as intermediaries also allowed the Blackfoot to control exactly what European technologies their neighbors could acquire, though they did provide some guns to the Kootenais. Their ties to mountain groups also allowed the Piikanis to acquire some beaver pelts in return, a valuable trade commodity Blackfoot people mostly resisted acquiring by their own hunting or trapping due to their religious beliefs. By shaping the region's economic geography to their advantage, Blackfoot people ensured that the fur trade always benefited them more than their neighbors.[36]

While Blackfoot people used the threat of violence to dissuade other Indigenous people from visiting the trading posts on the North Saskatchewan, they faced a far more delicate challenge in preventing the whites from going themselves to visit Indigenous nations. In September 1800, the NWC engaged experienced surveyor David Thompson to cross into the mountains, visit the Kootenais, and then explore onward until he reached the Pacific Ocean. Today remembered as one of the greatest explorers and geographers in Canadian history, Thompson rose from humble origins. Cast into poverty upon the death of his father, Thompson grew up in a charity hospital in London before being apprenticed to the HBC shortly after his fourteenth birthday in 1784. While employed at Manchester House in 1787, Thompson wintered with a Piikani family and developed a friendship with the aged Piikani warrior Young Man. In subsequent years, Thompson developed remarkable talent as a surveyor, and in 1797 he left the HBC for the NWC and became its chief western geographer. A man of unquestioned intelligence, confidence, and curiosity, Thompson had close personal ties to the Piikanis and could communicate in Blackfoot and Cree languages. He would make a formidable adversary to Blackfoot interests.[37]

The Piikanis first tried to turn Thompson away using personal appeals. When Piikani leaders learned that Thompson had hired a guide to take him to the mountains, they rushed to intercept him and did "all they could to persuade [him] to return" to Rocky Mountain House. They warned him that he and his horses would likely die of fatigue and hunger before he found the Kootenais. When Thompson proceeded anyway, a more experienced Piikani diplomat named Sakatow tracked him down. A renowned orator and the Piikanis' most prominent civil chief, the "remarkably well made" Sakatow wore two fine otter skins adorned with mother of pearl upon his back to indicate his high status. Sakatow implored Thompson to turn back, explaining that if the Kootenais and Flatheads acquired firearms, it would result in "great Hurt" to the Piikanis. In response, Thompson falsely claimed that his journey's main purpose was to settle a small group of NWC-affiliated Haudenosaunee (Iroquois) and Saulteaux trappers in the foothills between the mountains and plains to serve as a buffer between the warring groups. Though dismayed, Sakatow nonetheless allowed him to journey onward.[38]

When misinformation and diplomacy failed, the Piikanis turned to more forceful tactics in order to undermine Thompson. After Sakatow parted ways with Thompson, the Piikanis impeded the expedition however they could. Thompson later reported (and possibly exaggerated) that as he and his Kootenai guides moved westward, they "frequently had to fight [their] way thro' the [Piikani] Indians by force of Arms." Thompson sent two men ahead to spend the winter with the Kootenais, but Piikani attacks, ill health, and bad guides forced him to abandon his explorations by the spring of 1801. A few months later, Thompson hired a Kootenai guide to lead him on a second expedition into the mountains, but the guide was murdered by unnamed assailants within miles of Rocky Mountain House. Growing desperate, Thompson hired a Cree guide known as The Rook, along with an elderly Kootenai woman who had been taken captive years earlier. On their journey west, The Rook fretted constantly that he would be killed, and eventually led the entire party into a steep impasse in the mountains. Blaming his "worthless" and "timorous" guide for the expedition's failure, Thompson once again returned to Rocky Mountain House. Through violence and intimidation, the Piikanis thus thwarted the first attempts by whites to expand into the northern Rocky Mountains, preserving the Blackfoot people's regional superiority in the process.[39]

BY THE DAWN of the nineteenth century, Blackfoot people had begun to rebuild following the devastation of the 1781 smallpox epidemic. Through aggressive raiding they had driven nettlesome adversaries like the Shoshones and Flatheads from the northwest plains, and their territories once again expanded past the Marias and Missouri Rivers to the south. Blackfoot warriors mastered the art of raiding and traveled vast distances for horses and human captives. Blackfoot entrepreneurs became coveted trade partners for Indigenous nations in the intermountain West and grew wealthy by controlling the flow of European goods. Native peoples throughout the Northwest lived in the shadow of the growing Blackfoot ascendancy, and often in fear of it. In terms of sheer geography, the three Blackfoot nations had together become one of the most expansive and powerful polities in all of North America.

Above all else, Blackfoot people used the fur trade to drive their ascendancy. In the chaotic aftermath of the 1781 catastrophe, Blackfoot people harnessed direct trade with whites to improve their material circumstances and their security. By casting aside the middlemen, they gained crucial advantages over other Native people, and they carefully maintained their direct ties to British and Canadian traders. They created individual bonds of kinship and friendship with white traders using adoption, sexual exchange, and interpersonal diplomacy. They choreographed their trade visits to affirm peaceful relations, especially through gift exchange. They manipulated the plains environment by driving off bison to create a demand for their own products. And finally, they used both diplomacy and violence to prevent other Indigenous nations from gaining equal access to the whites. Together, these strategies laid the foundation for Blackfoot dominance throughout the region. Despite the dramatic changes that had unfolded on the northwest plains over the previous century, Blackfoot people remained determined to dictate the terms of European expansion into the Northwest, and not the other way around.[40]

PART II | Boundaries,

1806–1848

CHAPTER THREE

Now They Will Pretend to Equal Us

[The Kootenais] have always been our slaves (Prisoners) and now
they will pretend to equal us; no, we must not suffer this, we must
at once crush them, we know them to be desperate Men, and we
must destroy them, before they become too powerful for us.

—SAKATOW (Piikani), 1807

The Country about the sources of the Missouri, forms a part of the
tract wandered over by a nation of Indians, called the *Blackfoot*, a
ferocious savage race, who have conceived the most deadly hatred
to the Americans.

—HENRY MARIE BRACKENRIDGE (American), 1816

On July 26, 1806, Side Hill Calf and his fellow warriors rode north full of
pride. The eight young Piikanis had just completed a long journey to the lands
south of the Missouri River that had resulted in their capture of nearly thirty
horses from the Crows. Delighted with their success, they felt eager to return home astride their new mounts and resplendent in their war paint to
bask in the admiration of their friends and families. Ambitious young Blackfoot men lived for moments like these. Horse raids were keystones in the
lives of young warriors like Side Hill Calf, most of whom dreamed of accu-
mulating enough successes to one day become respected community leaders, not to mention attractive potential husbands. The young men also knew
that raids were essential to their community's well-being. People could use
the new mounts to hunt bison and carry lodges, to replace horses lost in
enemy raids, and to improve the overall prestige of the band within the
Piikani nation. Nearly a century after horses first arrived on the northwest
plains, horse raiding had become indispensable to the region's culture and
politics. The young men therefore had good reason to feel proud of their ac-
complishment. With Side Hill Calf in the lead, the cadre felt more confident the farther north they traveled.

The triumphant ride came to an abrupt halt that afternoon, however, as
the youths crossed the Two Medicine River in what is now northwest Montana. On a distant hillside, they spotted a cluster of strange men—white
men, hundreds of miles south of their usual trading posts. Their presence

raised immediate alarms. What were the náápiikoan doing here in the south, so far from their homes on the North Saskatchewan River? What were they looking for, and what did they want? The Piikanis hurried to gather their weapons and secure their new horses. On the other hillside, the whites felt similarly nonplussed at the unplanned encounter. When their leader, Meriwether Lewis, set off with three men to explore the area days earlier, he had remarked that he hoped "to avoid an interview" with the Blackfoot if at all possible. But as the two parties eyed each other from across the open prairie, they felt they had little choice but to approach one another and take their chances with a meeting. Following some awkward greetings and a handshake, Lewis gave a medal, a flag, and a handkerchief to three of the Piikanis, and the two groups set up camp together near the riverbank. Twelve in all, they passed the evening beside the fire, smoking and conversing in sign language.

It soon dawned on the Piikanis that these strangers did not come from the same place as the British and Canadian traders in the north. Through signings by George Drouillard, a mixed-ancestry French-Canadian and Shawnee man who served the strangers' expedition as a hunter and interpreter, they learned that Lewis claimed to represent a great power in the East led by a "Great Father," and that he had spent two years traveling throughout the West establishing peaceful trade with the many Indigenous peoples he met. Lewis told the Blackfoot youths that he had traveled a great distance, "and had seen a great many nations all of whom [he] had invited to come and trade . . . on the rivers on this side of the mountains." Lewis offered to broker a peace agreement between the Piikanis and the Flatheads, then added that he hoped to establish a trading post for both groups at the mouth of the Bear River (which the explorers renamed Maria's River, though the apostrophe was later dropped), in what is now northwest Montana. The stranger's audacity undoubtedly stunned the Piikanis, but Side Hill Calf and the others kept their feelings to themselves.

At daybreak the next morning, the Piikanis awoke and quietly warmed themselves at the campfire. When Side Hill Calf noticed that watchman Joseph Field had carelessly laid his gun down beside his sleeping brother Reuben, he gave his comrades a signal to act. Side Hill Calf crept silently to take the Fields' weapons, while two of the other Piikanis inched toward Drouillard and Lewis. But their stealth failed them, and suddenly the words "Let go my gun!" pierced the quiet morning air. Side Hill Calf leapt up and sprinted for safety but was overtaken and tackled to the ground by Joseph and Reuben. As the fledgling Piikani leader struggled desperately to free himself from their grasp, one of the Field brothers drove a knife into his heart. Meanwhile,

Meriwether Lewis shooting a Piikani man on the morning of July 27, 1806. This illustration, created later, depicts six men in Lewis's party instead of four. (*Captain Lewis shooting an Indian*, in Gass, *Journal of the Voyages*, opposite 245, courtesy of the Beinecke Rare Book and Manuscript Library, Yale University.)

one of the other Piikanis worked frantically to untie the reins that held the Americans' horses, but a single shot from Lewis's rifle struck him in the stomach and he crumpled to the ground. The six remaining Piikanis mounted their horses and rode north to safety. One of them—a thirteen-year-old named Wolf Calf—lived long enough to tell his story to ethnographers more than eighty years later. The four unharmed Americans recovered their weapons and horses and galloped away to the south, toward the Missouri River, William Clark, and the rest of the Corps of Discovery. Two months later they floated into St. Louis, to the rapturous reception of a nation fascinated with the strange lands and peoples of the so-called Louisiana Territory.[1]

Why did Side Hill Calf and his fellow warriors risk their lives trying to cripple Lewis's expedition? Capturing the Americans' horses and guns offered the ambitious youths more personal glory and advancement, of course, but communal concerns almost certainly motivated them as well. The Piikanis had to have recognized that Lewis and the other American explorers threatened the very foundation of Blackfoot prosperity and security: their privileged access to the fur trade. European trade goods and horses had enabled the Blackfoot people's ascendancy in the decades following the 1781 smallpox epidemic, and for years the Blackfoot had fiercely guarded their access to these technologies. Their blockade on the expansion of the fur trade preserved their military superiority over nations like the Flatheads and Shoshones—not to mention the Crows they had just raided—who lacked equal access to guns, knives, and metal arrowheads. By ascending the Missouri River and laying the groundwork for direct trade with these groups, Lewis and the Corps of Discovery threatened to destroy the balance the Blackfoot had meticulously crafted and leave them vulnerable to freshly armed enemies. Side Hill Calf and his companions thus recognized Lewis as an existential threat. When they saw their opportunity to take his horses and strand him on the prairie, they took it, despite great personal risk. The causes of the Two Medicine fight ran far deeper than Lewis or his fellow Americans understood.

The 1806 fight on the Two Medicine River marked the beginning of a dangerous and profoundly consequential period in Blackfoot history, as Blackfoot people found themselves increasingly enmeshed in violent conflicts with náápiikoan intruders. Beginning in 1806, Blackfoot warriors and their Gros Ventre allies mounted a determined resistance to any Americans who followed Lewis and Clark's path up the Missouri River. Their battles against the American explorers, trappers, and traders who ascended the river's uppermost portions ultimately closed off one of the United States' great western thoroughfares for a generation. During the same time period, they took a similar stance toward British and Canadian explorers along the Saskatchewan River in Rupert's Land, and their concerted campaigns forced the British and Canadians to abandon or reroute their plans for expansion into the intermountain West. Between 1806 and the 1820s, Blackfoot people used violence and intimidation to restrict colonial expansion and preserve crucial advantages over their neighbors. Their strategy, though often misconstrued as simply reactionary violence, would shape the course of British, Canadian, and American expansion throughout the North American West.

FOR YOUNG BLACKFOOT MEN like Side Hill Calf and his companions, conflict had become an inescapable and omnipresent reality by the early nineteenth century. As raiders and budding warriors, Side Hill Calf and the other young Piikanis followed a well-worn path toward prosperous manhood in Blackfoot society. Horses had become the key to social and economic mobility for men. They represented the ultimate source of individual wealth, since they could be used for hunting, carrying possessions or trade goods, raiding other nations, or could themselves be traded for other goods. Men could also reap provisions and hides by lending their horses to less fortunate hunters in return for a share of the kill. Possessing surplus horses to lend out instantly boosted one's social status as well, since people preferred to follow leaders who demonstrated generosity toward the younger and less fortunate. Lending or giving horses to the poor therefore allowed wealthy Blackfoot men to build the political support needed to ascend to chieftaincy. Wealth in horses also allowed men to support multiple wives, who of course provided emotional and physical companionship but who also helped build wealth by preparing the provisions and furs used in trade. Wealth begat more wealth, and over time Blackfoot society became increasingly stratified between the horse-rich and the horse-poor. The only way for men to break the cycle and rise up in society was by organizing or joining a successful horse-raiding party, like the one Side Hill Calf led against the Crows.[2]

Horse raids often led to warfare, which was equally essential to Blackfoot honor and prestige. Although the ideal horse raid ended by escaping undetected, raiders sometimes fought and died when they were discovered. Honor demanded revenge by family and friends, so survivors organized war parties. Unlike horse-raiding parties, who traveled out on foot in small groups, war parties were usually mounted and were much larger, sometimes numbering in the hundreds. As Siksika elder Crooked Meat Strings later explained, revenge parties never came back empty handed. Warriors sought to kill enemies and to capture their horses, their goods, and often their scalps. According to Crooked Meat Strings, proper vengeance did not necessarily require that the specific perpetrator of the initiating event be killed. Vengeance required only blood, for even if avengers could not locate a member of the offending nation, they could sometimes mete out revenge against a different enemy. For example, if Crows killed a Siksika horse raider but Siksika avengers could not find Crows to attack in turn, they might attack and kill enemy Crees instead, even if those Crees had been uninvolved in the initial killing. The violence perpetuated itself ad infinitum: the need for defense against horsebound attackers demanded the capture of horses, and every revenge killing inspired more men to seek revenge. Little wonder that Blackfoot men measured themselves by success in warfare, and that women soon far outnumbered men in Blackfoot communities.[3]

As in all aspects of Blackfoot life, religion and spiritual power played significant roles in warfare and raiding. Elders later explained to the Piikani researcher David Duvall that before leaving, young warriors would usually pay a visit to a more experienced warrior or medicine man in order to request some spiritual power. This usually came in the form of a war song, face paint, and a physical token of that power like a feather or feathers for the young warrior to wear in his hair. The elder Adam Young Man explained to another researcher that before battle a prudent warrior would be careful to tell his fellow travelers about his acquired powers, so that his companions could "show token and sing song . . . if he lost consciousness." On the eve of their departure from camp, warriors sang "wolf songs" together to bring them good fortune, while they reserved other war songs to sing just before the battle itself. If the raid or war party had success, upon returning, young warriors would then give a captured horse or gun to whoever provided them with their spiritual powers, and novices often received new names in recognition of their bravery. According to the Piikani elder Split Ears, if a war party killed enemies while losing few or none of their own, the women of the band would perform a scalp dance, in which they honored the returning warriors with an elaborate dance and sang unique songs heralding their victory. For example, one song celebrated a victory over the renowned Assiniboine warrior White Dog with the line "White Dog at last had to cry" when he realized he would die at Blackfoot hands. Spirituality, combined with political, economic, and social pressures, made intertribal conflict a deeply meaningful and increasingly inescapable aspect of Blackfoot life.[4]

Violence served vital purposes, but it could also have a corrosive effect upon life within Blackfoot bands, and even within Blackfoot lodges. Omnipresent conflict enabled the rise of chiefs who did not embody the values that traditionally led to power, such as generosity and calm wisdom. Aggressive and violent men sometimes gained followings, such as Big Man of the Siksikas, whose powerful physique and violent temperament made him a fearsome warrior but an impulsive and bullying leader. Chiefs like Big Man, while in the minority, exacerbated tensions with outsiders. Violence could also be redirected in more intimate spaces. As men became trained in violence, some may have grown inured to it. Brawls between men became more frequent, especially when British or Canadian alcohol flowed. Domestic violence may have increased as well. In its most severe manifestation, Blackfoot men sometimes mutilated wives they accused of adultery by cutting off their noses as a mark of shame. Although relatively few women suffered this fate, the well-documented presence of disfigured women raises the prospect that constant conflicts with other nations may have also given rise to more brutality in domestic life. Blackfoot country had become a more violent place than ever when Meriwether Lewis intruded in 1806.[5]

Conflicts grew more frequent during the early nineteenth century, as tensions across the northwest plains ratcheted up. The Blackfoot had been the region's ascendant power for decades, at least since they had begun trading directly with whites in 1782. Access to North Saskatchewan River trading posts like Edmonton and Fort Augustus formed the key to Blackfoot power. Ready access to European weaponry allowed Blackfoot bands to raid nations to their south and west for horses and captives with relative impunity. The aggression of Blackfoot raiders, particularly Piikanis, forced groups like the Flatheads, Kootenais, and Pend d'Oreilles to abandon their bison hunts on the plains, and a steady assault likewise forced Shoshone bands to retreat south of the Missouri River entirely by the end of the eighteenth century. But Blackfoot dominance was already facing challenges when Lewis and the Corps of Discovery arrived, particularly in the northern portions of their territory adjoining the North Saskatchewan.

In the north, Blackfoot relations with the British and Canadian traders had become increasingly tense by 1806. In the early years of the nineteenth century, both the HBC and the NWC concluded that they could not justify the cost of transporting less valuable furs like wolf and began to prioritize beaver furs and bison provisions in their western trade. In 1812, both companies officially cut off all purchases of wolf pelts, a change that impacted Blackfoot traders disproportionately, since they traded more wolf pelts than their neighbors and generally avoided killing beavers for religious reasons. White traders noted a growing "discontent" among Blackfoot visitors, some of whom became so frustrated that they threatened violent retaliation on the trading companies. Others tried to force the companies to purchase wolf pelts by withholding their few beaver pelts if they did not buy wolf pelts as well. Outside of provisions, company traders became less interested in what the Blackfoot offered. NWC trader Alexander Henry remarked, "The trade with the [Blackfoot] Indian Tribe is of very little consequence to us. . . . Their principal trade is Wolves, of which of late years we take none." The source of Blackfoot strength for decades, the fur trade on the North Saskatchewan River had grown frustratingly difficult during the early years of the nineteenth century.[6]

Equally troubling to the Blackfoot were their deteriorating relations with other Indigenous nations along the North Saskatchewan. For generations, trade had brought the Blackfoot together with their Cree and Assiniboine neighbors. Prior to European contact, the Blackfoot had relied on the Crees' seasonal trade rendezvous for access to trade goods, and beginning in the early eighteenth century they looked to Cree and Assiniboine middlemen to bring them European items. Generation upon generation of exchange intertwined the social lives of many Blackfoot, Cree, and Assiniboine people. Their warriors often joined forces to go on raids to the south and west. Some people moved between the different nations, such as the Piikani elder Young Man, who had been born a Cree but joined the Piikanis after his Cree wife left him for another man. Others intermarried and often became key intermediaries in trade and diplomacy. Relations between the groups remained relatively peaceful even after the middleman trade became obsolete in 1782. All three groups shared access to the North Saskatchewan posts, and they kept peace in order to maintain it. Deep social ties, as well as the mutual need for access to HBC and NWC, encouraged cordiality. For a while, the posts on the North Saskatchewan worked as a de facto neutral ground, where no group wielded total supremacy, and where it remained in every group's interest to maintain peace so they could trade with the whites.[7]

Despite generally peaceful ties, tensions began to build between the Blackfoot and the Crees and Assiniboines after 1782, when their trade partnerships ended and they began competing for trade and resources. After the middleman system ended, some Cree and Assiniboine bands began to expand onto the plains and parklands south of the North Saskatchewan River—territory that until then had been occupied mostly by Siksikas. These newcomers abandoned their annual round of hunting and trapping in woodland areas in favor of one much like that of the Blackfoot. They ditched their canoes in favor of horses and began to hunt bison for food and shelter, and like the Blackfoot traded bison provisions to whites. However, these plains Crees and Assiniboines struggled to replenish their horse herds as quickly as groups farther south, since their horses often died during the winter months for lack of forage. They had limited options to trade for horses, so they resorted to raiding and soon earned a reputation as the most aggressive horse thieves in the region by the end of the eighteenth century. The Blackfoot, who became their most common targets, raided in turn, and good relations between the groups frayed.[8]

In the summer of 1806, just weeks before the Two Medicine fight between the Piikanis and Lewis, the tenuous bonds between the Blackfoot and their Cree and Assiniboine neighbors reached a breaking point. In July, a large party of Kainais and Siksikas joined an encampment of Crees and Assiniboines in order to wage war against the Gros Ventres, who had attacked and killed several Assiniboines the previous April. During their journey south, a quarrel began over the ownership of a horse. The argument quickly escalated into a full-fledged battle, laying bare the tensions that had long been building between the groups. The Crees and Assiniboines fought the Kainais and Siksikas in a day-long fracas that left at least twenty-four of the latter dead, and three of the former. Traders noted that in the wake of the battle, many Crees and Assiniboines fled the plains "to conceal themselves in the woods" throughout the fall and winter while Blackfoot war parties sought revenge. Their fears proved well-founded, for in September 1806—just weeks after Lewis and his detachment from the Corps of Discovery had passed through—a Siksika war party ambushed a group of around forty oblivious Crees returning from a visit to Piikani camps and killed or captured all but three. As the conflicts intensified, traders on the North Saskatchewan complained about diminished trade returns, since most Native people avoided visiting posts that fall and winter for fear of enemy attacks.[9]

Open warfare with the Crees and Assiniboines threatened Blackfoot trade and security, and leaders sought out a peaceful resolution. After the winter ice thawed in April 1807, a Siksika civil chief named Old Swan led a small delegation to Edmonton. Old Swan seemed a natural fit to spearhead peace negotiations, having headed the largest Siksika band for over a decade, and having long maintained friendly relations with both the Crees and white traders. His task was urgent. Old Swan explained to HBC trader James Bird that "his Country Men all wish[ed] sincerely for Peace," having grown "accustomed to be supplied with Brandy Tobacco &c." He added that "these articles are become objects of primary necessity to them & nothing but absolute Danger can prevent their coming to procure them as usual." Blackfoot traders had been forced to avoid the trading posts throughout the previous fall and winter out of fear of meeting Cree or Assiniboine enemies. Old Swan's people had grown eager, even frantic, to reopen trade. Diplomacy seemed the surest route for securing their ability to exchange that winter's collection of wolf pelts, provisions and furs for alcohol, tobacco, iron awls, kettles, axes, cloth, knives, guns, ammunition, and more.[10]

During an April 1807 meeting outside of Edmonton, Old Swan succeeded in brokering a peace between the Blackfoot nations and the Cree-Assiniboine coalition. As part of the peace agreement, a young Siksika man stayed behind with the Crees, likely in the hope that his adoption would create family ties between the groups and that he could act as an intermediary if called upon. The arrangement worked and over the following months HBC traders at Edmonton reported frequent visits from Siksika, Kainai, and Piikani traders. But Old Swan's tenuous peace did not last. For reasons now lost to us, in September 1808 the young Siksika man was murdered by his Cree hosts. His relatives swore revenge, and relations between the groups again descended into open war. Despite the exertions of leaders like Old Swan, a lasting peace between Blackfoot people and the Cree-Assiniboine coalition never again materialized.[11]

The break between the Blackfoot and the Crees and Assiniboines had far-ranging effects on trade. Most damagingly for the Blackfoot, the conflict made it dangerous to visit British and Canadian trading posts on the North Saskatchewan River. When the trading posts first appeared during the 1780s and 1790s, the river marked the approximate boundary between the territories of plains groups like the Blackfoot and the mixed woodland groups like the Crees and Assiniboines. The gradual movement of Crees and Assiniboines onto the parklands and plains to the south, and the simultaneous southward expansion of the Blackfoot at the expense of groups like the Shoshones, had shifted Blackfoot territory gradually southward. Later oral histories from Cree elders sometimes noted that their territories on the prairies below the North Saskatchewan were "Blackfoot country originally," until the Crees "[drove] them back." Thus, the HBC and NWC posts on the North Saskatchewan stood in lands claimed increasingly by the Crees and Assiniboines—enemy territory to the Blackfoot after 1806. Blackfoot traders had to be careful. The Blackfoot "seldom go to the Fort but in smaller bands," wrote an HBC trader at Edmonton House in 1823, "owing to their dread of the Crees & Thick Woods Assiniboines." Piikani bands began to trade more frequently at Rocky Mountain House and Acton House, which had fewer Cree and Assiniboine visitors; however, the HBC and NWC only operated these posts irregularly. The Blackfoot continued to visit the North Saskatchewan despite the growing difficulty and danger of their journeys.[12]

As clashes with their neighbors worsened, the Blackfoot turned to new partnerships. The Gros Ventres, a plains nation whose territories mostly lay just east of Blackfoot lands, shared common adversaries and interests with the Blackfoot, and became essential allies after 1806. Like the Blackfoot, the Gros Ventres experienced frequent horse raids from the Crees and Assiniboines, with whom they had been in constant conflict since the 1790s. Also like the Blackfoot, the Gros Ventres enjoyed access to the North Saskatchewan posts and shared a desire to keep European arms and ammunition out of the hands of groups like the Flatheads and Shoshones. Beginning in 1806, Gros Ventre warriors frequently joined the Blackfoot in raids and war parties, especially into the mountainous regions to the west and south. They also joined the Blackfoot in trade, and joint trading parties of Gros Ventres and Kainai or Siksika traders became a common occurrence at Edmonton. In subsequent years, the Blackfoot and Gros Ventres became so linked that many outsiders had trouble telling them apart. American traders and trappers in particular almost always referred to Gros Ventres as "Blackfeet." In many ways, the groups became politically inseparable.[13]

In addition to forming new alliances, Blackfoot people responded to their mounting challenges by redoubling their commitment to suppressing enemies to the west and south. Although Blackfoot people could not disarm the Crees and Assiniboines to their north and east, they could still ensure that their southern and western neighbors lacked access to European weaponry. So long as they maintained this advantage over certain neighbors, they could gain strength by raiding them for horses and captives. They could also keep their position as trade intermediaries, shuttling a few European goods to mountain nations at a heavy markup. This became especially important after the HBC and NWC stopped purchasing wolf pelts, since Blackfoot traders could still acquire beaver pelts from mountain peoples instead of capturing them on their own, which would violate religious rules. If any white traders established direct ties to mountain nations, the Blackfoot would lose a great deal.

Meriwether Lewis therefore arrived in Blackfoot country at precisely the wrong time, with precisely the wrong message. His pronouncement that he had crossed over the mountains and invited "a great many nations" to trade fundamentally undermined the Blackfoot at a precarious moment in their history. Blackfoot leaders understood that their position had grown delicate, and they would act forcefully to safeguard their interests.

THOUGH THE BLACKFOOT and their homelands were still separated by more than a thousand miles from any American settlements, by 1806 Blackfoot interests had already begun to run afoul of those of the United States of America, a new nation that gained its independence from Great Britain just a year after Blackfoot people first visited trading posts. The freedom to expand west into Indigenous lands had motivated the Americans to break away from the British Empire, and after their revolution American farmers poured over the Appalachian Mountains to found states like Ohio, Kentucky, and Tennessee. To open these lands for settlement, government officials cajoled and coerced Indigenous nations—many of whom had sided with the British during the war—into signing treaties that dramatically reduced their lands or evicted them altogether. Thomas Jefferson, the author of the Declaration of Independence and America's first Secretary of State, supported expansion with particular verve. Jefferson believed that the United States could only fulfill its revolutionary ideals through a populace composed of independent, land-owning farmers. In Jefferson's vision, a national commitment to yeoman farming would eclipse the evil of slavery (which he hypocritically practiced himself) and would give each citizen a direct stake in the future of the republic. When Jefferson became the third president of the United States in 1801, he therefore prioritized opening up new land for settlers. He found the opportunity to supercharge his expansionary goals two years later, when French officials unexpectedly offered to sell preemption rights to the vast Louisiana Territory in order to finance its ongoing fight against a slave uprising in its Saint-Domingue colony. In 1803, the United States completed the Louisiana Purchase, which included the portions of Blackfoot territory south of the forty-ninth parallel.[14]

Expanding American involvement in the fur trade in the trans-Mississippi West played a key role in Jefferson's vision for the country. To him, trading with Indians in the newly acquired lands west of the Mississippi River could serve multiple ends. First, trade would provide a temporary livelihood for the many Native nations who were being pushed west by American farmers crossing the Appalachians. Second, forming alliances and trade partnerships with Native people could provide a protective barrier against Spanish, British, and Russian expansion and help ensure the integrity of American claims. Third, and perhaps most importantly, the lands could provide an economic boon to the fledging republic. Trading furs with Native people would infuse wealth into downriver cities like St. Louis and New Orleans, and if a water route could be found that connected the Mississippi with the Pacific Ocean—a "northwest passage"—Americans could transport furs west to trade in Chinese markets. Lewis and Clark's Corps of Discovery set out from St. Louis in 1804 to make Jefferson's vision a reality. Over the next two years, the explorers traveled more than seven thousand miles, from St. Louis to the Pacific Ocean and back again. They established diplomatic ties with dozens of nations while promising Native leaders that American traders would follow. Although the expedition also confirmed that no northwest passage existed, it succeeded in laying the foundation for American expansion.[15]

Although their ambitions directly contradicted Blackfoot ones, Americans coveted the new opportunities presented to them by the Louisiana Purchase and the Lewis and Clark Expedition. This was especially true in the growing mercantile hub of St. Louis. Trade with Indigenous people had been essential to the fabric of St. Louis since its founding in 1764 as a fur trading post by Auguste Chouteau and Pierre Laclede. Located at the junction of the Missouri and Mississippi Rivers, St. Louis offered a perfect launching point for trading parties to the north, south, and west, and even east along the Ohio River, and it offered easy access to coastal and European markets via New Orleans. Over time, St. Louisans gained piecemeal knowledge about the mysterious lands that adjoined the upper portions of the Missouri to the west, and expeditions launched from St. Louis traveled as far as the Black Hills during the late eighteenth century. Still, wealthy merchant families like the Chouteaus took a conservative approach and avoided the risks inherent in sending exploring parties too far upriver. By the beginning of the nineteenth century, bolder thinking took hold. The city briefly transferred out of Spanish hands to the French in 1802, then permanently to the United States in 1803. When the Corps of Discovery set off from St. Louis in 1804 to explore the Missouri River all the way to its sources, it inflamed the imaginations of a growing cohort of fur trader entrepreneurs who sought to challenge the city's elite and seize on America's expansionary energy.[16]

Even before the Corps of Discovery returned to St. Louis in September 1806, multiple parties of Americans followed their lead up the Missouri River. The first departed from St. Louis in secret in August 1806, led by a former army captain named John McClellan and financed by Brigadier General James Wilkinson, a former governor of Louisiana Territory whose position legally prohibited him from engaging in the Indian trade. Wilkinson tasked McClellan and around forty men with establishing a trading post at the mouth of the Platte River in what is now Nebraska. While ascending the river on September 17, McClellan encountered the returning Corps of Discovery and learned that the Upper Missouri River and the mountains to the west teemed with beavers and eager Indigenous trade partners. McClellan changed the plan and set out to re-create the Corps of Discovery's journey up the Missouri River and into the mountains. By July 1807, McClellan's party of around forty members reached Flathead territory and built a post on the lower Flathead River, just over the mountains from Piikani lands. By following Lewis and Clark's detailed instructions and avoiding Blackfoot or Gros Ventre entanglements, the McClellan party became the first Americans to trade with Native peoples of the northern Rockies. For the first time, the Blackfoot's western and southern neighbors hosted náápiikoan traders in their own lands.[17]

More trouble was on the way. Just behind McClellan, a French-Canadian named Charles Courtin led another group of trappers and traders up the Missouri. Like McClellan, Courtin crossed paths with the returning Corps of Discovery in September 1806, and likewise gleaned information about opportunities for wealth in the far West. The Corps' reports of large beaver concentrations on the farthest portions of the Upper Missouri — the unfamiliar five-hundred-plus mile stretch of water upriver from its westward bend near the Mandan villages in what is now central North Dakota — intrigued Courtin. In spite of warnings he surely received from Lewis about

Blackfoot opposition, Courtin became determined to use the Missouri River to enter the northwest plains and make his fortune. By the autumn of 1807, Courtin and his party built a small trading post near the Three Forks of the Missouri (the area in what is now southwest Montana where the Jefferson, Gallatin, and Madison Rivers come together to form the Missouri), where they planned to spend the winter of 1807–8 trapping beavers and trading with friendly nations like the Crows and Shoshones. Even more than McClellan, Courtin brazenly infringed upon Blackfoot-dominated lands and violated Blackfoot restrictions on trapping and trade.[18]

Close on the heels of McClellan and Courtin, Manuel Lisa led the most well-known of the three Upper Missouri expeditions upriver in the spring of 1807. A Spanish-speaking St. Louisan and longtime fur trade veteran, Lisa was likewise inspired by Lewis and Clark's journey. Lisa planned to move incrementally, using his friendly trading relationships with Lower Missouri nations to grant him safe passage upriver beyond the Mandan villages, where he would build a fort and dispatch trappers to hunt for beavers. In November 1807, Lisa established Fort Raymond at the confluence of the Bighorn and Yellowstone Rivers in the territory of friendly Crow people. By the late fall of 1807, then, three new American establishments ringed Blackfoot country: one among the Flatheads to the west, one on the Missouri River to the south, and one on the Yellowstone to the southeast, among their enemies the Crows. These establishments formed an unwelcome counterpart to the HBC and NWC posts that bordered Blackfoot country to the north.[19]

The Blackfoot had reason to distrust the latest American visitors, even beyond the arming of their enemies. Unlike most of the British and Canadians they knew, the Americans also sought to trap animals and collect furs themselves. American trappers reaped hefty profits using simple beaver traps made up of two powerful steel jaws, laid open with a flat sheet of metal between them. When an animal stepped on the center sheet, the steel jaws would instantly spring closed. Trappers placed their contraptions in shallow water near the edges of beaver ponds, and usually baited them with twigs dipped in a pungent beaver secretion known as castoreum. When beavers came to investigate the smell, the trap would spring shut, usually leading the frantic beaver to drown itself in panic. Brutally simple yet efficient, this mechanism offered quick financial rewards for trappers and would eventually be used to decimate beaver populations across the West. The Americans who came to the northwest in 1807, especially Lisa, wanted to use traps to collect as many beaver pelts as possible before returning downriver. The Americans all ignored or misunderstood long-standing Blackfoot restrictions on beaver hunting. The Blackfoot had long prohibited outsiders from trapping beavers in their territories, which would effectively cut them out of any resulting economic exchange. Outsiders' trapping could also reduce beaver populations and disrupt ecosystems, since beavers retained water in river valleys during dry periods. Moreover, beavers had special religious significance to the Blackfoot, which made their mass slaughter by strangers especially distasteful. The American interlopers, in wantonly killing beavers and trading with the Blackfoot's adversaries, undermined Blackfoot people's security and sovereignty.[20]

It did not take long for Blackfoot people to detect the Americans' presence. Sometime in the fall of 1807, a joint Kainai and Gros Ventre raiding party discovered Charles Courtin's Missouri River outpost. Rather than attack, the surprised raiders met with the whites to learn their intentions, and later told HBC traders that the Americans "received them in a very friendly manner" and "made them presents." The strangers readily offered to trade guns to the Indigenous visitors in exchange for beaver pelts and bison robes. Courtin also proposed a "general meeting" the following spring, in order to "settle a Peace" with neighboring nations, to trade, and to discuss the further expansion of his operations. Making peace between the Blackfoot, Gros Ventres, Crows, and Shoshones would have served Courtin's interests, but not the Kainais and Gros Ventres to whom he proposed the meeting, who sought horses and prestige by raiding gun-poor nations south of the Missouri. The meeting demonstrated that Blackfoot people were not reflexively hostile to Americans, but at the same time they could only accept Courtin if he stopped trading with their enemies and trapping on their lands.[21]

The Blackfoot and Gros Ventres quickly realized that none of the three American expeditions had any interest in respecting Native limitations on their trading and trapping. Sometime in the spring of 1808, a large party of Blackfoot and/or Gros Ventre warriors attacked a band of Crows near the Three Forks of the Missouri. At the time the Crows also hosted a sizable group of Flathead visitors, which on its own was unremarkable. The two nations had long-standing trading ties to one another, since Blackfoot blockades had forced the Flatheads to go through Crow intermediaries to obtain a trickle of European goods from Mandan and Hidatsa villages. The groups had probably come together that spring to trade or to visit one of the new American trading posts. More shocking to the raiders was that a white man named John Colter was with the Crows as well, and that he fought alongside his hosts when the battle began. A veteran of the Corps of Discovery, Colter had returned to the Upper Missouri with Lisa, and had traveled west from Fort

Raymond in order to invite western Indigenous nations to trade. Word of Colter's participation in the fight spread quickly among Blackfoot bands, stoking fears that the Americans had cast their lot with the Flatheads and Crows. Colter's very presence threatened Blackfoot interests.[22]

Blackfoot warriors found their chance for revenge on Colter a few months later, when he returned to the same area with a fellow trapper named John Potts. According to Colter's account, a large Blackfoot war party (Colter said the party consisted of five or six hundred men, but may well have exaggerated), perhaps accompanied by Gros Ventres, spotted and surrounded the two men as they canoed in a small creek to check their traps. When the warriors beckoned them ashore, Potts panicked and shot wildly, and was quickly killed. The warriors then stripped Colter naked and told him to run. After giving him a head start of several hundred yards, the warriors chased after him on foot. The athletic Colter outdistanced all but one Blackfoot man, who slipped and fell when Colter abruptly turned to face him, his face and chest smeared from a heavy nosebleed. Colter then escaped by hiding in a beaver dam for the rest of the day before hiking back to Fort Raymond. "Colter's Run" quickly became frontier lore, told and retold throughout the West as a tale of idealized white manhood and perceived Indian savagery. The dramatic encounter served as a warning to other Americans about the dangers of trapping and trading in Blackfoot country.[23]

After their two run-ins with Colter, the Blackfoot and their Gros Ventre allies abandoned all patience with the Americans. Sometime in the late summer or early fall of 1808, a joint party of Kainai and Gros Ventre raiders attacked and destroyed Courtin's fledgling post at the Three Forks of the Missouri, killing one man and stripping the ten others naked before allowing them to escape. In October they brought their fresh plunder, including three hundred of the Americans' beaver skins, north to Edmonton to trade to the HBC. Meanwhile, Courtin led his remaining employees west into Flathead territory and built a new post on the Jocko River. Two years later, Courtin decided to return to the plains to hunt bison, but a party of Piikanis quickly located him in a defile now called Hellgate Canyon, near present-day Missoula, Montana. In the ensuing fight, Courtin and a Native hunter died, and several other members of the party suffered wounds. When they described this event to NWC traders, Flathead observers "seemed to think that the imprudence of Mʳ Court[in], in going to the War Grounds, with a small party . . . was the cause of his death." Courtin's disregard for the Blackfoot and their opposition to his goals destined his expedition for disaster.[24]

The story of Colter's 1808 escape from Blackfoot warriors circulated widely, usually as an example of white heroism in the face of Indian "savagery," and bolstered the Blackfoot's reputation as hostile and aggressive toward Americans. This fanciful illustration lionizes Colter while badly misrepresenting Blackfoot dress and weaponry. (Hammatt Billings, *The Trapper and the Indians*, *Ballou's Pictorial*, May 10, 1856, p. 300.)

Blackfoot warriors likewise decided to drive out McClellan's party of traders and trappers. A war party of Piikanis and Gros Ventres attacked McClellan's men shortly after they first established a post on the lower Flathead River in the summer of 1807, which forced them to move north to Flathead Lake, farther from Piikani trails into the mountains. Over the next two years, perhaps due to fights with the Blackfoot and Gros Ventres, McClellan's party shrunk from over forty men to around twelve. Sometime in 1810, McClellan and his small cadre of survivors left their mountain outpost and moved onto the plains to hunt bison and trap beavers. In the fall of 1810, they, too, fell victim to Blackfoot attack, and word reached the HBC that Piikani warriors had "massacred an American force of 8 men near the sources of the Missouri . . . & scalped the whole lot." A handful of the Americans may have escaped, but the attack effectively ended the McClellan expedition. By destroying both the Courtin and McClellan parties in 1810, the Piikanis once again blocked the flow of trade to the Shoshones, Flatheads, and others, and in so doing preserved their own superiority over the mountains and plains.[25]

The Blackfoot found the opportunity to complete their expulsion of the Americans when Lisa, ignorant to the fate of his competitors, decided to expand his operations in 1810. Lisa incorporated his outfit as the Missouri Fur Company (MFC) in 1809, along with partners Pierre Menard and Andrew Henry. In the spring of 1810, Menard and Henry led thirty-two MFC employees to establish a new post at the Three Forks of the Missouri, where they began trapping beavers almost immediately. Over the ensuing weeks and months Blackfoot and/or Gros Ventre warriors systematically targeted the MFC trappers, killing eight within weeks of their arrival, including George Drouillard, the member of the Corps of Discovery who had clashed with eight Piikani youths on the Two Medicine River four years earlier. Soon, the surviving trappers felt too unsafe to leave their tiny fort. By the time the MFC abandoned the post in the fall of 1810, their tormenters had destroyed or plundered most of their equipment and furs, and twenty out of their original thirty-two men had died. The survivors fled south to take refuge among the Shoshones. In three years, the Blackfoot and their Gros Ventre allies eradicated all American presence in their homelands.[26]

The Blackfoot and Gros Ventres' wildly successful campaign against Americans on the Missouri between 1807 and 1810—though generally unknown or overlooked by historians—helped shift the course of American exploration and expansion in the West. Their attacks so decimated the first two American parties to follow the Lewis and Clark's footsteps into the mountains that those expeditions have been almost entirely forgotten to history. They likewise crippled the MFC, which lost most of its horses, equipment, and beaver pelts to the raiders. When they abandoned their Three Forks post in the fall of 1810, MFC employees had accumulated just thirty packs of beaver furs, far fewer than they had hoped. The losses dealt a death blow to the company, which was already struggling elsewhere, and in January 1812 Lisa and his partners dissolved the MFC. Although they soon reconstituted it with new financial backing, the outbreak of war with Great Britain limited their ambitions, and the reorganized MFC restricted its operations to the lower stretches of the Missouri River until Lisa's death in 1820. Despite some scattered reports of Blackfoot attacks on American trappers in ensuing years, the MFC's abandonment of the Three Forks effectively marked the end of American ambitions on the Upper Missouri for more than a decade. Blackfoot opposition blunted this initial thrust of U.S. expansion, and closed off the trail that Lewis and Clark blazed.[27]

By rendering the Upper Missouri region a dangerous no-man's-land for whites, the Blackfoot forced Americans to find new paths west, and after 1810 the bulk of American fur trading and trapping centered on the Pacific Northwest's Columbia River and on the central Rockies. In 1810, American John Jacob Astor's Pacific Fur Company (PFC) established a post called Astoria at the mouth of the Columbia River in present-day Oregon. Rather than follow Lewis and Clark's path, Astor's company opted to approach the northwest by sea, and Astor's employees maintained a deep-seated fear of Blackfoot country. For example, in 1812 a PFC employee named Robert Stuart led a party overland from Astoria to St. Louis in order to communicate with Astor, but sought a path "out of the walks of the Blackfoot Indians, who are very numerous, and inimical to the whites." Stuart and his companions eventually located a path across a desolate high plateau in what is now southern Wyoming but nearly resorted to cannibalism on the way. Stuart's route became known as the South Pass and would later serve as the primary migration route for the Oregon Trail. Instead of following the trails of Lewis and Clark, westward expansion proceeded by other routes: some, like Astor, sought to access the far west via the Pacific coast, while other Americans traveled overland via South Pass. Like a stream around a stone, the course of empire shifted to avoid Blackfoot country.[28]

AMERICAN TRADE WAS NOT the only challenge to Blackfoot dominance in the opening years of the nineteenth century. At the same time that the Blackfoot and Gros Ventres stifled American ambitions on the Upper Missouri, they faced an equally vexing challenge from the NWC in the north. Like the Americans, the Canadian traders of the NWC longed for new commercial opportunities in the intermountain West, and worried that the Americans would monopolize the region's fur trade if they did not act quickly. The NWC had tried to expand beyond the plains before, but David Thompson's 1800 and 1801 expeditions failed due in large part to Piikani interference. In 1807, Thompson organized a new expedition. Leaving Rocky Mountain House just after the winter ice thawed, Thompson, a Cree guide, and a handful of colleagues entered the mountains through a gap later known as Howse Pass. Finding the pass unguarded (perhaps as a result of Blackfoot preoccupations with the Two Medicine fight or their brewing conflicts with the Crees and Assiniboines), Thompson and his men crossed the continental divide in June and reached the headwaters of the Columbia River near what is now Invermere, British Columbia. There they erected a small cluster of log houses surrounded by a high stockade to protect them from the Blackfoot attacks they felt were sure to follow. Thompson named the new post "Kootenae House," and used it as a base to open trade with the area's Kootenai people. He sent word to the Flatheads to bring furs as well.[29]

Stunned Blackfoot leaders prepared their response. In early September 1807, a party of around thirty Piikanis visited Kootenae House saying they wanted to trade but left after a wary Thompson refused them entry. Thompson later learned that the Piikani visitors, led by respected war chief Kootenai Old Man, contemplated attacking the post from the outside but changed their minds when one of their leaders explained that he did not wish "to go and fight against Logs of Wood, that a Ball cannot go through, and with people we cannot see and with whom we are at peace." The decision to leave Kootenae House alone enraged the prominent Piikani civil chief Sakatow. Although Sakatow urged him to destroy the NWC post, Kootenai Old Man limited his actions to horse raiding and never attacked Kootenae House directly. Unable to dislodge Thompson by force, a delegation of Piikani leaders met with Kootenai, Flathead, and Nez Percé representatives at Kootenae House to negotiate a peace in December 1807, but their newly armed and emboldened counterparts rejected their overtures and boasted that they would fight them if necessary. Thompson's move into the mountains energized the Blackfoot's enemies, just as leaders like Sakatow had feared.[30]

Blackfoot people watched with concern as the NWC then expanded its footprint in the mountains. After two successful trading seasons at Kootenae House, Thompson established two more posts west of the continental divide: Kullyspell House in September 1809, on Lake Pend d'Oreille, and Saleesh House in November 1809, on the Clark Fork of the Columbia River, where he opened trade with Kalispell, Pend d'Oreille, and Flathead people. Commerce thrived. "Our arrival rejoiced them very much," Thompson recalled, as the Indigenous peoples of the Rockies eagerly exchanged beaver pelts for guns, ammunition, and iron arrowheads. Thompson's fellow trader Ross Cox remarked that the Flatheads "were overjoyed at having an opportunity of purchasing arms and ammunition, and quickly stocked themselves with a sufficient quantity of both." Although they bought few of the beads Thompson offered, women eagerly traded for metal awls, needles, and other "iron work." At long last, mountain peoples could experience the same transformations that nearby plains peoples had enjoyed some eighty years earlier.[31]

The fast success of Thompson's establishments highlighted their danger to Blackfoot people. Prior to Thompson's visit, warriors from mountain nations relied mostly on flint-headed arrows and lances for defense against

Blackfoot raiders, so their acquisition of metal technologies like iron arrowheads and firearms gave them equal footing with their Blackfoot enemies for the first time in generations. According to Thompson, the Piikani chief Sakatow had foreseen precisely this outcome when Thompson entered the mountains, warning fellow chiefs that the mountain nations had "always been our slaves (Prisoners) and now they will pretend to equal us." Since Blackfoot warriors could no longer strike with impunity, they turned to more clandestine tactics, which likely meant raiding by foot instead of horseback. Blackfoot people observed that their newly armed neighbors began to venture out beyond their mountain homelands, especially the Flatheads, Nez Percés, Kootenais, and Pend d'Oreilles, who hunted bison on the plains for the first time in a generation. The Blackfoot had forced each of these groups to abandon their bison hunts decades earlier, and mountain nations sought to reclaim what they felt was their ancestral right to hunt on the plains.[32]

Blackfoot people felt the full consequence of their failure in July 1810, when about 150 heavily armed Flatheads, along with three NWC employees, rode to the plains determined to resume their traditional bison hunt. When Piikani warriors spotted the intruders, they rushed to attack. For the first time, their charge was met with gunfire. The two groups battled throughout the day, at the end of which a handful of Flathead people and between seven and sixteen Piikanis lay dead. The Piikanis had no choice but to move their camp, and the Flatheads experienced their first successful bison hunt in decades. As Thompson remembered, "this was the first time the [Piikanis] were in a manner defeated." The Flatheads had borne the brunt of Blackfoot militarism for at least a generation, helplessly providing the horses that helped enable their well-armed enemies' ascendancy. Their 1810 victory over the Piikanis marked a significant shift in the political balance of the region, and the end of unchecked Blackfoot dominance over their western neighbors. The keeper of a Piikani winter count recorded it as the year "when we were driven in battle." It became an instructive, if unpleasant memory.[33]

Their defeat at the hands of the Flatheads forced Blackfoot leaders to redouble their efforts to isolate mountain nations from whites. By December 1810, they had driven out all three of the American expeditions, but Thompson's Canadian posts remained. Worse still, Blackfoot traders learned that the HBC had begun plotting to expand westward as well. Piikani leaders considered several strategies. According to Thompson, Piikani, Kainai, and Siksika leaders gathered in council immediately following the July battle, and several men proposed attacking the NWC traders at Rocky Mountain House and plundering the post in revenge for the company's arming the

Flatheads, but Kootenai Old Man convinced them that attacking the post would damage their own ability to trade. The Blackfoot saw the HBC and NWC as valued trade partners, unlike the Americans, so the idea of using the same sort of scorched earth tactics that they used against the Americans gave them pause. Instead of direct force, Blackfoot leaders opted first for intimidation. In the spring of 1811, a group of Piikanis visited Acton House and warned the HBC traders there that "if they again met a white man going to supply their Enemies, they would not only plunder & kill him, but that they would make dry Meat of his body." They conjured up the threat to terrify the traders, and it worked. HBC traders felt so alarmed that they abandoned their immediate plans to follow the NWC into the mountains.[34]

Blackfoot people also turned to a familiar European tactic — the blockade — to stifle trade. A Piikani chief named Black Bear stationed warriors along the North Saskatchewan River west of Rocky Mountain House to intercept NWC traders bound for Howse Pass. This came at an inopportune moment for the NWC. In the summer of 1810, the company's partners at Fort William voted to form a partnership with American John Jacob Astor, who had just founded the PFC and planned to establish trading operations on the Pacific coast. The NWC partners dispatched Thompson to lead a party across the mountains and meet the Americans at the mouth of the Columbia River. Thompson's task was twofold: in addition to notifying the PFC that his employers planned to accept Astor's terms, he was also tasked with discouraging the Americans from expanding inland, where the Canadians hoped to maintain their monopoly on trade. Thompson's mission did not go well. While Thompson himself managed to slip by the Piikanis, Black Bear stopped Thompson's reinforcements, and the famed cartographer had to spend several days hiding in a thicket beside the river. When his fellow employees finally managed to reach him, Thompson decided that they should try a new route farther north that would circumvent the Blackfoot entirely. Thompson's party marched thirty-four days north and crossed over Athabasca Pass in January 1811. When he finally reached the Pacific in July, he discovered that the PFC had already built Astoria at the mouth of the Columbia River just two months earlier. Astor had decided against the joint venture with the NWC, and Thompson had little success in discouraging the Americans' immediate ambitions to expand inland from the west. While Black Bear's blockade fell short of stopping all trade, it frustrated the Canadians' ambitions.[35]

Still, from the perspective of the Blackfoot, their campaign against the expansion of the fur trade represented an incomplete victory. They prevented mountain peoples from establishing lasting ties to Americans or the HBC, but the Canadians lingered stubbornly. Canadians continued to bypass them using Athabasca Pass, and in 1812 they purchased Astoria from the PFC. With the support of the British navy, the Canadians renamed it Fort George and used it as a base to export furs to Chinese markets. Saleesh House and Koo-tenae House became part of the Pacific-facing NWC's peripheral Spokane District. Although trade was limited due to irregular supplies via Fort George, guns and metal weapons continued to find their way into the hands of the Blackfoot's enemies, and conflicts intensified. Ross Cox, who traded at Saleesh House in 1813, wrote that the Flatheads' acquisition of guns and metal weapons had affected "a decided change in their favour." Relations be-tween the Blackfoot and the Kootenais took a similar turn. Despite their enormous effort and some successes, Blackfoot people faced a more danger-ous world.[36]

THE BLACKFOOT'S USE of violence and intimidation to advance their inter-ests in the early nineteenth century garnered them a fearsome reputa-tion, especially in the United States. The journals of the Lewis and Clark expedition, published in 1814, labeled both the Blackfoot and Gros Ventres as "vicious and profligate rovers," from whom whites had "everything to fear." (In his personal journal, Lewis called the Blackfoot "a vicious lawless and reather [sic] an abandoned set of wretches.") Although their actions against McClellan and Courtin remained mostly unknown, their conflicts with the MFC gained nationwide newspaper coverage in 1810 and 1811. A few years later, the incredible story of their pursuit of the naked Colter likewise made its way into newspapers as far away as Maine and Washington, D.C. Tales of their near-destruction of the MFC and their tormenting of Colter underscored the Blackfoot's supposed "hostility" and brutality, and gave rise to a portrayal of Blackfoot history that persisted long thereafter. Hiram Chittenden, who wrote the first major history of the fur trade in the United States, labeled them the "scourge of the Upper Missouri." Harvard historian Bernard De Voto followed suit in his 1952 fur trade opus The Course of Empire by declaring that the Blackfoot "were throughout the history of the fur trade to be nearly always hostile and always suspicious, bilious, and vicious."[37]

Americans' portrayals conveniently removed the Blackfoot from the his-torical context that moved them, and reduced Blackfoot motivations to a set of supposedly innate characteristics like hostility, viciousness, and lawless-ness. To American writers, Blackfoot warriors hounded American explorers and trappers because they were violent people, or because they were easily manipulated by crafty British rivals. These formulations implied that the

Blackfoot acted according to unchanging base impulses, not political, social, or economic considerations. This persistent mythology therefore obscured the extraordinary range of challenges that Blackfoot people faced in the century before Lewis's arrival. For nearly a century, the Blackfoot had lived in a world of profound and constant fluctuation, in which carefully deployed violence and hostility could serve important functions. Generations of people like Side Hill Calf came of age understanding that controlling the flow of European goods could give the Blackfoot a crucial upper hand on their neighbors and could protect them from the consequences of constant political destabilization, population loss, captive-raiding, horse-raiding, and war. By portraying the Blackfoot as the ultimate barriers to exploration and expansion, Americans overlooked the fact that colonialism had already shaped Blackfoot life for generations.[38]

A focus solely on Blackfoot hostility also obscures the powerful ways in which Blackfoot people dictated the limits of colonial expansion to meet their needs. For a generation after the Lewis and Clark Expedition ascended the Upper Missouri to the Rocky Mountains in order to lay the foundation for the expansion of the fur trade, no other Americans could replicate their success. The Blackfoot likewise slowed British and Canadian attempts to connect the North Saskatchewan River trade system with the Rocky Mountains. Across a large portion of northwestern North America, Blackfoot interests dictated the extent of Indigenous people's engagement with non-Native traders and explorers. In a landscape rife with uncertainty and conflict, the Blackfoot continually found new ways to assert themselves and to protect their way of life.

CHAPTER FOUR

Between Empires

> This morning eight blood Indians arrived . . . one of them is
> decorated in an American chief's Scarlet Coat of no inferior quality
> and a large green Blanket Powder horn and Blue bead wrought shot
> Bag thrown over his shoulders. The Indian told us that he gave four
> large Beaver for the Coat and three for the latter. He left us to judge
> the Price of them had they been disposed of by ourselves.
>
> —JOHN ROWAND (British), 1828

> Torment us they will till the last, [for] we are now on their territories
> and must take our chance.
>
> —PETER SKENE OGDEN (British), 1827

Early in the winter of 1830-31, a man named Ááhsa'paakii, or Good Woman, led a group of riders out of the Grease Melter band's winter encampment in the Belly River valley. The Piikani chief likely went in search of bison herds, which reliably retreated to the sheltered peripheries of the plains when temperatures dropped. Hunts in valleys and parklands provided crucial support for Blackfoot bands during the winter months. They broke up the monotony of the Closed season, a time when the Blackfoot by necessity stopped their communal travels and spent months on end in one spot, tending fires and clearing snow. Hunts also provided meat and fat to eat and to trade with the náápiikoan to the north, who conducted the majority of their trade during the winter. The thick wooly coats that bison developed during the winter had little value in trade with the British, but they kept the people warm when the cold winds blew. Like everyone in their community, Good Woman and his fellow riders knew that they had their role to play in the Grease Melters' fortunes. But on that day in 1830, they could scarcely have predicted that their routine foray would shake the very foundations of Piikani life.[1]

After perhaps a day's travel, Good Woman's Piikanis saw something truly unexpected: six white men, traveling by dogsled across the empty prairies north of the Missouri River. The sight of unexpected travelers in this area probably brought to the Piikanis' minds the well-known tale of Side Hill Calf, who a generation earlier had discovered Meriwether Lewis's

89

party of travelers on a nearby stretch of prairie under similar circumstances. That encounter had not ended well for either side. This time, Good Woman's Piikanis rode forth and made their unease known to the trespassers by threatening them and demanding to know their business. Good Woman restrained his young men before a fight could break out, perhaps because he recognized the whites' leader as a French-Canadian named Jacques Berger, who had visited Piikani and Kainai bands years earlier as a trader for the NWC. Why this familiar face would suddenly reappear after several years' absence in a corner of Blackfoot country where outsiders rarely trod was unclear. When tempers cooled, Good Woman allowed Berger to explain in broken Blackfoot that he had returned to Blackfoot land on behalf of a new American trading outfit called the American Fur Company (AFC), to meet with leaders like Good Woman and establish peaceful trade. In many ways, Berger's proposal closely echoed what Lewis had offered to Side Hill Calf in 1806 and came with no assurances that the AFC would steer clear of trading with the Blackfoot's many enemies. Nevertheless, Good Woman responded very differently than did his predecessors. Instead of fighting, he invited the strangers to spend the remainder of the winter as his guests.

The Piikani chief decided to take the Americans up on their offer. When the ice thawed in the spring of 1831, Good Woman and a delegation of around seventy Blackfoot people accompanied Berger to Fort Union, a newly constructed AFC trading post some two hundred miles east near the confluence of the Missouri and Yellowstone Rivers. Siksika and Kainai representatives came along as well, including the prominent Kainai chief Stámiksoosak, or Bull Back Fat. When they finally arrived at Fort Union, the chiefs smoked with AFC officials and formally invited them to build a trading post in Blackfoot territory, the first American post of its kind on the northwest plains. By the fall of 1831, AFC traders had built a fortified outpost near the confluence of the Missouri and Marias Rivers, in the heart of Piikani territory, where trade would flourish for nearly forty years. The Blackfoot blockade on the Upper Missouri fur trade had ended.[2]

If Blackfoot warriors had come upon Berger and his comrades in the same place peddling a similar message a decade or two earlier, they almost certainly would have responded with violence. However, a great deal had changed in the years leading up to 1830 that led Blackfoot people to embrace the Americans and their plans for the region. Although it seemed abrupt, Blackfoot leaders for years had envisioned peace with the Americans. Two major changes in the fur trade during the 1820s had demanded a bold rethinking of the Blackfoot's relationship to outsiders. First, their trade with the British and Canadians at the North Saskatchewan River posts had become an increasingly frustrating and less lucrative endeavor after 1821, when the British and Canadian companies merged and robbed Indigenous people of their hard-earned leverage in trade. Second, beginning in the early 1820s American and British traders and trappers flooded the Rocky Mountains in search of beaver furs and managed to provide guns and ammunition to the Blackfoot's adversaries, and by 1830 the Blackfoot nations had lost the material advantages over their neighbors that had enabled previous generations to dominate the region. These twin transformations upended the region's politics, but as always, the Blackfoot responded creatively and forcefully. Slowly, Blackfoot leaders formulated a new strategy, one that would turn American expansion from a hindrance into an advantage. Their shrewd diplomacy would turn Blackfoot country into one of North America's most vibrant borderlands.

IN THE DECADES prior to Good Woman's meeting with Berger in 1830, Blackfoot people generally regarded Americans as enemies while treating both the British and Canadians as valuable trade partners. They had good reason to oppose the Americans, who wanted to trade guns and ammunition to their enemies and often trapped beavers without Blackfoot permission. Good relations with the British and Canadians, on the other hand, contributed greatly to Blackfoot prosperity. Even though the NWC had themselves violated Blackfoot wishes by trading in the mountains, they remained important trade partners, and all three Blackfoot nations regularly visited plains NWC posts like Rocky Mountain House and Fort Augustus. Blackfoot people even protected the Canadians from harm. For example, when Gros Ventre warriors proposed a joint assault on the NWC's Rocky Mountain House in 1811 in revenge for the company's westward push, a Piikani chief named White Buffalo Robe convinced them not to, since it would damage trade. Blackfoot leaders kept their peace with Canadians, despite their fraught history.[3]

Along the North Saskatchewan River, Blackfoot people knew they benefited from working with two companies instead of one and pitted the British HBC and Canadian NWC against one another whenever possible. When they visited trading posts, Blackfoot parties almost always sent emissaries to both companies and decided where to bring their goods in part based on the prices and gifts the companies offered them. The close proximity of HBC and NWC trading posts (typically built directly alongside one another) therefore provided an advantage to Native traders, since it allowed them to exchange their goods at either post without undertaking additional travel. It also fueled intense competition between the companies, which evidently became so expensive by 1820 that employees of Edmonton and Fort Augustus met on the ground between their posts and agreed to stop "bribing" trade partners, though the HBC continued to accuse their NWC counterparts of providing extra gifts. The Blackfoot, like other Indigenous peoples, understood the rivalry and used it to extract key concessions. For example, when the HBC considered abandoning the Piikanis' preferred trading post of Acton House in 1820, chiefs threatened to take all of their trade to the NWC, which forced the HBC to keep the expensive post open. Competition empowered Indigenous people and handicapped the companies.[4]

Native people's savvy usage of the HBC-NWC rivalry across Rupert's Land fueled an intense and sometimes violent conflict between the companies, and eventually forced outsiders to intervene. The NWC had a more expensive transportation system for their goods than did the HBC, and therefore relied on high profits from their exclusive northern Athabasca district (what is now northern Alberta) posts to offset the high prices they paid Indigenous people in areas like the North Saskatchewan, where they competed directly with the HBC. The NWC saw its monopoly over the Athabasca country as essential to its survival, so when HBC traders began to arrive there in 1815, the Canadians retaliated by conspiring to starve sixteen HBC employees to death during the winter, which led to violence, arrests, and incriminations on both sides. The rivalry took a similarly dark turn along the Red River of what is now Manitoba, where British officials' attempts to restrict the pemmican trade by NWC-aligned locals led to a pitched battle that left twenty-two men dead in 1816. Partly in response to these reports of violence, British officials in London decided to end the rivalry in 1821 by forcing the two companies to merge. The NWC ceased to exist independently, and employees of both companies thereafter worked together under the Hudson's Bay Company name. As a result of the merger, the HBC gained a monopoly over all trade with Indigenous people in what later became western Canada.[5]

Native people throughout Rupert's Land saw the 1821 HBC-NWC merger as a disastrous development. Because the amalgamated HBC had no major competitors, Native traders like the Blackfoot lost their negotiating leverage. Edmonton trader Anthony Feistel described the first Siksika traders to learn of the merger in November 1821 as being "very much dejected, seeing no opposition, so that they cannot expect any further competition for their property." The Siksikas, short on ammunition, tobacco, and other necessary goods, had traveled across the cold prairies and parklands for fifteen days to reach Edmonton. The news that they no longer had a choice of trading partners was disheartening. Throughout the fall and winter of 1821–22, Native people bemoaned the changes to trade on the North Saskatchewan. Wrote one HBC employee, "The change of system . . . render[ed] the natives exceedingly turbulent, and discontented, and consequently more difficult to be dealt with." Freed from the threat of competition, the new HBC monopoly had less reason to meet Indigenous people's requests, and HBC officials closed Rocky Mountain (formerly Acton) House despite Piikani leaders' fervent objections. The HBC officials knew that without any other options, the Piikanis would have to make the longer and more dangerous trip to Edmonton. The merger robbed the Blackfoot of much of their bargaining power, and without the NWC it was unclear how they could regain it.[6]

Already reeling from news of the merger, Blackfoot traders were again stunned in 1822 when they learned that the HBC planned to build a new trading post on the South Saskatchewan River, in the heart of Blackfoot territory. The HBC had high hopes for their so-called Bow River Expedition. They imagined that moving south would offer them more access to beavers, which had declined along the North Saskatchewan; that it would provide employment for the surplus of employees they had incorporated in the recent merger; and that it would provide a deterrent to any future American competitors on the Missouri River. They kept their other ambition—that the expedition would yield a convenient route for trade with new partners like the Flatheads and Shoshones—to themselves. Opinion among the Blackfoot was split. Some Piikani leaders had encouraged the HBC to expand southward, believing that a new post would be convenient and would prevent clashes with the Crees and Assiniboines farther north. They promised the HBC that in return for the new post they would spend more time trapping beavers on the Missouri River and its southern tributaries, despite their well-known reluctance to killing the animal. Believing that the Bow River Expedition had the blessing of Blackfoot leaders, a former NWC trader named Donald McKenzie and around eighty employees built a new post near the junction of the Bow and Red Deer Rivers in September 1822, about two hundred miles south of the North Saskatchewan.[7]

Although some Blackfoot people encouraged the Bow River Expedition, others became convinced that the HBC's venture posed more danger than opportunity. Many of the Blackfoot and Gros Ventres correctly surmised that the HBC planned to use the new post as a launching point to trap beavers themselves and eventually to establish trade ties with their enemies. The Gros Ventres were especially suspicious of McKenzie, whom they remembered encountering in the mountains while he worked for the NWC. When McKenzie led an exploring party from the Bow River Post toward the sources of the Missouri River in October 1822, Piikani and Gros Ventre warriors blocked his way and informed him of "their firm determination of forcibly preventing him from proceeding one step farther in that direction." Two other HBC parties managed to explore the Marias and Bow Rivers but found few beavers. Tensions also arose at the post itself, where HBC employees reported frequent fights, thefts, and threats of violence. While some Blackfoot people had wanted the post because they felt it would make trade easier, others saw a golden opportunity to capture horses and other goods from the whites. Taking horses from the HBC men, who needed mounts to travel overland to Edmonton for supplies, forced them to buy replacement mounts from Native people. Some Blackfoot and Gros Ventre men, intoxicated with HBC alcohol, attempted to pilfer goods from the post as well. McKenzie and his employees abandoned the post and returned to Edmonton in June 1823. The Bow River Expedition proved an expensive failure, and deepened mistrust between the Blackfoot and the new HBC.[8]

At the same time that the merger roiled the British fur trade to the north during the early 1820s, a different set of transformations set off a burst of activity among American fur traders to the south. U.S. ambitions on the Upper Missouri had mostly languished since 1812, after Manuel Lisa's first expedition to the region failed and the outbreak of war between the United States and Great Britain temporarily closed off New Orleans and East Coast markets to U.S. traders. For most of the ensuing decade, St. Louis–based traders restricted their operations to the Lower Missouri River around Council Bluffs. By the early 1820s, a series of events reenergized Americans' ambitions to extend the fur trade into the far West. Mexican independence loosened restrictions on trade on the Santa Fe Trail and in the southern Rockies. More importantly, in 1822 Congress decided to ease up on its longtime (inconsistently enforced) requirement that all Indian trade in the West operate out of "factories" that were officially licensed by the Office of the Superintendent of Indian Trade. At the same time, constricted economic opportunities after the financial panic of 1819 led more men to try their hand at the difficult and dangerous profession of trading and trapping, and by 1822 the banking industry had recovered sufficiently to begin financially backing entrepreneurs.[9]

The new wave of American fur traders and trappers broke upon the northwest plains in the spring of 1823, in the immediate wake of the HBC's contentious merger and the collapse of the Bow River Expedition. The first party of interlopers bore the masthead of the Missouri Fur Company (MFC), the same outfit that the Blackfoot had nearly destroyed in 1810. After Blackfoot and Gros Ventre warriors killed twenty MFC employees near the Three Forks in the summer of 1810, the MFC had withdrawn to the Lower Missouri and had made no further attempts to ascend the river to its source. When founder Manuel Lisa died in 1820, his partner Joshua Pilcher took over management and again set his sights on the Upper Missouri. In 1821 Pilcher built a new post at the mouth of the Bighorn River, where Lisa's Fort Randall had once stood. Encouraged by their success, Pilcher dispatched partners Robert Jones and Michael Immell to lead a large party upriver to the Three Forks in the spring of 1823. The MFC employees hoped to trap beavers on their own, not to trade with Blackfoot people. The new MFC had done little to change their strategy since the 1810 expedition, and they probably expected a similar reception from the Blackfoot if detected.[10]

This time, at least one Blackfoot leader wanted to explore a new relationship with the Americans in the wake of the HBC merger. On May 18, 1823, a Piikani leader named Mi'ksskímmisöka'simi, or Iron Shirt, rode to the Americans' encampment along the Jefferson River, one of three tributaries that combined to form the Missouri. Later described by the German adventurer Maximilian of Wied as a "big, powerful man," who painted his face black with two vertical red stripes, Iron Shirt presented a formidable appearance to the MFC trappers who, as he later reported, "showed signs of hostilities" to him. Despite their jumpiness, the trappers recalled that Iron Shirt "came up boldly, and smoked . . . making every profession of friendship" to the Americans. Having quelled their fears, Iron Shirt invited the Americans to establish a trading post at the mouth of the Marias River, another tributary of the Missouri some 150 miles to the north and a favorite site for Piikani winter camps. Iron Shirt's invitation confused the Americans, since it departed drastically from the hostility they expected from the Blackfoot. Although Iron Shirt parted with them on good terms, the Americans showed little apparent inclination to build a permanent post, or to replace their trapping with trade.[11]

Although the Americans would soon have reason to doubt it, Iron Shirt had a genuine desire to make peace. The events of the previous two years had caused him to reconsider how Americans might fit on the northwest plains. Since the 1821 merger, the Blackfoot had grown frustrated at their inability to barter for goods or extract concessions from the HBC. The closure of Rocky Mountain House had forced the Piikanis to bring their wares to Edmonton House, where the presence of Cree and Assiniboine

The Piikani chief
Iron Shirt, who first
attempted to broker
American expansion
in 1823. (Karl Bodmer
[Swiss, 1809–1893],
*Mehkskéme-Sukáhs,
Piegan Blackfeet Chief,*
1833, watercolor, ink
and pencil on paper,
Joslyn Art Museum,
Omaha, Nebraska,
Gift of the Enron
Art Foundation,
1986.49.284.)

adversaries frequently put traders in danger. The closure of Rocky Mountain House had especially frustrated the Piikanis, one of whom told HBC
traders at Edmonton that he "regret[ted] exceedingly" its closure, "as the
distance from their general hunting grounds, is too great to come this length,
as well as being afraid to fall in with the [Stoney] Indians, on their way
hither." An American post on the Upper Missouri, however, would amelio-
rate each of these frustrations. If the Americans agreed to trade instead of
trap, their presence could undermine the new HBC monopoly and would
restore crucial trade leverage to the Blackfoot. An American establishment
would also provide a far more convenient trading location for the Piikanis,
many of whom spent their winters on the nearby Marias River, and would
provide a safer place to trade during times of conflict. Rather than confront
the Americans, why not welcome them, within limits?[12]

Despite Iron Shirt's diplomacy, a consensus among Blackfoot leaders had
yet to form, and some saw more benefit in destroying the Americans than
partnering with them. They resented the trespassers, whom they knew had

ties to their southern Crow enemies, and who flouted Blackfoot power by denuding nearby rivers and streams of beavers without permission. The Kainais and Siksikas lacked the Piikanis' geographic proximity to the Missouri River, and many had never traded at Rocky Mountain House and therefore had less interest in finding a replacement for it. Perhaps most importantly, there was more profit to be had in the short term by attacking the Americans than partnering with them, since the Americans had huge stores of beaver pelts, guns, horses, and other goods, all of which offered an enormous bounty to whoever could capture them. In fact, just a month before Iron Shirt met with the MFC trappers, a party of Blackfoot or Gros Ventre warriors had attacked an advance trapping party from one of the MFC's rivals, killed four men, and made off with their rifles and ammunition. Seeking an even greater reward, a party of several hundred Kainai warriors ambushed the MFC trappers on the Yellowstone River twelve days after their meeting with Iron Shirt. The Kainais killed seven of the Americans and seized as much as $15,000 in plunder, including fifty horses and 1,500 beaver pelts, which they then brought to the HBC to trade. In St. Louis, Iron Shirt's invitation became subsumed in the ensuing controversy over the captured goods, and American survivors and their eastern patrons assumed that his entreaty was a ruse calculated to lull the Americans into a false sense of security. The pattern of violence and distrust between the Blackfoot and Americans continued.[13]

The Kainais' 1823 expulsion of the MFC had the unexpected consequence of helping to launch the era of the American "mountain man." The MFC collapsed following the 1823 attack, but their primary competitors on the Upper Missouri, a firm led by partners William H. Ashley and Andrew Henry, remained. Ashley and Henry had established a post at the mouth of the Yellowstone River in the spring of 1822 and planned to send trappers to the Three Forks the following year, but Blackfoot attacks on both their advance party and their MFC competitors in early 1823, coupled with a devastating attack downriver by Arikara warriors that killed fourteen of their employees in early June, convinced Ashley and Henry that no part of the Upper Missouri was safe and that their scheme was therefore unworkable. Ashley and Henry hatched a new plan that would allow their trappers to bypass the Upper Missouri altogether. They dispatched employee Jedediah Smith to lead a party overland from Fort Kiowa, which was downriver from the Mandan villages, to enter the Rocky Mountains by land. In the spring of 1824, Smith led the first trappers through South Pass and into the fertile beaver-trapping regions of the intermountain West. Ashley and Henry's employees (followed by competitors) fanned out and trapped beavers as individuals or in small groups, and only met up with their employers at annual rendezvous to exchange their furs for money and supplies. The new system eschewed the use of fixed fortifications in favor of mobile, adaptive actors who became known as "mountain men," who spent more time trapping than trading. It proved enormously lucrative: at the 1825 rendezvous alone, Ashley collected between $40,000 and $50,000 worth of beaver furs, which would amount to more than a million dollars today. The mountain man system, formed by necessity largely due to Blackfoot hostility, rapidly transformed the fur trade of the far West.[14]

In the north, HBC officials watched the Americans' ventures into the mountains closely and soon adopted a similar strategy. Prior to their 1821 merger, the HBC had mostly avoided operating in the mountains due largely to their fear of Piikani attacks. After the merger, the new HBC governor, George Simpson, instigated a new westward push for the company, partly to take advantage of existing NWC infrastructure in the region, and partly to prevent Americans from dominating the Pacific Northwest, which had become jointly occupied British and U.S. territory in an 1818 treaty. Simpson was determined to prevent the Americans from muscling the British out of the region. In 1823, HBC employees entered the mountains through Athabasca Pass, reoccupied the NWC's abandoned Saleesh House, and renamed it Flathead Post. From there they began to dispatch large trapping and trading parties into the mountains, most of them led by former NWC trader Peter Skene Ogden. These so-called Snake River Expeditions set out to trap and to trade as many beaver furs as possible in order to create a "fur desert," thereby making the region unappealing to American competitors. The British took to their task with vigor, and in 1825 Ogden boasted to Americans that the Snake River expeditions had already collected more than eighty-five thousand beaver pelts in just two years.[15]

For the Blackfoot, the explosion of the náápiikoan activity across the mountains was both alarming and tantalizing. The trapping parties had large horse herds and beaver furs that, if acquired, could easily be traded to other Native people or to the HBC. The opportunity to capture beaver furs from the trappers held special appeal, since Blackfoot religious beliefs discouraged them from killing beavers themselves. In short order, Blackfoot and Gros Ventre (whom the Americans usually also called Blackfoot) warriors organized raiding and war parties to target the Americans, often as they went to and from their annual trade rendezvous. In 1825, for example, Blackfoot warriors ambushed Ashley as he returned from his rendezvous and stole more

These Shoshones, firing their guns during the 1837 fur trapper rendezvous in what is now Daniel, Wyoming, would have been an unwelcome sight for the Blackfoot, who had long denied the Shoshones access to firearms. American and British mountain men relied on allied warriors like these to protect them against Blackfoot attacks. (Alfred Jacob Miller, *Cavalcade*, ca. 1858–60, the Walters Art Museum.)

than fifty of his horses, and in 1828 between two and three hundred Black-foot and/or Gros Ventre warriors surprised a party led by Robert Campbell and captured nearly $5,000 in beaver furs, along with forty horses. Blackfoot and Gros Ventre raiders routinely traveled hundreds of miles and preyed on trappers as far away as the Great Salt Lake. These and other attacks forced the Americans to rely on mountain nations for their defense, as in 1832, when Flathead and Nez Percé auxiliaries killed twenty-six Gros Ventre attackers during the annual rendezvous. Fear of attacks became a feature of life for trappers in the mountains and helped burnish the Blackfoot's already fear-some reputation.[16]

Although the Americans often blamed British "incitement" for attacks on mountain men, Blackfoot and Gros Ventre raiders preyed on the HBC's Snake River expeditions with equal, if not greater, vigor as they did the Americans. Kainai and Piikani raiders stole several dozen horses from the HBC's 1825 Snake River expedition, for example, while also killing a freeman trapper and taking his beaver furs. Similar attacks plagued subsequent expeditions, and Ogden recorded around two dozen Blackfoot raids and attacks on his men between 1825 and 1829. "Torment us they will till the last," Ogden wearily lamented in his journals, for "we are now on their territories." The specter of Blackfoot raids hung thickly over the American and the British mountain men alike. During the 1820s, the mountains became an ideal place for Black-foot and Gros Ventres to prove themselves as warriors while capturing horses and furs for trade. American and British trappers had little recourse.[17]

Ironically, the Blackfoot's conflicts with American and British trappers in the mountains helped clear the path for their 1831 rapprochement with Americans on the plains. Although the mountain men spent most of their energy trapping beavers themselves, they also traded regularly with local Indigenous people for supplies, especially horses. The arrangement benefited nations like the Flatheads, Shoshones, Crows, and Nez Percés, who acquired a windfall of guns, ammunition, and metal goods. During the mid-1830s, between 450 and 500 white trappers and freemen annually attended the Rocky Mountain rendezvous, and it was not unusual for many more Native people to meet them there. At the July 1835 rendezvous, for example, an American missionary counted two thousand Shoshone, Flathead, Nez Percé, and Ute attendees. In time, the mountain men eviscerated whatever remaining technological advantage the Blackfoot still had over their neighbors to the south and west. The Blackfoot's primary objection to American expansion had long been that Americans would inevitably trade weapons to their neighbors, thereby undermining their technological superiority. By the end of the 1820s, however, that superiority had all but evaporated.[18]

As the 1820s wore on, more Blackfoot people became open minded about the possibilities of an American presence on the northwest plains. In the summer of 1827, a short-lived peace accord with the Flatheads allowed a joint Piikani and Kainai party to ride into Flathead territory and visit members of an American trapping outfit called Smith, Jackson & Sublette. As one of the surprised Americans remembered, the Blackfoot "had always been considered enemies to our traders; but about that time some of them manifested a friendly disposition, [and] invited a friendly intercourse and trade." After smoking, they invited the Americans to return with them to the plains "to establish a branch post in their country," just as Iron Shirt had suggested a few years earlier. Sublette dispatched his veteran employee James Beck-wourth to accompany the Piikanis and Kainais to their homes near the Missouri River, where he acquired several hundred beaver furs during a brief stay. Beckwourth's visit hinted at the possibility of a peaceful relationship with the Americans, but renewed conflicts with the Flatheads soon cut off the Blackfoot's access to American camps.[19]

Although their plan for enticing Americans onto the plains fizzled in 1827, Blackfoot traders recognized that they could use their brief trade with Beckwourth as leverage against the British. When Blackfoot traders first informed HBC employees at Edmonton about the exchange, the British accused them of lying in order to extract better trading terms (which, in fact, some Piikani traders had done the previous year). The HBC men's doubts disappeared when a Kainai trader arrived the following February, "decorated in an American chief's Scarlet Coat of no inferior quality and a large green Blanket Powder horn and Blue bead wrought shot Bag thrown across over his shoulders." The Kainai man told the HBC employees what he had presumably paid Beckwourth for the goods and left the whites "to judge the Price of them had they been disposed of by [them]selves." The visual proof of the American trade alarmed the HBC men, as did the direct challenge to match the Americans' prices. They blamed two former colleagues who were seen alongside the Americans, whom they charged with working "to depreciate the character of the HBC Traders and render them despicable" to the Blackfoot. The HBC traders did not relish the idea of new competition, but Blackfoot people knew such an arrangement would serve their interests well.[20]

The abortive 1827 Blackfoot-American exchange laid the groundwork for the lasting peace that the Piikani chief Good Woman established with the AFC four years later. Fortuitously, a former NWC and HBC trader named Jacques Berger attended the Kainais' and Piikanis' 1827 meeting with the Smith, Jackson, and Sublette party. Berger had more than two decades of experience trading with Blackfoot people, and he recognized that Blackfoot attitudes toward Americans had evolved during the 1820s. In 1830, Berger left the mountains and headed east to the Missouri River, where he was hired by the AFC's Kenneth McKenzie, who likewise had extensive experience in the region. A former NWC clerk, McKenzie left Rupert's Land in 1822 and became a partner in the Columbia Fur Company, an outfit that competed closely with the AFC's Western Department for trade on the Missouri River. In 1827, these competing outfits merged to create the AFC's Upper Missouri Outfit, which expanded aggressively under McKenzie's leadership. Just at the moment when McKenzie pondered pushing the AFC's operations toward the sources of the Missouri, Berger arrived and shared his knowledge that many Blackfoot people wanted the same thing. In the autumn of 1830, McKenzie dispatched Berger and five other men to travel west and open trade. When Berger returned to Fort Union the following spring, he brought Good Woman and around seventy other Blackfoot emissaries with him. In the ensuing meeting, Good Woman and McKenzie made an agreement that changed the northwest plains forever. Over the next three-plus decades, a new trading network flourished with traffic up and down the Missouri. In lands they once characterized as hostile and inaccessible, American traders could now ply their wares.[21]

THE 1831 PEACE represented a dramatic shift in Blackfoot-American relations, but AFC officials soon discovered that not all plains people shared the same enthusiasm as Good Woman and Bull Back Fat. In the fall of 1831, Kenneth McKenzie dispatched veteran trader James Kipp to build a new post near the confluence of the Missouri and Marias Rivers, which he named Fort Piegan. The post's namesakes, the Piikanis, proved enthusiastic from the start, and within days of Kipp's arrival, several hundred Piikani lodges assembled nearby. According to an interview Kipp gave decades later, he asked them to come back when the post was finished, and two months later they returned to trade more than six thousand pounds of beaver pelts to the Americans. Kainai people, Kipp claimed, remained far more suspicious. Several hundred Kainai warriors laid siege to Fort Piegan shortly after it opened, and the stalemate ended only when a pair of Kainai chiefs spoke directly to Kipp and learned that he was willing to buy bison robes and other goods from the Kainais.[22]

Assiniboine and Crow people presented more determined opposition. At the encouragement of Kenneth McKenzie, Blackfoot and Assiniboine leaders had concluded a "treaty of peace and friendship" during the 1831 visit to Ft. Union, but the agreement proved short lived. The Assiniboines, most of whom had moved southward during the early nineteenth century and therefore already traded with Americans at Fort Union, repeatedly sought to undermine the Blackfoot-American connection. When the AFC traders left Fort Piegan temporarily in the spring of 1832 to ferry their goods downriver, Assiniboine warriors burned it down. The following autumn, a rumor reached the HBC that a large party of Assiniboines had temporarily "surrounded" Fort Piegan's replacement, Fort McKenzie, and refused to allow the Americans to leave despite being offered eight kegs of rum. In August of 1833, an Assiniboine chief known to whites as the Gauche, or Left Hand, led a massive war party to attack Piikani traders at Fort McKenzie, and in 1834 the same force massacred an entire band of Gros Ventres about a day's ride from the fort. Crow people took a similar approach. In the spring of 1834, several hundred Crow warriors attempted to gain entry to Fort McKenzie in hopes of plundering and burning it once inside. Like the Assiniboines, the Crows lacked the same mobility as the Blackfoot and likely worried that trading with the Americans as well as the British would give their enemies an insurmountable advantage. When AFC trader Alexander Culbertson foiled their plans, they admitted to him that they had hoped to destroy the fort because it "supplied their enemies with fire-arms and rendered them too powerful for the Crows to withstand." Despite the efforts of their adversaries, Blackfoot people built a thriving trade with the Americans.[23]

The presence of the Americans, some of whom remained naïve to the region's trade protocols, sometimes also exacerbated tensions within Blackfoot communities themselves. Late in the summer of 1833, large numbers of Piikani and Kainai traders gathered at Fort McKenzie to begin their third year of trade with the AFC. At a meeting with chiefs and prominent warriors of both nations, American trader D. D. Mitchell broke etiquette by presenting an expensive new uniform to a Piikani chief named Kííhtsípinnoka, or Spotted Elk, and none of the others, proclaiming that it was a reward for not visiting the HBC. The other chiefs felt outraged and humiliated by the slight, especially the Kainais. The tension soon reached a boiling point, and six days later, word reached Mitchell that Kainais had killed Spotted Elk's nephew. The affray caused an unprecedented rupture between the Piikanis and Kainais, which continued for more than a year afterward. Disagreements over trade inflamed tensions within bands as well. In 1840, for instance, word reached HBC traders that one Kainai man had stabbed another after the two men argued over whether to cast their lot that year with the Americans or the British. As life and leadership increasingly came to revolve around the fur trade, it introduced new sources of instability into Blackfoot life.[24]

In the north, Blackfoot bands' embrace of the Americans caused grave concern for the British. The HBC worried most of all about losing contact with the Piikanis, who lived closest to the Missouri, so they hurriedly dispatched envoys to Piikani bands to convince leaders not to visit the American posts. When that failed, they decided to take more drastic measures. In the fall of 1832, the HBC once again abandoned Rocky Mountain House and built a new post around one hundred miles to the south, on the Bow River near what is now the eastern entrance to Banff National Park. The HBC reasoned that a more conveniently located HBC post could dissuade the Piikanis from trading with the Americans. HBC trader John Harriott sent delegations to Piikani bands to encourage them to visit the brand-new "Piegan Post," and plied chiefs who did arrive with "as much Rum as they could drink." Despite these inducements, the Piikanis and other Blackfoot people insisted on continuing to trade with the Americans. Unable to regain their monopoly, the HBC abandoned Piegan Post in early 1834. Due to the high prices they paid to compete with the Americans and the expense of maintaining the isolated post, the price the HBC paid to acquire goods at Piegan Post far exceeded their value. As the HBC discovered in its experiment, the advantages Blackfoot people gained from maintaining trade with both the HBC and the Americans far outweighed anything the HBC alone could offer.[25]

Blackfoot people gained more by stoking British-American competition than by picking one side over the other. First and foremost, the rivalry allowed them to demand higher prices for their furs and bison provisions. This was a luxury few Native people had, especially in Rupert's Land. During the 1820s and 1830s, the price northern plains Indigenous people received for provisions, particularly pemmican, declined as a result of the HBC's regional monopoly. Freed from Canadian competition, HBC traders simply paid less, thereby forcing Indigenous people to produce more. After 1831, however, Blackfoot traders avoided the full impact of this devaluation, and the price for some Blackfoot goods may have even risen during the 1830s. "There is no contenting these animals of the Plain," wrote Edmonton's John Rowand in 1835, "although we pay them four times as much for everything we get from them than we do the Crees." Equally problematic for the HBC, other Native traders grew resentful that the Blackfoot received better prices for their goods. Higher prices also led to lower returns from Blackfoot traders, some of whom simply brought in fewer goods in order to receive the same amount in return. Although Rowand and other traders recognized the problem, they had little recourse. In 1843, Rowand again complained that "guns is now given for 10 Robes each," when "in former times an Indian who would have been bold enough to ask a Gun for that number of Robes would have been turned out of the shop with a kick in the B.S." Rowand knew the source of his problem: "We may thank the Americans for spoiling the trade as it is," he complained. "When our Indians do not see those people, there is no change in the trade."[26]

Blackfoot traders also used their new position to extract more elaborate gifts from British and American traders. Prior to 1821, Blackfoot leaders had often received gifts from NWC and HBC traders as inducements to trade at one house over the other. The flow of gifts slowed after 1821, but the AFC's arrival empowered Blackfoot leaders once again to demand gifts from the whites, especially expensive clothing that would burnish their high status. For example, during a visit to Fort McKenzie in 1833, the Piikani chief Iron Shirt presented AFC traders with several small gifts, expecting

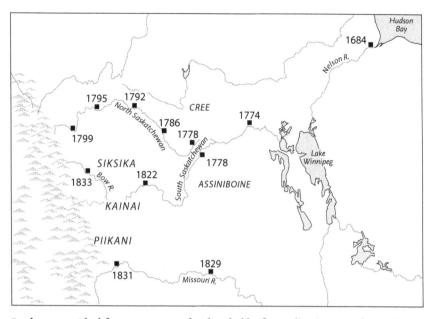

By the 1830s, Blackfoot country was bookended by fur trading posts to the north and south. After its establishment in 1670, the HBC established a string of posts on the North Saskatchewan River between 1774 and 1799, and tried unsuccessfully to expand onto the South Saskatchewan River in 1822 and 1833. The AFC established two major posts on the Missouri River: Fort Union (1829) and Fort Piegan (1831). The latter was then replaced with Forts McKenzie, Lewis, and Benton, all close by.

the Americans to provide an expensive new suit in return. In 1834, fourteen Blackfoot traders similarly "compelled" the AFC's James Kipp to provide new uniforms, along with gifts of alcohol, tobacco, and ammunition, despite their bringing far fewer beaver pelts than the previous year. Kipp groused that the Blackfoot traders were "expensive," and "in the habit of receiving too much for nothing." Traders in the north voiced similar frustrations. In 1837, HBC employees at Rocky Mountain House complained that one Piikani leader demanded clothing for himself and a new suit for each of his children, reminding traders that he had "resisted the temptation" of visiting the Americans instead. Although the HBC traders refused this particular request, the expectation of generous gifts to outshine competitors once again became central to Blackfoot trade encounters.[27]

Blackfoot traders could also use trade competition to gain greater access to alcohol. Since the earliest days of trade on the North Saskatchewan, Blackfoot visitors had grown accustomed to gifts of alcohol, often enjoying a small keg of rum to share among themselves on the eve of exchange.

These occasional revelries became a favorite diversion for many Blackfoot people, and they expected to receive similar gifts from the AFC, even though U.S. law prohibited the use of alcohol in trade with Indians. American traders skirted the rule as much as possible, fearing any disadvantage against the HBC. In 1833, Kenneth McKenzie brought a still to Fort Union to produce whiskey and circumvent federal inspectors, but officials soon learned of his scheme, and his superiors ordered him to dismantle the operation in the spring of 1834. Others lobbied federal officials to grant them an exemption from the law or to make an agreement with the British to outlaw alcohol trading in Rupert's Land as well. When these efforts failed, AFC employees simply smuggled barrels of liquor upriver. These efforts continued for years despite considerable changes in the company's organization. In 1834, the AFC's Western Department was purchased by Bernard Pratte & Company, which renamed itself Pratte, Chouteau & Company before finally reorganizing under the name Pierre Chouteau, Jr., & Company (Chouteau and Company) in 1839. Chouteau and Company traders continued to provide alcohol to the Blackfoot and other Native people on the Upper Missouri River, circumventing poorly enforced federal restrictions.[28]

Beyond material compensation, exchange with the Americans also allowed Blackfoot traders to diversify the goods they produced. Prior to the Americans' arrival, Blackfoot people traded a variety of bison products to the British and Canadians, including meat, grease, tallow, and pemmican. While Blackfoot people also sometimes traded beavers and other furs, British and Canadian traders had little interest in their abundant bison robes, which were too bulky to transport east by canoe or overland to Montreal. Bison robes therefore played little role in the fur trade before the 1830s. The arrival of Americans on the northwest plains changed this calculus, since American keelboats could easily transport bison robes down the Missouri and Mississippi Rivers. Blackfoot people embraced this new opportunity; after all, women had countless generations of experience in preparing robes, and men had long since become expert bison hunters on horseback. The robe trade grew quickly. In 1835, the AFC collected some three thousand robes at Fort McKenzie; in 1840, they collected twenty thousand. Fear of losing Native trade partners to the Americans led the HBC to begin purchasing more bison robes as well, but the majority of the robe trade centered on the Upper Missouri. In some cases, the robe trade may have conceivably allowed Blackfoot people to double their income from bison kills, by trading a bison's hide to the Americans and the same bison's meat to the British.[29]

The presence of American traders allowed Blackfoot warriors to pursue their enemies more aggressively. Freed from having to maintain the HBC's favor in order to trade after 1831, Blackfoot raiding and war parties targeted Cree and Assiniboine encampments outside the walls of Edmonton House, Rocky Mountain House, and even the more distant Fort Pitt and Carlton House, which were located deep in Cree territory in what is now central Saskatchewan. In September 1834, for example, a large party of Kainai warriors visited Edmonton and murdered a prominent Cree trader at his encampment outside the fort's palisade. Although the HBC mourned the death of the "very fine Cree Indian," there was little they could have done to discourage the Kainais, most of whom spent that season trading with the Americans at Fort McKenzie. HBC traders faced a similar problem a decade later, when a group of Siksikas attacked Cree traders near Rocky Mountain House before "mov[ing] off to the Americans." By moving freely over an expansive homeland that bridged north and south, Blackfoot people easily avoided retribution for such tactics.[30]

Conversely, having their choice of trading partners also allowed Blackfoot people to *avoid* entanglements with enemies if they desired. Since their schism with the Crees in 1806, visiting HBC posts on the North Saskatchewan had become an increasingly dangerous proposition for Blackfoot traders, because traveling and camping outside the forts' palisades exposed them to attacks from adversaries. Trips to Edmonton in particular brought them into close proximity of their enemies, in addition to being a long journey from Kainai and Piikani homelands. During the winter of 1830–31, some Piikanis traded their furs to Kootenai intermediaries rather than risk the journey to Edmonton. Concerns over safety surely helped motivate Blackfoot leaders to establish ties with the AFC in 1831. After the arrival of the Americans, the Blackfoot avoided long journeys to the north during periods of rancorous violence with their neighbors. For example, following several Cree and Assiniboine attacks on Gros Ventre, Piikani, and Kainai parties in the summer of 1835, almost all of the Blackfoot went south to trade at Fort McKenzie, thereby avoiding further clashes. Living in the borderlands provided safety, since the Blackfoot could avoid northern posts during times of extreme discord while maintaining trade in the south, and vice versa. Geographic mobility became a source of both power and security.[31]

Avoiding unwanted conflict grew more crucial after smallpox returned to Blackfoot country in 1837 for the first time in more than half a century. Opening up the Upper Missouri to American travelers had unwittingly put the Blackfoot in greater danger from disease. In June 1837, infected passengers traveling from St. Louis aboard the steamboat *St. Peter's* first transmitted smallpox to the agricultural Mandan people downriver. In a few short weeks, the scourge had nearly destroyed the Mandans and the neighboring Arikaras, who had already been weakened by food shortages. From there, the same steamboat brought the illness to Fort Union, where Assiniboine people likewise acquired it. Since steamboats could not ascend the river beyond Fort Union, Chouteau and Company's Alexander Harvey took a keelboat from Fort McKenzie to Fort Union to meet the *St. Peter's*. Even before they made it back to Fort McKenzie, members of Harvey's party began to show symptoms. According to Culbertson, the traders debated turning back, but eager Piikani and Kainai traders met them at the mouth of the Judith River and insisted they continue on to Fort McKenzie. They did, and from there smallpox spread like wildfire across the northwest plains. Some escaped the worst of the ravages, like the Crows, who hid in the mountains as the disease raged. Others had already acquired immunity, like many of the Gros Ventres, who had been exposed to the illness while visiting their Arapaho relatives a few years earlier. Many Crees likewise had gained immunity after receiving vaccines at HBC posts on the North Saskatchewan. The Blackfoot, the Tsuut'inas, and the Assiniboines, however, had no such luck, and they once again bore the terrible brunt of *Variola's* effects.[32]

A Siksika historian referred to the miserable summer and fall of 1837 as simply the "Big Small Pox." In a later interview, Culbertson recounted the grisly toll it took. After no visitors arrived at Fort McKenzie for two months, Culbertson rode out to investigate and found a Piikani encampment where the only remaining survivors were two old women who had lived through the 1781 outbreak when they were girls. Out of the band's sixty lodges, the rest had either fled or perished. (Abandoned lodges became a common sight in the region for years afterward.) The full scale of the devastation became clear as Piikani, Kainai, and Siksika survivors straggled into Fort McKenzie. Culbertson estimated that as much as two-thirds of the Blackfoot population perished. As in 1781, Blackfoot bands were forced to reorganize themselves, and as survivors formed new connections, some bands ceased to exist entirely. Social and religious organizations, whose existence depended on the transfer of knowledge among a select group of people, also disappeared, such as the Buffalo Bull Society, a religious organization among the Kainais whose headdresses and paraphernalia transferred to survivors in the Horn Society and the Old Women's Society. As in 1781, the 1837 outbreak left Blackfoot people disoriented, frightened, and disillusioned. In such times, building a stable future became all the more crucial.[33]

Reeling from the smallpox epidemic, Blackfoot bands suddenly found themselves more vulnerable to raids, particularly from the Plains Crees and Crows who had suffered far fewer losses during the outbreak. Beginning in 1838, Cree bands used the Blackfoot's weakness to consolidate their hold over the plains and parklands south of the North Saskatchewan River. The Crees' southward expansion forced Siksika bands to move the bulk of their activity about a hundred miles farther south from the Battle River valley to the Bow River valley, where they already frequented a shallow stretch of the river they called Ridge under Water, which later became known as Blackfoot Crossing. As Cree groups strengthened their position south of Edmonton, visiting the HBC post to trade became more dangerous than ever for the Siksikas, Kainais, and Piikanis. Assiniboine survivors, despite their own enormous losses to smallpox, maintained their alliance with the Crees and joined in attacks on Blackfoot trading parties. Due to their catastrophic population losses and the growing strength of the Crees, Blackfoot security became increasingly precarious.[34]

Weapons and ammunition provided strength to vulnerable Blackfoot communities following the 1837 smallpox outbreak, and many survivors eagerly returned to the trading posts. The American Fort McKenzie provided the safest and most convenient outlet once the sickness subsided in February 1838. One American trader wrote that while some Assiniboines swore vengeance on Americans for bringing the disease, "a different feeling seem[ed] to pervade the Blackfeet tribes," who were "humbled and very submissive and beg[ged] the whites not to desert them in their calamity." The influential Kainai chief Bull Back Fat, who had helped Good Woman broker the Americans' arrival seven years earlier, personally assured traders that he remained "as warm a friend to the company as heretofore." Despite the high mortality in their bands, Blackfoot traders actually brought more robes to the Americans in the years following the epidemic, and returns grew from seven thousand in 1837 to twenty-one thousand by 1841. The increased returns resulted partly from the fact that many Blackfoot survivors avoided visiting HBC posts for fear of Cree or Assiniboine attacks, and that hunters faced less competition, but they also reflected the importance of the bison robe trade to Blackfoot security and survival in the precarious aftermath of the epidemic. The Blackfoot depended upon consistent access to the náápiikoans' guns and ammunition in order to guard against outside threats. They also needed tobacco and paint for religious ceremonies that would reinforce their perhaps-strained relationships with the supernatural world. More than ever, trade was essential to their survival.[35]

Blackfoot traders leaned into the burgeoning bison robe trade to ensure that their relationships with the Americans remained strong after the smallpox epidemic. Fortuitously, demand for bison robes had already begun to eclipse demand for beaver furs. During the 1830s, beaver populations in the intermountain West plummeted as a result of more than a decade of overtrapping. The scarcity led most fur-trapping outfits to cease operating, and in 1840 American trappers held the last of their Rocky Mountain rendezvous. At the same time, demand for beavers fell in both Europe and the United States as silk and nutria emerged as popular substitutes for beaver felt. Fur trade interests in St. Louis, most prominently the venerable Chouteau family, accordingly shifted their energies toward the accumulation of bison robes. The flood of robes coming into Fort McKenzie and other Upper Missouri posts became essential for St. Louis–based traders. By the early 1840s, Chouteau and Company increasingly focused its attentions on the Upper Missouri, and by 1850 its northwest plains posts represented the only remnants of Chouteau and Company's once vast fur-trading operations. A matter of survival to the Blackfoot after the 1837 epidemic, their renewed collection of robes also helped stabilize the fur trade itself.[36]

Even as the American robe trade grew in importance and the North Saskatchewan grew more dangerous, Blackfoot people worked to maintain strong ties with the HBC. If they devoted too much of their attention toward the Missouri, they would lose the advantages that their borderland position afforded them. Maintaining ties with the HBC worried Blackfoot leaders for good reason. During the 1830s, Edmonton's chief trader, John Rowand, became frustrated with the comparatively high price of the Blackfoot trade. In letters to HBC governor George Simpson, Rowand even suggested abandoning the Blackfoot trade entirely. Blackfoot people, however, had no interest in severing their ties to the HBC, even though they traded more often with the Americans. When Simpson traveled to Edmonton in 1841, a delegation of nine leaders representing the Siksikas, Piikanis, Kainais, and Tsuut'inas visited him along with a combined encampment of nearly three thousand people. According to Simpson, the visitors came "dressed in their grandest clothes," and when Simpson presented them with gifts, "one of them vented his gratitude in a song; and another blessed the house in which he had been so well treated." The chiefs also presented Simpson with a gift of at least five ornately designed ceremonial shirts. The extraordinary gift reflected Simpson's influential stature, as well as his ability to reciprocate gifts of similar value. More importantly, it demonstrated the effort put forward by Blackfoot leaders to maintain strong ties with both British and American traders.[37]

Women likewise played a central role in maintaining the Blackfoot's relationships with whites, particularly in the south. The custom of "country marriage" between white traders and Native women most likely began shortly after the arrival of HBC and NWC traders to the North Saskatchewan in the 1780s, but company records reveal limited evidence of such unions with the Blackfoot. Marriages between Blackfoot women and American traders, on the other hand, yielded extensive documentation due to the high status that some women attained. In 1833, a Piikani woman whose name is now lost married Culbertson shortly after he helped to build Fort McKenzie. Seven years later, a Kainai woman named Natoyist-Siksina', or Medicine Snake Woman, likewise married Culbertson after he ascended to the position of chief trader and possibly after he divorced his first wife. Medicine Snake Woman came from a prominent Kainai family: her father, Two Suns, was chief of the Fish Eaters band, a title that transferred to her brother Seen from Afar after 1837. Other Blackfoot women formed unions with Culbertson's underlings. In 1844, a young Piikani woman named Coth-co-co-na, the daughter of a warrior named Under Bull and his wife Black Bear, married a newly arrived clerk named Malcolm Clarke, and another Piikani woman married Clarke's fellow trader Alexander Harvey.[38]

Marriages between Blackfoot women and company men strengthened Blackfoot relationships to the Americans. Family connections to prominent traders provided prestige to leaders like Two Suns and Seen from Afar and helped provide them with reliable access to trade, since men like Culbertson were unlikely to turn away family members. (Likewise, by marrying into the leading family of the Fish Eaters band, Culbertson ensured that Seen from Afar would travel to Fort McKenzie to trade, rather than going north to the HBC.) Marrying white traders provided a measure of power and prestige to women as well, and traders' wives often played prominent roles in diplomacy. Blackfoot women and fur trader husbands became experts in regional practices and protocols, and they often translated during trading interactions and helped to smooth over disagreements. By combining their knowledge of different cultures, they played an essential role in maintaining friendly relations between Blackfoot people and the small communities of white traders that lived in their midst.[39]

Personal relationships, and the mobility provided by the ability to trade in the north and south, proved crucial during times of crisis. In the summer of 1843, Chouteau and Company officials reassigned Culbertson (and by extension Medicine Snake Woman) to Fort Laramie, a newly acquired trading post on the North Platte River in what is now Wyoming in hopes that he

Medicine Snake Woman, a Kainai who married the prominent American trader Alexander Culbertson, became a crucial intermediary in the Upper Missouri fur trade. (John James Audubon, *Natawista Culbertson*, 1843, Audubon State Park Museum, Henderson, Kentucky.)

would reverse the post's sagging returns. To replace Culbertson as chief trader at Fort McKenzie, the company selected Francis Chardon, who had extensive experience with the Mandans downriver but none with the Blackfoot. During the winter of 1843–44, Chardon and his underling Harvey refused a party of Kainai men entry to the fort. Following a heated argument, the Kainais killed some of the fort's livestock, then shot one of their pursuers. Enraged, Chardon and Harvey plotted revenge. When a chief named Old Sun led an unrelated Siksika trading party to the fort a short time later, Chardon and Harvey fired a cannon at them from behind the fort's stockades. The Americans then killed several of the survivors and stole their goods. Fearing Blackfoot retaliation, Chardon and Harvey burned Fort McKenzie and retreated downriver, where they built a new post named Fort Chardon, which had little success, since few Blackfoot people were willing to trade at a post named for and operated by a known murderer. The killing of peaceful traders by whites had no precedent among the Blackfoot. Rather than continue to trade with Chardon, Piikani, Kainai, and Siksika bands all brought their trade goods north to the HBC in the winter of 1844–45.[40]

Blackfoot traders' refusal to trade with the Americans forced Chouteau and Company to adapt. Honoré Picotte, the company's partner in charge of the Upper Missouri, hurriedly dispatched Culbertson and Medicine Snake Woman to return to the region and construct a new fort in the fall of 1845. After sending an envoy north to distribute gifts of tobacco, Culbertson and Medicine Snake Woman received a delegation of Siksika chiefs and around fifty warriors in council in early 1846, including the powerful Siksika chief Big Swan. Culbertson assured them "of the dissatisfaction and anger with which the great chief of the traders had heard of the outrage inflicted upon them," and that "its perpetrators had been sent away from the country, and could not again enter the service of the great chiefs." Despite their anger, Blackfoot leaders felt pressure to resume trade with the Americans in order to unload their two years' backlog trade goods. In fact, many Blackfoot traders had deliberately withheld goods from the HBC in anticipation of making peace with the Americans. Restoring peaceful exchange on the Missouri was a priority for Blackfoot and American traders alike.

Heeding the assurances of Culbertson and Medicine Snake Woman, Blackfoot leaders acquiesced to their return, and trade soon resumed at a new post named Fort Lewis, which the company replaced with Fort Benton in 1847. When Culbertson finished trading in the spring of 1846, he had collected eleven thousand bison robes, along with many other furs, from Blackfoot traders. One Siksika winter count called it "the time when the good white men came." Not all Blackfoot people were ready to forget, however, as Old Sun and several Siksika bands refused to return to the south for more than a decade. Nevertheless, by resorting to the HBC when relations with the Americans soured, Blackfoot leaders forced Chouteau and Company to earn back their goodwill. In so doing, they also restored the borderland position on which they had come to depend.[41]

BEGINNING IN 1831, Blackfoot people deliberately positioned their homeland as the crossroads of the American and British fur trade. Choosing to become borderland people was a calculated risk. Welcoming Americans gave them the greatest opportunity to secure new advantages in trade and to maintain the upper hand on their neighbors. By playing the Americans and British against one another, Blackfoot traders gained greater access to weapons, ammunition, tools, ceremonial supplies, and gifts. Their flexible approach toward trade in the north and south helped them to protect their communities against raids, while also granting them the freedom to expand their own raiding and warfare against enemies. Having their choice of British or

American trade empowered them to demand key concessions from trading companies and to rid themselves of unwanted interlopers. Their borderland position helped Blackfoot people maintain their security in the terrifying aftermath of the 1837 smallpox outbreak. Despite major new developments, including the expansion of the American fur trade into the intermountain West, by the middle of the nineteenth century the Blackfoot remained the most powerful and prosperous people on the northwest plains.

Like other Indigenous people across North America, the Blackfoot found benefits in placing themselves at the borderlands of competing European and North American empires. In the colonial northeast, Haudenosaunee people famously pitted the French, British, and later Americans against one another for generations in what one scholar dubbed a "play-off system." In the Arkansas River valley, Quapaw and Osage people used their position between shifting French, Spanish, and later American claims to bolster their own influence. Perhaps most famously, in the Southwest the Comanches, and to a lesser extent the Apaches and others, used their position between Spanish, French, and later Mexican and American settlements to augment their own power through raiding and trade. By the beginning of the nineteenth century, the Comanches' military and economic dominance of the southern Great Plains gave them the leeway to launch uninhibited raids throughout northern Mexico. Though separated by half a continent from these other Indigenous borderlands, Blackfoot people pursued a like-minded approach, and positioning themselves between the British and Americans increased their power and autonomy. Their ascendancy likewise allowed them to extend their influence beyond their borders by hounding trappers throughout the intermountain West. By understanding and managing the rivalries of non-Native colonizers, the Blackfoot and other Indigenous people dictated the limits of colonial expansion well into the nineteenth century.[42]

Paradoxically, while the Blackfoot grew more influential and powerful, they also grew ever more dependent on their relationships with the náápiikoan. Ready access to weapons became more essential as warfare intensified during the 1820s and 1830s, and newly armed nations like the Flatheads, Nez Percés, Shoshones, Kootenais, and Crows sought to reassert themselves against the Blackfoot after decades of disadvantage. For Siksika, Kainai, and Piikani peoples, as well as their Gros Ventre allies, staying safe during this unstable era meant building and maintaining favorable relationships with non-Native people. They knew that their security and prosperity depended on their relationships with outsiders, and on the goods they provided. It also depended on the relative weakness of their British and American counterparts. Although both British and American officials saw the western fur trade as the leading edge of their empires, insofar as they claimed fur trading territories as their own, British and American people still only populated the northwest plains and mountains in vanishingly small numbers. Because their colonialism depended entirely on trade, Indigenous nations like the Blackfoot could control and manipulate them. For the time being, the emergence of the northwest plains borderland empowered the Blackfoot, just as Good Woman and others had imagined it would.[43]

PART III | Collisions,

1848–1870

CHAPTER FIVE

A Future They Were Resolved to Achieve

> We are satisfied that the white men are *our* friends, if they were not
> they would not go to the trouble of sending us so many valuable
> presents every year. We desire them to come & teach us about the
> Great Spirit & tell us plenty of good things.
>
> —LAME BULL (Piikani), 1857

> The Blackfeet are rich in all that constitutes the wealth of an
> Indian—Possessing a greater number of horses and living in a
> country abounding in Buffalo, they procure as many robes as they
> choose, which are traded at the trading posts on the Missouri, for
> Guns, Ammunition, Blankets, Scarlet Cloth, Calico, Knives, Beads
> and ornaments of various kinds.
>
> —JAMES DOTY (American), 1854

In their winter count, the family of Siksika historian Joe Little Chief marked 1848 as simply a "very good year" for all three Blackfoot nations. The entry departed from their usual historical practice of using singular events to remember each year, but Blackfoot people like Little Chief's ancestors had reason to think of 1848 in such straightforward terms. In many ways, the middle point of the nineteenth century represented a high point of Blackfoot power and prosperity. Blackfoot people traversed an expansive homeland that gave them the unique ability to trade with both the British and Americans, the latter of whom had recently returned to the region, and established a new post called Fort Benton. Trade thrived in both bison robes and provisions. More than ten years had passed since smallpox had last swept through the region and their improved health had allowed Siksika bands in the north to begin pushing back against the Crees who had expanded into their territory following the last outbreak. In the south, the Piikanis likewise asserted themselves against Flathead hunters who had encroached on the bison grounds from the west. Throughout the northwest plains, Blackfoot bands traveled, hunted, visited, prayed, and lived with more security than they felt in many years.[1]

If one were to ride directly south of Blackfoot country in 1848, he or she would soon discover far more unsettled circumstances. In the 1840s, the growing United States of America—a nation whose population had previously been confined mostly to the fertile agricultural regions east of the Great Plains—burst into the far West. In 1846, the United States acquired the Oregon Territory from Great Britain, and meanwhile declared war on Mexico, invaded it, and forced it to surrender a third of its territory. Although these acquisitions played out far from the northwest plains, they would profoundly change the way Americans viewed the entire West, including Native peoples like the Blackfoot. Federal officials quickly abandoned their old conceit that the Great Plains would remain Indian territory, and instead came to view the trans-Missouri West as an inevitable extension of the United States. They envisioned a future in which railways would link together communities of white settlers, who would eventually overwhelm Indian nations and force them to assimilate. In today's academic parlance, the Americans believed that *settler* colonialism (that is, filling new lands with settlers who would eventually outnumber and displace the previous inhabitants) would soon replace the *extractive* colonialism (that is, a presence based only on acquiring goods and materials from original inhabitants) of the fur trade era. The settler colonial future held no role for sovereign Indigenous powers like the Blackfoot.[2]

This new vision for expansion on the northwest plains put Blackfoot people and Americans on a collision course and would before long force the Blackfoot to rethink their relationships with non-Native people. In October 1855, just seven years after the "good year" of 1848, Blackfoot chiefs sought out and signed their first (and only) treaty with the U.S. government. The treaty ostensibly delineated Blackfoot territory south of the forty-ninth parallel for the first time, swore the Blackfoot to peace with their neighbors, and laid the groundwork for government institutions, farms, and religious missions. At first glance, this agreement seemed discordant with what motivated Blackfoot people at midcentury. Why would Blackfoot leaders pursue an agreement that gave concessions to the Americans when they continued to dominate the region and enjoyed greater security that they had in years? Why would they sign on to a treaty whose authors seemed determined to dismantle their way of life? To understand the treaty, one must grapple with the wildly different expectations that its signers held. Blackfoot leaders saw the purpose of the 1855 treaty in very different terms than did the Americans and used it to imagine a very different future for the northwest plains. Eventually, the agreement exposed the mutual misapprehensions and bad faith that would come to define a new era in Blackfoot history.

BLACKFOOT PEOPLE LIVED familiar lives in the 1840s, but change was already in the air in the decade before the treaty, most noticeably with the arrival of some peculiar black-robed men among the nations to their west. Sometime around 1820, a small group of Haudenosaunee (Iroquois) people settled among the Flatheads, bringing with them the Catholic faith they had acquired in their homeland of Caughnawaga, near Montreal. The Haudenosaunees convinced some of the Flatheads that Catholic teachings could provide them with the spiritual power to fight off European diseases and to protect themselves in conflicts with enemies like the Blackfoot and Gros Ventres. Beguiled by the potential of Christian power, the Flatheads and friendly Nez Percés sent four delegations to St. Louis between 1831 and 1839 to plead with the Catholics to send missionaries to them. In 1840, a priest named Pierre-Jean De Smet responded by leading a delegation of Jesuits upriver from St. Louis. In the summer of 1841, they established a small mission called St. Mary's in the Bitterroot Valley, just across the mountains from Piikani territory. For the first time in the history of the northwest plains and adjoining mountains, whites built a settlement that had nothing to do with the fur trade.[3]

Ever the opportunists when it came to the náápiikoan, many of the Blackfoot came to see potential benefits in the missionaries' arrival. Following a victory of Flathead warriors over the Crows in 1846, members of the Small Robes band of Piikanis became convinced that the strangers they called "Black Robe Medicine Men" wielded special spiritual powers that they could apply in warfare. Blackfoot people had a long tradition of selling, buying, giving, and receiving supernatural powers, and they logically viewed the priests the same way they saw other holy men: as potential purveyors of valuable skills and supernatural alliances. Many of the Small Robes wanted to acquire the Jesuits' power for themselves and had De Smet baptize eighty of their children during a visit to St. Mary's Mission. The Small Robes then allowed De Smet to dispatch his colleague Father Nicolas Point to establish a mission at Chouteau and Company's Fort Lewis (the short-lived predecessor to Fort Benton) in the summer of 1846. In less than a year, Point baptized between 650 and 700 Blackfoot people, most of them children. Some attempted to apply their newfound spiritual powers in daily life. For example, much to the delight of the observing Point, a group of Piikanis knelt to pray to the Virgin Mary after they spotted bison during a hunt the following fall. Perhaps only by testing the Black Robes' power for themselves could they know its true value.

The Catholics soon wore out their welcome among the Blackfoot. Blackfoot people viewed Catholic teachings as medicine—spiritual power they could add to their own—but not as a replacement for their own religious views. The Blackfoot refused to forsake practices like polygamy and to devote themselves to Catholicism, much to the consternation of Point, who realized that his mass baptisms had not had their intended effect. In the spring of 1847, less than a year after arriving, Point left Fort Lewis for good. The Jesuits' mission at St. Mary's likewise floundered, in part because Flathead leaders felt betrayed that the missionaries shared their spiritual power with their Blackfoot adversaries and grew loathe to defend the mission against frequent Blackfoot horse raids. In 1850, the Jesuits sold the mission buildings and farm to an independent trader named John Owen, in an exchange that is often called the first real estate transaction in what became Montana. The Black Robe Medicine Men abandoned the region, having failed to turn the Blackfoot into Christians, but their brief presence signaled greater changes to come.[4]

The 1840s also saw the arrival of other whites who, like the Black Robes, had no direct connection to the fur trade. Beginning in 1843, large numbers of American emigrants began to travel west in wagon trains along a route that became known as the Oregon Trail. Although the emigrants stayed well south of Blackfoot territory, following the mountain men's old paths along the Platte River valley and South Pass, Blackfoot people kept a wary eye on the travelers. According to Chouteau and Company traders, a Piikani raiding party first witnessed the emigrants' wagon trains winding past Fort Hall on the Snake River in what is now Idaho in 1843. The sight of dozens of wagons and hundreds of white men, women, and children astonished the Piikanis, since in their experience, náápiikoan visitors had always been men and had almost always come to the region by boat. They dubbed the new trail the "Great Medicine Road of the Whites." The wagon trains may have become tantalizing targets for some Blackfoot raiders, who sometimes appeared at Fort Benton with American mules and horses. At Fort Benton, a (quite possibly apocryphal) tale circulated that the Piikani chief Little Dog once captured a box of gold coins during a raid on an emigrant train but, thinking the coins were brass buttons, cached the box in a location he later forgot. Like the coins, however, the Medicine Road was a curiosity experienced by only a tiny handful of Blackfoot people.[5]

Despite interest in these strange developments, the fur trade still commanded far more Blackfoot attention during the 1840s. In the southern portions of Blackfoot territory, the American bison robe trade had made a roaring recovery following the attack on Old Sun's Siksikas in the winter of 1843–44. Medicine Snake Woman and Alexander Culbertson's return to the Upper Missouri in 1845 convinced most band chiefs that the American trading posts were once again safe to visit, and by 1846 Blackfoot traders returned to the Missouri in force. The bison robe trade during the winter of 1846–47 was one of the largest in the history of the region, and Blackfoot traders brought in more than twenty thousand robes—an average of eight bison killed for every Blackfoot hunter. The windfall took Chouteau and Company traders by surprise. When Fort Lewis's stock of trade goods ran out, the Americans resorted to trading their own bedding, clothing, and every other available item to Blackfoot visitors. The trade the following winter, after the Americans replaced Fort Lewis with Fort Benton, was nearly as robust.[6]

For the Blackfoot, the bison robe trade with Americans had long since surpassed the British provisions trade in importance. In the ten years prior to 1855, Blackfoot traders brought about seventeen thousand bison robes per year to trade at Forts Lewis and Benton. According to one observer, the Blackfoot traded six times as many goods to the Americans as they did to the British in the early 1850s. They preferred American posts in part because they were safer and more conveniently located than Edmonton, which after 1837 sat squarely in Cree territory. Piikani bands wintered on tributaries of the Missouri and rarely ventured significantly north of the Belly River. Preparing robes to trade during the winter also synced up with the Blackfoot's traditional communal bison hunts, which occurred in late fall, when bison cows and young bulls had already grown their thick winter coats. After the hunt, women dressed and prepared the robes for men to sell to Chouteau and Company traders. "They procure as many robes as they choose," noted one American who wintered with the Piikanis in 1854, which they "trade at the trading posts on the Missouri for Guns, Ammunition, Blankets, Scarlet Cloth, Calico, Knives, Beads and ornaments of various kinds." As he put it, "the Blackfeet are rich in all that constitutes the wealth of an Indian."[7]

Though they had more robust exchanges in the south in the 1840s and 1850s, Blackfoot traders still maintained their ties to the British in the north, just as they had done before. Blackfoot people knew that the HBC would continue to welcome them when they traveled north, since the company depended on pemmican (and, increasingly, tallow rendered from bison fat) to sustain their operations elsewhere. Kainai and Siksika bands in particular, who wintered on the southernmost tributaries of the Saskatchewan, continued to frequent Edmonton House during the late summer to trade bison meat, horses, and furs to the HBC in return for goods like tobacco, alcohol, guns, ammunition, and clothing. In addition to the obvious advantages of maintaining leverage with the Americans and occasional convenience, the availability of alcohol could also motivate the Blackfoot to make the trek north. In 1852, the chief factor at Edmonton reported that "the Blackfeet tribes . . . bring us provisions & Horses for sale in the summer. They come this far, for the sake of Rum and nothing else." While U.S. laws prohibited trading alcohol to Indians, Blackfoot traders could acquire rum at HBC posts well into the late nineteenth century. Blackfoot people had little reason to fear that the HBC would cut off their access to trade, and their ability to move freely between the Missouri and North Saskatchewan remained essential both strategically and materially.[8]

Buoyed by their thriving trade relationships, Blackfoot warriors raided their neighbors aggressively. Constant Blackfoot attacks took a toll on other nations. Conflicts with the Blackfoot drove Crow bands south of the Yellowstone River and crippled the Crows' robe trade with Chouteau and Company. Despite the company's repeated attempts to establish trading posts for the Crows on the Yellowstone River, the Crows' fear of Blackfoot attacks forced the Americans to conduct most of their trade through brigades that traveled directly to Crow villages. As a result, the Crows' robe trade lagged behind that of their Blackfoot neighbors. Assiniboine bands, many of whom had moved south toward the Missouri River to trade robes at Fort Union and later to receive annuity goods from the U.S. government, likewise complained to American traders that constant conflicts had left them destitute. Observers also noted that mountain nations like the Flatheads lived in "great dread" of Blackfoot horse raids. In 1853, Culbertson reported that Blackfoot warriors were out "at all seasons and times" on horse raids and war parties. Blackfoot warriors engaged in almost perpetual conflict with their neighbors, a cycle that was both enabled and motivated by the fur trade.[9]

The Kainai chief Mekaisto, or Red Crow, provided a window into the omnipresence of conflict in Blackfoot life during the 1840s and 1850s when he dictated his autobiography later in life. Born in 1830 in the Fish Eaters band, Red Crow grew up determined to make a name for himself as a warrior and became heavily involved in raiding and war parties as a teenager. He followed a familiar path. During his first two summers, he came on raids as an assistant, and his duties included gathering wood, tending fire, and carrying water for established warriors. By his third summer, he had earned enough trust to participate as a warrior instead of a servant. He began the summer by joining a massive war party of Kainais, Siksikas, and Tsuut'inas under the

The Kainai chief Red Crow, pictured here in 1895, first gained stature through his prodigious accomplishments in raiding and warfare during the 1840s. Later in life he would play a lead role in negotiating with the British Crown to create a separate reserve for the Kainai people. In this image, he wears a chief's jacket and treaty medal, which testify to his experience as a diplomat. (Glenbow Archives, NA-3281-2.)

leadership of the Siksika chief Old Sun that rode north to the North Saskatchewan area and killed three Cree bison hunters before disbanding. Days after returning to his band's camp near the Red Deer River, Red Crow joined a horse-raiding party going south toward Crow territory. After failing to capture horses, he again returned home, only to set out *again* a few days later on a joint Kainai-Siksika horse-raiding party against the Shoshones and Nez Percés, this one led by his relative Red Old Man, whose power famously derived from his supernatural alliance with a mouse. On his return home from the successful raids, Red Crow stayed with Piikani friends, then stopped in Fort Benton to visit his aunt Medicine Snake Woman and uncle Culbertson. By the end of the summer, Red Crow had traveled hundreds of miles, from the North Saskatchewan to the Missouri and from the plains to the mountains; had captured numerous horses and war honors; and was fast on his way to becoming one of the Kainais' most respected warriors. Such was the road to success.[10]

During Red Crow's youth, access to bison herds became a creeping source of anxiety and conflict across the Great Plains. Although Blackfoot territory remained home to some of the most robust and resilient bison herds on the continent, elsewhere in the West, bison populations began to creak under the stress of overhunting, disease, and habitat loss. The advent of horses more than a century earlier had led various nations to adopt a plains-based lifestyle, thus increasing the population of people who relied on bison for food, clothing, shelter, and domestic goods. During the nineteenth century, trade for bison robes and provisions had increased pressure on herds. By the 1840s, Indigenous people throughout the plains had gained access to markets for bison robes, often at trading posts along the North Saskatchewan or Missouri River in the northern plains, or along the Platte River or the Santa Fe Trail farther south. Hundreds of thousands of bison fell victim to eager hunters hoping to trade their robes. New diseases and parasites transmitted by horses and cattle likely had an impact on declining herds as well. But perhaps most damaging of all were the changes to the bison's physical environment. Indigenous nations' massive horse herds, especially on the central and southern plains, had begun to denude the river valleys that bison relied upon for forage during winters and droughts. Emigrants and oxen on the overland trail exacerbated the problem on the central plains. Although they had not yet reached the crisis point they would a few decades later, bison herds in much of the U.S. and Canadian plains began to shrink noticeably during the 1840s and 1850s.[11]

Blackfoot leaders took notice when Native bison hunters from other regions began to make forays onto Blackfoot territory, where herds remained robust. From the west, Flathead, Pend d'Oreille, Kootenai, and Shoshone hunters responded to shrinking game populations in the mountains by riding onto the plains to find food, and by the late 1840s, conflicts over bison-hunting grounds in the western portions of Blackfoot territory grew more frequent. Dwindling bison populations to the north and east caused a similar problem, as Crees, Lakotas, and Assiniboines pushed their hunting operations west toward Blackfoot territories. In 1854, an American noted with concern that Cree and Assiniboine hunters were encroaching on the Upper Missouri, and that "although for many years buffalo have been tolerably numerous through the country of the Crees and Assinaboines [sic] . . . they are rapidly diminishing." As a result, these nations had become "obliged to hunt on the tributaries of the Missouri," far to the south and west of their traditional hunting grounds. Lakota bands also experienced growing shortages of bison and began to hunt in the area of the Upper Missouri around the late

1840s. Rare to nonexistent before, conflicts between the formidable Lakotas and the Blackfoot became frequent during the 1850s and 1860s. The depletion of bison populations in surrounding regions rippled throughout the plains, and outside pressure on the Blackfoot grew.[12]

Not all Blackfoot bands were immune from growing scarcity. In the northern portions of Blackfoot country, some Siksika and Kainai bands had difficulty locating bison during the winter of 1854–55, in part because Cree hunters had used prairie fires to reroute bison herds away from their normal grazing grounds. Several winter count keepers marked the winter of 1854–55 as the "year we ate dogs"—a food supply to which Blackfoot peoples resorted only in desperation, since they so valued dogs as workers and companions. The prospect of desperate Lakota, Cree, and Assiniboine (and later, Métis) hunters moving into Blackfoot lands, driving off bison, and elbowing Blackfoot hunters out of their hunting grounds surely provoked intense anxiety, and leaders almost certainly feared the prospect of increased competition. Beaver bundle holders owned songs that could change the movements of bison herds, but such powers could only be used rarely, in times of great hardship. Finding a long-term means to preserve their access to bison weighed heavily on their minds.[13]

Traditionally, diplomacy represented the clearest solution to conflicts, and northern plains people had long made both informal and formal agreements that preserved access to resources. Leaders representing nations (though sometimes only representing their individual bands) periodically met for diplomatic councils in which they exchanged gifts, smoked, and hashed out agreements that allowed one another access to hunting grounds, trading posts, and other resources. Generally, Native people saw these agreements as practical solutions to temporary problems and did not expect them to be permanent. More informal arrangements over resources often emerged as well. Liminal areas between nations' territories often became de facto neutral grounds, where no nation's bands could feel comfortable enough to camp without being attacked, but where hunters of various stripes could visit temporarily in search of bison. Neutral grounds surrounding Blackfoot country had begun to shrink as other nations encroached during the 1840s and 1850s, leading to increased conflicts. Still, the region's long history of bison diplomacy gave hope to plains people that they could resolve their present conflicts. If the Blackfoot and other nations of the northwest plains could make an agreement over how to distribute their hunting, they could reduce pressure on the herds and minimize unnecessary clashes.[14]

To the south of Blackfoot country, plains people were already making agreements that addressed their growing conflicts over bison. In 1840, the Comanches, Kiowas, Cheyennes, and Arapahoes concluded a peace council that allowed them all to hunt bison in the Arkansas River valley. In the fall of 1851, an even larger council took place, this one organized by U.S. officials at Fort Laramie, on the Platte River in what is now Wyoming. The treaty council included representatives of the Lakotas, Cheyennes, Crows, Assiniboines, Mandans, Hidatsas, and Arikaras, many of whom had been in conflict with one another over access to shrinking bison herds in the Platte River valley. The treaty established peace between the many groups, as well as the U.S. government, and allowed for safe passage by white emigrants. Although the Blackfoot's familiar Chouteau and Company counterpart Culbertson played a role in organizing the Fort Laramie treaty, he did not invite Blackfoot or Gros Ventre representatives, since he could not send word to them in time. When Culbertson returned to the Upper Missouri a few weeks after the treaty signing, he concluded a smaller peace agreement between the Gros Ventres and Assiniboines, who had recently been at odds with one another, but did nothing with the Blackfoot nations. For Blackfoot people, a treaty like the one at Fort Laramie could help reduce the pressure they felt from their neighbors and perhaps reaffirm their preeminence in the region.[15]

In the summer of 1853, Medicine Snake Woman and Culbertson presented Blackfoot chiefs with an opportunity for diplomacy, sending them tobacco and other gifts along with a request to assemble for a council with visiting U.S. officials. More than thirty Blackfoot leaders heeded the call, including powerful Piikani civil chiefs like Lame Bull, Little Dog, and Low Horn, as well as several Kainai, Siksika, and Gros Ventre leaders. Clad in their finest clothing, they gathered inside the trading house at Fort Benton on September 21. Medicine Snake Woman translated and introduced the chiefs to Washington Governor Isaac Stevens, the short, bearded náápiikoan who had organized the gathering. As the council began, one chief pointedly noted that although the chiefs had dressed for the occasion, Stevens had greeted them out of uniform. "We dress up to receive you and why do you not wear the dress of a chief?" he demanded. Stevens's dress represented a serious faux pas in plains diplomacy. Although Stevens had made a poor first impression, Medicine Snake Woman and Culbertson vouched for him, and the chiefs stayed to hear him out.[16]

The chiefs listened patiently as the American declared his intention to organize a treaty that would create a lasting peace between the Blackfoot and

A Blackfoot war chief named White Man's Horse met with Stevens as Stevens was on his way to Fort Benton in 1853. According to Stevens, the chief regaled him with stories of his frequent horse raids in Flathead territory. (John Mix Stanley, *Council with White Man's Horse*, in Stevens, "Narrative of 1853," opposite 12:89.)

their neighbors, and that would also include safe passage through the region for whites. Stevens wanted to hold the treaty council the following summer and asked the assembled chiefs to cease sending raiding and war parties against their neighbors in the meantime. The assembled chiefs immediately expressed doubts about their ability to control young men who depended on raiding for prestige and wealth. (This was a common problem that emerged in peace talks, since raiding offered considerable rewards for young men, and even powerful chiefs generally lacked the unilateral authority to prohibit young warriors from raiding as their fathers and grandfathers had done.) Nevertheless, to show good faith toward Stevens, the Piikani chief Low Horn ended the council by exhorting the young men seated nearby to cease their raiding. Low Horn's display satisfied Stevens, who distributed presents to the assembled chiefs before the council departed. Even though their conflicts with neighboring nations continued after the 1853 council meeting, Blackfoot and Gros Ventre leaders demonstrated genuine interest in a peace treaty. Still, their unfamiliarity with Stevens must have gnawed at the chiefs. Who was this strange man who greeted the powerful Blackfoot in his muddy travel clothes?[17]

ISAAC STEVENS ESPOUSED an ideology fundamentally different from anything the Blackfoot had yet encountered during their century of direct interactions with the náápiikoan. Unlike those who came before him, Stevens's ultimate goal was not to facilitate economic exchange between Native and non-Native people but to enable the colonization of the northwest plains through settlement. To Stevens, recent history made it obvious that the northwest plains were destined to be consumed by the United States and its people. During the 1840s, the United States experienced a dramatic territorial expansion. In an 1846 treaty, officials resolved a long-standing dispute with Great Britain over the location of the international border west of the continental divide, affixing the boundary permanently at the forty-ninth parallel and bringing what became Washington, Oregon, Idaho, and parts of Montana and Wyoming into the United States. The same year, U.S. troops went to war with Mexico over contested territory in southern Texas. The conflict ended in 1848 with the Treaty of Guadalupe-Hidalgo, in which the United States took possession of over a third of what had once been Mexico. In late 1853, the United States acquired even more land from Mexico in a transaction known as the Gadsden Purchase. In less than a decade, the United States grew by more than 1.2 million square miles.[18]

Territorial expansion fueled a surge of overland migration into the trans-Missouri West that quickly eclipsed the fur trade in scope. Between the 1840s and the 1860s, as many as half a million Americans set out in caravans of covered wagons from places like Independence, Missouri, and Council Bluffs, Iowa, bound for the promised lands of California, Utah, and Oregon. Overland trail emigrants had very different goals than the trappers, traders, and explorers who preceded them. Rather than forge relationships with Native people, the new wave of emigrants imagined a future for themselves that did not include Native people at all. They came to farm, to mine for precious metals, to set up businesses, and to escape religious persecution. To them, commercial connections with Native people were not only unnecessary but detrimental to their goals; the fur trade had become nothing more than a relic of the past, along with the marriage and family relationships that had structured it.[19]

The flood of settlers across the plains led federal officials to develop new policies that would remove Native opposition and boost expansion. In the years prior to 1846, the fantasy of a so-called permanent Indian frontier had guided western Indian policy. During this period, federal officials sought to relocate Native peoples west of the Mississippi River, where they would supposedly remain in relative isolation from American settlements in perpetuity. But the rapid acquisition of more western lands, coupled with the increasing presence of squatters and passing migrants in Indian territories, had rendered this policy impractical. Following the formal annexation of northern Mexico and the Oregon Territory, the government's attention shifted toward facilitating settlement and integrating the interior West into the Union. Federal officials increasingly sought to confine Native peoples on specifically defined tribal territories, to keep them away from settlers, and to assign them agents from the Office of Indian Affairs who could instruct them on the supposed benefits of white civilization. On the central and southern plains, government officials organized massive treaty councils at Fort Laramie in 1851 and Fort Atkinson in 1853, which obligated Indian nations to keep peace and protect emigrants in return for yearly annuity payments. Using treaties like these to pacify and control Indigenous people, rather than simply remove them, would prove essential for expanding America's empire to the Pacific.[20]

Stevens fashioned himself as a personal torchbearer for expansionism. Possessor of a forceful presence that belied his five-foot, three-inch stature, Stevens graduated from West Point in 1839 and helped lead U.S. forces into Mexico during the Mexican-American War, fighting in numerous battles before suffering wounds during the 1847 invasion of Mexico City. By war's end he had risen from lieutenant to major. Stevens not only supported the Mexican-American War; he believed it to be divine prophecy. After the conflict, Stevens wrote that the Mexicans "succumbed to a people having a future they were resolved to achieve." Although Mexico was once a great nation, Mexicans' future was "in their past," while the Americans had "great destinies before them." After the war, white American settlers would continue the work that the war began, and Stevens advocated a strong military presence in the West to protect emigrant trains against Indian attacks and to keep a watchful eye on Mexico and Great Britain. Stevens believed firmly that the United States had a duty to expand across North America, a political ideology that became known as "Manifest Destiny."[21]

Stevens tied himself closely to the politics of westward expansion. An ardent Democrat, Stevens grew up admiring the aggressive nationalism of President Andrew Jackson and later supported Jackson's pro-expansionist protégé James Polk in the 1844 presidential election. Stevens fit sectional politics into his ideology as well, arguing that aggressive expansion into the northwest in particular would strengthen the North at the expense of the slaveholding South. After Stevens backed his candidacy in 1852, President Franklin Pierce appointed Stevens the first governor of Washington Territory, an assignment that made Stevens acting superintendent of Indian affairs in the region as well. Nothing if not energetic and ambitious, Stevens wrote to Secretary of War Jefferson Davis immediately after receiving the governorship to request an appointment to lead an exploration and survey of a transcontinental railroad route in the region as well. His new appointments would provide the perfect opportunity for him to put his ideology into action. One biographer rightly dubbed him a "young man in a hurry."[22]

Stevens thus traveled to Blackfoot country in 1853 determined to accelerate America's westward movement. While his position as commissioner of the railroad survey charged him with merely mapping the physical characteristics of the region, Stevens also sought, in his words, "to give great attention to the Indian tribes, as their friendship was important to be secured, and bore directly upon the question . . . of the Pacific railroad." The path that Congress wanted Stevens to scout, stretching from the Great Lakes to the Puget Sound, would have to pass through the territories of a variety of Native peoples, many of whom had yet to complete treaties with the United States. In Stevens's mind, his mission therefore also entailed making sure future travelers would be safe from attacks. In eastern publications, the Blackfoot had a particular reputation for violence and ranked as the largest and most powerful of the nations along the route (and therefore, naturally, would be the treaty partners who could earn Stevens the most prestige). Stevens and his eastern supporters decided that he should make the first formal agreement between Blackfoot peoples and the United States, one that would establish peace in the region, open it to more detailed surveys, and ultimately facilitate American emigration.[23]

Nationalism and fears about British meddling also motivated Stevens and his allies. All three of the Blackfoot nations maintained ties to the HBC and consistently traveled between U.S. territory and Rupert's Land. Many U.S. officials fretted that Indians living and trading in British territory might cross the border to raid or attack settlements on the U.S. side. They also worried that Indians living in the United States might raid north across the border, leading to anti-American recriminations by the British. In a letter to Stevens, Commissioner of Indian Affairs George Manypenny directed that Blackfoot people should be "induced" to remain permanently in the United States, and not to pass into British territories for any reason whatsoever. Stevens likewise stated that he was "determined, in [his] intercourse with the Indians, to break up the ascendancy of the Hudson [sic] Bay Company, and permit no authority or sanction to come between the Indians and the officers of this government." To allow Blackfoot nations to move freely across the international border, to have their own friends, to battle constantly with their neighbors, and to impose their own idea of order on the region was anathema to the goals of U.S. expansion. A treaty therefore offered the opportunity for Stevens to strengthen the integrity of the nation's northern border, and therefore of the United States itself.[24]

Beyond enabling settler expansion, Stevens believed that the treaty would prove a first step toward assimilating the Blackfoot to American culture. At his 1853 council with Blackfoot chiefs, Stevens warned that their reliance on dwindling bison herds clouded their future and that the bison robe trade stood in the way of progress. In Stevens's opinion, farms and cattle offered a more sustainable path forward. He argued that the northwest plains would make ideal farmland for white settlers and Blackfoot people alike, and if federal officials could only instruct the Blackfoot to farm effectively, they would soon abandon the chase for agriculture. His proposed treaty would therefore include provisions for a demonstration farm in Blackfoot territory. Stevens insisted that "the establishment of an agency or farm in their country" would change the Blackfoot "from a warlike and nomadic to a peaceable and agricultural nation." A true believer in the innate superiority of Americans, Stevens was determined to transform the lifeways of the Blackfoot. To Stevens, a treaty with the Blackfoot represented the crucial first step in turning the high plains into an extension of the agricultural Midwest.[25]

Finally, Stevens and his allies argued that a Blackfoot treaty would have positive ramifications for Indian policy and diplomacy across the Northwest. The lack of a treaty with the powerful Blackfoot and Gros Ventres, who continued to send raiding and war parties far beyond their own borders, undermined the Americans' existing Indian treaties in neighboring regions. The 1851 Fort Laramie Treaty defined Blackfoot territory as existing north of the Musselshell and Missouri Rivers in what became central Montana, but it had no Blackfoot or Gros Ventre signatories and therefore no direct influence upon them. Moreover, the Blackfoot and Gros Ventres' continued attacks on nations that had promised to maintain peace in 1851 threatened the stability of the arrangement. A government agent at Fort Pierre, a post on the Missouri River several hundred miles east of Blackfoot territory, noted in 1853 that Lakota, Assiniboine, and Crow leaders all complained of Blackfoot raids and said they would continue to respond if only out of "self-preservation."

Blackfoot conflicts with mountain nations likewise threatened the ambitions of missionaries and other officials there, and some officials worried about Blackfoot attacks on overland emigrants. Perhaps most importantly, the Blackfoot, and their Gros Ventre allies remained the only plains Indigenous nations that had yet to sign any treaty with the United States, an omission that surely bothered officials who sought to bring their idea of order to the region.[26]

Congressional debates over Stevens's Blackfoot treaty underscored the primacy of expansionist ideology. Buoyed by his reception at Fort Benton in September 1853, Stevens immediately afterward dispatched Culbertson to Washington, D.C., to lobby for congressional approval. Stevens's friends in the Democratic Party greeted Culbertson and assured him of their support, but many other congressmen balked at the council's $100,000 price tag, and Congress voted down the appropriation in May 1854. Expansion remained controversial to many, and the blistering sectional politics surrounding the Kansas-Nebraska Act complicated the appropriation, since a northern route for the transcontinental railroad would disproportionately benefit non-slave states. Fittingly, expansionist Democrats who played a key role in advocating for the Mexican-American War, including Senate president pro tempore David Atchison of Missouri, eventually helped to push the Blackfoot treaty appropriation through. Conversely, Whig senator John Bell of Tennessee, a vociferous opponent of the war with Mexico, opposed the Blackfoot appropriation. Congress finally agreed to an $80,000 cost in July 1854. The wrangling forced Stevens to delay the treaty for another year, but the governor had gotten his wish.[27]

Late in the summer of 1855, Blackfoot bands received word that the treaty council had at last been approved. From their temporary headquarters in Fort Benton, Stevens and his co-commissioner Alfred Cumming sent couriers to each of the Blackfoot nations, as well as the Gros Ventres, Flatheads, Nez Percés, Pend d'Oreilles, Kootenais, Shoshones, and Crows, that the treaty council would take place in the middle of October at the mouth of the Judith River downriver from Fort Benton. Many looked forward to having a forum to resolve their disputes and to provide more stability to their communities.[28]

IN THE DAYS leading up to October 16, 1855, thousands of Blackfoot people arrived at the cottonwood groves at the confluence of the Missouri and Judith Rivers, carrying their homes and belongings on travois behind their horses and dogs. As the southernmost, largest, and most powerful of the three Blackfoot nations, the Piikanis made up a plurality. The Kainais had a slightly smaller contingent, while only a fifth of the Siksikas made the long trek south. Among the Piikanis, Lame Bull of the Hard Top Knots band enjoyed the most influence, followed by Mountain Chief, a venerable leader of the Blood band, Low Horn of the Buffalo Dung band, and Little Dog of the Black-Patched Moccasins People. Most of the Blackfoot bands had been camped near the Belly River, north of the international border, when couriers summoned them to the council late in the summer of 1855. Their journey south for the treaty most likely represented their last movement before separating into camps for the long winter. Although they left few written accounts of their experience, Blackfoot leaders certainly discussed the upcoming council at length in the preceding days. The agreement would have momentous consequences for their people; otherwise, they would not have come.[29]

As the big day approached, the cottonwood grove pulsed with the anticipation of a wide array of peoples who came either to witness or to participate in the council. In a matter of days, some 3,500 people had erected their tipis in the shelter of the wide valley. Most of the lodges on the valley floor belonged to Blackfoot people, while the visiting Flatheads set up their lodges about a mile away. Nearly seven thousand more people camped within easy riding distance on the prairies above the river valley, including Nez Percé, Pend d'Oreille, and Gros Ventre bands. Altogether, Stevens reported that more than ten thousand people attended, making it one of the largest gatherings of Native people in American history. One American noted that in the days leading up to the council, members of the different nations were "mingling together in a friendly manner." Never before had the peoples of the northwest plains and mountains congregated in such numbers.[30]

On October 16, the long-awaited council finally convened, with all the ceremony and greetings appropriate to such a momentous occasion. Representatives from each of the bands arrived at the council grounds in a procession similar to fur trade ceremonies, with male leaders at the fore, faces painted and wearing their finest garments. They then gathered outside the commissioners' tents, in the shadows of the leafless cottonwoods. By noon, representatives of the Blackfoot, Gros Ventres, Flatheads, Pend d'Oreilles, Kootenais, and Nez Percés, as well as a handful of Shoshone and Cree observers, formed a large semicircle around the commissioners. Meanwhile, as the commissioners' secretary Henry Kennerly later recalled, "other bands and squads of Indians on horseback and on foot and gaily decorated were parading and chanting around the treaty grounds. This gave enchantment to our surroundings." At noon, the commissioners introduced and swore in

On October 16, 1855, representatives from nine nations gathered to make a treaty at the confluence of the Missouri and Judith Rivers. (Gustav Sohon, *Blackfoot Council Group*, 1855, Washington State Historical Society, Tacoma, Washington.)

the interpreters: two for the Flatheads, two for the Nez Percés, and three for the Blackfoot, including Culbertson and a mixed ancestry trader named James "Jemmy Jock" Bird. At one o'clock the proceedings began.[31]

In their short speeches to begin the council, Stevens and Cumming outlined how the proposed treaty would transform Blackfoot country. Both voiced hopes that the treaty would bring peace among all of the nations involved, as well as with the Crows, who were unable to attend. The treaty would end conflict, they said, by creating common hunting grounds, in which all tribes could pursue bison freely without fear of attack. In a departure from his 1853 message, Stevens also articulated his vision for civilizing institutions. "We want to establish you in your country on farms. We want you to have cattle and raise crops. We want your children to be taught," Stevens informed them. "Send word . . . where you want your farms to be, and what schools and mills and shops you want." The commissioners then read the entire treaty aloud, and the seven translators then communicated it to the gathered representatives. The commissioners reported that they frequently stopped to explain each provision to the assembly.[32]

Bison diplomacy, not "civilization" or cultural transformation, dominated the chiefs' debate over the treaty provisions, for the assembled chiefs wanted above all to bring order to the increasingly chaotic hunting situation on the plains. Blackfoot leaders hoped to prevent outsiders from overhunting or driving off herds, while neighboring nations wanted to preserve some access for themselves. The treaty proposed a familiar solution: the creation of two common hunting grounds, one in the rich hunting grounds at the base of the Rocky Mountains near the Three Forks of the Missouri, and one farther east on the prairies, north of the Missouri between Blackfoot and Assiniboine territories. Located on the eastern and southwestern fringes of Blackfoot territory, both areas had served as neutral zones in the past. Their locations inspired the council's most spirited debate. After hearing the articles of the treaty read aloud, the prominent Pend d'Oreille chief Alexander announced that his people had an ancestral right to hunt throughout the high plains near the mountains, and that they had lost that right only because better-armed Blackfoot warriors drove them into the mountains. Alexander's declaration threatened the basis of the entire agreement. He dropped the issue only after the Piikani chief Little Dog stood up and promised to show Alexander's people "hospitality" if they came to visit Piikani lands outside the common hunting ground. With the issue of bison settled, the council sped forward.[33]

The final draft of the treaty between the United States and the Blackfoot entailed three main concessions from Blackfoot and Gros Ventre peoples (whom the agreement erroneously identified as a fourth Blackfoot tribe). First, the Blackfoot were to maintain peace with all of the neighboring tribes. In order to facilitate this peace, the treaty created common hunting grounds in the southern and western sections of what the Fort Laramie Treaty had recognized as Blackfoot territory. There would be no reservation for now. The Blackfoot would likewise promise to allow U.S. citizens to pass freely through their territory, to utilize its resources, and to live there if they chose. (Sectional politics had recently scuttled any immediate dreams of a railroad in the area, but the commissioners remained keen on enabling overland and water travel.) In return, the Blackfoot would receive $20,000 in goods annually for ten years, and the United States agreed to spend up to $15,000 annually on agency buildings, farms, and other promotions of the Indians' "civilization."[34]

From the Blackfoot perspective, the treaty addressed pressing issues over access to bison and did not entail any radically new concessions. In fact, each of the concessions the treaty outlined resembled those already granted to fur traders or other Indigenous nations. Neutral grounds were a familiar diplomatic reality, and náápiikoan traders had often attempted to broker and maintain peace between the Blackfoot and other nations (and, like the government, had only fleeting success). Fur traders had also asked for the right

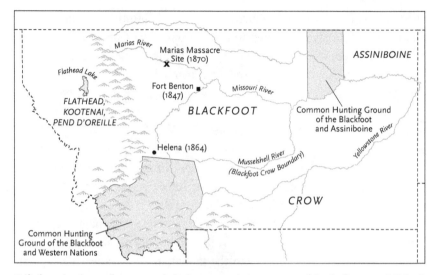

Tribal territories and common hunting grounds in Montana (shaded), as established in the 1855 treaty.

to build small settlements and to travel through the region safely. Blackfoot people had long accepted these concessions because of the considerable reward they entailed, especially the opportunity for material advancement and increased security. Blackfoot chiefs approached the treaty in much the same way: as an opportunity to strengthen their relationships with Americans, to ensure their access to bison, and to gain new insurance against scarcity and starvation.

Unlike Stevens and Cumming, the Blackfoot did not see the treaty as a precursor to widespread settlement. Though the Blackfoot were surely aware of the momentous changes happening elsewhere in the West, they had seen no indication that the northwest plains was on the verge of similar tumult. "The Blackfeet say they are a great and powerful people, but the whites are few and feeble," reported their government agent a few years later. "If the white men are so numerous, why is it the same ones come back to the country year after year, with rarely an exception?" Agents pleaded with their superiors to fund a delegation of Blackfoot chiefs to travel east, but they declined. Blackfoot people were not ignorant of events beyond their homelands. Medicine Snake Woman, for example, had made several trips between her husband's hometown of Peoria, Illinois, and Fort Benton over the years. But the Blackfoot recognized that a long distance separated them from the whites' cities and knew that the Americans had little power over them. Indeed, whites on the northwest plains had always seemed few and feeble when compared with the Blackfoot, and the treaty offered serious benefits in the present.[35]

The 1855 treaty council also bolstered peace and reinforced Blackfoot leadership in similar ways to fur trade interactions. During Stevens's first visit in 1853, he distributed $600 in gifts to Blackfoot chiefs, including the Piikani leaders Little Dog and Lame Bull. When the Blackfoot arrived at the council grounds in 1855, Stevens and Cumming piled $10,000 worth of goods within view of the council and promised a similar yearly windfall for the next decade. As at fur trading posts, band chiefs carefully mediated the distribution of these gifts, receiving the goods directly from officials before dispersing them among individual families. In following years, agents would ask the civil chiefs of each band to inform the officials of the number of families in each band, then to distribute the goods themselves. Careful adherence to this principle helped to fortify and elevate the position of chiefs. The distribution of gifts strengthened Blackfoot chiefs and demonstrated their ability to extract concessions from outsiders. The treaty conferred a new source of individual power and influence.[36]

The treaty's annuity goods provided more peace of mind for the assembled chiefs. If bison should become scarce for any reason, the government's promised annuity distributions would provide some insurance and stability. Although Blackfoot leaders showed limited interest in farming themselves, the establishment of a government farm and mission could also provide an emergency source of horses and food if necessary. The treaty thus provided increased security to the Blackfoot in the face of inevitable hardships. Leaders most likely saw the treaty as an opportunity to alleviate potential pressures, provide increased security, and maintain important relationships. Stevens offered to broker an already-desired peace with their neighbors, strengthen the power of chiefs, and provide a yearly windfall of goods, all in exchange for seemingly minor concessions. The Blackfoot chiefs who assembled at the mouth of the Judith in 1855 foresaw mostly positive results for their people.

Before the council concluded, the Piikani chief Little Dog gave a lengthy speech in favor of the treaty as Culbertson translated. Finally, Lame Bull, along with Little Dog, Low Horn, and Mountain Chief, as well as representatives of the Siksika, Kainai, Gros Ventre, Flathead, Pend d'Oreille, Kootenai, and Nez Percé peoples, assented to the agreement. At 3:00 P.M. on

October 17, 1855, the gathered commissioners and Native leaders signed the treaty. The council had lasted less than two days.

AS THE DISTRIBUTION OF goods commenced, Native leaders received the goods first, then divided them among the heads of different lodges. They distributed the goods "without creating much dissatisfaction," one official blithely observed, "which is rather strange, as they are very jealous." The mountain of goods included articles of clothing and blankets, as well as various types of food, including sugar, coffee, bacon, dried apples, and flour. Such goods may have reflected the staples of an 1855 American cupboard, but they offered little utility to equestrian people like the Blackfoot. Most had never drunk coffee or seen bacon (some thought, disgustedly, that it was a sort of fish) and did not know how to cook using flour or beans. Some women kept the goods and attempted to make bread and coffee; many others simply left the goods on the ground when they departed the council site. "Anyone who might have gone in pursuit of them could have easily followed their trail by observing the flour, beans, rice, hominy, dried apples etc. that had been strewn upon the ground along their path," one observer remembered. Some Blackfoot people even dumped out burlap sacks of goods to make clothing from the bags. Sugar and tea were among the only items that actually made it into Blackfoot homes.[37]

Despite the mountains of unused goods that sat rotting outside the commissioners' tents, the brief council's conclusion marked an unqualified success in the minds of Stevens and Cumming. Both men departed the council grounds on October 22 (glad to be rid of one another, having clashed frequently throughout the process). Stevens rode west to complete more treaties in Washington Territory, while Cumming floated downriver to St. Louis. Stevens proudly reported to his mother-in-law, "We have succeeded beyond our most sanguine expectations in establishing a peace between the Blackfeet and the Indians of Washington. . . . Nothing could have gone off better, nor could anything have been more successful." From their perspective, the men had good reason to feel accomplished. The accord they had organized ostensibly ended generations of violent conflict between the region's peoples, facilitated their future education and assimilation, and opened the region to white immigration.[38]

Blackfoot leaders likewise felt satisfied with the agreement, and many sought to strengthen the peace it created in the years immediately following the treaty, especially with the mountain nations. The spring following the treaty, Little Dog led a delegation west on a visit to the Flathead villages, where John Owens reported that they "traded some horses & roots, [and] made many trifling exchanges in tokens of friendship." Warfare with neighboring nations decreased significantly. By 1860, the Blackfoot's government agent Alfred Vaughan reported that "the Blackfeet Indians, a nation so dreaded in times past by the whites, have become the most peaceful nation on the Missouri River." Vaughan exaggerated, given that conflicts continued between the Blackfoot and Crees and Assiniboines north of the international border and became especially intense in 1859 and 1860. Nevertheless, the reduction in conflict south of the forty-ninth parallel showed that Blackfoot people had achieved what they wanted through the treaty. With less pressure on the bison herds, and with the promise of yearly gifts from U.S. officials, Blackfoot leaders felt more secure.[39]

The Blackfoot only saw reminders of the treaty's other provisions whenever they visited Fort Benton. As promised in the treaty, the Office of Indian Affairs assigned them an "agent," who set up a small agency building north of Fort Benton along the Sun River and once a year distributed annuity goods to Blackfoot bands. The agent also built a tiny demonstration farm and employed two white men to operate it. The Blackfoot spent the years following the treaty generally doing what they had always done: hunting bison, gathering plants, holding ceremonies, raiding, warring, and trading. They traveled to Fort Benton during the fall and winter months to trade bison robes for guns and other goods. In the winter of 1856–57 alone, Native traders brought a record twenty-three thousand bison robes to Fort Benton. As for the Indian Affairs agents, they took up little of the Blackfoot visitors' time and attention, besides their annual annuity distributions. Blackfoot people generally liked them, especially Vaughan, who took over the agency in 1857. Visitors described Vaughan as "an amusing old man," who was "fond of exaggeration."[40]

Blackfoot leaders sought to strengthen personal ties with government officials. When Vaughan's predecessor Edwin Hatch arrived to distribute their annuities in 1856, Lame Bull presented him with a white bison robe—an item of incalculable spiritual and material value to plains Native people. Although Hatch did not appreciate its significance and sold it to a visitor shortly thereafter, the gift was meant to strengthen bonds of mutual respect. "We are satisfied that the white men are *our* friends," Lame Bull told a visitor in 1856. "If they were not they would not go to the trouble of sending us so many valuable presents every year." Some Blackfoot people even took interest in the officials' educational projects, such as Little Dog, who resided on the government's demonstration farm between 1858 and 1860. Blackfoot chiefs also convinced government agents to send more useful annuity goods, and Blackfoot women learned how to use many of the previously unknown foods. Gifts demonstrated that Blackfoot chiefs had built a positive relationship with the government officials, just as they had with the Chouteau and Company traders next door. By signing the 1855 treaty, Lame Bull and his fellow signatories believed that they had entered into a mutually beneficial agreement, one that would strengthen the Blackfoot's position in the region, and one that would ensure friendship between the Blackfoot, white fur traders, and white officials.[41]

Neither Lame Bull nor Isaac Stevens lived long enough to see the results of the treaty they made. During a hunt in 1857, a bison bull charged and toppled Lame Bull's horse and the chief broke his neck in the fall. Stevens died during the Battle of Chantilly in September of 1862, felled by a Confederate ball that struck him in the forehead. Both men probably believed until their deaths that they had done well in the 1855 treaty. Neither foresaw the twisted aftermath that would unfold when the misapprehensions and misdirection that underlay the agreement finally became evident. Celebrated leaders both, Stevens and Lame Bull reflected the divergent realities of the nineteenth-century West, where nations often interacted on discordant levels.[42]

The 1855 treaty reflected the different goals of its signers, as well as a growing recognition on both sides that the fur trade no longer defined Indigenous-newcomer relations on the northwest plains. In the decade and a half prior to the treaty, Blackfoot leaders like Lame Bull saw significant changes on the horizon. The arrival of missionaries, the growing presence of overland emigrants, news of conflicts and diplomacy elsewhere in the West, and the worrisome diminution of the bison elsewhere on the plains all hung heavily in their minds. Stevens embodied the already-ominous specter of U.S. expansion. The vision he described during councils, in which cattle replaced bison, white settlers eventually took up permanent residence on Blackfoot lands, and Blackfoot people attended schools and missions, would represent a fundamental change from the fur trade era if it ever came to pass. Nonetheless, Blackfoot people did not sign the 1855 treaty as a capitulation to inevitable change. They sought to use the 1855 treaty to fortify existing advantages over their neighbors and to continue participating in the fur trade. The treaty would ensure access to resources like bison and would therefore allow the trade that had first enabled the Blackfoot's ascendancy to continue.

While Americans increasingly fixated on an ever-expanding settler frontier and the dispossession of Indigenous lands, Blackfoot people sought to maintain their relationships with whites on terms of economic exchange and carefully structured coexistence. Both sides read what they wanted in the treaty, investing it with meanings and intentions that reflected their own ideas for the future. The two resulting visions would never be reconciled. In the years to follow, the treaty would enable an assault on Blackfoot sovereignty that would imperil the Blackfoot's very survival as a people.

CHAPTER SIX

Nefarious Traffic

> In very early days we had old traders—we want the new traders to
> act like the old men who traded long ago, when there was nothing
> but peace and quietness. When we come to trading posts we do not
> want to be interfered with. We want good traders so that we may
> buy and live.
>
> —CALF SHIRT (Kainai), 1868

> It is most gratifying that my previsions were fully realized, and
> complete success was attained, not only in the severe punishment
> of the Piegans, but in the telling effect of that manifestation of our
> power on the whole of the Blackfeet nation.
>
> —COLONEL REGIS DE TROBRIAND (American), 1870

On July 17, 1859, the industrial age arrived in Blackfoot country. On that day, the Chouteau and Company steamboat *Chippewa* moored along the banks of the Missouri River twelve miles downstream from Fort Benton, a momentous achievement that marked the deepest penetration of steam-powered machines into the continent's interior by hundreds of miles. The epic journey of the *Chippewa*, which traveled more than 3,100 miles upriver from St. Louis, marked the culmination of four decades of efforts by St. Louis fur traders to overcome the wide Missouri's shallow waters and tempestuous currents: in 1819, the first steamers reached only so far as Council Bluffs before turning back, and in 1832, the steamboat *Yellowstone* ascended as far as Fort Union. Nevertheless, the final six-hundred-mile stretch of river to Fort Benton had remained elusive for the heavy steamers that became easily stranded in shallow waters. To overcome this challenge and at long last replace their small and inefficient keelboats, Chouteau and Company purchased the *Chippewa*, which was smaller and lighter than its predecessors, and hired expert captain John La Barge to navigate it through the treacherous Upper Missouri into Blackfoot territory.

No Blackfoot people were present to see the *Chippewa* unload its nearly 160 tons of cargo beside the ruins of old Fort McKenzie, since the fall and winter trading season had yet to begin and summer ceremonies likely demanded their attention instead. But Blackfoot people eventually acquired most of the boat's cargo nonetheless. A large portion went to stock Chouteau and Company's store at Fort Benton, where over the coming months Blackfoot visitors would bring in thousands of bison robes to exchange for the *Chippewa*'s cargo of rifles, ammunition, metal tools, paints, dyes, fabrics, and blankets. Another large portion belonged to the Office of Indian Affairs and was promised to Blackfoot and Gros Ventre bands per the 1855 treaty. Soon, the Blackfoot's new government agent would send word to them to assemble near Fort Benton, where they would receive several tons of clothes, blankets, northwest guns, powder horns, beads, kettles, tools, cutlery, coffee, sugar, tobacco, and other items. The third part of the goods, however, was not destined for the Blackfoot. Those goods consisted of supplies for a U.S. Army lieutenant named John Mullan, whose superiors had tasked him with building a road from Fort Benton to the sources of the Columbia River. Just like the annuities, Mullan's operation depended on the 1855 treaty and its provision that granted safe passage for whites. Still, the "Mullan Road" did not seem likely to impact Blackfoot people much at all. The coming of the *Chippewa* seemed like welcome news for Native people and whites alike.[1]

Few could have reckoned that the *Chippewa*'s arrival signaled the start of a devastating series of events that would unfold over the following decade. Soon, steamers arrived at Fort Benton carrying hundreds of white settlers who poured into Blackfoot lands. Unlike the generations who came before them, this new wave of arrivals came to build new lives in permanent settler colonies sustained by mining and agriculture, not to participate in the so-called Indian trade. By shortening the journey upriver, the steamboats also brought new viruses and other pathogens to the northwest plains. As this chaos unfolded, Blackfoot people watched with frustration as U.S. government officials mismanaged and abandoned their obligations in the region. The fragile peace between Blackfoot bands and their Indigenous neighbors on either side of the border collapsed, and new enemies emerged. Most troublingly of all, in the years following the *Chippewa*'s arrival, the fur trade went into a rapid decline in both the north and the south, disorienting Blackfoot people who had carefully cultivated relationships with white traders for generations. Blackfoot people responded to these growing challenges in a variety of ways—some productive, and some destructive. Some used their diplomatic skills to forge new relationships, while others responded with force, and used the emergent international border to their advantage. By the end of the 1860s, these forces begat a violent cataclysm that permanently re-shaped the northwest plains, and the place of Blackfoot people upon them.

THE YEARS IMMEDIATELY following the 1855 treaty had been largely unre-markable for Blackfoot people, who for the first time maintained a formal relationship with a settler government. For the time being, the southern por-tions of Blackfoot country fit under the auspices of a distant and mostly un-obtrusive U.S. federal bureaucracy known as the Office of Indian Affairs. Founded in 1824 as a part of the War Department, Indian Affairs adminis-tration transferred to the Department of the Interior in 1849 following the Mexican-American War. As the United States expanded in the 1840s and 1850s and ratified treaties with Indigenous nations throughout the Great Plains and Pacific Northwest, the Office of Indian Affairs grew. To adminis-ter the provisions of western treaties, Indian Affairs created new regional "su-perintendencies," which oversaw specific tribal "agencies." Each agency had an assigned "agent," who was a government employee authorized to deal with the agency's Native people on behalf of the U.S. government. More broadly, the task of every Indian agent was to maintain peace with Native people while slowly shepherding them toward their eventual cultural assim-ilation as Americans. With the signing of the 1855 treaty, Indian Affairs cre-ated the Blackfeet Agency for the three Blackfoot nations along with the Gros Ventres, which they then placed within the auspices of the larger Washing-ton Superintendency. Edwin Hatch served as agent for the first two years be-fore Alfred Vaughan took over in 1857.[2]

The Office of Indian Affairs' plan for Blackfoot country seemed orderly in theory, but in practice it soon became a confusing mess. Between 1855 and 1866, officials shuffled the Blackfeet Agency between five different superin-tendencies: the Washington, Central, Dakota, Idaho, and finally Montana. During the same period, the Office of Indian Affairs assigned the Blackfeet Agency six different agents, including three between 1861 and 1863 alone. Agents often expressed confusion over which superintendency they belonged to and who their superiors were, and as a result their official correspondence ended up in a variety of locations. The outbreak of the American Civil War in April 1861 worsened the confusion. When the war began, Vaughan, a Vir-ginian, immediately left his position as agent. Vaughan had built strong re-lationships with Blackfoot chiefs and had worked diligently to carry out the treaty's provisions, including the timely and equitable distribution of annu-ity goods. His successors would feel far less accountability toward their Black-foot "wards."[3]

Fort Benton, pictured here in 1853, would within a decade become a bustling gold rush town and an extremely dangerous place for Blackfoot visitors. (John Mix Stanley, *Fort Benton*, in Stevens, "Narrative of 1853," opposite 12:101.)

Blackfoot people grew frustrated with the Blackfeet Agency's disorder, especially when Vaughan's successors continually delayed or lost their promised annuity goods. In the summer of 1861, the steamboat carrying their goods up the Missouri River caught fire and exploded and therefore never reached Fort Benton. In 1863, the goods again failed to arrive, this time due to low water levels. In the meantime, the revolving door of new agents did little to inspire confidence. A local trader remarked that Vaughan's replacement Henry Reed's "unpopularity with the influential Indians cannot be disguised." Reed showed little enthusiasm for his work and spent 1863 at his home in Epsworth, Iowa, because he feared passing through Sioux territory on his way upriver. By leaving the agency unstaffed, Reed allowed newly arrived independent traders to sell alcohol openly and illegally to Native people and left the Blackfoot with no one to whom they could address their concerns. When a new agent finally arrived in December 1863, he noted that "No agent having been in the country for over eighteen months, the Indians began to feel as though they were forgotten by their 'Great Father,' and expressed themselves to that effect." The abysmal performance of agency employees eroded Blackfoot people's trust in the U.S. government.[4]

Blackfoot frustrations mounted when their agents engaged in corruption and outright theft. Gad Upson took charge of the neglected agency in December 1863, but as a local trader later recalled, the new agent "knew as much about an Indian as I did about the inhabitants of Jupiter," and had little interest in fair dealings. Upson distributed some much-delayed annuity goods in September of the following year, but his assistant later alleged that Upson distributed barely half the amount he reported, then kept the rest for himself and paid a group of white observers to attest that he had distributed the correct figure. Upson probably sold the leftovers to local merchants or directly to new immigrants disembarking at Fort Benton, as items marked "Blackfoot Annuity Goods" soon became a common sight in white settlements. His assistant later recalled that the theft "was an open secret," and that swindled Native people "were smart enough to know they were being robbed and resented it." Indian Affairs officials had little interest or capacity to prevent such illegal actions. Blackfoot people undoubtedly noticed the fraud, and their trust in the Blackfeet Agency floundered. What good was the treaty if its promises were so easily ignored by unscrupulous agents?[5]

As distrust toward the Americans set in, a new wave of outsiders descended on the region. During the summer of 1862, news spread throughout the United States that gold had been discovered in Grasshopper Creek, a small stream near one of the Three Forks of the Missouri. By the fall, hundreds of white prospectors had established a settlement nearby they named Bannack City. Thousands more—some seeking new opportunities after failing to make their fortunes in California or Colorado, and others seeking to avoid service in the Civil War—followed, in what soon became one of the largest mineral rushes in American history. Within two years, more than ten thousand newcomers crowded into boomtowns like Virginia City, Nevada City, and Helena. Most of the miners came by steamboat to Fort Benton, and from there embarked upon the new military trail known as the Mullan Road, which had first connected Fort Benton with Fort Walla Walla two years earlier. While the military rarely used the trail, it provided a perfect route for the miners, who used it to transport equipment to their new settlements near the Missouri River headwaters. The miners built their new towns and diggings within the prime hunting grounds that tribes had agreed in the 1855 treaty to use in common, and close to several key passes into the mountains, which restricted Native people's ability to travel for trading, hunting, and raiding. The sudden change must have been alarming to Native people on both sides of the mountains, who signed the treaty expecting that these areas would remain accessible for hunters, thus staving off conflicts over bison.[6]

Some Blackfoot people saw the influx of outsiders as an opportunity for trade. Early in 1863, a Métis prospector named Edward Bird returned to the Red River Settlement in what is now Manitoba and reported that he had met with a Piikani chief named Middle Sitter, who asked him to encourage other Métis to come to the gold regions to prospect or to hunt game for the Americans. Middle Sitter personally owned a herd of 300 horses and hoped to trade some to the Métis in exchange for British-manufactured goods. "Why do not the Half-breeds come and trade with me, and leave off dealing with the Crees for their saw-backed horses?" he asked Bird. Other prospectors reported that there was little to fear from the Blackfoot besides potentially losing horses to raids. Savvy Blackfoot traders imagined that the gold rush could complement existing markets.[7]

As newcomers' numbers swelled, however, many Blackfoot people grew more apprehensive about the newcomers' intentions. Although most of the mining towns (besides Helena) sprang up south of what the treaty defined as Blackfoot territory, miners repeatedly trespassed onto Blackfoot lands and even traveled as far north as Edmonton in search of new strikes. In July 1862, more than one hundred prominent Siksika, Piikani, and Kainai representatives met Agent Reed in Fort Benton to convey their concerns. "They manifested some little apprehension from seeing so many white men in their country," Reed reported, "lest there might be some design of getting their lands from them." Reed assured them that the government had no such intention, but Blackfoot leaders had good reason for worry. Miners soon began to crowd the dusty river valley around Fort Benton, lingering after their long riverboat trips to drink and buy goods before embarking overland for the mining encampments, and a cluster of stores and saloons sprouted up outside the fort to cater to the new clientele. The new establishments shared the valley with the Chouteau and Company trading post, which meant that Blackfoot traders frequently mingled with the unwashed newcomers. Seemingly overnight, Fort Benton transformed from a fur trade outpost to a gold rush town. Meanwhile, rather than limit the flood of prospectors and settlers, in 1864 Congress officially created Montana Territory to accommodate them, with its first capital at Bannack City.[8]

While a town quickly sprang up in the river valley around Fort Benton, the business that first gave the post life decayed. The Civil War had unsettled both national and international markets for robes, and Chouteau and Company forts throughout the Upper Missouri had fallen into disrepair. Charles Chouteau, the company's leader who was also a former slaveholder and a perceived Southern sympathizer, worried that Republican Office of

Indian Affairs appointees and territorial officials would deliberately impede his operations and that an eventual railroad would undercut his river-based business. In 1865, Chouteau sold most of his family's fur trade operations to Minnesota-based businessmen James Hubbell and Alpheus Hawley, who incorporated their new operation as the Northwest Fur Company. Fort Benton transferred to the new company the following year. Hubbell and Hawley repurposed Fort Benton as a store for outfitting white prospectors and settlers and moved their Native trading operations to smaller posts nearby, including one on the Marias River. As longtime producers in the fur trade economy, the Blackfoot found that they had little power to influence faraway capitalists like Chouteau once they decided to leave the fur trading business behind.[9]

The withdrawal of Chouteau and Company dealt a major blow to the fur trade in the southern portions of Blackfoot territory, and further reduced the avenues through which Blackfoot leaders could express their mounting grievances with Americans. They had already lost their most crucial intermediaries in 1857, when Alexander Culbertson and his wife Medicine Snake Woman retired to Peoria, Illinois. The couple's departure deprived the Blackfoot of their most important and influential advocates on the Upper Missouri just when they needed them most. The couple had been vital in in organizing the treaty in 1855 and in brokering the return of Chouteau and Company to Blackfoot territory in 1845 following the Chardon fiasco, but now they were nowhere to be found and Blackfoot leaders had few intermediaries they could trust to communicate with U.S. officials. Lame Bull, their most accomplished diplomat who had led the 1855 treaty negotiations, had died from a hunting injury in 1857. Isaac Stevens, his white counterpart, had died while fighting in the Civil War. And Vaughan, the government agent who had done the most to gain their trust, had resigned his government posting in 1861. Increasingly, Blackfoot leaders in Montana Territory dealt directly with officials who knew almost nothing about them.[10]

Miners' incursions and government neglect pushed Blackfoot-American relations to a breaking point. By 1863, some Blackfoot leaders came to feel that since the government was not living up to its treaty commitments, they likewise had no such obligation, and began violating the 1855 treaty by organizing larger and more frequent raiding parties against neighboring nations. A few Blackfoot men raided the Blackfeet Agency for horses as well, and employees complained that war parties often tried to steal tools and other implements from the agency farm. White immigrants to Montana likewise began to blame Blackfoot raiders for their missing horses. Blackfoot people likely saw horse-raiding as a form of recompense for the promised goods they had not received. By capturing horses from the agency, Blackfoot people registered their displeasure with the delayed annuities while augmenting their own herds. Of course, U.S. officials and white Montanans did not see the loss of horses as a reasonable response, but rather as a willful disregard of promises made in the 1855 treaty.[11]

An 1864 outbreak of "black pox," as they called it in their winter counts, was the last straw for many frustrated Blackfoot people. Most likely a combination of measles and scarlet fever, the black pox found easy transport among the hundreds of miners and speculators traveling through the region, and like smallpox, it had a devastating impact on Indigenous communities. Blackfoot people had rarely experienced either disease before and therefore had little biological immunity to protect themselves. Illness tore through Blackfoot bands during the winter of 1864–65. Decades later, Siksika elder Crooked Meat Strings remembered the black pox striking his band's hunting encampment in the autumn of his tenth year: when his band finally departed for its winter camp along the Red Deer River, he remembered that it left thirty tipis behind, "each with an entire family dead inside it." Observers at Edmonton estimated that by March 1865 more than 1,100 Blackfoot people had died, and American estimates ranged even higher. The epidemics led some Blackfoot people to lash out at the whites, whom they correctly identified as the source of the scourge. In March 1865, HBC traders at Rocky Mountain House complained that Blackfoot visitors had become "desperate," and "very hard to deal with & threatening the whites very much, blam[ing] us for the sickness." In the south, some Kainais claimed that Upson had included poisoned blankets among their annuity goods, upbraided him with threats, and stole goods from the agency.[12]

By the time the miserable disease winter ended, some Blackfoot warriors decided that they had had enough of the American interlopers. On April 23, 1865, a party of Kainai warriors stole forty horses in a daring raid on Fort Benton, which by then had become a bustling town of more than 1,500 residents. Over the following weeks, rumors abounded of horses and equipment stolen during other Blackfoot raids. Some Fort Bentonians blustered that they would kill the next "hostile" Indian who entered the town. The editor of the *Montana Post*, a fledgling newspaper in Virginia City, repeated the unverified rumor that a party of white travelers had been killed, and puffed that the only way to "quiet" Indians was to shoot them. On May 22, three Kainais arrived in Fort Benton, unaware of the anti-Native sentiment seething among the miners and merchants there. A drunken brawl soon broke out, and the townspeople shot all three of the outnumbered visitors. The whites dragged two of the bodies to the river and shoved them into the water; the third victim managed to escape but died soon thereafter.[13]

With these murders, the conflict had crossed a bloody threshold that incensed the Kainais. A respected Kainai warrior named Calf Shirt, who was war chief of the Lone Fighters band, organized a revenge party that numbered around two hundred men and rode south toward the American settlements. On May 25, 1865, a few days after the Fort Benton murders, the party came upon a group of eleven woodcutters who were working to clear a prospective town site named Ophir on the banks of the Marias River. Calf Shirt and his raiders killed all eleven. (The Kainais later claimed that when they arrived, the woodcutters insulted and threatened them, and that the whites fired first.) Residents of Fort Benton and beyond reacted to the Ophir killings by calling for military assistance and even outright extermination of Montana's Native people. "We deny the Indians' rights to the lands," one particularly outraged editor wrote. "Robbers and murderers have no such rights." In Fort Benton, an angry mob rounded up and shot the few Native people they could find. Fearing reprisal, Calf Shirt fled to the British side of the border and did not return south for several years.[14]

Montana newspapers had now dubbed the conflict an "Indian War," thus grouping it with other conflicts that had begun to rage across the U.S. West during the early 1860s. Indeed, much of the West had become engulfed in violence as American settlers poured into Indigenous lands. In 1862, Dakota Sioux people in Minnesota, starving due to reduced game populations and crop failures, lashed out against corrupt government agents and killed around five hundred settlers before the state militia crushed their uprising. Later that year, Apaches and Navajos in the Southwest became the target of a U.S. Army effort ostensibly intended to halt those nations' raids on white settlements. Former mountain man Kit Carson led a merciless scorched earth campaign that forced many Apaches to flee into the mountains or across the border, then rounded up most of the Navajos and marched them to a desolate reservation called Bosque Redondo. Meanwhile, in the newly created Colorado Territory, some Cheyennes and Arapahoes responded to settlers' invasion of their homelands by attacking wagon trains and driving off livestock, which led the state's governor to raise a regiment of volunteers led by Colonel John Chivington. In November 1864, Chivington's regiment attacked the camp of the Cheyenne chief Black Kettle on Sand Creek and massacred some two hundred Cheyenne men, women, and children. The era of the "Indian wars" had commenced, and many Montanans hoped military officials would apply a similarly ruthless approach to the Blackfoot that they had used against the Cheyennes, Navajos, Dakotas, and others.[15]

Many Blackfoot chiefs likewise sensed that the recent killings could lead to an all-out war like those occurring elsewhere and sought a diplomatic solution to the crisis. By 1864, the white population of Montana Territory had soared to nearly thirty thousand people, more than triple the population of all three Blackfoot nations combined. Going to war with the whites could end very poorly, as it had for the Cheyennes and Dakotas. Hoping to smooth things over, Siksika and Piikani civil chiefs met with citizen representatives from Fort Benton, returned some stolen horses, and publicly repudiated any alliance with the Kainais. The gesture encouraged U.S. officials, who sought to reset relations by negotiating a new treaty with the Blackfoot that would replace the 1855 agreement that was coming up on its ten-year expiration date. The proposed treaty would oblige Blackfoot people to relinquish parts of their territory south of the Missouri River that were already under increasing pressure by settlers and miners. In return, the government would provide gifts and increased annuity payments to Blackfoot bands. The Office of Indian Affairs provided $15,000 to conduct the treaty in the fall of 1865, and appointed Upson as treaty commissioner. Territorial officials would attend as well, including the new acting governor and superintendent of Indian Affairs Thomas Meagher.[16]

Blackfoot chiefs attended the November 1865 treaty council eager to forge accommodation but faced government officials with different goals in mind. For the third time in five years, their promised annuity goods had been delayed by several months and did not arrive until the time of the treaty council. Moreover, Governor Meagher began the council by insulting his Blackfoot counterparts. An Irish immigrant who rose to the rank of brigadier general during the Civil War, Meagher had only recently arrived to the territory and was keen to establish himself as a strong leader and advance his political career. When Meagher arrived at the council, a delegation of Piikani chiefs visited him, and each presented him a choice bison robe as well as one valuable horse. To their shock, Meagher refused the gifts, telling them that he was paid by the government and that they needed their property lest they go cold and hungry during the coming winter. The new governor's rejection of the gifts, though perhaps well intentioned, reflected a combination of ignorance and a misplaced desire not to appear corrupt or accommodating toward Indians. It represented an outright rejection of centuries of plains diplomatic tradition and had no precedent in the generations of Blackfoot dealings with whites. Blackfoot chiefs suddenly found themselves in very unfamiliar territory.[17]

Forty-one Kainai, Piikani, and Gros Ventre representatives signed the new treaty on November 16, 1865, but many Blackfoot people remained dissatisfied and resentful of the whites. Some chiefs were eager for a successful negotiation, especially the Piikani Little Dog, who worked directly with treaty commissioners to rewrite their speeches in order to make them more understandable. Most attendees were more skeptical. Several thousand Native people camped at Fort Benton during the treaty negotiations, but as longtime trader Bill Hamilton remembered, the vast majority only came to trade and receive their delayed annuities. According to Hamilton, many of them distrusted the U.S. treaty commissioners and resented accommodationist leaders like Little Dog. Some even made a game of their contempt. After the council concluded and the assembled Blackfoot people received their goods, many of the young men took long swaths of calico fabric and tied them to their horses' tails, then rode in all directions trying to step on the cloths pulled by other horses. The resulting spectacle "was such as neither I nor anyone else had ever beheld," Hamilton remembered. "We would all of us have been glad to have had the Commissioners see in what contempt the valuable presents that their Great Father had sent them were held by the Indians."[18]

The U.S. Senate never ratified the 1865 treaty, dashing the hopes of negotiators like Little Dog that it would stem the bloodshed. Stories of violence in the immediate aftermath of the treaty muddied the diplomatic waters. Settlers claimed that even during the treaty council, Blackfoot raiders ran off nearby ranchers' stock. In late November and early December, a party of Piikanis conducted horse raids along the Prickly Pear Creek north of Helena and killed a mixed ancestry herder who had connections to their enemies the Pend d'Oreilles. Reports circulated that winter that Kainai and Piikani warriors had massacred a party of miners along the Musselshell or Yellowstone rivers, and in December Piikanis killed two white men in the Bears Paw Mountains north of Fort Benton. Despite the ongoing tensions, Upson left for Washington, D.C., in February 1866, treaty in hand, but died after a short illness before boarding a ship in San Francisco and never made it to the capital. Officials in the Office of Indian Affairs heard the continued reports of violence and chose not to recommend the treaty for ratification.[19]

Blackfoot people who remained south of the international border faced a bleaker path after the 1865 treaty failed. Chiefs who had signed the agreement reacted indignantly when the U.S. officials abandoned their promises. According to one official's account, many never understood the ratification process and grew incensed when their promised annuity goods failed to arrive. At the same time, the reports of post-treaty raiding inflamed anti-Blackfoot anger among whites, and some Montana leaders probably viewed the ongoing violence as a political opportunity. The February 3, 1866 issue of the *Montana Democrat* included a letter from several Fort Benton merchants, who declared that the town's citizens needed protection from the "murderous [Indian] thieves" who supposedly killed whites without hesitation. To the merchants' delight, Governor Meagher immediately responded by calling for five hundred volunteers to mount an expedition against the Blackfoot. He had little success recruiting men from mining camps, however, who rarely had contact with the Blackfoot and saw no reason to put themselves at risk. Eventually, Meagher rode north with just forty men who dispersed after receiving a token gift of ten horses from a Piikani band. A nearby Indian agent groused that Meagher's Indian-fighting campaign was "the biggest humbug of the age," intended solely to burnish the ambitious governor's political reputation.[20]

While some Blackfoot people retreated north into Rupert's Land, others sought to escalate the conflict with Americans and began to focus their violence more directly on government institutions. In April 1866, a Piikani war chief named Bull's Head attacked the government agency's Sun River demonstration farm, killed a white laborer, and burned the surrounding buildings. The same party then rode to a nearby Jesuit mission (which had been established a few years earlier, with little success) and killed a herder along with several cattle. The terrified missionaries fled to Helena and did not return for years. Bull's Head's party concluded their rampage at a nearby ranch, where they killed a laborer named Charley Carson, an unfortunate nephew of the famous frontiersman Kit Carson. Unlike other raids, the attacks on the agency and the mission offered scant material reward and the raiders captured little property. Bull's Head almost certainly intended the attack as an assault on the primary institutions enabled by the treaties of 1855 and 1865: the government agency and the missionaries' church.[21]

As the turmoil south of the forty-ninth parallel intensified, a schism deepened between Kainai and Piikani leaders like Calf Shirt and Bull's Head, who favored conflict, and those who still advocated diplomacy, including Little Dog. Still the most influential chief of the Piikanis south of the border, Little Dog had long sought to coexist with the Americans. In the late 1850s he had taken up residence on the agency's demonstration farm, and in 1865 he had conferred privately with white negotiators and given long speeches in support of the updated treaty. By early 1866, he began to provoke the ire of his less-accommodating peers. On May 27, he visited Fort Benton and in a gesture of goodwill delivered twelve horses to Agent Hiram Upham that Piikani raiders had recently captured from whites. As he rode out of town, a group of Piikanis confronted him and demanded that he surrender his weapon. When he refused, a fight broke out and the assailants shot him and his son. In a letter to his superiors, Upham explained that Little Dog had been killed for being "too friendly" with whites. Four days later, a group of Piikani chiefs visited Fort Benton, renounced the murderers, and declared their continued desire to maintain peace between their bands and whites in Montana. These chiefs were known among whites as the "Medal Men" for their tactic of wearing silver peace medals they had received at the 1865 treaty council. Among them was a respected Piikani civil chief named Heavy Runner.[22]

Little Dog's murderers were probably drunk when they attacked him, and alcohol fueled much of the violence in Montana Territory. U.S. federal law had banned trading alcohol to Native people since 1822, much to the consternation of American fur traders who believed the ban gave the British an unfair advantage. The Montana gold rush, however, made the American ban almost impossible to enforce, and independent merchants often transported liquor upriver and sold it indiscriminately to both whites and Native people. Blackfoot buyers were unprepared for this change. Alcohol had been a central component to Blackfoot trade interactions since the 1780s, but consumption was confined to occasional trading visits and Blackfoot people rarely acquired enough to last more than a few days. Unlimited access to alcohol therefore presented new challenges, and violence often resulted when prospectors and Native people drank to excess in close proximity. In his 1865 report, Gad Upson called the illegal sale of alcohol to Indians "the first cause of all our troubles," and argued that "not a depredation is committed that cannot be traced back to this nefarious traffic." One missionary likewise claimed that horse raids increased in part because some Native men needed to replace horses they traded for whiskey while intoxicated. Alcohol did not explain well-organized campaigns like those of Calf Shirt and Bull's Head, but it did contribute to many smaller confrontations and relaxed inhibitions against using violence. Alcohol made an already bad situation much worse.[23]

Leaders on both sides tried unsuccessfully to solve the alcohol problem. Many pointed out the difficulty of preventing clashes since the Blackfeet Agency was located in Fort Benton, a bustling commercial center filled with thirsty prospectors. In September 1866, a drunken white mob killed seven

Piikanis in and around Fort Benton, which frightened those Native people who came there to meet their agent and to trade. Kainai and Siksika leaders told their agent, George Wright, that they were too afraid to enter the settlement, and Wright was forced to deliver goods directly to some of their camps. In response, Wright attempted to ban the sale of alcohol in the town in the spring of 1867. Governor Meagher blocked the order, arguing that Fort Benton was not on a reservation and that the agent had no legal authority to restrict commerce there. He directed Wright to withdraw all such notices and warned others against aiding "in wantonly interrupting the legitimate business and pursuits of the citizens of the Town." Following their public disagreement, Meagher refused to approve Wright's requisitions for agency funds, and as the agency racked up debt, Wright was forced to travel to Washington, D.C., and apply for money directly. The thriving alcohol trade in Fort Benton continued to undermine any chance for preventing violence.[24]

The international border also complicated efforts to make peace in Montana. Although they maintained stronger commercial connections in the south, the majority of Blackfoot territory remained north of the forty-ninth parallel, in the HBC dominion still known as Rupert's Land. Blackfoot people understood and used the border to their advantage. During the 1860s and 1870s, Indigenous people throughout the northern plains realized that the border could provide safe haven from settler governments on either side. Most famously, the Métis leader Louis Riel used the border to escape British officials after his people's first resistance movement in 1870, and the Lakota leader Sitting Bull fled north of the border to avoid U.S. recriminations for destroying the Seventh Cavalry at Little Big Horn in 1876. Northern plains Indigenous people would later dub the border the "Medicine Line," for the extraordinary political power it held. The north provided safety for Blackfoot raiding parties, who frequently escaped north of the border after raiding or attacking settlers in Montana. Following the 1865 attack on Ophir, for example, Calf Shirt fled north and reputedly did not return for years. Bull's Head, who led the attacks on the agency and mission buildings in 1866, resided in the north as well. Such geographic mobility frustrated some officials who cited it as a reason to distrust the Indians. Agents also suspected that many Blackfoot bands resided in the north full time and crossed the border only to receive their annuities. Although the border had been legally established in 1818, it only became significant for Blackfoot people during the 1860s. They saw that the imaginary line had a powerful pull over American officials, who hesitated to cross it even to pursue Blackfoot warriors like Calf Shirt.[25]

The Blackfoot found safety in the north, but over the previous decade their relations with the British had become almost as fractious as their relations with the Americans. During the 1840s and 1850s, Crees had come to dominate the lands surrounding Edmonton, and the last fifty miles of the journey northward had become a deadly gauntlet for Blackfoot traders. As Blackfoot energies shifted toward the American robe trade, HBC officials turned their attention to the Crees. Blackfoot people who did make the journey to Edmonton and Rocky Mountain House often accused HBC traders of favoring the Crees over them, and of offering them inferior goods at higher prices. In 1858, Kainai traders discovered an HBC employee riding among a Cree war party, which deepened their suspicion that the HBC had cast in with their longtime enemies. In 1860, Cree warriors killed the prominent Siksika chief Old Sun of the All Medicine Men band as he attempted to trade at Edmonton. His killing inflamed the Siksikas' suspicions toward the HBC while also helping to consolidate the power of confrontational Siksika chiefs like Big Swan of the Bad Guns band. In response to Old Sun's murder, Siksika warriors destroyed Edmonton's crops, stole horses, and even threatened to burn Edmonton to the ground. They did the same at Rocky Mountain House, forcing the HBC to abandon the post in 1861. One HBC trader lamented that the Siksikas became "unbearable" following Old Sun's death.[26]

Growing violence south of the border during the 1860s, however, gave Blackfoot chiefs reason to soften their growing hostility toward the HBC and to restore the northern connections that had long been essential to their security. In December 1862, Kainai, Piikani, Siksika, Tsuut'ina, and Cree chiefs gathered in Edmonton and made peace with one another. In subsequent years, many Blackfoot bands, especially among the Siksikas and Kainais, turned north and avoided going south of the border at all. For example, no Siksikas and only a fraction of the Kainais attended the 1865 treaty council in Fort Benton. HBC traders happily noted the increase in Blackfoot people fleeing north from the American side. In the summer of 1866, they reopened Rocky Mountain House and rebuilt the fort with high palisades, thick walls, and sliding doors. As a further inducement for Blackfoot and other plains peoples to bring them much-needed provisions, the HBC boosted their bison robe purchases during the 1860s as well, thus undercutting one of the main reasons for Native people to travel south of the border. Hundreds of Siksika and Kainai traders, as well as some Piikanis, arrived at the rebuilt post during its first season. Some Blackfoot traders came a long way to avoid the trouble in Montana, like the members of one joint Kainai-Siksika party who claimed to have lost fifteen horses to the cold during their long ride to Rocky Mountain House in March 1868. Such sacrifices were worth the cost for Blackfoot people seeking to avoid the violence in Montana. Rupert's Land became a vital refuge, and many Blackfoot people would never again return south of the international border.[27]

While the situation in the north stabilized, tensions continued to fester south of the border due to the ongoing invasion by white miners, settlers, and whiskey traders. In 1868, Indian Affairs officials decided to make another attempt at a treaty. They struggled to convince Blackfoot chiefs to gather for yet another treaty council, however, since the United States had not honored their 1865 agreement. Treaty commissioners decided to recruit intermediaries who might engender more trust among the Blackfoot, including Vaughan, their trusted agent from before the Civil War, and Culbertson, the retired fur trader and husband of Medicine Snake Woman. Vaughan and Culbertson convinced many key Kainai and Piikani leaders to gather once again for a treaty council at Fort Benton in July, though most of the Siksikas chose to stay in the north. The Kainai chief Calf Shirt made his first recorded visit south of the border since his raid on Ophir and explained, "We did not intend to come, but when we saw these old men [Vaughan and Culbertson] we thought it was good, so we come." Calf Shirt gave a speech during the treaty council in which he lamented the changes that had so swiftly transformed the region. "We want the new traders to act like the old men who traded long ago, when there was nothing but peace and quietness. When we come to trading posts we do not want to be interfered with. We want good traders so that we may buy and live." A great deal had changed during the previous decade, and Calf Shirt yearned to restore the prosperous and peaceful exchanges that characterized the fur trade era.[28]

Blackfoot chiefs once again made a treaty with U.S. officials in 1868, only to see the agreement once again rejected when it reached Washington, D.C. Like the 1865 version, the 1868 treaty called for the Blackfoot to relinquish all claims to land south of the Missouri River and to relocate permanently onto a reservation north of the river. In return, the government would guarantee increased annuity payments, which had slowed to a trickle following the expiration of the 1855 treaty three years earlier. In all, sixty-two Blackfoot representatives signed the treaty, including Mountain Chief, the most prominent Piikani chief, and Three Bulls of the Siksikas. Calf Shirt of the Kainais signed two months later, but ongoing violence soon extinguished any optimism for the new treaty. During negotiations, Mountain Chief requested the removal of a few white merchants from Fort Benton, presumably for selling liquor to Blackfoot buyers. After the council, two of the men confronted

The most powerful Piikani leader after the death of Little Dog, Mountain Chief was often blamed for harboring Blackfoot warriors accused of raiding Montana settlements. (Gustav Sohon, *Nen-ne-as-ta-cui Chief Mountain Piegan Chief*, 1855, Washington State Historical Society, Tacoma, Washington.)

Mountain Chief, struck him, and shot at him. Commissioner Cullen issued a warrant for the arrest of the perpetrators, but the local sheriff and justice of the peace both resigned rather than arrest the white assailants. In revenge for the rough treatment of their chief, Piikani warriors made a brazen raid on the mining community of Diamond City and captured eighty horses. Commissioner Cullen took eighteen Piikani men prisoner at Fort Benton and demanded the return of the stolen animals. A week later, Mountain Chief returned many of the horses and the men were released. The well-publicized episode caused Indian Affairs officials to reject the 1868 treaty, just as they had in 1865.[29]

Blackfoot chiefs complained bitterly when the 1868 treaty again went unfulfilled, and Culbertson worried that an attitude of "contempt and distrust" began to swell among the disaffected Piikanis in particular. Violence grew more intense when raiding and war parties went out the following summer. On July 17, 1869, a party of Crows attacked a wagon train near Fort Benton. Assuming that the perpetrators were Blackfoot, a group of white men in Fort Benton murdered four Piikanis from Mountain Chief's people (known as the

Blood band) who were then in town, including the chief's elderly brother. The whites lynched three of them and attached a note to one of the hanging bodies that read, "There are three good Indians." The attack further hardened the most powerful Piikani chief's disdain toward the Americans. "I despise the whites," one early Montana settler claimed to have heard Mountain Chief declare. "They have treated my nation like dogs; and hereafter I shall no longer be responsible for the depredations which may be committed by my young men." Following the killings, whites increasingly accused Mountain Chief of harboring Piikanis who raided white settlers, and Piikani war parties attacked several freighting parties on the road between Fort Benton and Helena over the following weeks and months. One marshal estimated that the Blackfoot killed fifty-six whites and stole a thousand horses in 1869 alone. He neglected to guess how many Blackfoot people were killed by whites during that same period.[30]

At the same moment when the most important Piikani chief retreated from diplomacy, policymakers in Washington, D.C., likewise revised their policy toward Native people. In the spring of 1869, the recently inaugurated U.S. president Ulysses Grant outlined a new approach to Indian affairs that he called his "Peace Policy," which he hoped would stem the tide of conflicts that had swelled throughout the West during and after the Civil War. The new policy ended the treaty system and made explicit the government's goal to confine Indigenous people on reservations in order to "civilize" them. The new policy also allowed church leaders to nominate Indian agents, thereby undercutting the corrupt web of patronage that had long characterized Indian Affairs. Nevertheless, the Peace Policy's name belied its violent and coercive aspects. In order to force Native people onto reservations, the U.S. Army tolerated civilian bison hunters' violation of treaties and sometimes directly undermined Native people's subsistence by hunting bison themselves. Grant also transferred control over many western superintendencies to the War Department, thereby showing Indigenous people that the threat of violence lay behind any resistance to the new order.[31]

In July of 1869, an Army general named Alfred Sully arrived in Montana Territory to take over as superintendent of Indian Affairs, and he immediately sensed that the situation was primed to explode. Sully was a keen judge of such matters, having fought in wars of conquest across the country since the early 1840s, including against the Seminoles in Florida, various nations in California and Oregon, the Dakotas in Minnesota, and the Cheyennes, Arapahoes, and Sioux on the plains. The general knew how vicious such conflicts could become and noted with concern that since the 1868 treaty had failed, he had no annuities to offer Blackfoot bands and little to incentivize them to keep the peace. Meanwhile, white Montanans wanted more soldiers, not more diplomacy. Fur trappers had first proposed the idea of using military force on the Blackfoot half a century earlier, but such pleas usually fell on deaf ears, since the region had long seemed too remote, vast, and thinly populated to justify the expense. But now, following the failed treaties and seemingly ceaseless violence, calls for military aid grew louder and more plausible. In 1867, the U.S. Army had built Fort Shaw near what is now Great Falls and stationed a garrison of soldiers to protect travelers on the Mullan Road, but the small and poorly manned fort had little impact on Indigenous peoples' movements or raids in the area. In the summer of 1869, there were no more than two hundred soldiers in the entire territory. Sully, one of America's most prolific Indian fighters, called for more.[32]

The excuse to use the military came later that summer, when Piikani warriors struck directly at one of Montana's leading families. The family's patriarch, Malcolm Clarke, was one of the most venerable white settlers in Montana, having arrived around 1841 as a trader for Choteau and Company at Fort McKenzie. Clarke married a Piikani woman named Coth-co-co-na, had several children, and enjoyed a successful career before retiring in 1863 to start up a cattle ranch north of Helena. By most accounts, whites and Indigenous people alike respected Clarke. Among Piikanis he was known as Four Bears, a name he apparently garnered for a prolific day of hunting shortly after his arrival two decades earlier. He helped found the Montana Historical Society, and his ranch was a favorite stopping point for travelers on the road between Helena and Fort Benton. Montanans held the handsome pioneer in awe. Years later, one settler remembered that with his "iron gray hair and beard . . . resembling some of the portraits of General Jackson," Clarke was "one whom you would be inclined to stop and look at after you had passed him on the street."[33]

Not everyone fawned over Four Bears. The aging trader was also known to have an ornery streak, which one pioneer called a "fierce and ungovernable temper." Prior to his joining Chouteau and Company, for example, the U.S. Military Academy at West Point had expelled Clarke not once but twice (the first time he was reinstated by President Andrew Jackson himself after beating a classmate over the head with a stick). In 1867, his temper resurfaced when a group of Piikani relatives visited his ranch. During the visit, Clarke found himself at odds with his wife's cousin, a young man named Ne-tus-che-o, known to whites as Pete Owl Child. According to the Clarke family, Malcolm and his son Horace caught Owl Child trying to steal their horses and, in a fit of rage, whipped the humiliated Piikani in front of his peers while calling him a "dog" and an "old woman." Many Piikanis maintained that the truth was far worse, and that Clarke had raped Owl Child's wife. Whatever its cause, the two men never resolved their quarrel, and Owl Child harbored a bitter grudge toward Four Bears.[34]

On the evening of August 17, 1869, Owl Child and three other young Piikanis rode to Clarke's ranch, and the old trader invited them to dine with his family. Malcolm's daughter Helen, who at the time was in her early twenties, remembered the visitors acting strangely throughout the evening, with one even breaking down in tears during the meal. After dinner, as Clarke stepped outside with Owl Child for a smoke, one of the Piikanis shot him in the chest, and Owl Child cleaved his forehead with an axe. Nearby, another of the Piikani men shot Horace in the face and left him for dead. The rest of the terrified Clarke family barricaded themselves inside the ranch house until the killers left. When word of their ordeal reached Helena the next day, it caused a sensation. As Pete Owl Child and his companions rode through the Prickly Pear Canyon and emerged onto the plains to the north, they could scarcely have imagined the consequences they had helped unleash.[35]

In the meantime, Blackfoot bands soon had bigger worries than Owl Child's actions and the fury brewing in Helena, for the dreaded smallpox made a sudden reappearance at the worst possible moment in the fall of 1869. Part of a larger epidemic sweeping northward through the Great Plains, the virus most likely arrived via steamboat on the Missouri River sometime during the late summer. One Montana newspaper reported that a Piikani man snuck onto a steamboat and stole a blanket from a quarantined passenger, then unwittingly transmitted the disease to his band when he returned home. Wherever it came from, the virus spread quickly among the Indigenous peoples of the northwest plains, who had gone more than thirty years since a major outbreak. The disease hit the Piikanis first, then traveled north and reached Kainai, Siksika, and Tsuut'ina camps over the ensuing months, before moving on to the Crees and Assiniboines the following spring. The disease devastated Blackfoot communities, just as it had in 1781 and 1837. In a report on the outbreak, an HBC investigator estimated that about one-fourth of all Blackfoot people died, reducing the total population to around seven thousand. The disease robbed them of wizened leaders like the Kainai chief Seen from Afar and the Siksika chief Three Suns. Their close allies the Tsuut'inas suffered even more terribly, shrinking from fifty lodges to only twelve. Throughout the northwest plains, Blackfoot people spent the fall and winter of 1869–70 caring for the sick, tending to the dead, and desperately hoping to avoid infection.[36]

While Blackfoot people focused on staying alive during the fall of 1869, Montana's military and civilian officials plotted their response to Clarke's murder. In the weeks and months before smallpox laid them low, some Piikani raiders had continued to attack white travelers and settlers and to run off livestock. In September the body of James Quail, a rancher whom some implicated as one of the murderers of Mountain Chief's brother, was found riddled with Piikani arrows. Quail had reportedly set off to pursue some Piikani raiders who had driven off horses and mules from his ranch when he died. Several wagons were attacked on the Fort Benton–Helena Road as well, and in December Piikanis reportedly ambushed a party of twelve white hunters near Fort Shaw, killing one. In October, a U.S. marshal named William Wheeler indicted Owl Child and the other Piikanis accused in the killing of Clarke. Wheeler presented the warrant to General Sully in Helena, who in turn forwarded it to Commissioner of Indian Affairs Ely Parker. Parker bade Sully and Wheeler to demand that the Blackfoot hand over Owl Child and the other indicted Piikanis.[37]

A handful of Blackfoot chiefs, sensing imminent bloodshed, sought to protect their bands using diplomacy. When scouts summoned Blackfoot chiefs to a meeting at the Blackfeet Agency on January 1, 1870, the Piikani chief Heavy Runner heeded the call, along with fellow Piikanis Big Lake and Little Wolf, as well as a Kainai chief named Gray Eyes. No other chiefs attended. The low turnout disappointed Wheeler and Sully, especially the absence of the most powerful Piikani Mountain Chief, whom they believed harbored Owl Child. Sully told the four chiefs who did attend that the government was prepared to wage a full-scale war on the Blackfoot and bluffed that the U.S. Army would pursue the Indians north across the border if necessary. Sully reported that the chiefs begged him to spare their bands if such a campaign indeed commenced. They had no power to capture Owl Child and his fellow perpetrators, since the killers were in Mountain Chief's camp, but they promised to kill Owl Child themselves if they found the chance. They also promised to return any captured horses they could find. As the council broke up, Heavy Runner requested a note of safe passage from Sully that attested to his peaceful inclination. Heavy Runner then returned to his band's winter camp on the banks of the Marias River, where many of his people were still suffering and dying from smallpox.[38]

Mountain Chief's absence from the unsatisfying council served as a final justification for war. On January 14, four regiments of U.S. cavalry under the command of Major Eugene M. Baker rode from Fort Ellis (near what is now Bozeman) to Fort Shaw. Upon their arrival, General Phil Sheridan—hero of the Appomattox Campaign and commander of the Military Division of the Missouri—telegraphed instructions from Chicago: "If the lives and property of citizens of Montana can best be protected by striking Mountain Chief's band, I want them struck. Tell Baker to strike them hard." On January 19, Baker and nearly four hundred men marched north from Fort Shaw to destroy the hostile Piikanis of Mountain Chief's band, camped along the Marias River about fifteen miles downstream from Heavy Runner's people.[39]

IN JANUARY 1870, the Heron band of Piikanis took shelter next to a crook of the Bear River known as the Big Bend. The Bear—or Marias River, as it was known to whites—had sheltered Piikani bands for winters beyond memory. The river carved a deep, snaking gouge in the undulating monotony of the Montana prairie, which provided a crucial shelter from the biting winds that ripped across the treeless landscape. The Bear had been central to the yearly round of the Piikanis for centuries. This winter was different from others, however. From his lodge near the center of the camp, their chief Heavy Runner worried greatly about the rising tide of violence with the Americans, and about the cold reception he had received during his last meeting with General Sully. Still, he felt confident that his friendly reputation would protect him from any reprisals. More worrisome to Heavy Runner was the fact that smallpox had recently reached the Heron band and begun to wreak havoc, especially among the younger people. To prevent the spread of the disease, Heavy Runner had deliberately isolated his people from other bands who camped at different spots up and down the river valley. The Heron band had little choice but to suffer in solitude as the White Scabs Disease brought agony to lodge after lodge.[40]

At dawn on the morning of January 23, the people of the Heron band awoke to the sound of dogs barking. It was a cold morning, even by the standards of northern Montana, and temperatures had plunged to well below zero degrees Fahrenheit. Many of the healthy Piikanis crawled to their tipi flaps and looked to see what had startled their dogs. Looking up, they saw a line of náápiikoan soldiers on horseback, looming over them from the dimly lit bluff overhead. A messenger awoke Heavy Runner. The chief exited his lodge, holding the papers he had received from General Sully weeks earlier, which attested to his peacefulness and innocence in the matter of Clarke's murder. As he walked forward, he assured his people that they had nothing to fear, for he was a friend to the whites. Surely when the strangers saw that he was one of the Medal Men, they would move on.

As Heavy Runner ascended the rise toward the whites, paper in hand, a single shot rang out, and the chief crumpled to the frozen ground. Believing that the blast signaled an order to open fire, the other soldiers began shooting furiously into the tipis below. (Some stories maintain that the soldiers' half-Piikani guide Joe Cobell fired the shot in hopes that an attack on Heavy Runner's band would protect his relatives in Mountain Chief's camp.) The Piikanis had no time to mount a resistance, and even if they did, most of the healthy young men were away from camp hunting at the time. After the initial barrage, the soldiers descended the hill and cut open the bullet-riddled lodges with butcher knives. They then used their knives, rifles, and bayonets to slaughter dozens of survivors, many of whom had not even had the strength to emerge from beneath their bison robes. Within an hour, between 173 and 217 Blackfoot people lay dead, mostly women and children. The soldiers then seized hundreds of Piikani horses and declared victory. Major Baker left a company of men behind to burn what was left of the camp. The few surviving members of the Heron band traveled on foot to seek the safety of other Blackfoot bands, but many froze to death on the way. The slaughter became known as the Marias Massacre, or sometimes the Baker Massacre.[41]

In Helena, citizens celebrated what they felt was a long overdue chastisement of the hostile Indians. From the perspective of American officials, the massacre of Heavy Runner's band served its purpose, insofar as it terrorized all of the Blackfoot bands. Sick, scared, and recently banned from trading per official orders, the Blackfoot in Montana had little choice but to seek peace. A week after the massacre, one official wrote that "all the [Piikani] Indians are begging for peace. . . . They are in a stunning condition and the laws of humanity if nothing else ought allow them to trade for provisions." General Regis de Trobriand gleefully noted that the Piikanis were "completely cowed. They had never dreamed of such an execution." The Kainais were likewise "terrified by the punishment of the Piegans, [and] deem it very fortunate not to have brought upon themselves such a severe retribution." In the months and years following the massacre, Blackfoot raids on the settler population of Montana effectively ended. The "war" was over.[42]

Most Blackfoot bands retreated north of the border in 1870. Men, women, and children marched up to a hundred miles in freezing weather to escape Montana and set up new winter camps in British lands. The following summer, Culbertson found Mountain Chief and his band camped in the Cypress

Major Eugene Baker, slouching, bearded, center right, led the massacre of some 200 Piikani people on the morning of January 23, 1870. (Courtesy of the Library of Congress Prints and Photographs Division, LC-USZ62-51644.)

Hills, just north of the international boundary. In Culbertson's eyes, the seventy-year-old partially blind Mountain Chief, so feared and derided in Montana over the previous two years, seemed suddenly aged and diminished in influence. The old chief told Culbertson he was desperate for peace and determined "toward cultivating & reestablishing that friendly feeling, which at one time existed between [the Piikanis] and the whites." Over the long winter, smallpox had reduced Mountain Chief's once formidable band to a small handful of lodges. Among the dead was Owl Child, whose body they laid to rest along the Belly River that spring.[43]

Despite Blackfoot people's hope that British lands would provide refuge, the north was itself primed for an explosion of settler colonial activity that mirrored that of the United States. British North Americans' westward march had for decades lagged behind the Americans' for several reasons. Until 1867, British North America remained a collection of distinct British colonies and lacked a domestic centralized political authority that could protect settlers and put expansionary policies in place. Their population paled in comparison to that of the United States, which meant they had fewer demographic pressures pushing them west, and most of the soon-to-be Canadian West remained the domain of the HBC according to their 1670 charter. By the 1850s, however, things had begun to change. Interest in western settlement spiked, especially in the agricultural heartland of Upper Canada (later Ontario), where Crown lands had grown difficult for settlers to acquire. Much-publicized western expeditions led by Henry Youle Hind and John Palliser in the late 1850s further stoked interest by playing up the agricultural potential of certain parts of Rupert's Land. HBC officials read the writing on the wall and slowly began to reorient the company, long resistant to the prospect of settlement, toward increased investment in mining and settler infrastructure like telegraphs and railroads. As British North American expansion picked up steam, boosters advocated a cautious approach toward Indigenous nations in order to prevent wars like those south of the border, since the British North Americans lacked the same military resources that the United States deployed to prop up settlements. While they hoped to avoid the same chaos that unfolded in the U.S. West, British North Americans increasingly sought the same end goal.[44]

In 1867, representatives from the British North American colonies of Nova Scotia, New Brunswick, and Upper and Lower Canada (which became Ontario and Quebec) ratified a deal that united them as the Dominion of Canada. In addition to facilitating westward expansion, the authors of confederation believed that uniting the disparate colonies would protect British domains for future settlers against the Americans. The threat of American annexation had become all too real over the previous two decades, especially now that Americans were no longer inhibited by the need to maintain a balance between new free states and new slave states. From the British perspective, linking the four eastern colonies together would strengthen them politically and economically, but leaders worried that western British possessions remained vulnerable. The U.S. purchase of Alaska in March 1867 fueled fears that the HBC was an ineffective bulwark against Americans on the prairies. The only way to ensure British control over the West would be to populate it with British settlers, who would be linked to the eastern provinces by a railroad. In November 1869, the HBC surrendered its charter to Rupert's Land to the British Crown in return for £300,000 in compensation, and the vast Hudson Bay drainage became part of the Dominion of Canada the following summer. Although the HBC continued to operate, the transfer signaled that a new economic and political order lay on the horizon.[45]

Confederation and the transfer of Rupert's Land had dire implications for Blackfoot people in both the short and long term. After the transfer, the HBC no longer had the legal authority to enforce British restrictions on the liquor trade, which opened the door for American traders to go north of the border. Opportunistic Americans from Fort Benton established their first trading posts north of the border late in 1869, led by merchants John Healy and Alfred Hamilton, who built Fort Whoop-Up at the confluence of the Oldman and St. Mary River near what later became the city of Lethbridge. The Americans chose the site wisely, as it lay in the heart of Kainai hunting grounds and had recently become home to many Piikani bands that had fled north from Montana. Healy and Hamilton offered an alluring trade to their new neighbors. Unlike their predecessors, they offered unlimited whiskey in return for bison robes. They also offered breech-loading repeating rifles, which represented a huge upgrade from the muzzle-loading trade guns that the HBC and Chouteau and Company had offered without significant change for generations. The new "many-shots" guns were easier to load, could fire faster, and were more accurate and more powerful. They could even be used on horseback. These goods attracted enough Blackfoot traders that Hamilton and Healy made $50,000 during their first winter north of the border, which would amount to more than $1,000,000 today.

The whiskey trade made Americans rich, but it wreaked havoc on Blackfoot communities. Some may have looked to alcohol as an escape from the sorrows of disease and war. Others, accustomed to drinking only occasionally on visits to trading posts, were simply unprepared for unfettered access to alcohol, which the whites often laced with substances like chewing tobacco, peppers, and molasses for extra potency. Between 1869 and 1874, when the forts closed, scores of Blackfoot people died of alcohol-related causes, including exposure and violence. As Kainai elder Camoose Bottle later explained, "the bringing of this liquor was very harmful to the Indian people," and quickly ravaged the Blackfoot communities that gathered at the "drinking place" where the rivers met.[46]

Some saw opportunity in the Blackfoot's vulnerability. Driven out of much of their territory, decimated by disease and war, and weakened by alcohol, Piikani, Kainai, and Siksika people faced a desperate situation as 1870 drew to a close. They had also lost their strongest allies, the Gros Ventres, after a series of quarrels during the 1860s. Seeking to capitalize on the Blackfoot's perceived weakness, Cree and Assiniboine chiefs decided to launch a surprise attack on the Kainai and Piikani bands that were camped near Fort Whoop-Up. Led by the Cree chiefs Big Bear, Piapot, and Little Pine and the Assiniboine chief Little Mountain, a force of between six hundred and eight hundred Cree and Assiniboine warriors charged upon one of the Kainai camps just before dawn on November 1, 1870, hoping to catch their enemies still drunk from trading. The attackers made two major miscalculations, however, beginning with underestimating the number of Blackfoot bands in the area. The sounds of their initial assault, along with the barking of the Kainais' dogs, alerted nearby Piikani camps to the attack. Throughout the nearby river valleys, Blackfoot men awoke, grabbed their weapons, and rode toward the sounds of their kinspeople in distress. Kainai elder Mike Mountain Horse later said that as daylight broke, "warriors from the Blackfoot camps north and south could be seen approaching on horseback, in twos, and threes, over hills and knolls, chanting their war songs in anticipation of battle."

As Kainai and Piikani warriors surrounded the Crees and Assiniboines, the attackers' other miscalculation came into play, for the Blackfoot's recently purchased repeating rifles were far superior to the Crees' and Assiniboines' antiquated muzzle-loaders. The attackers realized that the battle had turned against them and retreated to a coulee near the Oldman River. After a few hours, the Kainais and Piikanis charged into the coulee and forced their attackers to rush into the river, where the Blackfoot warriors fired down on their thrashing enemies. In the final accounting, around forty Kainais and Piikanis died during the battle, but nearly two hundred of the Cree and Assiniboine attackers perished (though some accounts claimed as many as four hundred). The Battle of the Belly River, as it became known in Alberta, provided a desperately needed victory for Blackfoot people. At a time when despair and disorder threatened to overwhelm Blackfoot communities, they asserted their resilience, bravery, and commitment to one another. It was the last major battle between Indigenous people on the northwest plains.[47]

As the Closed season began in 1870, the peoples of the Kainai, Piikani, and Siksika nations faced an uncertain future. In just one year, they had lost countless friends and family members to disease and violence. Deep sorrow lingered in the heart of every survivor. The relationships with outsiders that had enabled them to prosper throughout their ancient homelands for more than a century had crumbled, leaving confusion and disorder in their wake. The fur trade companies they had so adroitly managed for generations had either left or become hollow shells of their former selves. The vast bison herds that had been the staff of life for countless generations had begun to shrink noticeably, hounded by hunters who intruded into Blackfoot hunting grounds on both sides of the border. Fort Whoop-Up and its bottomless whiskey barrels could offer a brief reprieve, but they introduced volatile and destructive new elements into Blackfoot life.

Nevertheless, Blackfoot people remained committed to preserving their homelands, and to one another. As hundreds of Cree and Assiniboine warriors fled northward across the prairie on the morning of November 1, 1870, it was clear that despite the great challenges they faced, Blackfoot people would not be destroyed or dislodged from the lands that Náápi made for them so many generations before.

Epilogue
Blackfoot Crossing

> [The Wise Man] come out of his tent, call out saying to people: "Have your good times now! Times are changing. Buffalo will soon leave!" Women used to laugh at him, saying: "Look how many buffalo there are! He's wrong." He'd say: "All the animals you see on prairie will not live! Animals you see will live only on foothills! Buffalo will be shown to you only by white men! You'll not meet them!" Those things have all come true.
>
> —MANY GUNS (Siksika), 1938

> Our ability to adapt to the environment and to change is infinite and assures our survival.
>
> —EARL OLD PERSON (Chief of the Blackfeet Nation), 2001

In the autumn of 1875, twelve Blackfoot chiefs gathered in the Hand Hills, about eighty miles northeast of the newly established Fort Calgary, to chart a path forward for their people. From the Kainais, Bad Head, Red Crow, Many Spotted Horses, Bull Back Fat (probably a younger relative of the chief who visited Fort Union in 1832), and White Striped Dog attended. Many of the Piikanis chose to remain south of the international border, and only the chiefs Sitting on an Eagle Tail, Walking Forward, and Stakkas came to the meeting. The Siksika chiefs Old Sun, Eagle, and Low Horn came as well, along with the man who had become perhaps the most respected Blackfoot chief of all, the Siksika leader Crowfoot. Using an interpreter, the assembled chiefs dictated a petition that called for the new Canadian Governor of the North West Territories, Alexander Morris, to send an Indian Commissioner to the Hand Hills immediately to hold a general council with the Blackfoot nations. They had urgent need of one, they explained, for white settlers had begun building houses in Blackfoot hunting grounds despite previous assurances that no one would take their land without their consent. Also invading their land were parties of well-armed Crees and Métis "Half-breeds," who came to hunt rapidly dwindling bison herds. The chiefs implored the governor to put "a stop to the invasion of our Country, till our Treaty can be made with the Government." They added that they felt "perfectly confident that the representative of Our Great Mother, Her Majesty the Queen, will do prompt Justice to her Indian children." The time had come to once again make a treaty with the náápiikoan, this one north of the border.[1]

The chiefs found themselves in a desperate position. The years following the cataclysms of 1870 had taken a terrible toll, especially in the north. American whiskey traders from Fort Benton who sought to replicate the success of Fort Whoop-Up built at least a dozen new trading forts on the Canadian side between 1870 and 1874. Many Blackfoot people, demoralized from the smallpox epidemic, the invasion of their lands, and the massacre of the Heron band of Piikanis, turned to alcohol for escape. Some traded everything they had for it, including their beloved horses. Drunken violence ran rampant in Blackfoot communities. According to one observer, eighty-eight Siksikas died in drunken brawls in 1871 alone, while many others died of cold, exposure, or neglect. Some oral histories explain that the alcohol trade made Blackfoot women vulnerable to sexual assault and abuse by whiskey traders. The alcohol-fueled chaos carried away key leaders like Mountain Chief, who died in a fight with other Piikanis in 1872, and the Kainai war chief Calf Shirt, whom American traders killed in an argument in February 1874. A staggering amount of hard alcohol flooded Blackfoot lands: U.S. officials estimated that the Americans traded more than ten thousand gallons of liquor north of the border during the winter of 1872–73 alone, which amounted to nearly two gallons each for every Blackfoot man, woman, and child. Crowfoot and other chiefs grew desperate for a solution. "Our people have been woefully slain and impoverished," Crowfoot lamented to a missionary in 1874, "by the coming of the [Americans], with their firewater and their quick-shooting guns."[2]

Salvation of a sort came in the summer of 1874, when the North-West Mounted Police arrived to expel the whiskey traders. Later renamed the Royal Canadian Mounted Police and known popularly as "Mounties," the police force was created by the Canadian Parliament in 1873 partly in response to the shocking reports about the whiskey trade, though Parliament had other motives as well. Many felt that the time had come to open up the western prairies to white farmers, which could only happen once Mounties pacified the "lawless" region and subdued the Indigenous people who lived there. Canadian officials also received pressure from the HBC and commercial traders in Fort Benton, who felt that the whiskey traders cut into their profits, and the U.S. Army, who worried about the diffusion of repeating rifles among plains Indigenous people. The Mounties worked quickly, ousting most of the whiskey traders by the fall of 1874 and setting up a headquarters called Fort

Macleod on the Oldman River. While some Blackfoot people continued to purchase alcohol surreptitiously south of the border, the worst excesses of the whiskey trade ended. Leaders like Crowfoot afterward expressed gratitude for the police, in part to flatter their government counterparts but also because they had witnessed the trade's devastating impact firsthand. In their 1875 petition to the government, Crowfoot and his fellow Blackfoot chiefs included a provision that they were "perfectly willing" for the Mounties to remain in the area, since they were "much indebted to them for important services."[3]

While chiefs like Crowfoot welcomed the Mounties, they also worried over what their presence meant for the Blackfoot. White settlers had already begun to take up, in the words of the 1875 petition, "the best location[s]" and built farms and ranches near Fort MacLeod and Fort Calgary, both in prime Blackfoot hunting grounds. The arrival of settlers in the north surely reminded Blackfoot people of their experiences south of the border, where settlers, miners, and ranchers came a decade or two earlier. In the United States, the settlement of Montana lands, the violence of the 1860s, and the end of the treaty system in 1871 had emboldened government officials to shrink Blackfoot territories without consultation. In 1873, President Ulysses Grant signed an executive order that set aside a joint reservation for the Blackfoot, Gros Ventres, and Assiniboines north of the Missouri and Sun Rivers. The following year, U.S. officials moved the southern boundary north to the Marias River, which opened up Montana's best grazing lands to ranching and deprived the Blackfoot of many of their richest hunting grounds. Increasingly, the southern Piikanis who remained in Montana—around one-fourth to one-third of the total Blackfoot population—were restricted to the far-northern areas of their territory in the United States. As they watched this process unfold for their southern Piikani brethren, northern chiefs knew that Canadian settlers' appetite for land would likewise be voracious. They sought a way to mitigate a similar invasion north of the border.[4]

Whites were not the only group pressing into Blackfoot lands. For decades, the Blackfoot had witnessed incursions by Indigenous hunters who faced declining game populations in their own territories. By the middle of the 1870s, this invasion reached crisis levels. The central parts of Blackfoot country that straddled the international border hosted the last major bison herds on the continent and therefore drew desperate hunters from far afield. Several thousand Métis people—among the most seasoned and prolific hunters on the continent—migrated west into the South Saskatchewan River Valley following their failed 1870 resistance movement in Manitoba.

From there, the Métis launched frequent hunting expeditions into Blackfoot lands surrounding the Bow River. As those herds shrunk, Métis hunters moved south, and by 1875 the Métis became a fixture around the Cypress Hills near the border. Cree hunters likewise responded to the collapse of herds by extending their hunts deep into Blackfoot country, and Lakota exiles from the United States joined them in congregating around the Cypress Hills. Blackfoot homelands became a magnet for Indigenous hunters whose own lands had become habitable only by relying on government rations. The northwest plains offered their only chance to maintain their old way of life.[5]

New technologies put even greater pressure on the bison herds. Prior to the 1870s, most Native people on the northern plains preferred to hunt by firing arrows from horseback. Although they had possessed muzzle-loading trade guns for more than a century, bison hunters found the guns far too cumbersome to fire and reload during a chase. After 1870, however, American breech-loading repeating rifles gave hunters the chance to fire guns from horseback, and in turn motivated hunters to kill more bison in order to purchase more guns. Demand for bison products also grew during the 1870s, as American industrialists perfected new chemical processes that allowed them to turn bison hides into leather belting for heavy machinery. The value of shorn bison hides soon outpaced that of woolly robes on both sides of the border. Unlike robes, which had to be collected during fall and winter and required women's expertise and labor to prepare, hides could be collected during summer and required little preparation. White, Métis, and Native hunters could kill with abandon and earn themselves a tidy three to four U.S. dollars for each hide they sold.[6]

It became clear to Blackfoot leaders that bison herds faced unsustainable pressure, and that the day would soon come when they could no longer rely on hunting to meet their needs. In a meeting with police subinspector Cecil Denny in August 1876, Crowfoot lamented that his people were becoming "shut in" by hunters and settlers on all sides: "We all see that the day is coming when the buffalo will all be killed, and we shall have nothing more to live on, and then you will come into our camp and see the poor Blackfeet starving." He told Denny that he had rejected overtures from messengers sent by the Lakota chief Sitting Bull (who fled to Canada following his defeat of American cavalry at the Battle of Little Big Horn) to join in their war against the Americans. Without the bison, Crowfoot knew that his people would need to work with the whites in order to survive. Given their increasingly desperate circumstances, sustained violent conflict like what they had experienced in Montana was out of the question. By rejecting Sitting Bull's offer,

Crowfoot and other Blackfoot chiefs signaled their willingness to negotiate with the Crown.[7]

Leaders like Crowfoot were experienced diplomats and had dealt with British subjects their entire lives, but they also realized that circumstances north of the border had changed fundamentally since 1870. Rupert's Land no longer belonged to the HBC, and Canadian leaders had grown determined to strengthen their new nation by extinguishing Indigenous title across the country. Between 1871 and 1876 Canadian officials conducted six multilateral treaties with Indigenous nations, starting in what is now Manitoba, then moving into Ontario and what is now Saskatchewan and Alberta. In 1876, they completed Treaty Six with the Plains and Woodland Crees, just north of Blackfoot territory. Officials designed the "Numbered Treaties" to enable rapid settler colonization of these lands, and Blackfoot country stood next in line. Officials felt especially eager to treat with the Blackfoot nations, since their lands stood in the proposed path of a transcontinental railroad, which they had promised British Columbians to build when they granted them provincehood, and to prevent any possible alliance with American refugee nations. More broadly, Canadian officials believed that opening new lands to settlement would transform their new confederation into a unified and strong country. Like the Americans before them, the Canadians saw their Blackfoot treaty in nationalist terms. Crowfoot and other chiefs saw treaty-making as a pragmatic way to stabilize their communities in the face of outside pressures.[8]

The Treaty Seven council commenced on September 19, 1877 at Blackfoot Crossing on the Bow River. Around eight thousand people attended, including six thousand Indigenous people and around two thousand white traders and mounted police. During the negotiations, the treaty commissioners proposed limiting Blackfoot territories to two "reserves"—the Canadian equivalent of American reservations. The treaty would create one shared reserve for the Siksikas, Kainais, and Tsuut'inas at Blackfoot Crossing, and a separate reserve for the northern Piikanis about one hundred miles to the southwest. (The Kainais would later move to their own reserve near Fort Macleod in 1882, and the Tsuut'inas to a reserve near Calgary.) The Stoneys—who made their homes in the foothills and were close relatives of the Assiniboines—would move to a reserve near the base of the mountains between present-day Calgary and Banff. All of the Native signatories would retain the right to hunt throughout their erstwhile territories, on lands that had not yet been claimed directly by the government or by settlers who had the permission of the Crown. The treaty guaranteed all tribal members a onetime payment of twelve dollars, with annual payments of five dollars thereafter, and chiefs were guaranteed suits of clothing and a variety of tools. The treaty also promised funding for schoolteachers, cattle, and farming implements.[9]

As in 1855, the negotiations for Treaty Seven focused almost exclusively on access to the region's diminishing resources, the source of greatest anxiety for the Indigenous signatories. The Siksika chief Old Sun, named for his late father, asked the commissioners to ban wolf poisons, since the poisons killed horses and bison as well. The Kainai chief Medicine Calf requested that the North-West Mounted Police pay for the firewood they had collected from river valleys since their arrival in 1874. More crucially, Medicine Calf also pushed the commissioners to ban Cree and Métis hunters from Treaty Seven territory entirely. The Canadian commissioner David Laird replied that newly implemented restrictions on killing bison calves and cows in winter would provide a sufficient deterrent but that he could never "exclude any class of the Queen's subjects" from Canadian lands. After conferring among themselves, representatives from each of the five nations signed Treaty Seven on September 22, 1877.[10]

While they debated resource rights at length, neither the commissioners nor the chiefs discussed the treaty's massive transfer of territory from Indigenous nations to the Crown. Many Blackfoot people to this day maintain that Treaty Seven was above all a peace treaty, not a land surrender, and that the signers agreed to share and not cede their traditional lands. Poor communication probably limited many of the Indigenous signers' understanding of the land transfer. According to one observer, when Laird began the council the lead translator, Jerry Potts, "stood with his mouth open. He had not understood the words as spoken, and if he had he would have been utterly unable to convey the ideas they expressed." The commissioners called on other translators to assist Potts, but confusion persisted. For example, few Blackfoot people had experience with the units of measurement used to determine and describe the size of the reserves, especially the baseline requirement of "one square mile" per family of five persons. Debates over the true meaning and intent of the treaty continue to the present day, and many still feel that the lack of proper communication should call the entire agreement into question.[11]

Whatever their understanding, the attendees went their separate ways after the council ended. The commissioners distributed payments amounting to around $60,000 and then departed, as did the Mounties. Many of the Native signatories stayed to spend their new money on goods from the white

Blackfoot Crossing, a shallow stretch of the Bow River east of Calgary, has been home to the Siksika Nation Reserve since Crowfoot negotiated Treaty Seven in 1877. (Sydney Prior Hall, *The Blackfoot Indians under Crowfoot Crossing the Bow River, September 10, 1881*, Library and Archives Canada, MIKAN no. 2839018.)

traders camping nearby. By Tuesday, October 1, the traders had left as well. One by one, the Blackfoot bands made their departure from the treaty grounds. Siksika, Kainai, and Piikani women carefully packed their families' belongings, fed their dogs, wrapped their food, untied their lodge covers, and carefully fitted their tipi poles into travois. The autumn bison hunts would come soon, and then it would be time to settle into the river valleys for the winter, as they had always done.[12]

AFTER CROWFOOT DIED IN 1890, the people of the Siksika Nation buried him in a place of honor overlooking the heart of the reserve, the river valley where the Blackfoot negotiated their first and only treaty with the Canadian government. The site was well chosen. Looking down upon Blackfoot Crossing, one cannot help but reflect upon the legacy of Crowfoot and his peers, who were faced with almost unimaginable circumstances and had to make unbearable choices. The twilight of Crowfoot's life brought him and his people even more heartache. Blackfoot people faced destitution in the years following the 1877 treaty, as the plains bison herds finally disappeared and settler governments on both sides of the border failed to provide enough nutrition and medical care to prevent disease, malnutrition, and mass starvation. On both sides of the border, Blackfoot people confronted federal bureaucracies designed to destroy Indigenous culture through forced assimilation, residential schooling, and allotment. Only through a fierce commitment to their communities, cultural identities, and sovereign land bases did the Blackfoot nations survive the attempted cultural genocide of the early reservation and reserve era.[13]

Blackfoot people are determined to honor this history. About a half a mile away from Crowfoot's gravesite stands the jewel of the reserve: a gleaming multimillion-dollar museum complex dedicated to preserving Blackfoot history and culture called Blackfoot Crossing Historical Park. As the museum's exhibits make clear, the Siksika Nation reserve is one of several Blackfoot homelands. Drive about two hours to the southwest, and you will find the Piikani Nation reserve. Next door to the Piikanis, you will find the Kainai Nation's reserve, which was created at the insistence of the great Chief Red Crow. About an hour south of that is the Blackfeet Reservation, home to the southern Piikanis who remained in the United States. Today there are approximately thirty-seven thousand Blackfoot people enrolled in the four nations, slightly over half of whom live on these tribal lands.[14]

When Crowfoot and his peers touched pen to paper in 1877 and created the reserves, they drew from more than a century and a half of experience with confronting, resisting, and adapting to colonial transformation. Since at least the 1720s, Blackfoot people had responded to an almost constant barrage of change. They mastered horses. They fit new tools and technologies to their way of life. They became expert hunters and negotiators with Indigenous middlemen. When whites arrived, the Blackfoot built personal relationships, crafted new ceremonies, and strategized for leverage. They fought back against those who tried to weaken those ties and forced outsiders either to respect their lands or to go to tremendous lengths to avoid them. Later, they formulated a grand strategy of borderland management that made them one of the most powerful Indigenous nations in North America. Eventually, the Blackfoot faced forces they could not control or manipulate. As miners, settlers, soldiers, and merchants besieged their lands and the bison dwindled, the Blackfoot faced fewer and fewer options. By 1877, only diplomacy could ensure that they retained a distinct political identity within their homelands.

Blackfoot people's creative engagement with colonial change between 1720 and 1877 shaped not only their own experience but the world around them as well. For well over a century, Indigenous peoples through much of north-western North America lived the shadow of Blackfoot influence. The Blackfoot controlled the pace of colonial change by managing the diffusion of metal tools, weapons, guns, and other goods across the plains and mountains. At the same time, their traffic in furs, provisions, horses, and sometimes people defined the region's economy. Generations of non-Native outsiders likewise found that their experiences and ambitions in the West were inextricably tied to the Blackfoot, and continually found their plans subordinated to Blackfoot interests. At times, the Blackfoot thwarted U.S., British, and Canadian expansion, and at other times, they carefully negotiated the pace and extent of outsiders' presence in the region. Although settler society eventually overwhelmed the northwest plains and its peoples, the Blackfoot dictated their own path for generations. By acting creatively in their own interests and projecting their power onto countless others, Blackfoot people ensured that their story should be central to understanding the history of the early North American West.

Blackfoot people long understood their homeland as a central and powerful place—a place of both convergences and divisions, whose unique geography could bring either opportunity or peril. The northwest plains were essential to Blackfoot religion and identity, and as the Blackfoot confronted radical changes starting three hundred years ago, this place became all the more essential to their story. Blackfoot country was the meeting place of the mountains, plains, and northern forests, and it bridged waters that drained all the way to frigid northern bays and to balmy southern seas. It attracted people from far afield. Throughout the era of the fur trade, Blackfoot people used the unique geography of their homelands to preserve and augment their way of life. The Blackfoot experience, in all its triumph and tragedy, comes fully into focus only when it is seen first and foremost as the history of a changing Indigenous homeland, not merely as a chapter in U.S. or Canadian history. Only by putting Indigenous places at the center of our histories can we understand the changing face of North America over the last five hundred years.

Blackfoot history goes on. That today the Blackfoot nations remain where they have always been, deep in the storied prairies beneath the Backbone of the World, is a profound testament to their resiliency and persistence in the face of colonial change.

Notes

Abbreviations

ARCIA   Department of the Interior, *Annual Report of the Commissioner of Indian Affairs*

BRBL   Beinecke Rare Book and Manuscript Library, New Haven, Conn.

EHPJ   Edmonton House Post Journal, Hudson's Bay Company Archives, Winnipeg, Man.

GMA   Glenbow Museum Archives, Calgary, Alta.

HBCA   Hudson's Bay Company Archives, Winnipeg, Man.

IHFP   Indian History Film Project, Canadian Plains Research Center, University of Regina

LR:OIA   Letters Received by the Office of Indian Affairs, 1824–81, RG 75, Records of the Bureau of Indian Affairs, M234, National Archives Microfilm Publications

MHS   Montana Historical Society Research Center, Helena

NAMP   National Archives Microfilm Publications

PSLFT   Papers of the St. Louis Fur Trade

RCSIA   Records of the Central Superintendency of Indian Affairs, RG 75, Records of the Bureau of Indian Affairs, M856, National Archives Microfilm Publications

RMSIA   Records of the Montana Superintendency of Indian Affairs, RG 75, Records of the Bureau of Indian Affairs, M833, National Archives Microfilm Publications

RWSIA   Records of the Washington Superintendency of Indian Affairs, RG 75, Records of the Bureau of Indian Affairs, M5, National Archives Microfilm Publications

Introduction

1. Catlin, *Illustrations of Manners, Customs & Condition*, 30, 51; Schultz, *Signposts of Adventure*, 31.

2. John Sanford to William Clark, July 17, 1832, LR:OIA, roll 750, p. 304. Sanford attributes his quotes to an unnamed chief he also met the previous summer, which likely indicates it was Bull Back Fat, since we know Bull Back Fat was at Fort Union in 1832 and is named in other sources as one of the visitors to Fort Union in 1831. For Bull Back Fat's 1831 visit, see Schultz, *Signposts of Adventure*, 23–27. For modern orthography of name, see Maximilian, *North American Journals*, 2:409n.

3. November 2, 1833, EHPJ, 1833–4, fol. 20v, B.60/a/28, HBCA.

4. Unless otherwise noted, the Blackfoot orthography in this book comes from Frantz and Russell, *Blackfoot Dictionary*.

5. For a useful definition of prenational borderlands, see Aron and Adelman, "From Borderlands to Borders," 816. See also Hämäläinen, *Comanche Empire*; R. White, "Winning of the West"; Delay, *War of a Thousand Deserts*; DuVal, *Native Ground*.

6. Merrell, *Indians' New World*. For changes in the early West, see Blackhawk, *Violence over the Land*; Calloway, *One Vast Winter Count*; Fenn, *Encounters*, 1–176; Fenn, *Pox Americana*; Binnema, *Common and Contested Ground*; Silverman, *Thundersticks*. See also Ferguson and Whitehead, *War in the Tribal Zone*.

7. Saunt, "Go West"; Blackhawk, *Violence over the Land*, 5.

8. Key social and cultural histories of the western fur trade include A. Hyde, *Empires, Nations, and Families*; Van Kirk, *Many Tender Ties*; Graybill, *Red and the White*; Coleman, *Here Lies Hugh Glass*; Podruchny, *Making the Voyageur World*. Historiography of the Great Lakes fur trade is more robust, and includes R. White, *Middle Ground*; Witgen, *Infinity of Nations*; McDonnell, *Masters of Empire*; Richter, *Ordeal of the Longhouse*.

9. The fur trade has received far more attention in Canada, where it has been seen as essential to the formation of a national identity. The foundational text of Canadian fur trade historiography is Innis, *Fur Trade in Canada*. See also Podruchny and Saler, "Glass Curtains and Storied Landscapes."

10. Turner, *Rereading Frederick Jackson Turner*; R. White, *Western History*; Lewis, "WHA at Fifty."

11. Canadian historiography of the Saskatchewan River fur trade includes Ray, *Indians in the Fur Trade*; Ray and Freeman, *"Give Us Good Measure"*; Russell, *Eighteenth-Century Western Cree*; Milloy, *Plains Cree*; Thistle, *Indian-European Trade Relations*. U.S. historiography on the Upper Missouri River fur trade includes Barbour, *Fort Union*; Wischmann, *Frontier Diplomats*; Sunder, *Fur Trade*; Judy, "Powder Keg"; and Ewers, *Blackfeet*. Despite extraordinary ethnographic work, Ewers never had the opportunity to research extensively using Hudson's Bay Company records, which were housed in London until 1974. Works that seek to understand the region in transnational context include Binnema, "Allegiances and Interests"; Binnema and Dobak, "'Like the Greedy Wolf'"; Smyth, "Niitsitapi Trade"; Hall, "Before the Medicine Line."

12. J. Wilson, "Agency, Narrative, and Resistance"; Johnson, "On Agency." For critiques of agency on the Great Plains in particular, see Anderson, "Illusions of Independence."

13. For more on the need for non-Native scholars to think critically about their engagement with archives and communities, see Smith, *Decolonizing Methodologies*.

14. Most influential for me has been LaPier, *Invisible Reality*. Other Blackfoot scholarship includes Fox, "Using Geographic Information Systems"; McMillan and Yellowhorn, *First Peoples in Canada*; Yellowhorn, "Never-Ending Journey"; Bastien, *Blackfoot Ways of Knowing*; Chambers and Blood, "Love Thy Neighbour"; Treaty 7 Elders et al., *True Spirit*; Blackfoot Gallery Committee, *Story of the Blackfoot People*; and *Blackfeet Encounter* (DVD). I have also learned a great deal from Blackfoot curation at the Museum of the Plains Indian in Browning, Montana; the Blackfoot Crossing Histori-

cal Park in Cluny, Alberta; the Head-Smashed-In Buffalo Jump World Heritage Site near Fort MacLeod, Alberta; and the Glenbow Museum in Calgary, Alberta.

15. Today there are four nations, since the imposition of the international border divided the Piikanis between a reserve in Alberta (the Piikani Nation) and a reservation in Montana (the Blackfeet Reservation). The Piikanis are also known as the Piegan or Pikuni in the United States and the Peigan in Canada. The Kainais are also known as the Blood tribe, and the Siksikas are sometimes called the Blackfoot proper. While "Blackfeet" and "Blackfoot" are often used interchangeably in the United States, in Canada generally only the latter word is used. Ties between the nations remain strong, and representatives from each of the four nations meet annually at the Blackfoot Confederacy Conference.

Chapter One

1. Wissler and Duvall, *Mythology of the Blackfoot Indians*, 19–39. For other nineteenth-century and early twentieth-century versions of the creation story, see Henry, *Journal of Alexander Henry*, 2:379–80; Hale, "Ethnology," 209; and Maclean, "Blackfoot Mythology," 165–66. Henry heard his version from a prominent Siksika chief named Painted Feather in 1808; Hale recorded his from Albert Lacombe, an Oblate missionary to Blackfoot people between 1861 and 1872; and Maclean gathered his version while ministering to Kainai people between 1880 and 1889. Related stories appear in Grinnell, *Blackfoot Lodge Tales*, 137–44; Calf Robe, *Siksika'*, 3–5; and Bullchild, *Sun Came Down*, 5–126. See also Ewers, *Blackfeet*, 1–4; and Bastien, *Blackfoot Ways of Knowing*, 8–9. For "Backbone," see McClintock, *Old North Trail*, 13; Welch, *Fools Crow*, 3, 38, 52, 368.

2. For Blackfoot longevity on the northwest plains, see Vickers and Peck, "Identifying the Prehistoric Blackfoot," 473–97; Greiser, "Late Prehistoric Cultures," 47–48. For an overview on early Algonquian origins, see Foster, "Language and the Culture History," 97–100. Foster notes that the wide geographic distribution of Algonquian languages, including two in California, raise the slight possibility that the language group could have originated farther west than typically thought, perhaps even on the northwest plains. For more on the Canadian Shield hypothesis, see Schlesier, *Wolves of Heaven*, 43–44, 111, 164–66; and Calloway, *One Vast Winter Count*, 56–57. Some archaeologists have critiqued this hypothesis for having weak evidence. See Fagan, *Ancient North America*, 188.

3. McMillan and Yellowhorn, *First Peoples in Canada*, 155–56; Wissler, "Social Life," 7; Weasel Tail interview by Claude Schaeffer, November 11, 1948, book 2, p. 35, Claude E. Schaeffer Field Notebooks, M-1100-165, GMA; Middleton, *Kainai Chieftainship*, 39. Although "Niitsitapi" has become the most commonly cited endonym for the Blackfoot, some Blackfoot writers point out that the word actually refers to all Indigenous North Americans, and a more correct designation for the Blackfoot would be "Niitsi-poi-yksi," which means "Speakers of the Real Language," or "Siksikaitsipoyi," which means "Blackfoot-speaking real people." For the former, see Blackfoot Gallery Committee, *Story of the Blackfoot People*, 18; for the latter, see Bastien, *Blackfoot Ways of Knowing*, 212.

4. For precontact Blackfoot territory, see Vickers and Peck, "Identifying the Prehistoric Blackfoot," 82; Chambers and Blood, "Love Thy Neighbour," 254–55; Oetelaar and Oetelaar, "People, Places and Paths," 380; Binnema, "How Does a Map Mean." For a general description of northwest plains environments, see Duke, *Points in Time*, 46–54. For population estimates, see Hall, "Blackfoot Country," 24n–25n; Wissler, "Population Changes," 3–10. The devastating impact of European diseases beginning in 1781, coupled with the dearth of firsthand estimates prior to that date, makes it conceivable that the precontact population may have been higher than fifteen thousand.

5. For twin buttes, see Grinnell, *Blackfoot Lodge Tales*, 137. For Nááp effigies, see Vickers and Peck, "Identifying the Prehistoric Blackfoot," 486–89. For Old Women's Buffalo Jump, see Bryan, *Buffalo People*, 144. For Nááp's playing ground, see Yanicki, *Old Man's Playing Ground*, 1–12; Ewers, *Blackfeet*, 4–5. The location of this boulder was known as Ohkotok, or Big Rock, which later lent its name to the Calgary suburb of Okotoks.

6. Oetelaar and Oetelaar, "Structured World," 69–94; E. Wilson, "Report on the Blackfoot Tribes," quote on 188; Fox, "Using Geographic Information Systems," 21; Rides at the Door, *Nááp Stories*; Blackfoot Gallery Committee, *Story of the Blackfoot People*, 18. Citations refer to Firefly edition. For more on Indigenous sacred geographies, see Basso, *Wisdom Sits in Places*.

7. LaPier, *Invisible Reality*, 23–43, 64–81; Oetelaar, "Archaeological Imprint of Oral Traditions," 338–39; Bastien, *Blackfoot Ways of Knowing*, 11–12, 55–56; George First Rider interview by J. C. Hellson, June 27, 1969, IHFP, http://hdl.handle.net/10294 /617. A vivid description of these alliances can be found in Welch, *Fools Crow*.

8. Hellson and Gadd, *Ethnobotany of the Blackfoot Indians*; Kehoe, "How the Ancient Peigans Lived," 87–103; McMillan and Yellowhorn, *First Peoples in Canada*, 148. For settler perceptions of the Great Plains, see Webb, *Great Plains*, 152–60; Baltensperger, "Plains Booms," 59–73.

9. Verbicky-Todd, *Communal Buffalo Hunting*, 10–158; Brink, *Imagining Head-Smashed-In*, 71–178; Brink and Rollans, "Structure and Function of Drive Lane Systems," 152–67; Binnema, *Common and Contested Ground*, 35; Audubon, *Audubon and His Journals*, 144–46. Quote from Henday, *Year Inland*, 107.

10. Morgan, "Beaver Ecology/Beaver Mythology," 34–41; LaPier, *Invisible Reality*, 66–74; Daschuk, *Clearing the Plains*, 7; Blackfoot Gallery Committee, *Story of the Blackfoot People*, 22–23; Fox, "Using Geographic Information Systems," 23, 134–35. For early references to beaver taboos, see Fidler, *Southern Alberta Bicentennial*, 21–22; Henry, *Journal of Alexander Henry the Younger*, 2:380; Thomas Hutchins, "Observations on Hudson's Bay" [ca. 1775], p. 108, WA MSS S-2409, BRBL. Blackfoot terminology and spellings from LaPier, *Invisible Reality*. For more on beaver bundles, see Wissler, "Ceremonial Bundles." For oral history, see George First Rider interview by J. C. Hellson, July 22, 1969, IHFP, http://hdl.handle.net/10294/685; Joe Gambler interview by J. C. Hellson, October 21, 1968, IHFP, http://hdl.handle.net/10294/462.

11. LaPier, *Invisible Reality*, 44–98; Peck and Vickers, "Buffalo and Dogs," 55–86; Morgan, "Beaver Ecology/Beaver Mythology," 37–49; Binnema, *Common and Contested Ground*, 37–54; Ewers, *Horse in Blackfoot Indian Culture*, 123–29, 301; Kehoe,

"How the Ancient Peigans Lived," 89–90. Kehoe estimates that mounted Blackfoot bands moved between seventeen and twenty-three times per year; however, pre-equestrian movements were probably less frequent due to the greater difficulty of travel and the fact that they did not need to find fresh forage for horses. For dogs specifically, see Reeves, "Communal Bison Hunters," 170; Ewers, *Indian Life*, 8–9; Ewers, *Blackfeet*, 10. I am also especially grateful for the insights I received at the Piegan Institute Annual History Conference, "Imitaiks: When the Spirit Moved with Us," Browning, Montana, August 20, 2010.

12. For Blackfoot marriage practices and gender roles, see Carter, *Importance of Being Monogamous*, 104–44; and B. Hungry Wolf, *Ways of My Grandmothers*, 59–71. For Blackfoot childhood, see Mountain Horse, *My People, the Bloods*, 6–13; White Headed Chief (Spumiapi) interview by Jane Richardson, September 2, 1938, series 1, pp. 106–8, Lucien and Jane Hanks Fonds, M-8458-6, GMA; Crooked Meat Strings interview by Jane Richardson, September 12–13, 1938, series 1, p. 187, Lucien and Jane Hanks Fonds, M-8458, GMA; Bradley, "Characteristics, Habits and Customs," 272–77; McClintock, *Old North Trail*, 390–93; Wissler, "Social Life," 29–30; Thompson, *Writings*, 1:310.

13. Ewers, *Blackfeet*, 39, 96–98; Ewers, *Horse in Blackfoot Indian Culture*, 245–48; Binnema, "Old Swan, Big Man," 1–4.

14. McMillan and Yellowhorn, *First Peoples in Canada*, 134. For boundary making, see Raczka, "Posted: No Trespassing," 2, 6–7; Bouchet-Bert, "From Spiritual and Biographic," 27–46; Oetelaar, "Archaeological Imprint," 337–38; Bernstein, *How the West Was Drawn*, 21–29. Non-Native observers typically ignored or delegitimized Indigenous borders, which served the purpose of weakening Indigenous claims to land. For more on the importance of recognizing Indigenous borders and territoriality, see Bobroff, "Retelling Allotment."

15. For Kootenais, see McMillan and Yellowhorn, *First Peoples in Canada*, 180–83; Brunton, "Kootenai," 223–26; Wissler, "Material Culture," 17. For Flatheads and Pend d'Oreilles, see Malouf, "Flathead and Pend d'Oreille," 297–98; Wissler, "Material Culture," 17; Binnema, *Common and Contested Ground*, 73; Bamforth, *Ecology and Human Organization*, 87; Teit, "Salishan Tribes," 297, 303, 314–16. The descendants of Flathead people today generally refer to themselves as Bitterroot Salish; however, this name refers to the eventual location of their reservation and would therefore be anachronistic when referring to the prereservation era. For Nez Percés, see Walker, Jr., "Nez Perce," 420–21; West, *Last Indian War*, 12–14. For mountain trade rendezvous and trade routes, see Teit, "Salishan Tribes," 357–59. This route was likely part of the Old North Trail, which followed the front range of the Rocky Mountains. McClintock, *Old North Trail*, 434–40.

16. For Crees, see Darnell, "Plains Cree," 640. The extent of Cree presence in western plains and parklands prior to the arrival of horses has generated debate among scholars, with some tying the western migration of Crees to the fur trade and the advent of horses, and others arguing that the Cree presence in the West predated colonial contact. For arguments in favor of postcontact migration, see Milloy, *Plains Cree*, 5–20; and Mandelbaum, *Plains Cree*, 15–50. For works that argue for an earlier arrival,

see Russell, *Eighteenth-Century Western Cree*, 217–18; and Innes, *Elder Brother*, 44–54. For Assiniboines, see DeMallie and Miller, "Assiniboine," 572. For Tsuut'ina's, see Dempsey, "Sarcee," 629. For Saskatchewan River trade sites, see Meyer and Thistle, "Saskatchewan River Rendezvous Centers," 403–22.

17. For Gros Ventres, see Fowler and Flannery, "Gros Ventre," 677–78; Fowler, *Shared Symbols, Contested Meanings*, 1–40. For Crows, see Voget, "Crow," 695–96; Hoxie, *Parading through History*, 31–59. For Shoshones, see Calloway, "Snake Frontiers," 84; Shimkin, "Eastern Shoshone," 308–9; Bamforth, *Ecology and Human Organization*, 88–89; Greiser, "Late Prehistoric Cultures," 47–52. For Missouri River trade centers, see Ewers, *Indian Life*, 14–33; Swagerty, "Indian Trade," 351–53; Fenn, *Encounters*, 8–30.

18. For ethnic intermixing, see Albers, "Symbiosis, Merger, and War," 94–132; Rzeczkowski, *Uniting the Tribes*, 21–47. For plains sign language, see Ewers, *Blackfeet*, 203–4; Henry, *Journal of Alexander Henry the Younger*, 1:226, 264; Wissler, "Social Life," 7; Taylor, "Nonspeech Communication Systems," 275–82.

19. Binnema, *Common and Contested Ground*, 55–71; Thompson, *Writings*, 1:289–91; B. Hungry Wolf, *Ways of My Grandmothers*, 71–74; Bamforth, "Indigenous People, Indigenous Violence," 95–115. J. Rod Vickers has suggested that Young Man's adversaries in this story may have been Hidatsas or Crows, though the majority of scholarship identifies them as Shoshones. Vickers, "Cultures of the Northwestern Plains," 29–30.

20. Rich, *Fur Trade*, 19–44; Radisson, *Pierre-Esprit Radisson*, 1:48–49; Ray and Freeman, *"Give Us Good Measure,"* 23–25; Nute, "Chouart des Groseilliers, Médard."

21. The most thorough study of the Cree and Assiniboines' role in the fur trade is Ray, *Indians in the Fur Trade*, 1–116. See also Russell, *Eighteenth Century Western Cree*, 11–13, 47–83; Milloy, *Plains Cree*, 5–20.

22. Ray, *Indians in the Fur Trade*, 57–69; Binnema, *Common and Contested Ground*, 94–97; La Vérendrye, *Journals and Letters*, 248; Thompson, *Writings*, 1:289–91; Henday, *Year Inland*, 184. For annual round, see Ray, *Indians in the Fur Trade*, 85–88; Isham, *Observations on Hudsons Bay*, 313–14. The identity of the group Henday met has been the subject of debate. See chapter 2 in this book.

23. For gradual adoption of European goods, see Pyszczyk, "Use of Fur Trade Goods," 45–84. For technology and cooking, see Dempsey, "Blackfoot," 605. For more on Blackfoot clay vessels, see Kehoe and Kehoe, "Probable Late Blackfoot Clay Vessel," 43–45; Cocking, "Adventurer from Hudson Bay," 111; John Ewers, "Blackfoot Indians—Pottery," Southern Alberta Research Project Collection, M-4561-8, GMA, 1–3; Ewers, *Indian Life*, 8–11. For axes and hatchets, see Henry, *Journal of Alexander Henry the Younger*, 2:536. For fires, see Fenn, *Encounters*, 88–89. For clothing preparation, see Kehoe, "Blackfoot Persons," 114–16; Wissler, "Social Life," 26–28; Spector, *What This Awl Means*, 19–29. See also Hine and Faragher, *American West*, 139.

24. Bohr, *Gifts*, 4–8, 79–81; Pyszczyk, "Historic Period Metal," 163–87; Thompson, *Writings*, 1:59, 289–91; Henry, *Journal of Alexander Henry the Younger*, 2:528.

25. Davies, *Letters from Hudson Bay*, 318; Henday, *Year Inland*, 135.

26. Thompson, *Writings*, 1:294; Ewers, *Horse in Blackfoot Indian Culture*, 18; Ewers, *Indian Life*, 12–13; Dempsey, *Amazing Death of Calf Shirt*, 27. For other Blackfoot

stories about the arrival of horses, see Thompson, *Writings*, 1:293–94; Scalp Roller, interview by R. N. Wilson, 1893, p. 344, transcript, R. N. Wilson Fonds, M-4421, GMA; Grinnell, *Story of the Indian*, 232–37; E. Wilson, "Report on the Blackfoot Tribes," 185; Tom Kiyo, interview by David Duvall, February 20, 1911, p. 212, transcript, David C. Duvall Fonds, M-4376, GMA; John Drunken Chief, interview by Jean-Louis Levern, June 1, 1910, pp. 65–66, transcript, "Notes et Souvenirs Concernant Les Piednoirs," Jean-Louis Levern Fonds, M-8521, GMA; Ita Ruchow and Calf Bull, interview by Levern, June 20, 1911, p. 126, transcript, Jean-Louis Levern Fonds, M-8521, GMA.; Joe Little Chief, "History of the Blackfeet," pp. 13–14, Joe Little Chief Fonds, M-4394, GMA; Jim Blood interview by Wilhelm Uhlenbeck-Melchior, August 5, 1911, in Uhlenbeck-Melchior, *Montana 1911*, 317; Crowshoe, *Weasel Tail*, 79.

27. Ewers, *Horse in Blackfoot Indian Culture*, 2–19; Hämäläinen, "Rise and Fall," 845; Calloway, "Snake Frontiers," 85–89; Murphy and Murphy, "Northern Shoshone and Bannock," 300–302.

28. For examples of Blackfoot exploration, see Raczka, "Traditions of Northern Plains Raiders," 47–54. For the impact of horses more broadly, see Hämäläinen, "Rise and Fall," 833–62; *West, Episode One* (DVD); Wishart, *Great Plains Indians*, 15–28.

29. Henday, *Year Inland*, 108; Fagan, *Ancient North America*, 139–40; Bamforth, *Ecology and Human Organization*, 97–128.

30. Ewers, *Horse in Blackfoot Indian Culture*, 28–29, 129–47, 155–56; Cocking, "Adventurer from Hudson Bay," 111; Kehoe, "Blackfoot Persons," 114–15; Morgan, "Beaver Ecology/Beaver Mythology," 41–45; Binnema, *Common and Contested Ground*, 42–46; Landals, "Horse Heaven," 241–51. Blackfoot people continued to use dogs as pack animals after the arrival of horses as well.

31. For horse care, see Ewers, *Horse in Blackfoot Indian Culture*, 36–38; Pitoxpikis (Sleigh), interview by Jane Richardson, August 24, 1938, pp. 15–16, transcript, Jane and Lucien Hanks Fonds, M-8458-3, GMA. For horses as wealth, see Henry, *Journal of Alexander Henry the Younger*, 2:378; Ewers, *Horse in Blackfoot Indian Culture*, 28–30, 240–45; Binnema, "Old Swan, Big Man," 6–8; D. Nugent, "Property Relations, Production Relations," 336–62; and Conaty, "Economic Models," 403–9. Conaty rightly critiques Nugent for eliding the continuing importance of gift exchange and ideals like generosity in Blackfoot culture, but Nugent is correct in his assessment that horses increased social stratification.

32. For pre-equestrian warfare, see Ewers, *Blackfeet*, 16; Ewers, *Indian Life*, 11–12; Binnema, *Common and Contested Ground*, 57–59; Greiser, "Late Prehistoric Cultures," 55. For references to pre-equestrian Blackfoot armor, see Calf Robe, *Siksiká*, 76–77; James Willard Schultz, "How Man Got Idea of Fire," n.d., pp. 1–2, Eleanor Luxton Papers, M-4561-9, GMA. For post-equestrian warfare, see Thompson, *Writings*, 1:291; Secoy, *Changing Military Patterns*, 45–64; Wishart, *Great Plains Indians*, 21–25; Blackhawk, *Violence over the Land*, 1–293; Binnema, *Common and Contested Ground*, 86–106; Hämäläinen, *Comanche Empire*, 29–65; Hämäläinen, "Rise and Fall," 833–62.

33. Binnema, *Common and Contested Ground*, 84–106; Calloway, *One Vast Winter Count*, 295–97; Calloway, "Snake Frontiers," 84–88; Russell, *Eighteenth-Century Western Cree*, 196; Peter Fidler, September 9, 1792, "A Journal from York Fort Hudson's Bay

to Cumberland, Hudson's, Manchester & Buckinham Houses, up the Saskatchewan River, by Way of Lake Wennepeg in 1792," fol. 93, E.3/1, HBCA. Secondary sources often state the Shoshones "expanded" their territory north into southern Alberta, but there is little evidence in oral history or archaeology that the Shoshones supplanted Blackfoot people, or that the latter abandoned their core homelands. A more accurate assessment would be that the Shoshones expanded their raiding and warfare into traditional Blackfoot lands.

34. Cocking, "Adventurer from Hudson Bay," 112; Thompson, *Writings*, 1:317; William Tomison, April 13, 1786, Hudson House Post Journal, 1785–86, fol. 35r, B.87/a/8, HBCA; Ewers, *Horse in Blackfoot Indian Culture*, 171–215. For more on the movement of Cree bands onto the Plains, see Binnema, *Common and Contested Ground*, 109, 116–19; Milloy, *Plains Cree*, 21–26; Darnell, "Plains Cree," 638–40. Dale Russell argues that despite increasing plains activity, the Plains Cree remained "a parkland group," in Russell, *Eighteenth-Century Western Cree*, 218. For examples of early Cree and Assiniboine raids on Blackfoot horse herds, see Hutchins, "Observations on Hudson's Bay," 107; Tomison, May 5, 1786, Hudson House Post Journal, 1785–6, fol. 39, B.87/a/8, HBCA; Tomison, July 9, 1787, Manchester House Post Journal, 1787–8, fol. 5–5v, B.121/a/2, HBCA; Henry Hallett, October 7, 1800, Island House Post Journal, 1800–1, fol. 5, B.92/a/1, HBCA.

35. For Blackfoot captive-taking, see Henday, *Year Inland*, 106; Cocking, "Adventurer from Hudson Bay," 112; R. N. Wilson and Red Arrow, "Taboos and Customs," 1890, p. 123, R. N. Wilson Fonds, M-4421, GMA; Raczka, *Winter Count*, 22. For discussions of pre-equestrian captive-raiding, see Ewers, *Blackfeet*, 16; Ewers, *Horse in Blackfoot Indian Culture*, 310–11; and Fenn, *Encounters*, 20, 214–15, 392–93n. For Blackfoot people as captives, see Henday, *Year Inland*, 151–56; Isham, *Observations on Hudsons Bay*, 113–15; Smyth, "Niitsitapi Trade," 94–96.

36. For captive trading in the intermountain West, see Calloway, *One Vast Winter Count*, 297; Blackhawk, *Violence over the Land*, 16–87; De La Vérendrye, *Journals and Letters*, 412. For captive trading in the Canadian interior, see Umfreville, *Present State of Hudson's Bay*, 177; Calloway, "Snake Frontiers," 88–89; West, *Last Indian War*, 21. For more on Indigenous slavery in New France, see Rushforth, *Bonds of Alliance*. For Henday's visit, see Henday, *Year Inland*, 108–9, 156–57. For more on captives as social and political capital, see Barr, "From Captives to Slaves"; Brooks, *Captives and Cousins*. See also Gallay, *Indian Slave Trade*; and Reséndez, *Other Slavery*. The northwestern dimensions of this trade remain underexplored.

37. Saunt, *West of the Revolution*, 1–212; Alan Taylor, *American Colonies*, 446–54.

Chapter Two

1. Henday, *Year Inland*, 94–109, 179–84, quote on 104; Yellowhorn, "Never-Ending Journey of Anthony Henday," 87–110. Henday's journals present unique challenges because they exist in four different versions, all of which were mediated transcriptions of his original journal, which is now lost. One version of the journals suggests that the Blackfoot eventually agreed to Henday's request, though the other three record the opposite. In any case, none of the York Factory journals indicate that

such a visit ever occurred. Henday, *Year Inland*, 180; Smyth, "Niitsitapi Trade," 88–104. Writers have disagreed regarding the identity of the Indigenous people Henday met on October 14, 1754. Henday referred to them as "Archithinee," an apparent mispronunciation of the Cree word *ayaciyiniwak*, a generic term they used to refer to strangers or enemies. Clark Wissler and John Ewers have argued that Henday's counterparts were probably Gros Ventres, since the meeting took place on the far eastern margins of Blackfoot territory, apparently out of sight of the Rocky Mountains. However, as Philip Godsell has pointed out, the large size of the encampment (likely numbering between 1,400 and 2,000 people) likely precluded the possibility that it was composed solely of Gros Ventres. Although Gros Ventres may have been present, the majority of the camp was probably Blackfoot. Ewers, *Blackfeet*, 26; Wissler, "Population Changes," 4–5; Philip Godsell, ed., "Life and Adventures of Red Crow," p. 234n, R. N. Wilson Fonds, M-4421, GMA; Parks, "Enigmatic Groups," 973.

2. Ray, *Indians in the Fur Trade*, 51–71; Ray and Freeman, *"Give Us Good Measure,"* 190–91.

3. Ray and Freeman, *"Give Us Good Measure,"* 33–35; Smyth, "Niitsitapi Trade," 76–88; Ewers, *Blackfeet*, 24; Meyer and Thistle, "Saskatchewan River Rendezvous," 403–44.

4. For the 1751 incident, see Saint-Pierre, "Journal of Jacques Repentigny Legardeur St. Pierre," clxiii–clxv; Smyth, "Niitsitapi Trade," 81–88. In a related vein, in 1741 an ayahciyiniwak captive told Isham that visiting the York Factory would be impossible without permission from the Assiniboines. Isham, *Observations on Hudsons Bay, 1743*, 113; Smyth, "Niitsitapi Trade," 95–96.

5. Binnema, *Common and Contested Ground*, 104–5; Ray and Freeman, *"Give Us Good Measure,"* 34, 192; Rich, *Fur Trade and the Northwest*, 127–29; Meyer and Thistle, "Saskatchewan River Rendezvous," 418.

6. Smythe, *Thematic Study of the Fur Trade*, 172–73; Binnema, *Common and Contested Ground*, 109–13; Ray, *Indians in the Fur Trade*, 58, 125–28; Stewart, *Documents Relating to the North West Company*, 39–40; Smyth, "Niitsitapi Trade," 134–37; Saunt, *West of the Revolution*, 124–47.

7. Thompson, *Writings*, 1:289–92, quote on 292. See also Secoy, *Changing Military Patterns*, 39–47; Three Bears, interview by David Duvall, March 3, 1911, pp. 623–26, David C. Duvall Fonds, M-4376, GMA; Rich, *Cumberland House Journals*, 263; Cocking, "Adventurer from Hudson Bay," 103, 106, 112.

8. Thompson, *Writings*, 1:295–96, quotes on 296. A similar provenance for smallpox is suggested in Matthew Cocking to Edward Jarvis, August 1782, in Rich, *Cumberland House Journals*, 298. Due in part to the lack of specific dates and the uncertainties of David Thompson's translation, Young Man's narrative lends itself to a broad range of interpretation. Historian James Daschuk has argued that Young Man's anecdote actually referred to a smallpox epidemic striking the northwest plains sometime around the 1730s. Daschuk relies mostly on his own reading of Young Man's account and much later Kootenai and Flathead oral histories that do not specify dates. However, Young Man's narrative makes clear that the smallpox epidemic occurred after the Piikanis gained a steady supply of guns, suggesting it occurred after the 1760s. Contemporary accounts from HBC traders likewise state that the 1781–82 epidemic was

the first of its kind on the northwest plains. While an early eighteenth-century epidemic is possible, more substantial evidence is needed, especially in Blackfoot oral histories and fur trade records. Daschuk, *Clearing the Plains*, 24–26; Fenn, *Pox Americana*, 192; Umfreville, *Present State of Hudson's Bay*, 92; Thompson, *Writings*, 1:285.

9. Fenn, *Pox Americana*, 13–43; Shurkin, *Invisible Fire*, 25–39, 101–8.

10. Thompson, *Writings*, 1:296; Fenn, *Pox Americana*, 186–89; Farnham, *Travels in the Great Western Prairies*, 33–35; Binnema, "With Tears, Shrieks, and Howlings," 111–32; Henry, *Journal of Alexander Henry the Younger*, 2:381, 535; Umfreville, *Present State of Hudson's Bay*, 203; Raczka, *Winter Count*, 21. Raczka dated this entry as 1764; however, the epidemic occurred in 1781. For challenges locating food in the aftermath, see Thompson, *Writings*, 1:296; Binnema, *Common and Contested Ground*, 127. Adam R. Hodge argues that climate variability in the years leading up to the epidemic exacerbated the disease's effects and further complicated efforts to locate bison afterwards. Hodge, "In Want of Nourishment," 365–403.

11. For social reorganizations, see Thompson, *Writings*, 1:285; Weasel Tail and Cecile Black Boy, interview by Claude Schaeffer, November 6, 1947, pp. 92–93, transcript, "Peigan Bands," Claude E. Schaeffer Fonds, M-1100-135, GMA; Binnema, *Common and Contested Ground*, 124–25; Binnema, "With Tears, Shrieks, and Howlings," 120. For religious crisis and reorganization, see Fieldnotes by Esther Goldfrank, 1939, p. 489, Esther Schiff Goldfrank Fonds, PD 90, GMA; Thompson, *Writings*, 1:60–61, 286–87; Binnema, *Common and Contested Ground*, 124–28; Binnema, "With Tears, Shrieks, and Howlings," 117–20. Although his conclusions have often been contested by historians, Martin's *Keepers of the Game* remains one of the only works to investigate the impact of diseases on Indigenous people's spiritual relationships to the environment. For critiques of Martin, see Krech, *Indians, Animals, and the Fur Trade*.

12. Thompson, *Writings*, 1:284–85; William Walker, December 4, 1781, in Rich, *Cumberland House Journals*, 226; Matthew Cocking to Edward Jarvis, August 1782, in Rich, *Cumberland House Journals*, 297; Fenn, *Pox Americana*, 194–95.

13. Rich, *Cumberland House Journals*, 282; William Walker to William Tomison, August 12, 1782, Hudson House Post Journal, 1782, fol. 9v, B.87/a/5, HBCA; Walker, August 18, 1782, Hudson House Post Journal, 1782, fol. 10, B.87/a/5, HBCA.

14. For middlemen's opposition to expansion, see Peter Fidler, October 8, 1795, "A Journal from the Long Point Cedar Lake, to Swan River House, Somerset & Carlton Houses, also the upper parts of the Red River, in 1795," fol. 80, Peter Fidler Fonds, E.3/1, HBCA. Fidler remarked that "before the smallpox [the Crees and Assiniboines] were so very numerous that had not this destructive disorder attacked them it was the opinion of every one that no traders could with safety visit these interior parts." For a description of tensions between Canadians and middlemen on the Saskatchewan before 1781, see Binnema, *Common and Contested Ground*, 111–13.

15. Rich, *Fur Trade and the Northwest*, 172–85; Smythe, *Thematic Study of the Fur Trade*, 165–220.

16. For goods traded, see Henry, *Journal of Alexander Henry the Younger*, 2:548; Unknown author, September 9, 1783, Cumberland House Post Journal, 1783–4, fol. 43v, B.49/a/14, HBCA (entry written at Hudson House); M'Gillivray, "Some Account of

the Trade," 68–69. For improved trade terms, see Binnema, *Common and Contested Ground*, 136; Graham, *Observations on Hudson's Bay*, 257. For improved quality, see William Tomison, February 17, 1789, Manchester House Post Journal, 1788–1789, fol. 36v, B.121/a/3, HBCA; Tomison, January 27 and February 3, 1792, Manchester House Journal, 1791–1792, fols. 23–24, B.121/a/7, HBCA. The frequency of visits increased from between one and two Blackfoot visits per year to the HBC's Hudson House between 1782 and 1787, to around twenty-one annual visits at Edmonton and Buckingham Houses between 1795 and 1799. This is a measure of each recorded visit of Indian people explicitly identified as Blackfoot. Figures collected from Hudson House Post Journals, 1782–1787, B.87/a/6-9, HBCA; Manchester House Post Journals, 1786–1793, B.121/a/1-8, HBCA; Buckingham House Post Journals, 1795–1799, B.24/a/3-6, HBCA; Johnson, *Saskatchewan Journals*, 16–236. There are few extant records for NWC posts, but the pattern was probably similar. For discussion of how horses enabled and incentivized trade, see Jablow, *Cheyenne in Plains Indian Trade Relations*, 1–24. For the size of parties, see Johnson, *Saskatchewan Journals*, 16–36. For larger parties, see Johnson, *Saskatchewan Journals*, 107–8, 112. In the winter of 1795–96, William Tomison variously described the size of ten Blackfoot trading parties as ranging between two and thirty people. Traders explicitly noted when women and children were present, which suggests that trade was usually conducted solely by men. For Yellow Sun's description of trade, see Augustine Yellow Sun and Joe Poor Eagle interview by Allan Wolf Leg, 1974, IHFP, http://hdl.handle.net/10294/591.

17. For hunting of canines, see William Pink, January 17, 1770, York Factory Inland Journal, 1769–70, fol. 15v, B.239/a/63, HBCA. Piikani elders Weasel Tail and Cecil Black Boy told of a similar method involving a miniature surround made of willow branches, in Weasel Tail and Cecile Black Boy, interview by Claude Schaeffer, November 6, 1947, p. 94, transcript, "Peigan Bands," Claude E. Schaeffer Fonds, M-1100-135, GMA. For transportation barriers to the bison robe trade, see Marchildon, *History of the Prairie West Series*, 62; Ray, *Indians in the Fur Trade*, 210–12; Wise, *Producing Predators*, 7. For examples of small furs, see Johnson, *Saskatchewan Journals*, 156, 160; Henry, *Journal of Alexander Henry the Younger*, 2:548. For beaver trading, see Henry, *Journal of Alexander Henry the Younger*, 2:396-97. Binnema has observed that Piikani traders brought in far more beavers than other Blackfoot groups. However, the Piikanis also raided and traveled more expansively than their peers, which suggests that they may have acquired many of their beaver pelts through plunder or trade, or perhaps by trapping in other nations' homelands instead of their own. Binnema, *Common and Contested Ground*, 134. For horse trading, see Henry, *Journal of Alexander Henry the Younger*, 2:398; M'Gillivray, *Journal of Duncan M'Gillivray*, 31.

18. For the provisions trade, see Colpitts, *Pemmican Empire*, 1–103; Binnema, *Common and Contested Ground*, 117–19; Colpitts, "Provisioning the HBC," 179-203. See also M'Gillivray, "Some Account of the Trade," 67, 69. For Blackfoot people trading provisions, see William Tomison, February 19, 1788, Manchester House Post Journal, 1787–1788, fol. 26, B.121/a/2, HBCA. See also Henry, *Journal of Alexander Henry the Younger* 2:548; MacKenzie, *Voyages from Montreal*, lxvii.

19. For trade envoys, see Francis Heron, Edmonton District Report, 1818-9, quote on fol. 4v, B.60/e/3, HBCA; James Bird, February 19, 1815, EHPJ, 1814-5, fol.

33, B.60/a/13, HBCA; Bird, April 1, 1815, EHPJ, 1814–5, fol. 51, B.60/a/13, HBCA.; M'Gillivray, *Journal of Duncan M'Gillivray*, 41; Henry, *Journal of Alexander Henry the Younger*, 2:415. For competition and gift-giving, see Bird, November 11, 1808, EHPJ, 1808–9, fol. 9, B.60/a/8, HBCA; Bird, March 4, 1816, EHPJ, 1815–6, fol. 46, B.60/a/15, HBCA; Ray, *Indians in the Fur Trade*, 140–42.

20. Henry, *Journal of Alexander Henry the Younger*, 2:540–41. For HBC cannon salutes, see Richard Grant and [unknown name] Small, October 17, 1832, EHPJ, 1832–3, fol. 38, B.60/a/27, HBCA; and Grant and Small, January 29, 1833, EHPJ, 1832–3, fol. 73, B.60/a/27, HBCA.

21. Henry, *Journal of Alexander Henry the Younger*, 2:539–42. The HBC also traded brandy during the eighteenth century, though by the early nineteenth century they had joined the NWC in relying almost exclusively on rum. Ens and Binnema, *Edmonton House Journals, 1806–1821*, 126n.

22. For Blackfoot gift-giving and diplomacy, see Fidler, *Southern Alberta Bicentennial*, 32; Johnson, *Saskatchewan Journals*, 313; Ewers, *Horse in Blackfoot Indian Culture*, 255–56. For a detailed description of Cree and Assiniboine trade visits, see Thomas Hutchins, "Observations on Hudson's Bay," ca.1775, pp. 112–15, WA MSS S-2409, BRBL. For broader conversations on the importance of gift exchange to Indigenous diplomacy, see Sahlins, *Stone Age Economics*, 149–84; B. White, "'Give Us a Little Milk,'" 2–12; Thistle, *Indian-European Trade Relations*, 8–32; Hämäläinen, *Comanche Empire*, 40–41; DuVal, *Native Ground*, 15, 19, 40–42; A. Hyde, *Empires, Nations, and Families*, 36–37, 164; Witgen, *Infinity of Nations*, 29–68.

23. Mrs. Night Gun, interview by Claude Schaeffer, April 15, 1951, book 10, pp. 16–17, transcript, Claude E. Schaeffer Field Notebooks, M-1100-165-8, GMA; Grinnell, *Blackfoot Lodge Tales*, 219; Bradley, "Characteristics, Habits and Customs," 280–82; Ewers, *Horse in Blackfoot Indian Culture*, 255–56. The similar importance of gift exchange to Gros Ventre peoples is described in Fowler, *Shared Symbols, Contested Meanings*, 34–40. Quote in Maximilian, *Travels in the Interior*, 127.

24. John Edward Harriott, "Memoirs of Life and Adventure in the Hudson's Bay Company Territories" [ca. 1860], p. 107, WA MSS 245, BRBL; William Tomison, April 10, 1786, Hudson House Post Journal, 1785–6, fol. 36, B.87/a/8, HBCA; Tomison, March 5, 1791, Manchester House Post Journal, 1790–1, fol. 25v, B.121/a/6, HBCA. See also Maximilian, *North American Journals*, 364; Ens and Binnema, *Edmonton House Journals, 1806–1821*, 69; Fidler, *Southern Alberta Bicentennial*, 30; Hanson, "Laced Coats and Leather Jackets," 105–17.

25. M'Gillivray, *Journal of Duncan M'Gillivray*, 41, quote on 73; second quote in William Tomison, April 13, 1786, Hudson House Post Journal, 1785–1786, fol. 36, B.87/a/8, HBCA. Following a peacemaking ceremony in 1808, Cree leaders adopted a Blackfoot boy, "for the purpose of cementing more firmly the Peace between them & the Crees." James Bird, September 3, 1808, EHPJ, 1808–9, fol. 4, B.60/a/8, HBCA. For more on adult adoption, see Henry John Moberly, *When Fur Was King* (Toronto: J. M. Dent & Sons, 1929), 47; Smyth, "Niitsitapi Trade," 39–42, 72–73, 181–96. For more on the importance of "fictive" kinship, see Albers, "Symbiosis, Merger, and War," 94–132; Carter, *Importance of Being Monogamous*, 105.

26. For descriptions of sexual liaisons, see Henry, *Journal of Alexander Henry the Younger*, 2:422, 493, 545. Maximilian of Wied described similar transactions in Maximilian, *Travels in the Interior*, 2:109–10. For sex as gift exchange or diplomacy, see Hurtado, "When Strangers Met," 54; Colpitts, *Pemmican Empire*, 117. In other contexts, extramarital sex by women was generally considered disgraceful within Blackfoot bands. For Blackfoot beliefs on sex and adultery, see Wissler, "Social Life," 9–11.

27. For the winter of 1799–1800, see Johnson, *Saskatchewan Journals*, 235. The following April, Thompson also reported that all the lands between Edmonton and Rocky Mountain House were burnt, which may also have been the result of purposeful Indigenous manipulation of bison herds. Thompson, April 3, 1800, "Journal from Fort George to Rocky Mountain House, March 25th to May 5th, 1800," p. 4, David Thompson Papers, Thomas Fischer Rare Book Library, University of Toronto. For the use of fire to drive off herds generally, see M'Gillivray, *Journal of Duncan M'Gillivray*, 33; Colpitts, *Pemmican Empire*, 109–10.

28. Binnema, "Old Swan, Big Man," 1–32. Quote from M'Gillivray, *Journal of Duncan M'Gillivray*, 50.

29. Henry, *Journal of Alexander Henry the Younger*, quote on 2:546. R. White, *Middle Ground*.

30. Cox, *Adventures on the Columbia River*, 237–39, quote on 238; Robert Stuart, August 12, 1812, "Journal of a Voyage across the Continent of North American from Astoria," pp. 75–76, WA MSS 457, Robert Stuart Papers, BRBL; Henry, *Journal of Alexander Henry the Younger*, 2:523; Thompson, *Writings*, 1:317; Thompson, "Discoveries from the East Side," 43; Thompson, *Columbia Journals*, 7; Ewers, *Horse in Blackfoot Indian Culture*, 22–28; Binnema, *Common and Contested Ground*, 141–42; Silverman, *Thundersticks*, 252–63.

31. Hämäläinen, "Rise and Fall," 845–54; Thompson, *Writings*, 1:317; Johnson, *Saskatchewan Journals*, 309–10, 317n, quote on 310; M'Gillivray, *Journal of Duncan M'Gillivray*, 69; Binnema, *Common and Contested Ground*, 141–43.

32. Thompson, *Writings*, 1:320. Although Thompson dated this raid as 1807 in his memoir, the actual year was probably 1787. See Thompson, *David Thompson's Narrative*, 370; Calloway, *One Vast Winter Count*, 300; Thompson, *Writings*, 1:297; Bad Head, "Bad Head's Winter Count," p. 2, R. N. Wilson Fonds, M-4421, GMA. Thompson called the Piikani war chief "Kootanae Appee," likely a different spelling of the name Maximilian of Wied spelled "Kutonápi," when referring to a chief in 1833. Whether Maximilian referred to the same man, or a relative, is unclear. Maximilian, *North American Journals*, 356n. Pekka Hämäläinen has similarly demonstrated how the Comanches turned to captive-raiding to rebuild their population after disease outbreaks, in Hämäläinen, *Comanche Empire*, 220–23, 251–55.

33. Calloway, *One Vast Winter Count*, 300–301; Calloway, "Snake Frontiers," 88–90; G. Hyde, *Indians of the High Plains*, 181–85; Binnema, *Common and Contested Ground*, 182–83; Swagerty, "History of the United States Plains," 268; quote in William Tomison, April 10, 1786, Hudson House Post Journal, 1785–6, fol. 35v, B.87/a/8, HBCA; Peter Fidler, "A Journal from York Fort Hudson's Bay to Cumberland, Hudson's, Manchester & Buckingham Houses, up the Saskatchewan River, by Way of Lake Wennepeg in

1792," fol. 93, Peter Fidler Fonds, E.3/1, HBCA; Thompson, *Writings*, 1:288–89; quote from Moulton, *Journals of the Lewis and Clark Expedition*, 8:278.

34. Binnema, *Common and Contested Ground*, 183–85; Farr, "Going to Buffalo, Part 1," 4–14; Thompson, *Writings*, 1:188–89; Ewers, *Indian Life*, 12; Schultz, *Signposts of Adventure*, 12–14. According to some Kootenai oral histories, prior to 1781 at least one Kootenai band had even lived on the plains year-round. For more on Kootenais, see Brunton, "Kootenai," 223–25; Turney-High, *Ethnography of the Kutenai*, 11 (James Daschuk uses this passage as evidence that the Kootenai moved west after an earlier epidemic in the 1730s, but the source itself does not indicate such a date; Daschuk, *Clearing the Plains*, 203n.); E. Wilson, "Report on the Blackfoot Tribes," 197–98. For Flatheads and Pend d'Oreilles, see Malouf, "Flathead and Pend d'Oreille," 297–305. For Nez Percés, see West, *Last Indian War*, 12–18; Walker Jr., "Nez Perce," 420–21; Moulton, *Journals of the Lewis and Clark Expedition*, 7:246–51, 301.

35. For Kootenai attempts at trade, see Fidler, *Southern Alberta Bicentennial*, 68; M'Gillivray, *Journal of Duncan M'Gillivray*, 56. For reliance on Crow intermediaries, see Larocque, *Journal of Larocque*, 72–73; Calloway, *One Vast Winter Count*, 303–5; Calloway, "Snake Frontiers," 88.

36. Peter Fidler, February 19, 1811, Ile-a-la-Crosse Post Journal, 1810–11, fols. 24–24v, B.89/a/2, HBCA; Thompson, *Columbia Journals*, 62; Fidler, *Southern Alberta Bicentennial*, 42–45, 49. See also Ens and Binnema, *Edmonton House Journals, 1806–1821*, 36–37; Brunton, "Kootenai," 225. For Blackfoot gun trading to the Kootenais, see Thompson, *Columbia Journals*, 15; Fidler, *Southern Alberta Bicentennial*, 51.

37. J. Nicks, "Thompson, David (1770–1857)."

38. Occasional visits from Native emissaries from mountain nations fueled the companies' ambitions in the mountains. See, for example, the visit of two Kootenai envoys to Edmonton House in 1798, in Johnson, *Saskatchewan Journals*, 112–13. For Thompson's 1800 expedition, see Thompson, *Columbia Journals*, 3–15, quotes on 5, 15; Thompson, *Writings*, 1:302. For more on the role of Haudenosaunee, Nipissing, and Algonquian company employees in the West, see Ens and Binnema, *Edmonton House Journals, 1806–1821*, l–lii; Grabowski and St-Onge, "Montreal Iroquois Engagés"; T. Nicks, "Iroquois and the Fur Trade," 85–101.

39. For Thompson's attempts in 1800 and early 1801, see Thompson, "Discoveries from the East Side," 42–43; Thompson, *Columbia Journals*, 3–15. For his failed 1801 expedition with The Rook, see Thompson, *Columbia Journals*, 21–34; Thompson, "Discoveries from the East Side," 43; Fidler, *Southern Alberta Bicentennial*, 52.

40. For related interpretations of how European colonialism unfolded among Native people who had already experienced dramatic change, see Merrell, *Indians' New World*, 8–91; Witgen, *Infinity of Nations*, 1–167; and DuVal, *Native Ground*, 29–102.

Chapter Three

1. For Wolf Calf's account and other Blackfoot perspectives of this event, see Wheeler, *Trail of Lewis and Clark*, 2:311–12; George Grinnell to Olin Wheeler, March 16, 1903, box 7, George Bird Grinnell Papers, Yale University Manuscripts and Archives; Eric Newhouse, "Blackfeet Recollections Differ from Those Recorded in Lewis'

Journal," *Great Falls Tribune* (Great Falls, Mont.), April 23, 2003; *Blackfeet Encounter* (DVD); and James Bird to John McNab, December 23, 1806, EHPJ, 1806-7, fol. 6, B.60/a/6, HBCA. For Lewis's account, see Moulton, *Journals of the Lewis and Clark Expedition*, 8:113, 127-36, quote on 131; and Lewis to Unknown Correspondent, September 29, 1806, in Jackson, *Letters*, 335-43. See also Ronda, *Lewis and Clark*, 238-43.

2. Ewers, *Horse in Blackfoot Indian Culture*, 216-20, 249-50; D. Nugent, "Property Relations, Production Relations," 336-62.

3. Ewers, *Blackfeet*, 124-44; Ewers, *Horse in Blackfoot Indian Culture*, 194-96; Crooked Meat Strings interview by Jane Richardson, September 12-13, 1938, Lucien and Jane Hanks Fonds, series 1, pp. 167-71, 180, M-8458, GMA; Káinaikoan interview by Wilhelm Uhlenbeck-Melchior, June 12, 1911, in Uhlenbeck-Melchior, *Montana 1911*, 221-22.

4. David C. Duvall Fonds, Series 2, pp. 157-61, 637-38, 413-16, M-4376, GMA; Adam White Man interview by Claude Schaeffer, April 15, 1950, book 6, pp. 75-76, Claude E. Schaeffer Field Notebooks, M-1100-165, GMA; Mountain Horse, *My People, the Bloods*, 29-30; Ewers, *Horse in Blackfoot Indian Culture*, 178-81. See also Philip Godsell, ed., "Life and Adventures of Red Crow," R. N. Wilson Fonds, M-4421, GMA.

5. For violence and leadership, see Binnema, "Old Swan, Big Man," 12-20. For fighting and alcohol, see Henry, *Journal of Alexander Henry the Younger*, 2:534-35; William Walker, October 23, 1789, Manchester House Post Journal, fol. 24v, B.121/a/4, HBCA; William Tomison, May 1, 1789, Manchester House Post Journal, fol. 47, B.121/a/3, HBCA. For violence against women, see Ewers, *Blackfeet*, 100; Wissler, "Social Life," 9-11. For examples of nose cutting, see Donald McKenzie, February 19, 1823, Bow River Expedition (Chesterfield House) Journal, 1822-3, fol. 29, B.34/a/4, HBCA; Maximilian, *Travels in the Interior*, 109-10; Jean L'Heureux, "Description of a Portion of the Nor'West and the Indians," 1871, p. 18, Jean L'Heureux Fonds, GMA; Thompson, *Writings*, 2:307; Harmon, *Journal of Voyages and Travels*, 73-75. For connections between social conflicts and domestic violence in a different context, see Faragher, *Eternity Street*, xii, 214-24.

6. Henry, *Journal of Alexander Henry the Younger*, 2:397, 424, 496, 663n. A reminiscence by HBC trader Hugh Monroe similarly describes a violent reaction by Siksika traders to an increase in the price for goods at Edmonton during the late 1810s, in Grinnell, "White Blackfoot," 70-73; James Bird, November 22, 1812, Edmonton House Journal, 1812-13, fol. 3v, B.60/a/11, HBCA; Smyth, "Niitsitapi Trade," 262-66; Binnema, "Allegiances and Interests," 332.

7. For Blackfoot relations with the Crees and Assiniboines, see Smyth, "Niitsitapi Trade," 122-30, 161; Milloy, *Plains Cree*, 6-37; Binnema, *Common and Contested Ground*, 161-94. Binnema and Milloy have argued that the Blackfoot and the Crees and Assiniboines were military and economic allies throughout much of the eighteenth century, and that 1806 represented a drastic break between the groups. These historians have relied heavily on the testimony of Young Man in David Thompson's 1850 *Travels*, which is the only primary source to mention alliances specifically. Smyth contends that there is little evidence for such an alliance. Smyth is correct to point out that scholars may have been too quick to apply rigid formulations like

"alliance" to this period, but he undervalues the marked increase in Blackfoot-Cree violence in the period following 1806. For social and kinship connections between plains groups, see Albers, "Symbiosis, Merger, and War," 94–132; Rzeczkowski, *Uniting the Tribes*, 21–47. For Young Man, see Thompson, *Writings*, 1:63–65, 289–99, quote on 295; Fidler, *Southern Alberta Bicentennial*, 41. For intermarriage, see Henry, *Journal of Alexander Henry the Younger*, 2:532. Although few such stories survive, Henry provided a rare glimpse of Cree-Blackfoot intermarriage in 1811, when a Cree woman had a fight with her Piikani husband and went to NWC traders at Fort Augustus. After discussing current events among the Piikanis and Gros Ventres with the whites, the woman left to stay with some Cree relatives encamped nearby. For the North Saskatchewan as neutral ground, see Binnema, *Common and Contested Ground*, 174–75; Milloy, *Plains Cree*, 5–20.

8. Thompson, *Writings*, 1:131–32; Milloy, *Plains Cree*, 21–30; Darnell, "Plains Cree," 638–41; Binnema, *Common and Contested Ground*, 119, 174–75; Hämäläinen, "Rise and Fall," 851–52; Ens, "Fatal Quarrels," 140–42. There remains substantial disagreement about the chronology of the Crees' movement to the plains region, which may have begun earlier, but most scholars agree that the establishment of direct trade in the region accelerated the process. For examples of conflicts between Cree-Assiniboine and Blackfoot groups prior to 1806, see William Tomison, May 5, 1786, Hudson House Post Journal, 1785–6, fol. 39, B.87/a/8, HBCA; Tomison, July 9, 1787, Manchester House Post Journal, 1787–8, fols. 5–5v, B.121/a/2, HBCA; Henry Hallett, October 7, 1800, Island House Post Journal, 1800–1, fol. 2, B.92/a/1, HBCA.

9. For the July 1806 joint war party, see Harmon, *Journal of Voyages and Travels*, 119–20. For the subsequent battle, see James Bird, August 25, 1806, EHPJ, 1806–7, fols. 1–1v, B.60/a/6, HBCA; Harmon, *Journal of Voyages and Travels*, 120–21. See also Milloy, *Plains Cree*, 35; Binnema, "Old Swan, Big Man," 26–29; Ens and Binnema, *Edmonton House Journals, 1806–1821*, 2–3, 23–25. For the September 1806 Siksika attack, see James Bird, September 22, 1806, EHPJ, 1806–7, fol. 2, B.60/a/6, HBCA. Blackfoot war parties sometimes took women and children captive but did not engage extensively in slave trading. Ewers, *Blackfeet*, 16. For diminished trade returns, see James Bird, August 25, 1806, EHPJ, 1806–7, fols. 1–1v, B.60/a/6, HBCA; Bird to Peter Fidler, December 23, 1806, EHPJ, 1806–7, fol. 4v, B.60/a/6, HBCA.

10. James Bird, April 7, 1807, EHPJ, 1806–7, fol. 8v, B.60/a/6, HBCA. For more on Old Swan, see Binnema, "Old Swan, Big Man."

11. For the 1807 peace and adoption, see James Bird, April 7, 1807, EHPJ, 1806–7, fol. 8v, B.60/a/6, HBCA. For the return of Blackfoot groups, see James Bird, April 15, 1807, EHPJ, 1806–7, fol. 9, B.60/a/7, HBCA; Bird, May 10, 1807, EHPJ, 1806–7, fol. 10v, B.60/a/7, HBCA.; Bird, October 4, 1807, EHPJ, 1807–8, fol. 3v, B.60/a/8, HBCA; Bird, February 21, 1808, EHPJ, 1807–8, fol. 13, B.60/a/8, HBCA. For the 1808 murder and breakdown of peace, see James Bird, April 7, 1807, EHPJ, 1806–7, fol. 8v, B.60/a/6, HBCA; Bird, September 3, 1808, EHPJ, 1808–9, fol. 2v, B.60/a/8, HBCA. See also Milloy, *Plains Cree*, 31–37, 83–99; Binnema, "Old Swan, Big Man," 26–30. Henry's journal relates a slightly different set of events, stating that the Crees killed three and the Siksika killed four in revenge. Henry, *Journal of Alexander Henry the Younger*, 2:358, 366.

12. For Cree and Assiniboine expansion, see Thompson, *Writings*, 1:303; Milloy, *Plains Cree*, 21–66; John Rowand to George Simpson, March 1, 1823, George Simpson Inward Correspondence Book, 1822-3, fol. 28, D.4/117, HBCA. For Cree oral histories, see Ask hkapimuxta da (Walking Earth) interview by D. G. Mandelbaum, July 4, 1934, IHFP, http://hdl.handle.net/10294/1732; Asiniwikijik (Rocky Sky) interview by D. G. Mandelbaum, July 13, 1934, IHFP, http://hdl.handle.net/10294/1748. For Piikani preference of Rocky Mountain and Acton House, see Smythe, *Thematic Study of the Fur Trade*, 217–18.

13. For Gros Ventre conflicts with the Crees and Assiniboines, see Binnema, *Common and Contested Ground*, 144–60; Harmon, *Journal of Voyages and Travels*, 51–56, 78, 119–20. For joint Blackfoot-Gros Ventre raiding and trading, see James Bird, October 4, 1807, EHPJ, 1807-8, fol. 3v, B.60/a/7, HBCA; Bird, January 21, 1808, EHPJ, 1807-8, fol. 11v, B.60/a/7, HBCA; Bird, February 23, 1808, EHPJ, 1807-8, fol. 14, B.60/a/7, HBCA; Bird, October 31, 1808, EHPJ, 1808-9, fol. 4v, B.60/a/8, HBCA; Bird, October 7, 1813, EHPJ, 1813-4, fol. 3, B.60/a/12, HBCA; Bird, March 28, 1814, EHPJ, 1813-4, fol. 13, B.60/a/12, HBCA. For Americans' conflation of Blackfoot and Gros Ventres, see Binnema, "Allegiances and Interests," 328–30; Fowler, *Shared Symbols, Contested Meanings*, 45–49.

14. Wood, *Empire of Liberty*, 357–99; Lee, "Accounting for Conquest," 921–42; Lass, "Northern Boundary," 27–50.

15. Ronda, *Lewis and Clark*, 1–255; Ambrose, *Undaunted Courage*, 51–58, 68–79.

16. Goetzmann, *Exploration and Empire*, 3–20; Dolin, *Fur, Fortune, and Empire*, 166–88; Gitlin, *Bourgeois Frontier*, 26–67.

17. See Majors, "John McClellan." Considerable uncertainty has surrounded the McClellan party in historical studies. Because Wilkinson funded their venture illegally, the McClellan party avoided disclosing their names in the few documents they produced. Upon arriving to the Rocky Mountains, McClellan dispatched a letter outlining American trade regulations to the NWC's David Thompson through Native couriers, which he signed using the pseudonym "Zachary Perch" (see James Bird, November 10, 1807, Edmonton House Journal, 1807-8, fols. 6–8v, B.60/a/7, HBCA). McClellan sent another letter to Thompson the following September, which he signed "Jeremy Pinch" (transcription in Elliott, "Strange Case," 190). These letters remained a mystery to historians until Majors exhaustively reconstructed the history of the McClellan expedition in his 1981 article. John C. Jackson's 2010 biography of McClellan contains interesting speculation but fails to substantiate key claims about McClellan's time in the region (see note 21). Jackson, *By Honor and Right*.

18. For more on Courtin, see L. Morris, "Charles Courtin," 21–39. See also Majors, "John McClellan," 556, 611; and Josephy, *Nez Perce Indians*, 660–63. Like McClellan, Courtin remained largely mysterious until the investigations by Majors and Morris meticulously reconstructed the chronology of his journey.

19. Wishart, *Fur Trade of the American West*, 41–44; Chittenden, *American Fur Trade*, 1:113–19; Oglesby, *Manuel Lisa*, 40–64; Bradley, "Bradley Manuscript, Book II," 184–90. For Lisa's early relations with the Crows, see Hoxie, *Parading through History*, 54.

20. For Lisa's trapping scheme, see Wishart, *Fur Trade of the American West*, 41–46. For beaver trapping, see Dolin, *Fur, Fortune, and Empire*, 181–82. For the significance of beavers, see chapter 1 in this book.

21. James Bird, January 22, 1808, Edmonton House Journal, 1807–8, fol. 12, B.60/a/7, HBCA. There has been substantial disagreement among scholars about the identity of the Americans described in this entry. Alvin Josephy, Ens, and Binnema claim the meeting was with Manuel Lisa at Fort Randall. Although Lisa never directly reported meeting Blackfoot or Gros Ventres in 1807, Thomas Biddle later reported that Lisa's first party was "met by the Blackfeet" and "treated civilly" (Thomas Biddle to Henry Atkinson, October 29, 1819, in *Report of the Committee on Indian Affairs*, 16th Cong., 1st Sess., Senate Executive Document 47, 2); Ens and Binnema, *Edmonton House Journals, 1806–1821*, 115; Josephy, *Nez Perce Indians*, 652. Larry Morris, however, contends that the group identified in this entry was Charles Courtin's party. While Morris does not cite the Biddle letter, he reasons that Courtin's party was the only American group located on the Missouri River in the fall of 1807, as the Edmonton journal indicates, and that Fort Randall's distant location made it unlikely that a party of Kainai and Gros Ventres would stumble upon it and that the news would have time to reach Edmonton by January, especially since Fort Randall was only founded in late November. See L. Morris, "Charles Courtin," 38. John C. Jackson claims that the meeting was with John McClellan but offers little supporting evidence. Jackson, *By Honor and Right*, 161–64. The most likely explanation is that the post was Courtin's.

22. Thomas Biddle to Henry Atkinson, October 29, 1819, in *Report of the Committee on Indian Affairs*, 16th Cong., 1st Sess., Senate Executive Document 47, 2; James, *Three Years*, 52–53; Brackenridge, *Views of Louisiana*, 143; "Anecdote of Colter," *Village Record* (West Chester, Pa.), February 25, 1818. See also Oglesby, *Manuel Lisa*, 54–56; Ronda, *Lewis and Clark*, 243–44; Chittenden, *American Fur Trade*, 2:714; Harris, *John Colter*, 122–23; Binnema, "Allegiances and Interests," 335–36. Contemporary sources referred to Colter's adversaries only as "Blackfeet," which may also have referred to Gros Ventres. For more on Flathead-Crow ties, see Calloway, *One Vast Winter Count*, 303–5. See also chapter 1 in this book.

23. Harris, *John Colter*, 124–34; Coleman, *Here Lies Hugh Glass*, 74–80. The large size of the war party likely precluded the possibility that it was composed solely of Gros Ventres, though they may have participated as well.

24. For the 1808 attack on Courtin's Three Forks post, see James Bird, October 2, 1808, EHPJ, 1808–9, fol. 4, B.60/a/8, HBCA; Bird, October 31, 1808, EHPJ, 1808–9, fol. 4v, B.60/a/8, HBCA; Oglesby, *Manuel Lisa*, 85–89; L. Morris, "Charles Courtin," 33. Ens and Binnema identify this event described in the EHPJ as John Colter's unintended battle with the Blackfoot in early 1808. However, the particulars of these entries, especially the identification of a fully constructed post and eleven French-speaking inhabitants, make it far more likely that they referred to Charles Courtin. It is unclear why the entries refer to multiple posts: it may simply be a reference to multiple buildings, or it may reveal the presence of other trappers in the area at the time, including those dispatched from Fort Raymond. Ens and Binnema, *Edmonton House Journals, 1806–1821*, 123. For the later attack in Hellgate Canyon, see Thompson, *Writ-*

ings, 2:168–69; Thompson, *Journals Relating to Montana*, 88–94; L. Morris, "Charles Courtin," 33–34.

25. For the 1807 attack on the Flathead River, see Majors, "John McClellan," 606–10. For subsequent attacks, see Peter Fidler, February 19, 1811, Ile-a-la-Crosse Post Journal, 1810–1811, fol. 24, B.89/a/2, HBCA; David Thompson to Alexander Fraser, December 21, 1810, in McDonald of Garth, "Autobiographical Notes," 41; Majors, "John McClellan," 611–12; Ens and Binnema, *Edmonton House Journals, 1806–1821*, 40–42. This event may also appear in Henry, *Journal of Alexander Henry the Younger*, 2:545–46, which identifies Kainais as the attackers of the American party on the Missouri.

26. For contemporary accounts, see James, *Three Years*, 66–84; Pierre Menard to Pierre Chouteau, April 21, 1810, Pierre Chouteau, Jr. and Company Collection, MC 4, MHS; "St. Louis, July 25," *New York Commercial Advertiser*, August 20, 1810; "Indian News. St. Louis, August 8," *The Columbian* (New York, N.Y.), September 3, 1811; Thomas Biddle to Henry Atkinson, October 29, 1819, in *Report of the Committee on Indian Affairs*, 16th Cong., 1st Sess., Senate Executive Document 47, 2–3. See also Wishart, *Fur Trade of the American West*, 45–46; Chittenden, *American Fur Trade*, 1:140–44; Oglesby, *Manuel Lisa*, 93–116.

27. For the MFC, see Wishart, *Fur Trade of the American West*, 46; "Commerce with Asia," *St. Louis Enquirer* November 3, 1820, 4; Oglesby, *Manuel Lisa*, 116–19. For references to Americans killed or attacked by the Blackfoot and/or Gros Ventres between 1811 and 1813, see Thompson, *Journals Relating to Montana*, 213; Luttig, *Journal of a Fur-Trading Expedition*, 101–3. These vague accounts are difficult to reconcile with existing knowledge of the Courtin, McClellan, and MFC expeditions.

28. Stuart, *Discovery of the Oregon Trail*, 128; Wishart, *Fur Trade of the American West*, 146, 116–20. See also Ewers, *Blackfeet*, 53. A group of Astorians heading west under the leadership of Wilson Price Hunt likewise deliberately avoided Lewis and Clark's route up the Missouri in order to avoid the Blackfoot. Ronda, *Astoria and Empire*, 165–95; Bradbury, *Travels in the Interior*, 232–34; Brackenridge, *Journal of a Voyage*, 214.

29. Thompson, *Columbia Journals*, 35–74; Thompson, "Discoveries from the East Side," 43; Thompson, *Writings*, 2:135; Rich, *Fur Trade and the Northwest*, 199–200.

30. For the September 1807 visit and aftermath, see Thompson, *Columbia Journals*, 62–66; Thompson, *Writings*, 2:135–41, 144; Thompson, "Discovery of the Source," 43–46; Thompson, "Discoveries from the East Side," 43–44. See also Ens and Binnema, *Edmonton House Journals, 1806–1821*, 35–36. Thompson's later account of the summer of 1807 was somewhat inconsistent with his journals. In his 1848 *Travels*, he inflates the number of attackers to 300 and indicates that they laid a protracted siege on the post. For modern orthography of Kootenai Old Man, see Maximilian, *North American Journals*, 356n. For the December 1807 council, see partial transcription of Thompson journal in Elliott, "Strange Case," 189. See also Thompson, December 18–29, 1807, David Thompson Fonds, Journal 19, pp. 291–92, MS4426, Archives of Ontario, Toronto.

31. Thompson, *Writings*, 2:158–67, quote on 162; C. White, "Saleesh House," 251–63; Cox, *Adventures on the Columbia River*, quote on 1:238. Women traders were a rarity at plains posts, but more common in the mountains.

32. For the impact of technology on Blackfoot raids into the mountains, see Thompson, *Writings*, 2:162; Henry, *Journal of Alexander Henry the Younger*, 2:527; Ewers, *Horse in Blackfoot Indian Culture*, 184–86. For mountain nations' return to the plains, see Thompson, *Writings*, 2:200–201; Farr, "Going to Buffalo, Part 1," 2–21. For Sakatow, see Thompson, *Writings*, 2:139. The term "slave" likely referred to their groups' relative power differential, not literal bondage.

33. Thompson, *Writings*, 2:111–12; Henry, *Journal of Alexander Henry the Younger*, 2:527; James Bird, October 31, 1810, EHPJ, 1810-1, fols. 2–2v, B.60/a/9, HBCA; Thompson, *Travels in Western North America*, 264–67; Fidler, February 19, 1811, Ile-a-la-Crosse Journal, 1810-1, fol. 24v, B.89/a/2, HBCA. In his *Travels*, Thompson erroneously remembered this event as occurring in the summer of 1809. Raczka, *Winter Count*, 37–38. While this entry does not identify the Flatheads specifically, it likely refers to the summer 1810 battle given its importance to Piikani people in particular.

34. For Blackfoot deliberations, see Thompson, *Travels in Western North America*, 267–69. For threats to traders, see James Bird, May 13, 1811, EHPJ, 1810-1, fols. 13–13v, B.60/a/9, HBCA; Bird, May 5, 1813, EHPJ, 1812-3, fol. 8, B.60/a/11, HBCA. For HBC retreat, see Bird to Mr. Auld, August 9, 1811, Churchill Correspondence Book, 1811, fol. 19, B.42/b/55, HBCA. An HBC group led by Joseph Howse traveled to the mountains in 1810 and 1811 and conducted some trade with the Kootenais, but the HBC decided these journeys were too risky to continue. Robertson, *Colin Robertson's Correspondence Book*, 222–23. Despite the threat, there is no direct historical evidence of cannibalism among the Blackfoot.

35. Ronda, *Astoria and Empire*, 55–64, 232–35; Henry, *Journal of Alexander Henry the Younger*, 1:lii–liii; 2:480–86, quote on 480; Thompson, *Writings*, 2:112, 181–83; Thompson, "Discoveries from the East Side," 43–45; Thompson to Alexander Fraser, December 21, 1810, in McDonald of Garth, "Autobiographical Notes," 41; Rich, *Fur Trade and the Northwest*, 199–202.

36. For changes in trade, see Thompson, *Writings*, 2:262–66; Mackie, *Trading beyond the Mountains*, 13–34; Ronda, *Astoria and Empire*, 277–301. For Flatheads and Kootenais, see Cox, *Adventures on the Columbia River*, 236–38; Thompson, *Writings*, 2:259; Henry, *Journal of Alexander Henry the Younger*, 2:523; Brunton, "Kootenai," 225, 232–33.

37. For coverage of MFC conflicts, see, for example, "St. Louis, July 25," *New York Commercial Advertiser*, August 20, 1810; "Indian News: St. Louis, August 8," *The Columbian* (New York, N.Y.), September 3, 1811. Both articles were reprinted widely. For publicization of the Lewis and Clark fight, see Moulton, *Journals of the Lewis and Clark Expedition*, 8:113; Gass, *Journal of the Voyages and Travels*, 295–96. The Lewis and Clark journals incorrectly identified their adversaries at the Two Medicine Fight as Gros Ventres, but Americans rarely distinguished between the groups. For coverage of Colter's run, see Bradbury, *Travels in the Interior*, 25–31; "Anecdote of Colter," *Village Record* (West Chester, Pa.), February 25, 1818. This article was duplicated in newspapers throughout the eastern United States in the spring and summer of 1818. The first newspaper accounts of Colter's escape appeared in 1809 and 1810 but were not published as widely. Thomas, "Journey to the Mandans," 191–92. For historians' interpretations, see Chittenden, *American Fur Trade*, 2:850; De Voto, *Course of Empire*,

219–20. For historiography of Blackfoot violence, see Hall, "Blackfoot Country," 3–11, 71–74.

38. Similarly, in his study of the intermountain West, Ned Blackhawk demonstrates that nineteenth-century Americans often portrayed that region's Indigenous Paiute and Shoshone people as ahistorical relics, consigned to poverty and violence through innate characteristics. He goes on to show that those circumstances were in fact the result of generations of colonial destabilizations like captive raiding, disease, and warfare. Blackhawk, *Violence over the Land*.

Chapter Four

1. Observers also referred to Áähsa'paakii by the name Pretty Woman or Generous Woman. See Maximilian, *North American Journals*, 403n; Claude Schaeffer, "Biographies of Blackfoot Leaders," p. 98, M-1100-150, Claude E. Schaeffer Fonds, GMA; Donald Frantz, e-mail message to author, July 13, 2017.

2. While no direct contemporary accounts remain, the most useful secondhand accounts of this event are Nicolas Point, "Extract from Father Point's Journal," in Chardon, *Chardon's Journal at Fort Clark*, 401–4; and Bradley, "Affairs at Fort Benton," 201–3. See also Larpenteur, *Forty Years a Fur Trader* (1933), 93–97; Maximilian, *Travels in the Interior*, 2:90–92; Schultz, *Signposts of Adventure*, 23–27; Kenneth McKenzie to Agent of American Fur Company, June 7, 1831, Fort Tecumseh and Fort Pierre Letterbook, November 1, 1830–December 14, 1832, Papers of the St. Louis Fur Trade, PSLFT, reel 1:17, 44. For secondary sources, see Smyth, "Niitsitapi Trade," 420–27; Smyth, "Jacques Berger, Fur Trader," 44–47; Chittenden, *American Fur Trade*, 1:329–31. Point and Bradley identify the leader as Good Woman. Schultz's account, as well as Smyth's article and dissertation, identifies Bull Back Fat. The closer contemporaneousness of Point and Bradley's writings and the fact that the AFC named its first post "Fort Piegan," indicate strongly that the leaders most involved with this event were Piikani, although Kainai and Siksika representatives were involved as well. For proper translation of Bull Back Fat's name, see Maximilian, *North American Journals*, 409n.

3. For visits to both HBC and NWC, see James Bird, Edmonton District Report, 1815, fol. 4v, B.60/e/1, HBCA. See also, for example, Bird, March 5, March 29, April 17, May 1, 1816, EHPJ, 1815–6, fols. 23v, 29v, 32v, 36v, B.60/a/15, HBCA; Arima, *Blackfeet and Palefaces*, 205. For the thwarted 1811 attack, see Henry, *Journal of Alexander Henry the Younger*, 2:532–34.

4. For gifts, see Ray, *Indians in the Fur Trade*, 140–42; Francis Heron, October 12, 1820, EHPJ, 1820–1, fol. 14v, B.60/a/19, HBCA; Francis Heron to J. McBean, December 3, 1820, EHPJ, 1820–1, fols. 19v–20, B.60/a/19, HBCA; James Bird to McBean, February 7, 1821, EHPJ, 1820–1, fols. 28v–29, B.60/a/19, HBCA. For Acton House, see James Heron and Francis Heron, March 15, 1820, EHPJ, 1819–20, fols. 22–22v, B.60/a/18, HBCA.

5. Ens and Binnema, *Edmonton House Journals, 1806–1821*, 48–65; Rich, *Fur Trade and the Northwest*, 209–35; Friesen, *Canadian Prairies*, 75–84.

6. For reactions to merger, see Anthony Feistel, November 10, 1821, EHPJ, 1821–2, fol. 14, B.60/a/20, HBCA; and Francis Heron, Chesterfield House (Bow River) Report

on District, 1822-3, fol. 5, B.34/e/1, HBCA; Feistel, November 28, 1821, EHPJ, 1821-2, fol. 15, B.60/a/20, HBCA; Feistel, October 30, 1821, EHPJ, 1821-2, fol. 12v, B.60/a/20, HBCA; Feistel, April 17, 1822, EHPJ, 1821-2, fol. 27, B.60/a/20, HBCA. See also Smyth, "Niitsitapi Trade," 278-354; Ens and Binnema, *Edmonton House Journals, 1821-1826,* xlix-liv. For closing of Rocky Mountain House, see Colin Robertson, Edmonton District Report, 1822-3, fol. 3v, B.60/e/5, HBCA.

7. For the expedition and its goals, see Ens and Binnema, *Edmonton House Journals, 1821-1826,* lxi-lxxvi; Richard Grant, November 25, 1822, EHPJ, 1822-3, fol. 7, B.60/a/21, HBCA; Rich, *Fur Trade and the Northwest,* 245-46; Smyth, "Niitsitapi Trade," 293-95. For Piikani encouragement, see James Bird, Edmonton District Report, 1815, fol. 4v, B.60/e/1, HBCA. For other references to Blackfoot "inducements," see John Rowand to George Simpson, March 1, 1823, George Simpson Inward Correspondence Book, 1822-3, fol. 28v, D.4/117, HBCA; Francis Heron, Chesterfield House (Bow River) Report on District, 1822-3, p. 6, B.34/e/1, HBCA. See also Smyth, "Niitsitapi Trade," 289-93.

8. For suspicions, see Donald McKenzie, October 24, 1822, Bow River Expedition (Chesterfield House) Post Journal, 1822-3, fol. 15, B.34/a/4, HBCA. For October 1822 encounter, see Francis Heron, Chesterfield House (Bow River Expedition) Report on District, 1822-3, pp. 6-7, B.34/e/1, HBCA. For explorations of Marias and Bow Rivers, see Donald McKenzie to George Simpson, March 1, 1823, George Simpson Inward Correspondence Book, 1822-3, pp. 41-42, D.4/117, HBCA; Francis Heron, Chesterfield House (Bow River Expedition) Report on District, 1822-3, p. 7, B.34/e/1, HBCA; Harriott, "Memoirs of Life and Adventure," 5-26. See also Smyth, "Niitsitapi Trade," 289-99; Binnema, "Allegiances and Interests," 342-43. For tensions at the post, see Francis Heron, Chesterfield House (Bow River Expedition) Report on District, 1822-3, p. 6, B.34/e/1, HBCA; Harriott, "Memoirs of Life and Adventure," 101-4; John Rowand to George Simpson, March 1, 1823, George Simpson Inward Correspondence Book, 1822-3, fol. 28v, D.4/117, HBCA.

9. A. Hyde, *Empires, Nations, and Families,* 57-62; Wishart, *Fur Trade of the American West,* 46-51, 77-81.

10. Chittenden, *American Fur Trade,* 1:150-52; Wishart, *Fur Trade of the American West,* 46-48.

11. Maximilian, *North American Journals,* 355n, 362; William Gordon to Unknown, June 15, 1823, in Morgan, *West of William H. Ashley,* 49; Duncan Finlayson, November 28, 1823, EHPJ, 1823-4, fols. 27-27v, B.60/a/22, HBCA.

12. Duncan Finlayson, November 30, 1823, EHPJ, 1823-4, fol. 28v, B.60/a/22, HBCA.

13. For April 1823 Blackfoot attack on the advance party sent by Ashley and Henry, see Utley, *Life Wild and Perilous,* 47; Morgan, *West of William H. Ashley,* 72. For Kainai attack on the MFC, see Joshua Pilcher, July 1, 1823, in Morgan, *West of William H. Ashley,* 41-42. For Arikara conflict, see Nichols, "Arikara Indians," 85-91. The HBC's purchase of plundered furs caused an international controversy. See Binnema and Dobak, "'Like the Greedy Wolf,'" 423-34.

14. Wishart, *Fur Trade of the American West,* 121-27; Utley, *Life Wild and Perilous,* 55-67; A. Hyde, *Empires, Nations, and Families,* 59-70.

15. Wishart, *Fur Trade of the American West*, 129–31; "Official Documents. In Senate of the U. States—Feb. 9, 1829" *Daily National Intelligencer*, April 22, 1829, Dale Lowell Morgan Transcripts, WA MSS S-2221, box 3, folder 37, BRBL. For Peter Skene Ogden's extensive published journals, see Ogden, *Snake Country Journals, 1824-25 and 1825-26*; Ogden, *Peter Snake Country Journal, 1826-27*; Ogden, *Snake Country Journals, 1827-28 and 1828-29*. For a general overview of Ogden, see Williams, "Ogden Peter Skene."

16. Morgan, *West of William H. Ashley*, 129–30, 183, 187; Chittenden, *American Fur Trade*, 1:296–304; "Official Documents. In Senate of the U. States—Feb. 9, 1829," *Daily National Intelligencer*, April 22, 1829. For raids in Salt Lake, see Bradley, "History of the Sioux," 136; Hamilton, *My Sixty Years on the Plains*, 89; Ferris, *Life in the Rocky Mountains*, 145.

17. McLoughlin, *Letters of John McLoughlin*, 296–99; Ogden, *Snake Country Journals, 1824-25 and 1825-26*, 19, 23, 34, 78–82, 218–29. See also Ogden, *Snake Country Journals, 1827-28 and 1828-29*, 19–20, 81–92. For Blackfoot plunder, see John Rowand to George Simpson, January 7, 1835, George Simpson Inward Correspondence, 1821–1860, fol. 100, D.5/4, HBCA.

18. Robert Campbell, "A Narrative of Col. Robert Campbell's Experiences in the Rocky Mountain Fur Trade from 1825 to 1835," ca. 1870, PSLFT, roll 3:1, p. 16; Ogden, *Traits of American-Indian Life and Character*, 24–25; Mackie, *Trading beyond the Mountains*, 108; West, *Last Indian War*, 25–29.

19. For 1827 meeting, see Morgan, *West of William H. Ashley*, 187–88; Beckwourth, *Life and Adventures*, 112–22; Morgan, *Jedediah Smith and the Opening of the West*, 290–94; Smyth, "Niitsitapi Trade," 409–12. Beckwourth's penchant for exaggeration and mythmaking make his memoir a problematic source, but other sources corroborate his claim to have traded with the Blackfoot. For more on using Beckwourth's writings as primary sources, see Blackhawk, *Violence over the Land*, 333; and Coleman, *Here Lies Hugh Glass*, 80–87. For subsequent Flathead clashes, see Morgan, *West of William H. Ashley*, 188; Morgan, *Jedediah Smith*, 290–94; Richard Grant, June 15, 1828, EHPJ, 1828-9, fol. 4v, B.60/a/26, HBCA; Grant, August 4, 1828, EHPJ, 1828-9, fol. 17, B.60/a/26, HBCA; Smyth, "Niitsitapi Trade," 409; Binnema, "Allegiances and Interests," 345.

20. John Rowand and George Linton, October 31, 1827, November 29, 1827, and February 3, 1828, EHPJ, 1827-8, fols. 29, 34v, and 46v, B.60/a/25, HBCA. See also Rowand and Linton, September 17, 1827, EHPJ, 1827-8, fols. 18v–19, B.60/a/25, HBCA. For the Piikanis' 1826 deception, see George Linton and John Rowand, November 17, 1826, EHPJ, 1826-7, fol. 19v, B.60/a/24, HBCA; Linton and Rowand, December 7, 1826, EHPJ, 1826-7, fols. 23–23v, B.60/a/24, HBCA. See also George Simpson, Report to Governor and Committee, July 25, 1827, fol. 24, D.4/90, HBCA.

21. Smyth, "Jacques Berger, Fur Trader," 39–50; Wishart, *Fur Trade of the American West*, 52–60; Graybill, *Red and the White*, 32–33; Mattison, "Kenneth McKenzie," 217–21.

22. Chittenden, *American Fur Trade*, 1:335–36; Bradley, "Bradley Manuscript, Book F," 244–50. Kipp's narrative emphasized his own skill and bravery, and may well have exaggerated the Kainai "siege," which was not mentioned in sources from the time.

23. For Assiniboines, see Maximilian, *North American Journals*, 393–97, 508; Bradley, "Bradley Manuscript, Book F," 249–50; Richard Grant and [unnamed] Small, December 8, 1832, EHPJ, 1832–3, fols. 27v–28, B.60/a/27, HBCA; Audobon, *Audobon and His Journals*, 2:133–36; Kenneth McKenzie to Samuel Tulloch, January 8, 1834, Fort Union Letterbook, October 28, 1833 to December 10, 1835, PSLFT, roll 1:22, p. 33; DeMallie and Miller, "Assiniboine," 572. The autumn 1832 siege, or possibly an Assiniboine attack on Fort Piegan the previous year, may have been referenced by Charles "Rondi" Mercier in William F. Wheeler, "Personal Histories of Early Pioneers of Chouteau County, Mont.," 1884, William F. Wheeler Papers, MC 65, p. 4, MHS. For the 1834 massacre of Gros Ventres, see Bradley, "Affairs at Fort Benton," 210; Denig, *Five Indian Tribes*, 77. The same event is probably mentioned in Larpenteur, *Forty Years a Fur Trader* (1933), 76–77; and De Smet, *Life, Letters and Travels*, 3:1126. For Crows, see Bradley, "Affairs at Fort Benton," 210–16; Audobon, *Audobon and His Journals*, 2:179–80.

24. For 1833 row, see Maximilian, *Travels in the Interior*, 127–39; Harriott, October 11 and December 17, 1833, Bow River (Piegan Post) Post Journal, 1833–4, fols. 5, 10, B.21/a/1, HBCA; December 22, 1833, EHPJ, 1833–4, fol. 28v, B.60/a/28, HBCA; Rowand to Gov., Chief Factors, and Chief Traders, January 10, 1834, Governor George Simpson Inward Correspondence Books, p. 118, D.4/126, HBCA; Kipp to McKenzie, September 5, 1834, PSLFT, roll 1:23, pp. 2–3. For 1840 fight, see Rowand to James Hargrave, July 8, 1840, in Hargrave, *Hargrave Correspondence*, 317.

25. For HBC concerns and envoys, see George Simpson to Governor and Committee, July 18, 1831, Official Reports to Governor and Committee, 1831, fols. 31v–33v, D.4/98, HBCA. Colpitts, "Provisioning the HBC," 203; Richard Grant and [unknown] Small, June 4, 1832, EHPJ, 1832–3, fol. 2v, B.60/a/27, HBCA. For Piegan Post, see John Harriott, December 8, 1833, Bow Fort (Piegan Post) Post Journal, 1833–4, fol. 9, B.21/a/1, HBCA; George Simpson to Governor and Committee, July 21, 1834, Official Reports to Governor and Committee, 1834, fol. 18, D.4/100, HBCA; MacLeod, "Piegan Post and the Blackfoot Trade," 273–79.

26. John Rowand to George Simpson, January 7, 1835, George Simpson Inward Correspondence, 1821–1860, fol. 99v, D.5/4, HBCA; Rowand to Simpson, January 5, 1840, George Simpson Inward Correspondence, 1821–1860, fol. 223, D.5/5, HBCA; Simpson to Governor and Committee, June 10, 1835, Reports to Governor and Committee, 1835, fols. 38–39, D.4/102, HBCA; Rowand to John Hargrave, June 20, 1843, in Hargrave, *Hargrave Correspondence*, 441. For Blackfoot traders using similar tactics with American traders, see Maximilian, *North American Journals*, 403. For HBC price increases elsewhere, see Colpitts, "Provisioning the HBC," 190–203.

27. Maximilian, *North American Journals*, 362; James Kipp to Kenneth McKenzie, September 5, 1834, PSLFT, roll 1:23, pp. 1–2; Unknown author, January 23, 1837, Rocky Mountain House Post Journal, 1836–7, fols. 11–12, B.184/a/4, HBCA. John Rowand noted that Blackfoot people felt free to be "troublesome" at HBC posts once Americans arrived. Rowand to Simpson, January 1, 1844, George Simpson Inward Correspondence, 1821–1860, fol. 11, D.5/10, HBCA.

28. For alcohol on North Saskatchewan, see Henry, *Journal of Alexander Henry the Younger*, 2:535; M'Gillivray, "Some Account of the Trade," 68–69. For U.S. prohibi-

tions, see Unrau, *White Man's Wicked Water*, 17–22. For American attempts to circumvent law, see Wischmann, *Frontier Diplomats*, 127–40; Barbour, *Fort Union and the Upper Missouri Fur Trade*, 167–75. After 1834, I will refer to this outfit as Chouteau and Company. For an overview of the company's reformations, see Lecompte, "Chouteaus," xix–xx.

29. Dobak, "Killing the Canadian Buffalo," 41; Ray, *Indians in the Fur Trade*, 210–12; Bradley, "Bradley Manuscript, Book II," 156. Alternately, Charles Larpenteur reported that nine thousand robes were collected at Fort McKenzie in 1835, in Larpenteur, *Forty Years a Fur Trader* (1898), 79n. For more on the switch from beaver to bison robes, see Unknown author to Alexander Culbertson, May 5, 1835, Fort Union Letterbook, October 28, 1833 to December 10, 1835, PSLFT, roll 1:22, p. 68.

30. Rowand to Simpson, January 7, 1835, George Simpson Inward Correspondence, 1821–1860, fol. 99, D.5/4, HBCA; John Harriott to Simpson, August 23, 1847, George Simpson Inward Correspondence, 1821–1860, fol. 135v, D.5/20, HBCA.

31. For fears of Crees, see John Rowand to George Simpson, March 1, 1823, George Simpson Inward Correspondence Book, 1822–3, fol. 28, D.4/117, HBCA; George Simpson to Governor and Committee, July 18, 1831, Official Reports to Governor and Committee, 1831, fol. 32, D.4/98, HBCA. For summer 1835 trade, see Rowand to Simpson, December 31, 1835, George Simpson Inward Correspondence, 1821–1860, pp. 143–44, D.5/4, HBCA; Unknown author, July 25, 1836, Carlton House (Saskatchewan) Post Journal, 1836–7, fol. 6v, B.27/a/22, HBCA; Unknown author, October 1, 1836 to March 6, 1837, Rocky Mountain House Post Journal, 1836–7, fols. 2–14v, B.184/a/4, HBCA. For other examples, see Unknown author, July 4, 1833, EHPJ, 1833–4, fol. 4, B.60/a/28, HBCA; Rowand to Simpson, December 30, 1845, George Simpson Inward Correspondence, 1821–1860, fols. 623–623v, D.5/15, HBCA.

32. Fenn, *Encounters*, 311–25; Chardon, *Chardon's Journal at Fort Clark*, 123–81; Bradley, "Affairs at Fort Benton," 221–25.

33. Bradley, "Affairs at Fort Benton," 221–26; Wischmann, *Frontier Diplomats*, 67–76; Ewers, *Blackfeet*, 66; Siebelt, *Die Winter Counts Der Blackfoot*, 397. For examples of abandoned lodges, see Kane, *Paul Kane's Frontier*, 82; Point, *Wilderness Kingdom*, 171. For more on the 1837 smallpox epidemic that devastated the northern plains, see Daschuk, *Clearing the Plains*, 66–69; Fenn, *Encounters*, 311–25; Trimble, *Ethnohistorical Interpretation*.

34. Daschuk, *Clearing the Plains*, 66–69; De Smet, *Life, Letters and Travels*, 3:1187; John Rowand to James Hargrave, December 31, 1838, in Hargrave, *Hargrave Correspondence*, 273; Denig, *Five Indian Tribes*, 38. See also Joe Little Chief, "From 1830 the Year Crowfoot Was Born," pp. 2–3, Joe Little Chief Fonds, M-4394-18, GMA.

35. J. A. Hamilton to Pierre Chouteau Jr., February 25, 1838, PSLFT, roll 1:25, pp. 2–3; Ramsay Crooks to Chouteau, March 4, 1838, PSLFT, roll 1:25, p. 2; Bradley, "Bradley Manuscript, Book II," 156.

36. Lecompte, "Chouteaus," xx; Chittenden, *American Fur Trade*, 2:626–27; Sunder, *Fur Trade on the Upper Missouri*, 16–19; Wishart, *Fur Trade of the American West*, 161–66; Dolin, *Fur, Fortune, and Empire*, 279–93; Lecompte, "Pierre Chouteau, Junior," 108–19.

37. For Rowand's complaints, see Rowand to Simpson, January 5, 1840, George Simpson Inward Correspondence, 1821–1860, p. 223, D.5/5, HBCA. For Simpson's visit, see Simpson, *Overland Journey round the World*, 70–71; Peers and Brown, *Visiting with the Ancestors*, 35–38. For the importance of clothing, see Hanson, "Laced Coats and Leather Jackets," 105–17.

38. For an overview of family life at Edmonton and neighboring posts, see Ens and Binnema, *Edmonton House Journals, 1806–1821*, 65–66, 74–80. For American marriages and spellings, see Wischmann, *Frontier Diplomats*, 45, 85–95; Ewers, *Indian Life on the Upper Missouri*, 61–62; Graybill, *Red and the White*, 45–53; Bradley, "Affairs at Fort Benton," 247.

39. See also Lansing, "Plains Indian Women and Interracial Marriage," 413–33; Graybill, *Red and the White*, 48–50. For examples of Medicine Snake Woman's diplomatic reputation specifically, see Wischmann, *Frontier Diplomats*, 222–24, 255–59; Isaac Stevens, Report of Explorations, September 16, 1854, *ARCIA*, 1854, 403–4.

40. Bradley, "Affairs at Fort Benton," 235–39; Larpenteur, *Forty Years a Fur Trader* (1933), 187–93; Kane, *Paul Kane's Frontier*, 149; Wischmann, *Frontier Diplomats*, 106–17; Graybill, *Red and the White*, 76–77; Ewers, *Blackfeet*, 66–67.

41. Bradley, "Affairs at Fort Benton," 240–44; John Harriott to George Simpson, May 1, 1845, George Simpson Inward Correspondence, 1821–1860, fol. 7v, D.5/14, HBCA; Wischmann, *Frontier Diplomats*, 114–26; McDonnell, "Fort Benton Journal," 63; "Many Guns' Winter Count," folder 1, box 1, Tom Many Guns Family Fonds, PR0185, Provincial Archives of Alberta, Edmonton.

42. Aron and Adelman, "From Borderlands to Borders," 814–41. For Haudenosaunee borderlands, see Wallace, *Death and Rebirth of the Seneca*, 111–14; Alan Taylor, *Divided Ground*. For the colonial Southwest, see Hämäläinen, *Comanche Empire*; Delay, *War of a Thousand Deserts*; Barr, "Geographies of Power," 5–46. For Quapaws and Osages, see DuVal, *Native Ground*. For more on borderlands historiography, see Hämäläinen and Samuel Truett, "On Borderlands"; Johnson and Graybill, "Borders and Their Historians."

43. In his study of the Teton Sioux and the fur trade, Kurt Anderson argues that the Sioux became beholden to an unseen and "unimagined global economy" that gave them "illusions of independence." Like the Sioux, the Blackfoot indeed became increasingly dependent on access to European goods but were far from delusional about the vital role of exchange in their lives. Anderson, "Illusions of Independence." For more on dependency theory and Native Americans, see R. White, *Roots of Dependency*. In a similar vein, Alan Michael Klein has argued that plains people, including the Blackfoot, assumed the role of a "proletariat" class during the fur trade era, thus ceding economic agency to the capitalist class. Klein, "Adaptive Strategies."

Chapter Five

1. Joe Little Chief, "From 1830 the Year Crowfoot Was Born," p. 4, Joe Little Chief Fonds, M-4394-18, GMA.

2. On colonialisms, see Shoemaker, "Typology of Colonialism," 29–30; Eckstrom and Jacobs, "Teaching American History," 259–72; Faragher, "Commentary," 181–91.

3. Ewers, *Gustavus Sohon's Portraits*, 54–57; E. White, "Worlds in Collision," 26–45; Malouf, "Flathead and Pend d'Oreille," 306; Cebula, *Plateau Indians*, 92–98. A Methodist named Robert Rundle operated a mission at Edmonton between 1840 and 1847, but despite attracting some curiosity, he gained less traction among Blackfoot people than did the Jesuits. Rundle, *Rundle Journals*, xxv–xxix, 54, 129, 240–42, 263–71; John Rowand to George Simpson, January 9, 1841, George Simpson Inward Correspondence, 1821–1860, fols. 19–19v, D.5/6, HBCA.

4. Peterson with Peers, *Sacred Encounters*, 83–116; Wischmann, *Frontier Diplomats*, 141–60; Harrod, *Mission among the Blackfeet*, 19–38; Point, *Wilderness Kingdom*, 180–212; McClintock, *Old North Trail*, 154–61. There is some disagreement about whether the Small Robes, or Inaksis, were a large Piikani band or actually constituted an entirely separate nation. The Small Robes suffered devastating losses in a battle with the Crows in 1846 and lived on in a much-reduced state. See LaPier, *Invisible Reality*, 6–7, 48; Ewers, *Blackfeet*, 185–89.

5. Bradley, "Oregon Trail," 337–40; Alexander Culbertson to D. D. Mitchell, ca. 1851, RCSIA, roll 3, pp. 3–6.

6. Bad Head, "Bad Head's Winter Count," p. 4, R. N. Wilson Fonds, M-4421, GMA; Bradley, "Affairs at Fort Benton," 257; Bradley, "Bradley Manuscript, Book II," 156; Overholser, *Fort Benton*, 30. For population of warriors, see Doty to Stevens, December 20, 1854, pp. 1–2, Claude Schaeffer Fonds, M-1100-145, GMA. Edwin Hatch noted in 1856 that some Siksika groups continued to avoid American posts for more than a decade after Chardon's atrocity. Hatch to Alfred Cumming, July 12, 1856, *ARCIA, 1856*, 76.

7. Culbertson to Stevens, ca. 1853, RWSIA, roll 22, pp. 1–2; Bradley, "Bradley Manuscript, Book II," 156; Stevens to Commission, September 28, 1855, LR:OIA, roll 30, p. 8; J. M. Stanley, "Report of Mr. J. M. Stanley's Visit to the Piegan Camp, at the Cypress Mountain," in U.S. Department of War, *Report of Explorations and Surveys* (1855), 449; quote from Doty to Stevens, December 20, 1854, p. 5, M-1100-145, Claude E. Schaeffer Fonds, GMA. For a description of bison robes, see Clayton, "Growth and Economic Significance," 210–11. For Blackfoot wintering grounds at mid-century, see James H. Bradley Papers, p. 179, MC49, MHS.

8. For alcohol in the north, see John Rowand to George Simpson, December 8, 1852, George Simpson Inward Correspondence, 1821–1860, fol. 281, D.5/35, HBCA; Culbertson to Stevens, ca. 1853, RWSIA, roll 22, p. 1; Doty to Stevens, December 29, 1853, in Department of War, *Reports of Explorations and Surveys* (1855), 444. For British traders' worries about Americans, see Harriott to Simpson, May 1, 1845, George Simpson Inward Correspondence, 1821–1860, fols. 7–7v, D.5/14, HBCA; Harriott to Simpson, January 5, 1848, George Simpson Inward Correspondence, 1821–1860, fol. 34v, D.5/21, HBCA; Rowand to Simpson, December 30, 1848, George Simpson Inward Correspondence, 1821–1860, fol. 548, D.5/23, HBCA; Gladstone, *Gladstone Diary*, 17–26. For tallow, see Colpitts, "Provisioning the HBC," 198–99.

9. Culbertson to Stevens, ca. 1853, RWSIA, roll 22, pp. 1–3. See also Alexander Culbertson to D. D. Mitchell, ca. 1851, RCSIA, roll 3, p. 5. For conflicts with Crows, see Hoxie, *Parading through History*, 67, 72–73, 87; Bradley, "Affairs at Fort Benton," 261–63; Culbertson to Mitchell, ca. 1851, RCSIA, roll 3, pp. 3–5. For Assiniboines,

see Culbertson to Mitchell, ca. 1851, RCSIA, roll 3, pp. 3-4; Elwood Evans, October 11, 1853, pp. 25-26, Journal and Notes Kept by Elwood Evans, box 1, folder 1, Elwood Evans Papers, WA MSS 172, BRBL; Report of Alfred D. Vaughn, September 20, 1853, *ARCIA, 1853*, 76; Vaughn to Alfred Cumming, October 19, 1854, *ARCIA, 1854*, 289-90; Denig, *Five Indian Tribes*, 93-94. For more on the Plains Assiniboines' move southward, see DeMallie and Miller, "Assiniboine," 572-75. For Flatheads, see Elwood Evans, October 11, 1853, pp. 34-36, Journal and Notes Kept by Elwood Evans, box 1, folder 1, Elwood Evans Papers, WA MSS 172, BRBL.

10. Philip Godsell, ed., "Life and Adventures of Red Crow," pp. 141-50, R. N. Wilson Fonds, M-4421, GMA; Dempsey, *Red Crow*, 17-28.

11. West, *Way to the West*, 51-79; Isenberg, *Destruction of the Bison*, 93-122; Flores, "Bison Ecology and Bison Diplomacy," 482-85; Dobak, "Killing the Canadian Buffalo," 33-52.

12. For conflicts with mountain nations, see Pierre De Smet to H. H. Harvey, December 4, 1848, LR:OIA, roll 884, pp. 1-3; De Smet to Directors of the Association, June 10, 1849, in De Smet, *Western Missions and Missionaries*, 1:54; Wilkes, *United States Exploring Expedition*, 474. For conflicts in the east, see Alfred Vaughan, Report on Upper Missouri Agency, October 19, 1854, *ARCIA, 1854*, 290-91; De Smet to Bishop Hughes, April 16, 1846, in De Smet, *Life, Letters and Travels*, 2:533; Cowie, *Company of Adventurers*, 305-6; Isenberg, *Destruction of the Bison*, 111-13; Dobak, "Killing the Canadian Buffalo," 47-48. For Lakota intrusions, see De Smet to Directors of the Association, June 10, 1849, in De Smet, *Western Missions and Missionaries*, 1:52; Doty to Stevens, December 20, 1854, pp. 6-7, Claude Schaeffer Fonds, GMA; Edward Shelley, October 27 and November 1, 1862, pp. 107 and 109, "Diary of Travels in North America," WA MSS S-1908, BRBL; and John Healy, "The First Sioux Invasion," *Benton Record*, August 30, 1878. See also R. White, "Winning of the West," 331-38. Kainai elder Wilton Goodstriker wrote that the Kainais and Sioux made a treaty in 1810 that established the Cypress Hills as a boundary between the two groups. Treaty 7 Elders et al., *True Spirit and Original Intent of Treaty 7*, 7.

13. For 1854-55 starvation, see December 3, 1854, EHPJ, 1854-5, fol. 6v, B.60/a/29a, HBCA; Teddy Yellow Fly, "Teddy Yellow Fly's Winter Count," p. 3, Teddy Yellow Fly Fonds, M-4423, GMA; Bad Head, "Bad Head's Winter Count," p. 6, R. N. Wilson Fonds, M-4421, GMA; Houghton Running Rabbit, "Houghton Running Rabbit's Winter Count," p. 3, Houghton Running Rabbit Fonds, M-4233, GMA; Joe Little Chief, "From 1830 the Year Crowfoot was Born," p. 4, Joe Little Chief Fonds, M-4394-18, GMA; Tom Many Guns, "Many Guns' Winter Count," folder 1, box 1, p. 1, Tom Many Guns Family Fonds, PR0185, Provincial Archives of Alberta, Edmonton. Starvation that winter occurred among Siksika and northern Kainai bands that did not attend the treaty council, and not among the Kainai and Piikani bands that constituted most of the 1855 signatories. Doty to Blackfoot Council Commission, September 19, 1855, in Documents Relating to the Negotiation of Ratified and Unratified Treaties with Various Tribes of Indians, 1801-69, RG 75, Records of the Bureau of Indian Affairs, T494, NAMP, roll 5, p. 13. No extant Piikani winter counts mark it as a starvation year, nor did that of Iron Shirt, a Kainai, in McClintock, *Old North Trail*, 422. Traders at Fort Benton met regularly with Piikani and Kainai parties during the winter of 1854-55 and

made no mention of starvation, in McDonnell, "Fort Benton Journal," 3–27. For declining bison populations in neighboring regions, see Culbertson to Stevens, ca. 1853, RWSIA, roll 22, p. 1; Doty to Stevens, December 20, 1854, p. 5, Claude Schaeffer Fonds, M-1100-145, GMA; Hatch, Report of Blackfeet Agency, July 12, 1856, *ARCIA, 1856*, 76; Bradley, "Bradley Manuscript, Book II," 156; Stevens to Commission, September 28, 1855, LR:OIA, roll 30, p. 5. For the Charming the Buffalo song, see LaPier, *Invisible Reality*, 77–78.

14. For formal agreements, see Dempsey, *Great Blackfoot Treaties*, 16–30. For neutral ground, see Farr, "'When We Were First Paid,'" 140; Colpitts, "Peace, War, and Climate Change," 420–41; Palliser, *Exploration—British North America*, 53–54.

15. Flores, "Bison Ecology and Bison Diplomacy," 483; Denig, *Five Indian Tribes*, 91–93.

16. Ewers, *Blackfeet*, 208–10; Isaac Stevens, "Narrative of 1853," in U.S. Department of War, *Reports of Explorations and Surveys* (1860), 115.

17. Stevens, "Narrative of 1853," 116; Stevens to Manypenny, September 16, 1854, *ARCIA, 1854*, 409–11; Elwood Evans, October 11, 1853, Journal and Notes Kept by Elwood Evans while a Member of the Northern Pacific Railroad Expedition, folder 1, box 1, pp. 35–36, Elwood Evans Papers, WA MSS 172, BRBL; James Doty to Stevens, December 20, 1854, p. 11, Claude Schaeffer Fonds, M-1100-145, GMA.

18. For more on midcentury expansion, see Merk, *Manifest Destiny and Mission*; W. Nugent, *Habits of Empire*, 187–236; R. White, "*It's Your Misfortune*," 74–76; Hine and Faragher, *American West*, 159–233; Billington, *Westward Expansion*, 489–508; Trachtenberg, *Incorporation of America*, 11–37; Howe, *What Hath God Wrought*, 701–836.

19. A. Hyde, *Empires, Nations, and Families*, 347–450; Faragher, *Women and Men on the Overland Trail*, 66–188; Unruh, *Plains Across*; West, *Contested Plains*, 115–72; Keyes, "Beyond the Plains."

20. Utley, *Indian Frontier of the American West*, 31–64; Richards, *Isaac I. Stevens*, 210. For Fort Laramie and Fort Atkinson Treaties, see R. White, "*It's Your Misfortune*," 90, 95; Hine and Faragher, *American West*, 217–18; Hämäläinen, *Comanche Empire*, 300–304.

21. Stevens, *Campaigns of the Rio Grande*, 107–8; Richards, *Isaac I. Stevens*, 9, 58, 75; Stevens, *Life of Isaac Ingalls Stevens*, 1:280.

22. Richards, *Isaac I. Stevens*, 13–103. For more on patronage in western territorial politics, see Lamar, *Dakota Territory*, esp. 123–26.

23. Stevens, "Narrative of 1853," 31; Farr, "When We Were First Paid," 135–39.

24. Manypenny to Cumming, Stevens and Joel Palmer, May 3, 1855, *ARCIA, 1855*, 531; Hazard Stevens, *Life of Isaac Ingalls Stevens*, 1:297.

25. Stevens, "Narrative of 1853," 116; Partoll, "Blackfoot Indian Peace Council," 6; Stevens to Manypenny, September 16, 1854, *ARCIA, 1854*, 415; Stevens to Commission, September 28, 1855, LR:OIA, roll 30, pp. 1–5.

26. Ewers, *Blackfeet*, 205–7. For conflicts with plains nations, see Alfred Vaughan, Report on Upper Missouri Agency, September 20, 1853, *ARCIA, 1853*, 357. For conflicts with mountain nations, see John Mullan to Stevens, November 18, 1853, folder 36, box 1, pp. 1–5, Isaac Ingalls Stevens Papers, 1848–1859, WA MSS 443, BRBL; Mullan to Stevens, January 25, 1854, folder 36, box 1, p. 5, Isaac Ingalls Stevens Papers,

1848–1859, WA MSS 443, BRBL; Culbertson to Mitchell, ca. 1851, RCSIA, roll 3, pp. 3–6.

27. *House Journal*, 33rd Cong., 1st Sess. (1854), 564; *Congressional Globe*, 33rd Cong., 1st Sess. (1854), April 24, 1854, 972–79; Culbertson to Stevens, December 26, 1853, U.S. Office of Indian Affairs Records, 1853–1875, SC 1280, MHS; Bradley, "Affairs at Fort Benton," 269–70; Manypenny to R. McClelland, November 25, 1854, *ARCIA, 1854,* 223; Wischmann, *Frontier Diplomats,* 224–33.

28. James Doty, Minutes of Official Proceedings of the Commissioners, August 15, 1855, LR:OIA, roll 30, p. 1; Stevens and Cumming to Manypenny, August 29, 1855, LR:OIA, roll 30, p. 1; Stevens to the Commission, September 18, 1855, LR:OIA, roll 30, p. 1; Cumming to the Commission, September 19, 1855, LR:OIA, roll 30, p. 1; Stevens to the Commission, September 28, 1855, LR:OIA, roll 30, p. 8; Thomas Adams to Cumming and Stevens, October 2, 1855, LR:OIA, roll 30, p. 2; Stevens and Cumming, Official Report to Manypenny, October 22, 1855, LR:OIA, roll 30, pp. 8–9.

29. Isaac Stevens and Alfred Cumming to Commissioner George Manypenny, October 22, 1855, LR:OIA, roll 30, p. 7; Kennerly, "1855 Blackfeet Treaty Council," 48–50; Claude Schaeffer, "Biographies of Blackfoot Leaders," pp. 57–65, 72–80, 101–24, Claude E. Schaeffer Fonds, M-1100-150, GMA. Some historians have noted that treaty commissioners often identified pro-treaty leaders as "head chiefs" to facilitate councils. Some Blackfoot oral histories similarly indicate that Lame Bull was selected despite not being the most powerful Piegan at the time (Green Grass Bull interview by Claude Schaeffer, April 23, 1951, book 10, p. 23, Claude E. Schaeffer Field Notebooks, M-1100-168, GMA; and Juniper Old Person interview by Schaeffer, November 27, 1951, book 11, pp. 51–52, Claude E. Schaeffer Field Notebooks, M-1100-168, GMA.). However, most contemporary sources indicate that Lame Bull was the most prominent chief among the Piikanis. Furthermore, his foremost contemporaries—Little Dog, Mountain Chief, and Low Horn—also supported and signed the treaty of 1855, so selective recognition of Indian leadership cannot explain the treaty.

30. Isaac Stevens and Alfred Cumming to Commissioner George Manypenny, October 22, 1855, LR:OIA, roll 30, p. 7; Edwin Hatch, October 12, 1855, Edwin A. C. Hatch Diary, 1855–6, Ayer MS 3060, Newberry Library, Chicago, p. 280.

31. Partoll, "Blackfoot Indian Peace Council," 3–4; Kennerly, "1855 Blackfeet Treaty Council," 50; Stevens, *Life of Isaac Ingalls Stevens,* 2:116–17.

32. Partoll, "Blackfoot Indian Peace Council," 4–6.

33. Farr, "'When We Were First Paid,'" 132–39; Partoll, "Blackfoot Indian Peace Council," 6–8.

34. Treaty between the United States and the Blackfoot and Other Tribes of Indians, October 17, 1855, LR:OIA, roll 30.

35. Culbertson to D. D. Mitchell, ca. 1851, RCSIA, roll 3, p. 6; Alfred Vaughan, Report of Blackfeet Agency, July 24, 1859, *ARCIA, 1859,* 119; Wischmann, *Frontier Diplomats,* 269–98.

36. For 1853 gifts, see Stevens, "Narrative of 1853," 12:116; J. M. Stanley, "Report of Mr. J. M. Stanley's Visit to the Piegan Camp, at the Cypress Mountain," in *Report of Explorations and Surveys* (1855), 447. For 1855 gifts and distribution, see Bradley,

"Affairs at Fort Benton," 274–75; Ewers, *Blackfeet*, 214; Kennerly, "1855 Blackfeet Treaty Council," 50; Vaughan, Report of Blackfeet Agency, September 10, 1858, *ARCIA, 1858*, 77–78.

37. Hatch, October 19, 1855, Edwin A. C. Hatch Diary, 1855-6, p. 292; Kennerly, "1855 Blackfeet Treaty Council," 50; Bradley, "Affairs at Fort Benton," 274–75; Frank Monroe, "My Father's Trapping," folder 23, box 5, James Willard Schultz Papers, Collection 2307, Merrill G. Burlingame Special Collections, Montana State University, Bozeman, pp. 3–4.

38. Stevens to "Dear Mother," October 22, 1855, p. 1, Isaac Ingalls Stevens Letters, 1855–1861, WA MSS S-192, BRBL; Stevens, "Narrative of 1855," in Department of War, *Reports of Explorations and Surveys* (1860), 222.

39. Vaughan, Report of Blackfeet Agency, August 31, 1860, *ARCIA, 1860*, 85. For peace with Flatheads, see John Owen to Stevens, May 11, 1856, RWSIA, roll 22, p. 5. See also R. H. Lansdale to Stevens, April 1, 1856, RWSIA, roll 22, p. 3; McDonnell, "Fort Benton Journal, 1854–1856," 72, 98. For conflict with Crees and Assiniboines, see Edwin Hatch, Report on Blackfeet Agency, July 12, 1856, *ARCIA, 1856*, 75–76; Alfred Vaughan to A. M. Robinson, September 10, 1858, *ARCIA, 1858*, 81; Chambers, "Fort Sarpy Journal, 1855–1856," 157, 164–65; April 27, 1859, EHPJ, 1858–60, B.60/a/30, HBCA, 97; William Christie to Governor, Chief Factors, and Chief Traders, January 2, 1860, fol. 27v, D.5.51, George Simpson Loose Inward Correspondence, HBCA. In September 1855, a Piikani party visited Edmonton House and made a "compact of peace" with Cree leaders, but it is unclear how long this peace lasted, or if it extended to Kainai and Siksika bands as well. September 29, 1855, EHPJ, 1855-6, fol. 1v, B.60/a/29a, HBCA.

40. James Bradley, "Bradley Manuscript, Book II," 155–56; Kautz, "From Missouri to Oregon in 1860," 206.

41. For Lame Bull, see Edwin Hatch, September 20, 1856, Edwin A. C. Hatch Diary, 1856, SC 810, MHS, p. 17; "Scarce Article," *Peoria Daily Transcript*, November 6, 1857; Klett, "Missionary Endeavors of the Presbyterian Church," 343, emphasis in original. For negotiation of goods, see Vaughan to Cumming, August 29, 1857, *ARCIA, 1857*, 122. For Little Dog's farm, see Vaughan to A. B. Greenwood, August 31, 1860, *ARCIA, 1860*, 83; Henry Reed to W. Jayne, October 1, 1862, *ARCIA, 1862*, 180–81. Outsiders generally assumed they were incapable or uninterested in farming, but in fact many northern plains nations zealously pursued agricultural knowledge, especially after bison populations declined. See Carter, *Lost Harvests*, 36–78.

42. Ewers, *Blackfeet*, 223; Richards, *Isaac I. Stevens*, 387.

Chapter Six

1. Charles P. Chouteau, "Charles P. Chouteau Report, 1859," pp. 1–4, SC 532, MHS; Alfred J. Vaughan, Report of Blackfoot Agency, July 24, 1859, *ARCIA, 1859*, 115–16; Chittenden, *Early Steamboat Navigation*, 1:216–19; Sunder, *Fur Trade on the Upper Missouri*, 202–7.

2. Hill, *Office of Indian Affairs*, 1–3, 17; Prucha, *Great Father*, chs. 7–8; Utley, *Indian Frontier of the American West*, ch. 2.

3. For superintendencies, see Hill, *Office of Indian Affairs*, 17; William Dole to H. B. Branch, April 12, 1862, RCSIA, roll 14, pp. 1–2; Dole to William Jayne, April 12, 1862, Records of the Dakota Superintendency of Indian Affairs, RG 75, Records of the Bureau of Indian Affairs, M1016, NAMP, roll 1, pp. 1–2. For Vaughan, see Ewers, *Blackfeet*, 234; William Dole to A. M. Robinson, April 25, 1861, RCSIA, roll 11, pp. 1–2.

4. Chittenden, *Early Steamboat Navigation*, 1:220–21; Hill, *Office of Indian Affairs*, 17–18; Ewers, *Blackfeet*, 237; John Mason Brown to Frank Blair, June 30, 1862, LR:OIA, roll 30, p. 1; Gad Upson, Report of Blackfoot Agency, September 1, 1864, *ARCIA*, *1864*, 293; H. B. Branch, Report of Central Superintendency, October 22, 1861, *ARCIA*, *1861*, 50.

5. William Hamilton, "Council at Fort Benton," *Forest and Stream* 68, no. 17 (April 27, 1907): 4; Frederick Wilson and Benjamin Arnold to Alfred Sully, May 4, 1866, folder 57, box 3, Alfred Sully Papers, p. 1, WA MSS S-1311, BRBL; Gladstone, *Gladstone Diary*, 81.

6. Malone, Roeder, and Lang, *Montana*, 64–71; Hoxie, *Parading through History*, 88–89; Farr, "Going to Buffalo, Part 2," 28; Graybill, *Red and the White*, 85–89; Milner and O'Connor, *As Big as the West*, 57–59, 69–101.

7. "Gold on the Missouri," *Nor'Wester*, May 12, 1863; "Saskatchean Gold District," *Nor'Wester*, September 14, 1861; "Gold in the Rocky Mountains," *Nor'Wester*, January 22, 1862; "Important Gold News from the Interior," *Nor'Wester*, March 5, 1862; "Information for Miners," *Nor'Wester*, May 28, 1862.

8. For miners north of the border, see April 22, 1865; May 5, 1865; and July 3, 1865, all in Edmonton Post Journal, 1864–5, fols. 15, 16v, and 23, B.60/a/34, HBCA; "From Red River," *Globe*, January 14, 1864; "The Saskatchewan," *Nor'Wester*, December 20, 1865. For Blackfoot worries, see Henry Reed, Report of Blackfeet Agency, October 1, 1862, *ARCIA*, *1862*, 179. For Fort Benton, see Ewers, *Blackfeet*, 236–38; Wischmann, *Frontier Diplomats*, 307–8.

9. Wischmann, *Frontier Diplomats*, 307–8; Sunder, *Fur Trade on the Upper Missouri*, 260–63; Lass, "History and Significance," 24–40. See also Klein, "Adaptive Strategies," 467–76.

10. Ewers, *Indian Life on the Upper Missouri*, 61–62; Isaac Stevens, Report of Explorations, September 16, 1854, *ARCIA*, *1854*, 403–4; Wischmann, *Frontier Diplomats*, 93–94, 222–24, 255–59, 273. See also Lansing, "Plains Indian Women," 413–33.

11. James Vail to Gad Upson, December 26, 1863, LR:OIA, roll 30, pp. 1–2; Gad Upson, Report of Blackfeet Agency, September 1, 1864, *ARCIA*, *1864*, 293; Bradley, "Bradley Manuscript, Book II," 147–48; Tovías, "Diplomacy and Contestation," 275–80.

12. For "black pox," see Crooked Meat Strings interview by Jane Richardson, August 8–10, 1938, Lucien and Jane Hanks Fonds, series 1, p. 259, M-8458, GMA; Houghton Running Rabbit, Winter Count, p. 2, Houghton Running Rabbit Fonds, M-4233, GMA; Joe Little Chief, "From 1830 the Year Crowfoot was Born," p. 5, Joe Little Chief Fonds, M-4394, GMA. U.S. agent Gad Upson identified the disease as measles, but HBC traders identified the illness as scarlet fever, as has historian James Daschuk. Upson, Report of Blackfeet Agency, October 2, 1865, *ARCIA*, *1865*, 511–12; March 24, 1865, EHPJ, 1864–5, fol. 58, B.60/a/34, HBCA; Daschuk, *Clearing the Plains*,

77. For estimates of deaths, see March 24, 1865, EHPJ, 1864–5, fol. 58, B.60/a/34, HBCA. Upson heard reports of 1,780 deaths, though he expected the actual total was slightly less. Upson, Report of Blackfeet Agency, October 2, 1865, *ARCIA, 1865,* 511–12. U.S. officials estimated Blackfoot population to be between 5,800 and 7,600 in the decade prior to the outbreak. The epidemic therefore took between 14 and 31 percent of Blackfoot lives. Alfred Vaughan, "Memorandum of the Census, Wealth &c. of the Blackfeet Indians," July 4, 1860, RCSIA, roll 9, p. 1; Edwin Hatch to Alfred Cumming, December 25, 1855, LR:OIA, roll 30, p. 1. For Blackfoot blaming of whites, see March 28, 1865, EHPJ, 1864–5, fol. 59, B.60/a/34, HBCA; Upson, Report of Blackfeet Agency, October 2, 1865, *ARCIA, 1865,* 511–12; James O'Neil, Report of Nez Percé Agency, August 3, 1865, *ARCIA, 1865,* 240.

13. For April raid, see Gad Upson, Report of Blackfeet Agency, October 2, 1865, *ARCIA, 1865,* 511; "Items from Last Chance and Prickly Pear," *Montana Post,* May 20, 1865, 4. "Danger from Indians," *Montana Post,* May 20, 1865, 4. For May murders, see "Particulars of the Massacre at the Marias," *Montana Post,* July 8, 1865; Gad Upson, Report of Blackfeet Agency, October 2, 1865, *ARCIA, 1865,* 511.

14. For Ophir raid, see Gad Upson, Report of Blackfeet Agency, October 2, 1865, *ARCIA, 1865,* 511; Bradley, "Bradley Manuscript, Book II," 144–46; Bradley, "Blackfoot War with the Whites," 252–55. Calf Shirt's party may also have sought revenge for the killing of two Kainai horse raiders by hunters the previous December. For white reactions, see "The Indian Troubles," *Montana Post,* June 10, 1865; "Indian Troubles on the Missouri," *Montana Post,* July 1, 1865; "The Indian War," *Montana Post,* June 10, 1865, transcript in box 1, folder 3, Granville Stuart Papers, WA MSS S-1120, BRBL; Gladstone, *Gladstone Diary,* 83; Shirley Ashby, "Story as Told by Col. S. C. Ashby," pp. 4–5, S. C. Ashby Papers, SC 283, MHS; Dempsey, *Amazing Death of Calf Shirt,* 54–55.

15. "The Indian War," *Montana Post,* July 8, 1865; Hine and Faragher, *American West,* 226–32; R. White, *"It's Your Misfortune,"* 94–102.

16. For chiefs' diplomacy, see "Particulars of the Massacre at the Marias," *Montana Post,* July 8, 1865; "The Indian War," *Montana Post,* June 10, 1865, transcript in box 1, folder 3, Granville Stuart Papers, WA MSS S-1120, BRBL; Utley, *Indian Frontier,* 72. For treaty planning, see D. N. Cooley to James Harlan, October 31, 1865, *ARCIA, 1865,* 31; "Official Announcement to Maj. G. E. Upson of His Nomination, and His Reply thereto," *Montana Post,* August 19, 1865; Wylie, *Irish General,* 238–39.

17. Meagher, "Some Letters," 86; Athearn, "Early Territorial Montana," 15–16; W. P. Dole to Gad Upson, March 24, 1865, *ARCIA, 1865,* 250–52; Bradley, "Bradley Manuscript, Book II," 132–33; Ewers, *Blackfeet,* 240.

18. Hamilton, "Council at Fort Benton," 5; "Treaty between the United States and the Blackfoot Nation of Indians, Etc., November 16, 1865."

19. For raids during and after council, see "Letter from Fort Benton," *Montana Post,* February 3, 1866; Hiram Upham, Report of Blackfeet Agency, July 25, 1866, *ARCIA, 1866,* 202; Upham to Upson, January 9, 1866, *ARCIA, 1866,* 199; Hiram Upham, "Affidavit in Regard to Indian Affairs," March 15, 1866, folder 2, box 1, Thomas Francis Meagher Papers, SC 309, MHS; William Christie (Fort Edmonton) to Colvin [illegible], February 27, 1866, and Christie (Fort Edmonton) to [illegible] March 5, 1866, both

in Edmonton Correspondence Book, 1864–8, pp. 393, 400–401, B.60/b/2, HBCA; "Letter from Fort Benton," *Montana Post*, February 3, 1866. For treaty's failure, see D. N. Cooley, Report of the Commissioner, October 22, 1866, *ARCIA, 1866*, 13–16, 40; D. N. Cooley to James Harlan, April 12, 1866, in Documents Relating to the Negotiation of an Unratified Treaty in July and September 1868, with the Gros Ventre, Blackfeet, Shoshoni, and Bannock Indians, RG 75, Documents Relating to the Negotiation of Ratified and Unratified Treaties with Various Tribes of Indians, 1801–69, T494, NAMP, roll 10, pp. 3–5.

20. For Blackfoot frustration, see W. J. Cullen, Report of Treaty, September 2, 1866, *ARCIA, 1868*, 222. For Meagher's expedition, see Bradley, "Blackfoot War," 252–55; "To His Excellency, Thomas Francis Meagher," *Montana Democrat*, February 1, 1866; Thomas Meagher, "Proclamation," *Montana Democrat*, February 1, 1866; "Indian Hunting," *Montana Post*, February 10, 1866; Augustus Chapman, Report of Flathead Agency, July 5, 1867, *ARCIA, 1867*, 259–60.

21. Hiram Upham, Report of Blackfeet Agency, July 25, 1866, *ARCIA, 1866*, 202–3; Palladino, *Indian and White in the Northwest*, 180–84; Father Joseph Giorda, "Indian Depredations," *Montana Post*, April 4, 1866.

22. "A Trip from Virginia to Fort Benton," *Montana Post*, June 9, 1866; Upham, Report of Blackfeet Agency, July 25, 1866, *ARCIA, 1866*, 203.

23. For American ban on alcohol, see Morgan, *West of William H. Ashley*, 33; Wischmann, *Frontier Diplomats*, 127–40; Unrau, *White Man's Wicked Water*, 17–22. For alcohol sales, see Gad Upson, Report of Blackfeet Agency, October 2, 1865, *ARCIA, 1865*, 514; Father Giorda to Gad Upson, January 22, 1864, LR:OIA, roll 30, p. 3.

24. For September killings, see George Wright, Report of Blackfeet Agency, July 5, 1867, *ARCIA, 1867*, 256–57. For Wright's attempted ban, see Thomas Francis Meagher, "Proclamation and Official Notice: To the Citizens of Fort Benton," 1867, BrSide4 Zc43 866mo, BRBL; "From Benton," *Montana Post*, May 25, 1867; George Wright to N. G. Taylor, March 5, 1868, LR:OIA, roll 30, p. 3.

25. For border crossing concerns, see Ashby, "Story," 4–5; George Wright, Report of Blackfeet Agency, August 30, 1866, *ARCIA, 1866*, 204; Gad Upson, Report of Blackfeet Agency, September 28, 1864, *ARCIA, 1864*, 300; Alfred Sully to J. T. McGinniss, January 3, 1870, in House of Representatives, *Piegan Indians: Letter from the Secretary of War*, 37. For a broader discussion of the Medicine Line and its use by Indigenous people, see LaDow, *Medicine Line*; Hogue, *Metis and the Medicine Line*; Hogue, "Disputing the Medicine Line"; Sharp, *Whoop-Up Country*; Rensink, *Native but Foreign*; Ens, "Border, Buffalo, and Métis"; McManus, *Line Which Separates*.

26. For tensions with HBC and Crees, see Palliser, *Exploration*, 8; Joe Brown and James Schultz, "In Fur Trade Days," *Forest and Stream* 51, no. 4 (July 23, 1898): 62; Southesk, *Saskatchewan and the Rocky Mountains*, 422–23; Hind, *Canadian Red River Exploring Expedition*, 2:126. For Old Sun's killing and aftermath, see Dempsey, *Red Crow*, 56–57; September 26, 1860, EHPJ, 1860–1, fol. 39, B.60/a/31, HBCA; Dempsey, *Crowfoot*, 45–46; February 13, 1861, EHPJ, 1860–1, fol. 66, B.60/a/31, HBCA; Brown and Schultz, "In Fur Trade Days," 62.

27. For 1862 council, see December 5–11, 1862, EHPJ, 1862–4, fols. 13v–14v, B.60/a/33, HBCA. For Rocky Mountain House reopening, see William Christie (Fort

Edmonton) to Colvin [illegible], February 27, 1866, and Christie (Fort Edmonton) to [illegible] March 5, 1866, both in Edmonton Correspondence Book, 1864–8, pp. 393 and 400, B.60/b/2, HBCA. For HBC and robes, see Hogue, *Metis and the Medicine Line*, 70; Ray, *Indians in the Fur Trade*, 211–12. For Blackfoot trading in north, see December 12, 1866, EHPJ, 1866–9, fol. 3, B.60/a/36, HBCA; Dempsey, *History of Rocky Mountain House*, 22–23; Robinson, *Great Fur Land*, 197–203; March 7, 1868, Rocky Mountain House Post Journal, 1866–8, fol. 44v, B.184/a/5, HBCA; "Personal," *New Nation*, May 17, 1870.

28. W. J. Cullen, Report of Treaty, September 2, 1868, *ARCIA, 1868*, 221; "Treaty with Bloods and Blackfeet," *Montana Post*, September 11, 1868; Dempsey, *Amazing Death of Calf Shirt*, 55; Wischmann, *Frontier Diplomats*, 316–19.

29. For 1868 treaty, see "Treaty with the Blackfeet, etc. 1868"; "Treaty Matters," *Montana Post*, August 7, 1868; "Treaty with Bloods and Blackfeet," *Montana Post*, September 11, 1868. For conflicts in aftermath, Nathaniel Pope, Report of Blackfoot Agency, October 9, 1868, *ARCIA, 1868*, 215; W. J. Cullen, Report of Treaty, September 2, 1868, *ARCIA, 1868*, 221–22; Curtis, *North American Indian*, 8.

30. For post-treaty frustrations, see Alexander Culbertson, "Regarding the Alleged Massacre of Piegan Indians by Col Baker," June 20, 1870, RMSIA, roll 2, pp. 4–5; Alfred Sully, Report of Montana Superintendency, September 23, 1869, *ARCIA, 1869*, 290; F. D. Pease, Report of Blackfeet Agency, August 10, 1869, *ARCIA, 1869*, 300. For July lynchings, see Dempsey, *Firewater*, 34–35; Ewers, *Blackfeet*, 246; Chewing Black Bones interview by Claude Schaeffer, November 13, 1950, Claude E. Schaeffer Field Notebooks, 7:32b. For Mountain Chief's affiliation with the Blood band, see Hayden, *Contributions to the Ethnography*, 264. For Mountain Chief's disaffection, see F. D. Pease, Report of Blackfeet Agency, August 10, 1869, *ARCIA, 1869*, 300; Clarke, "Sketch of Malcolm Clarke," 260–61. For 1869 attacks on whites, see Ewers, *Blackfeet*, 247; James Hardie to George Hartsuff, January 29, 1870, in U.S. House of Representatives, *Piegan Indians*, 29–32. Estimates of Blackfoot killings may have been inflated to justify settler violence.

31. Utley, *Indian Frontier of the American West*, 130–34; Hill, *Office of Indian Affairs*, 3; Isenberg, *Destruction of the Bison*, 128–29; R. White, *"It's Your Misfortune,"* 102–4; Hämäläinen, *Comanche Empire*, 324–39.

32. Johnson, "List of Officers of the Territory of Montana to 1876," 329; Sully, Report of Montana Superintendency, September 23, 1869, *ARCIA, 1869*, 290; Sully, Report of Montana Superintendency, September 20, 1870, *ARCIA, 1870*, 190–91; Ewers, *Blackfeet*, 244.

33. Alvin Wilcox, "Alvin H. Wilcox Reminiscence, 1901–1904," 2–3, SC 981, MHS; Van Cleve, "Early Life of Malcolm Clarke," 97; Historical Society of Montana, "Act of Incorporation," 16.

34. Graybill, *Red and the White*, 98–100; Van Cleve, "Early Life of Malcolm Clarke," 94–95; Helen Clarke, "Sketch of Malcolm Clarke," 259–60; Charlie Revais interview by Schaeffer, January 15, 1951, book 9, p. 23, Claude E. Schaeffer Field Notebooks, M-1100, GMA; Ege, *Tell Baker to Strike Them Hard*, 8–9; Schultz, *My Life as an Indian*, 40.

35. Clarke, "Sketch of Malcolm Clarke," 255–68; unknown author, "Horace J. Clarke Reminiscence," pp. 7–8, Horace J. Clarke Reminiscences, SC 540, MHS; Historical

Society of Montana, "Transactions," 27; Wischmann, *Frontier Diplomats*, 321–24; Graybill, *Red and the White*, 97–103.

36. For arrival and spread, see Dempsey, *Crowfoot*, 59–60; Butler, *Great Lone Land*, 368–71; W. J. Christie, "Brief Sketch of the Origin and the Spread of Smallpox in the Saskatchewan District," ca. 1870, p. 104, Richard C. Hardisty Fonds, M-477, GMA. The origins of the 1869–70 smallpox epidemic remain unclear, and there are several alternate possibilities. One newspaper reported the disease appearing in Fort Benton as early as June, though this report is uncorroborated and does not indicate whether it was transmitted to Indigenous people. "Local and Miscellaneous," *Montana News-Letter*, Helena, June 19, 1869. Alternately, William Christie of the HBC reported that it was first communicated to the Crows at Fort Union, then onto the Piegans, but Frederick Hoxie has argued that the Crows successfully avoided the disease until 1870. Hoxie, *Parading through History*, 100. For impact, see Christie, "Brief Sketch," 1; Dempsey, *Crowfoot*, 59–60; Statement Showing the Population of Various Indian Tribes by Superintendency, *ARCIA, 1868*, 352. Christie estimated that 2,386 Blackfoot people died in the outbreak; coupled with the Office of Indian Affairs' 1868 estimate of 9,560 total Blackfoot population, this would suggest that almost exactly one-fourth of the Blackfoot population perished.

37. U.S. Army Military Division of the Missouri, *Record of Engagements with Hostile Indians*, 25–29; James Hardie to George Hartsuff, January 29, 1870, in U.S. House of Representatives, *Piegan Indians*, 29–32; Ege, *Tell Baker to Strike Them Hard*, 28–30.

38. Alfred Sully to J. T. McGinniss, January 3, 1870, in U.S. House of Representatives, *Piegan Indians*, 36; Regis De Trobriand to O. D. Greene, January 3, 1870, Regis De Trobriand Papers, 1869–1870, SC 5, MHS; Ege, *Tell Baker to Strike Them Hard*, 30–32.

39. Wylie, *Blood on the Marias*, 145–80; Ege, *Tell Baker to Strike Them Hard*, 31–33.

40. For references to Heavy Runner's band as the Heron band, see Schaeffer, "Blackfoot Bands," pp. 61–63, Claude E. Schaeffer Fonds, M-1100, GMA; A. Hungry Wolf, *Blackfoot Papers, Volume One*, 214. A Piikani elder named Yellow Kidney later claimed that Heavy Runner was chief of the Blood band, but most sources indicate that the Blood band was led by Mountain Chief (see note 30). Spear Woman interview by Schaeffer, May 6, 1952, book 12, p. 34, Claude E. Schaeffer Field Notebooks, Claude Schaeffer Fonds, M-1100, GMA.

41. See William Birth to Percy Hobbs, January 31, 1870, pp. 1–2, William Birth Letters, Accession Number 2011.wa.39 (uncatalogued acquisition), BRBL; John Ponsford, "Reminiscences, 1910," pp. 1–2, John W. Ponsford Reminiscences, SC 659, MHS; Spear Woman interview by Schaeffer, May 6, 1952, book 12, pp. 32–34, Claude E. Schaeffer Field Notebooks, Claude Schaeffer Fonds, M-1100, GMA. By far the best collection of firsthand Piikani accounts can be found in the Heavy Runner Records, 1914-1921, MF 53, MHS. The best secondary source accounts of the massacre are Graybill, *Red and the White*, 124–30; and Wylie, *Blood on the Marias*. See also Ewers, *Blackfeet*, 236–53; Ege, *Tell Baker to Strike Them Hard*; Henderson, "Piikuni," 48–70. The Marias Massacre is also sometimes known as the Baker Massacre.

42. For Helena celebration, see Regis de Trobriand to "Dear Lina," March 9, 1870, and De Trobriand to Alfred Sully, February 2, 1870, both in Regis de Trobriand

Papers, 1869–71, SC 1201, MHS. For Blackfoot reactions, see Regis De Trobriand to O. D. Greene, February 2, 1870, pp. 1–2, Regis De Trobriand Papers, 1869–1870, SC 5, MHS; J. H. Eastman to Sully, February 3, 1870, RMSIA, roll 2, pp. 1–2.

43. For escape to Canada, see Culbertson, "Regarding the Alleged Massacre of Piegan Indians by Col. Baker," June 20, 1870, RMSIA, roll 2, pp. 4–5; Culbertson, "Journey from the Marias River to the Bow River, Canada, July–August, 1870," p. 10, Alexander Culbertson Papers, SC 586, MHS. For Mountain Chief and Owl Child, see Culbertson to Sully, June 8, 1870, RMSIA, roll 2, pp. 1–3; C. Imoda to Sully, April 11, 1870, RMSIA, roll 2, pp. 1–2. In a recent article, Rodger Henderson states that Owl Child survived to have his photo taken in 1903, but it is much more likely that the image is of a different Owl Child. Henderson, "Piikuni," 53; DeMarce, *Blackfeet Heritage, 1907–1908*, 200–201n.

44. Miller, *Compact, Contract, Covenant*, 129–33; Carter, *Lost Harvests*, ch. 2. For concerns about American-style wars, see Hector, *Notice of the Indians Seen*, 15; "Red River Indians: Memorial to the Duke of Newcastle," *Nor'Wester*, May 14, 1862; "The North-West Papers," *New Nation*, April 22, 1870.

45. Hogue, *Metis and the Medicine Line*, 66–67; Owram, *Promise of Eden*, 38–68; Tough, "Aboriginal Rights," 225–50. For an overview of Confederation, see Bothwell, *Penguin History of Canada*, 187–214.

46. Dempsey, *Firewater*, 1–225; Kennedy, "Whiskey Trade Frontier," 1–207; Sharp, *Whoop-Up Country*, 33–54; Dempsey, *Crowfoot*, 73–75; Ewers, *Blackfeet*, 254–76; Ewers, *Indian Life on the Upper Missouri*, 34–44; Camoose Bottle interview by Harry Shade, October 24, 1973, IHFP, http://hdl.handle.net/10294/502.

47. For battle, see Dempsey, *Firewater*, 67–70; Milloy, *Plains Cree*, 115–17; Ewers, *Blackfeet*, 260–61; Johnston, *Battle at Belly River*; Dixon, *Vanishing Race*, 112–15; Mountain Horse, *My People, the Bloods*, 49–51, "Indian Fight—The Crees Astonished by Breech-Loaders," *Manitoban and Northwest Herald*, March 4, 1871. For break with Gros Ventres, see Fowler, *Shared Symbols, Contested Meanings*, 49–51; Ewers, *Blackfeet*, 242–43.

Epilogue

1. Treaty 7 Elders et al., *True Spirit*, 276–77; Dempsey, *Crowfoot*, 83–85.

2. Dempsey, *Firewater*, 108; Ewers, *Blackfeet*, 254–76; Kennedy, *Whiskey Trade*, 1–207; McDougall, *On Western Trails*, 186; Claude Schaeffer, "Biographies of Blackfoot Leaders," pp. 122–24, Claude E. Schaeffer Fonds, M-1100-150, GMA. For a less condemnatory perspective on the whiskey traders, see Ens, "Dissenting Perspectives." While Ens rightly points out that the whiskey trade's excesses were a "symptom" of larger problems, the trade's devastating impact is clear in the primary sources, and the whiskey traders deserve blame for profiting off of despair, disorder, and alcoholism. For oral histories, see Camoose Bottle interview by Harry Shade, October 24, 1973, IHFP, http://hdl.handle.net/10294/502; Jim Bottle interview by Harry Shade, October 25, 1973, IHFP, http://hdl.handle.net/10294/503; Chris Bull Shields interview by Mike Devine, ca. 1973, IHFP, http://hdl.handle.net/10294/505; Bad Man interview by Harry Shade, January 1974, IHFP, http://hdl.handle.net/10294/2210; Chief One Gun

interview by Christine Welsh and Tony Snowsill, February 21, 1983, IHFP, http://hdl
.handle.net/10294/2166; Willie Scraping White interview by Harry Shade, November 12, 1983, IHFP, http://hdl.handle.net/10294/580; Useless Good Runner interview by Dila Provost and Albert Yellowhorn, ca. 1973, IHFP, http://hdl.handle.net/10294/546.

3. Treaty 7 Elders et al., *True Spirit*, 276; Graybill, *Policing the Great Plains*, 23–63; Dempsey, *Firewater*, 184–200; Ewers, *Blackfeet*, 262–63; A. Morris, *Treaties of Canada*, 248; Ens, "Dissenting Perspectives," 121, 125–26.

4. Malone, Roeder, and Lang, *Montana*, 120–21; Ewers, *Blackfeet*, 270–73. For populations in 1874, see George Hyek to Assistant Adjutant General, August 6, 1874, vol. 2, p. 3, Letters Sent, 10/1869–5/1881, RG 393, Records of U.S. Army Continental Commands, 1817–1947, Identifier 643345, National Archives Building, Washington, D.C.; William T. Ensign, Report of Blackfeet Agency, September 1, 1873, *ARCIA, 1873*, 251; R. F. May, Report of Blackfeet Agency, September 10, 1874, *ARCIA, 1874*, 260.

5. Hogue, *Metis and the Medicine Line*, 103–4, 172–75; Dobak, "Killing the Canadian Buffalo," 47–48; Ray, *Indians in the Fur Trade*, 225–28.

6. Isenberg, *Destruction of the Bison*, 131–63; Ewers, *Blackfeet*, 260–61; Howard, *Montana*, 21–29; Ray, *Indians in the Fur Trade*, 210–13; Hansen, "Tanner's View," 227–44.

7. Canada Department of the Secretary of State, *Report of the Secretary of State for Canada for the Year Ended 31st December, 1876* (Ottawa: Maclean, Roger, 1877), 22; Dempsey, *Crowfoot*, 87–92; Ewers, *Blackfeet*, 263–64; LaDow, *Medicine Line*, 68.

8. Miller, *Compact, Contract, Covenant*, 129–85; Treaty 7 Elders et al., *True Spirit*, 206–19. See also Belich, *Replenishing the Earth*, 406–17.

9. For council attendance, see William Scollen to parents, October 14, 1877, pp. 2–3, Scollen Family Fonds, M-1108-2, GMA; A. Morris, *Treaties of Canada*, 250. The commissioners' official tally counted 4,392 Indians, not including Bobtail's Crees. For treaty provisions, see Robert, "Negotiation and Implementation of Treaty 7," 59–63; Treaty 7 Elders et al., *True Spirit*, 230–39.

10. A. Morris, *Treaties of Canada*, 251–62, 267–75, quote on 258.

11. For differing views on treaty's meaning, see J. Taylor, "Two Views," 40–45; Treaty 7 Elders et al., *True Spirit*, 111–45; Dempsey, *Great Blackfoot Treaties*, 173–83. Dempsey argues that saying the signers misunderstood the concept of land cessions does them "a disservice," but it seems clear that at the very least several factors limited Blackfoot signers' understanding of the treaty provisions. For translation problems, see Frank Oliver, "The Blackfeet Indian Treaty," *Maclean's Magazine*, March 15, 1931, p. 28; Calf Robe, *Siksiká*, 21; White Headed Chief (Spumiapi) interview by Jane Richardson, September 2, 1938, series 1, p. 114, Jane and Lucien Hanks Fonds, M-8458-6, GMA; Treaty 7 Elders et al., *True Spirit*, 69–77, 143–44; Jack Crow interview by Albert Yellowhorn, January 1, 1973, IHFP, http://hdl.handle.net/10294/508; Useless Good Runner interview by Dila Provost and Albert Yellowhorn, ca. 1973, IHFP, http://hdl.handle.net/10294/546; Mrs. Buffalo interview by Johnny Smith, March 12, 1975, IHFP, http://hdl.handle.net/10294/504.

12. Oliver, "Blackfeet Indian Treaty," 28; John Bunn to Richard Hardisty, October 8, 1877, pp. 1–2, Richard C. Hardisty Fonds, M-477-896, GMA; Jane Richardson, "Life in Crowfoot's Camp, ca. 1870–1877," p. 17, Jane and Lucien Hanks Fonds, M-8458-17,

GMA; William Parker, "History of Captain William Parker, Life in the North-West Mounted Police, 1874–1912," p. 49, William Parker Fonds, M-934-22, GMA.

13. For histories of the early reserve/reservation era, see Daschuk, *Clearing the Plains*, 99–180; McManus, *Line Which Separates*, 57–105; Ewers, *Blackfeet*, 277–315; Treaty 7 Elders et al., *True Spirit*, 146–88.

14. Indigenous and Northern Affairs Canada, "Aboriginal Connectivity Profiles of Alberta," http://www.aadnc-aandc.gc.ca/eng/1352223782819/1353504825398?p=ab; Montana Governor's Office of Indian Affairs, "Blackfeet Nation," http://tribalnations .mt.gov/blackfeet.

Bibliography

Primary Sources: Archival

Bozeman, Montana
   Merrill G. Burlingame Special Collections, Montana State University
      James Willard Schultz Papers
Calgary, Alberta
  Glenbow Archives
     Arthur Family Fonds
     Claude E. Schaeffer Fonds
     David C. Duvall Fonds
     Eleanor Luxton Papers
     Esther Schiff Goldfrank Fonds
     Houghton Running Rabbit Fonds
     Jane and Lucien Hanks Fonds
     Jean L'Heureux Fonds
     Jean-Louis Levern Fonds
     Joe Little Chief Fonds
     R. N. Wilson Fonds
     Richard C. Hardisty Fonds
     Scollen Family Fonds
     Southern Alberta Research Collection
     Teddy Yellow Fly Fonds
     William Parker Fonds
Chicago, Illinois
  Newberry Library
     Edwin A. C. Hatch Diary
Edmonton, Alberta
  Provincial Archives of Alberta
     Tom Many Guns Family Fonds
Helena, Montana
  Montana Historical Society Archives
     Alexander Culbertson Papers
     Alvin H. Wilcox Reminiscence
     Charles P. Chouteau Report
     Edwin A. C. Hatch Diary
     Heavy Runner Records
     Horace J. Clarke Reminiscences
     James H. Bradley Papers

John W. Ponsford Reminiscences
Pierre Chouteau, Jr. and Company Collection
Regis De Trobriand Papers
S. C. Ashby Papers
Thomas Francis Meagher Papers
U.S. Office of Indian Affairs Records
William F. Wheeler Papers
New Haven, Connecticut
Beinecke Rare Book and Manuscript Library, Yale University
Alfred Sully Papers
Dale Lowell Morgan Transcripts
Edward Shelley Diary
Elwood Evans Papers
Granville Stuart Papers
Isaac Ingalls Stevens Letters
Isaac Ingalls Stevens Papers
John Edward Harriott, "Memoirs of Life and Adventure in the Hudson's Bay
    Company Territories"
Robert Stuart Papers
Thomas Francis Meagher Proclamation
Thomas Hutchins, "Observations on Hudson's Bay"
William Birth Letters
Yale University Manuscripts and Archives
George Bird Grinnell Papers
Regina, Saskatchewan
Canadian Plains Research Center (University of Regina Press)
Indian History Film Project
St. Louis, Missouri
Missouri Historical Society
Papers of the St. Louis Fur Trade
Toronto, Ontario
Archives of Ontario
David Thompson Fonds
Thomas Fischer Rare Book Library, University of Toronto
David Thompson Papers
Washington, D.C., and College Park, Maryland
National Archives and Records Administration
Records of the Bureau of Indian Affairs, Record Group 75, Central
    Classified Files
    Documents Relating to the Negotiation of Ratified and Unratified Treaties
        with Various Tribes of Indians, 1801–69, Microfilm T494
    Letters Received by the Office of Indian Affairs, 1824–81, St. Louis Superin-
        tendency, Upper Missouri Agency, and Blackfeet Agency, Microfilm 234
    Records of the Central Superintendency of Indian Affairs, 1813–78,
        Microfilm 856

Records of the Dakota Superintendency of Indian Affairs, 1861–70, Microfilm 1016

Records of the Montana Superintendency of Indian Affairs, 1867–73, Microfilm 833

Records of the Washington Superintendency of Indian Affairs, 1853–61, Microfilm 5

Records of U.S. Army Continental Commands, 1817–1947, Record Group 393

Records of the War Department, Fort Benton, Montana, 1869–81, Identifier 643345

Winnipeg, Manitoba

  Hudson's Bay Company Archives, Provincial Archives of Manitoba

    Bow Fort Post Journal, 1833–34

    Bow River District Report, 1822–23

    Buckingham House Post Journals, 1792–99

    Carlton House (Saskatchewan District) Post Journals, 1795–1839

    Chesterfield House Post Journals, 1799–1802, 1822–23

    Churchill Correspondence Books, 1753–1910

    Cumberland House Post Journals, 1774–1940

    Edmonton Correspondence Books, 1857–86

    Edmonton, Edmonton District, and Saskatchewan District Reports, 1815–25, 1862, 1875, 1886–97

    Edmonton Post Journals, 1795–1885

    Fort Pitt Post Journals, 1830–32

    George Simpson Inward Correspondence Books, 1821–35

    Governor George Simpson Loose Inward Correspondence, 1821–60

    Governor George Simpson Official Reports to the Governor and Committee, 1822–43

    Hudson House Post Journals, 1778–87

    Ile-a-la-Crosse Post Journals, 1805–1940

    Island House Post Journal, 1800–1801

    Manchester House Post Journals, 1786–93

    Peter Fidler Fonds, 1790–1809

    Rocky Mountain House Post Journals, 1828–37, 1866–68

    South Branch House Post Journals, 1786–94

    York Factory Inland Journals, 1766–70

Primary Sources: Published

Government Documents

Canada Department of the Secretary of State. *Report of the Secretary of State for Canada for the Year Ended 31st December, 1876.* Ottawa: Maclean, Roger, 1877.

Congressional Globe. 33rd Cong., 1st Sess., 1854.

House Journal. 33rd Cong., 1st Sess., 1854.

Indigenous and Northern Affairs Canada. "Aboriginal Connectivity Profiles of Alberta—As of March 2013." Accessed July 9, 2018. http://www.aadnc-aandc.gc .ca/eng/1352223782819/1353504825398?p=ab.

Montana Governor's Office of Indian Affairs. "Blackfeet Nation." Accessed July 9, 2018. http://tribalnations.mt.gov/blackfeet.

"Treaty between the United States and the Blackfoot Nation of Indians, Etc., November 16, 1865." In *Indian Affairs: Laws and Treaties*, edited by Charles Kappler, vol. 4, 1133–37. Washington, D.C.: Government Printing Office, 1929.

"Treaty with the Blackfeet, etc., 1868." In *Indian Affairs: Laws and Treaties*, edited by Charles Kappler, vol. 4, 1138–42. Washington, D.C.: Government Printing Office, 1929.

U.S. Army Military Division of the Missouri. *Record of Engagements with Hostile Indians within the Military Division of the Missouri, from 1868 to 1882, Lieutenant General P. H. Sheridan, Commanding*. Chicago: Headquarters Military Division of the Missouri, 1882.

U.S. Congress. *Report of the Committee on Indian Affairs*. Senate Executive Document 47. 16th Cong., 1st Sess., 1820.

U.S. Department of the Interior. *Annual Report of the Commissioner of Indian Affairs to the Secretary of the Interior*. Washington, D.C.: Government Printing Office, 1853–1870, 1873–74.

U.S. Department of War. *Reports of Explorations and Surveys to Ascertain the Most Practicable and Economical Route for a Railroad from the Mississippi River to the Pacific Ocean*. Vol. 1. Washington, D.C.: Beverly Tucker, 1855.

———. *Reports of Explorations and Surveys to Ascertain the Most Practicable Route for a Railroad from the Mississippi River to the Pacific Ocean*. Vol. 12. Washington, D.C.: Thomas H. Ford, 1860.

U.S. House of Representatives. *Piegan Indians: Letter from the Secretary of War*. House Executive Document 269. 41st Cong., 2nd Sess., 1870.

Periodicals

The Benton Record (Fort Benton, Montana)
The Columbian (New York, New York)
Daily National Intelligencer (Washington, D.C.)
Forest and Stream
The Globe (Toronto, Ontario)
Great Falls Tribune (Great Falls, Montana)
Maclean's Magazine (Toronto, Ontario)
The Manitoban and Northwest Herald (Winnipeg, Manitoba)
The Montana Democrat (Virginia City, Montana)
Montana News-Letter (Helena, Montana)
The Montana Post (Helena, Montana)
The Montana Post (Virginia City, Montana)
The New Nation (Winnipeg, Manitoba)
New York Commercial Advertiser (New York, New York)

The Nor'Wester (Red River Settlement, Manitoba)
Peoria Daily Transcript (Peoria, Illinois)
St. Louis Enquirer (St. Louis, Missouri)
The Village Record (West Chester, Pennsylvania)

Books and Articles

Audobon, John James. *Audobon and His Journals*. Edited by Elliott Coues. 2 vols.
   New York: C. Scribner's Sons, 1897.
Beckwourth, James. *The Life and Adventures of James P. Beckwourth, Mountaineer,
   Scout, and Pioneer, and Chief of the Crow Nation of Indians*. London: S. Low, 1856.
Brackenridge, Henry Marie. *Journal of a Voyage up the River Missouri; Performed in
   Eighteen Hundred and Eleven*. 2nd ed. Baltimore: Coale and Maxwell, Pomeroy &
   Troy, 1816.
———. *Views of Louisiana: Containing Geographical, Statistical and Historical Notices of
   That Vast and Important Portion of America*. Baltimore: Schaeffer & Maund, 1817.
Bradbury, John. *Travels in the Interior of North America in the Years 1809, 1810, and
   1811*. London: Sherwood, Neely, and Jones, 1819.
Butler, William Francis. *The Great Lone Land: A Narrative of Travel and Adventure in the
   North-West of America*. London: S. Low, Marson, Low & Searle, 1872.
Catlin, George. *Illustrations of the Manners, Customs & Condition of the North American
   Indians. With Letters and Notes, Written during Eight Years of Travel and Adventure
   among the Wildest . . . Tribes Now Existing*. London: Chatto & Windus, 1876.
Chambers, James. "Fort Sarpy Journal, 1855–1856." In *Contributions to the Historical
   Society of Montana*, edited by Anne McDonnell, vol. 10, 100–187. Helena, Mont.:
   Rocky Mountain, 1940.
Chardon, Francis. *Chardon's Journal at Fort Clark, 1834–1839*. Edited by Annie Heloise
   Abel. Iowa City, Ia.: Athens, 1932.
Chittenden, Hiram, ed. *Life, Letters and Travels of Father Pierre-Jean De Smet*. 4 vols.
   New York: Francis P. Harper, 1905.
Cocking, Matthew. "An Adventurer from Hudson Bay: Matthew Cocking's Journal."
   Edited by Lawrence Burpee. *Proceedings and Transactions of the Royal Society of
   Canada* 2, no. 2 (1908): 89–121.
Cowie, Isaac. *The Company of Adventurers: A Narrative of Seven Years of Service of the
   Hudson's Bay Company*. Toronto: W. Briggs, 1913.
Cox, Ross. *Adventures on the Columbia River: Including the Narrative of a Residence of Six
   Years on the Western Side of the Rocky Mountains, among Various Tribes of Indians
   Hitherto Unknown: Together with a Journey across the American Continent*. Vol. 1.
   London: H. Colburn & R. Bentley, 1831.
Davies, K. G., ed. *Letters from Hudson Bay, 1703–40*. London: Hudson's Bay Record
   Society, 1965.
De La Vérendrye, Pierre Gaultier de Varennes. *Journals and Letters of Pierre Gaultier
   De Varennes De La Vérendrye and His Sons: With Correspondence between the
   Governors of Canada and the French Court, Touching the Search for the Western Sea*.
   Edited by Lawrence J. Burpee. Toronto: Champlain Society, 1927.

De Smet, Pierre-Jean. *Life, Letters and Travels of Father Pierre-Jean De Smet, S.J., 1801–1873; Missionary Labors and Adventures among the Wild Tribes of the North American Indians*. Edited by Hiram Chittenden. 3 vols. New York: F. P. Harper, 1905.

———. *Western Missions and Missionaries: A Series of Letters*. 4 vols. New York: James B. Kirker, late Edward Dunigan & Bro., 1863.

Ens, Gerhard, and Theodore Binnema, eds. *The Hudson's Bay Company Edmonton House Journals, Correspondence & Reports, 1806–1821*. Calgary: Historical Society of Alberta, 2012.

———, eds. *Hudson's Bay Company Edmonton House Journals: Reports from the Saskatchewan District including the Bow River Expedition, 1821–1826*. Calgary: Historical Society of Alberta, 2016.

Farnham, Thomas. *Travels in the Great Western Prairies, the Anahuac and Rocky Mountains, and in the Oregon Territory*. Vol. 2. London: R. Bentley, 1843.

Ferris, Warren Angus. *Life in the Rocky Mountains: A Diary of Wanderings on the Sources of the Rivers Missouri, Columbia, and Colorado, 1830–1835*. Edited by Le Roy Hafen and Paul C. Philips. Denver, Colo.: Old West, 1983.

Fidler, Peter. *Southern Alberta Bicentennial: A Look at Peter Fidler's Journal, 1792–93: Journal of a Journey over Land from Buckingham House to the Rocky Mountains in 1792 &3*. Edited by Bruce Haig. Lethbridge, Alta.: Historical Research Centre, 1991.

Gass, Patrick. *A Journal of the Voyages and Travels of a Corps of Discovery, under the Command of Capt. Lewis and Capt. Clark of the Army of the United States, from the Mouth of the River Missouri through the Interior Parts of North America to the Pacific Ocean, during the Years 1804, 1805 and 1806 . . . With Geographical and Exploratory Notes*. 1807. Reprint, Minneapolis: Ross & Haines, 1958.

Gladstone, William. *The Gladstone Diary: Travels in the Early West*. Edited by Bruce Haig. Lethbridge: Historic Trails Society of Alberta, 1985.

Graham, Andrew. *Andrew Graham's Observations on Hudson's Bay, 1767–91*. Edited by Glyndwr Williams. London: Hudson's Bay Record Society, 1969.

Hamilton, William. *My Sixty Years on the Plains, Trapping, Trading, and Indian Fighting*. New York: Forest and Stream, 1905.

Hargrave, James. *The Hargrave Correspondence, 1821–1843*. Edited by G. P. Glazebrook. Toronto: Champlain Society, 1938.

Harmon, Daniel Williams. *A Journal of Voyages and Travels in the Interior of North America, between the 47th and 58th Degree of North Latitude*. New York: Allerton Book Co., 1922.

Hector, James. *Notice of the Indians Seen by the Exploring Expedition under the Command of Captain Palliser*. London: Ethnological Society of London, 1861.

Henday, Anthony. *A Year Inland: The Journal of a Hudson's Bay Company Winterer*. Edited by Barbara Belyea. Waterloo, Ont.: Wilfrid Laurier University Press, 2000.

Henry, Alexander. *The Journal of Alexander Henry the Younger, 1799–1814*. Edited by Barry Gough. 2 vols. Toronto: Champlain Society, 1988.

Hind, Henry Youle. *Narrative of the Canadian Red River Exploring Expedition of 1857: And of the Assinniboine and Saskatchewan Exploring Expedition of 1858*. 2 vols. London: Longman, Green, Longman and Roberts, 1860.

Historical Society of Montana. "Act of Incorporation." In *Contributions to the Historical Society of Montana*, vol. 1, 16–19. Helena, Mont.: Rocky Mountain, 1876.

————. "Transactions." In *Contributions to the Historical Society of Montana*, vol. 1, 27–35. Helena, Mont.: Rocky Mountain, 1876.

Isham, James. *Observations on Hudsons Bay, 1743, and Notes and Observations on a Book Entitled A Voyage to Hudsons Bay in the Dobbs Galley, 1749*. Edited by E. E. Rich. Toronto: Champlain Society, 1949.

Jackson, Donald, ed. *Letters of the Lewis and Clark Expedition, with Related Documents, 1783–1854*. Urbana: University of Illinois Press, 1962.

James, Thomas. *Three Years among the Indians and Mexicans*. 1846. Reprint, St. Louis: Missouri Historical Society, 1916.

Johnson, Alice, ed. *Saskatchewan Journals and Correspondence: Edmonton House 1795–1800; Chesterfield House 1800–1802*. London: Hudson's Bay Record Society, 1967.

Kane, Paul. *Paul Kane's Frontier: Including Wanderings of an Artist among the Indians of North America*. Edited by J. Russell Harper. Austin: University of Texas Press, 1971.

Kautz, August. "From Missouri to Oregon in 1860: The Diary of August V. Kautz." Edited by Martin Schmitt. *Pacific Northwest Quarterly* 37, no. 3 (July 1946): 193–230.

Kennerly, Henry. "The 1855 Blackfeet Treaty Council: A Memoir by Henry A Kennerly." Edited by David Walter. *Montana: The Magazine of Western History* 32, no. 1 (Winter 1982): 44–51.

Klett, Guy, ed. "Missionary Endeavors of the Presbyterian Church among the Blackfeet Indians in the 1850's." *Journal of the Department of History of the Presbyterian Church in the U.S.A.* 20, no. 8 (December 1941): 327–54.

Larocque, Francois-Antoine. *Journal of Larocque from the Assiniboine to the Yellowstone, 1805*. Edited by Lawrence Burpee. Ottawa: Government Printing Bureau, 1910.

Larpenteur, Charles. *Forty Years a Fur Trader on the Upper Missouri: The Personal Narrative of Charles Larpenteur, 1833–1872*. Edited by Milo Milton Quaife. Chicago: Lakeside Press, 1933.

————. *Forty Years a Fur Trader on the Upper Missouri: The Personal Narrative of Charles Larpenteur, 1833–1872*. Edited by Milo Milton Quaife. 2 vols. New York: F. P. Harper, 1898.

Luttig, John C. *Journal of a Fur-Trading Expedition on the Upper Missouri, 1812–1813*. Edited by Stella M. Drumm. St. Louis: Missouri Historical Society, 1920.

M'Gillivray, Duncan. *The Journal of Duncan M'Gillivray of the North West Company at Fort George on the Saskatchewan, 1794–5*. Edited by Arthur Silver Morton. Toronto: Macmillan Company of Canada, 1929.

————. "Some Account of the Trade of the North West Company (1809)." In *Report of the Public Archives for the Year 1928*, 56–73. Ottawa: F. A. Acland, 1928.

MacKenzie, Alexander. *Voyages from Montreal on the River St. Laurence through the Continent of North America to the Frozen and Pacific Oceans in the Years 1789 and 1793*. Vol. 1. New York: W. B. Gilley, 1814.

Maximilian, Alexander Philipp Prinz zu Wied. *Maximilian, Prince of Wied's Travels in the Interior of North America, 1832–1834*. Edited by Reuben Gold Thwaites. Vol. 2. Cleveland: A. H. Clark, 1906.

———. *The North American Journals of Prince Maximilian of Wied*. Edited by Stephen S. Witte and Marsha V. Gallagher. Vol. 2, *April–September 1833*. Norman: University of Oklahoma Press, 2010.

———. *Travels in the Interior of North America*. Translated by H. Evans Lloyd. London: Ackermann, 1843–1844.

McDonald of Garth, John. "Autobiographical Notes, 1791–1816." In *Les Bourgeois de la Compagnie du Nord-Ouest*, edited by L. R. Masson, vol. 2, 1–59. Quebec: A. Cote, 1890.

McDonnell, Anne, ed. "Fort Benton Journal, 1854–1856." In *Contributions to the Historical Society of Montana*, vol. 10, 1–99. Helena, Mont.: Rocky Mountain, 1940.

McDougall, John. *On Western Trails in the Early Seventies: Frontier Pioneer Life in the Canadian North-West*. Toronto: William Briggs, 1911.

McLoughlin, John. *The Letters of John McLoughlin from Fort Vancouver to the Governor and Committee*. Edited by E. E. Rich. Toronto: Champlain Society, 1941.

Meagher, Thomas. "Some Letters of General T. F. Meagher." *Journal of the American Irish Historical Society* 30 (1932): 83–87.

Morris, Alexander. *The Treaties of Canada with the Indians of Manitoba and the North-West Territories: Including the Negotiations on Which They Were Based, and Other Information Relating Thereto*. Toronto: Belfords, Clarke, 1880.

Moulton, Gary, ed. *The Journals of the Lewis and Clark Expedition*. Vol. 7, *From the Pacific to the Rockies*. Lincoln: University of Nebraska Press, 1991.

———, ed. *The Journals of the Lewis and Clark Expedition*. Vol. 8, *Over the Rockies to St. Louis*. Lincoln: University of Nebraska Press, 1993.

Ogden, Peter Skene. *Peter Skene Ogden's Snake Country Journals, 1824–25 and 1825–26*. Edited by E. E. Rich, K. G. Davies, and Glyndwr Williams. London: Hudson's Bay Record Society, 1950.

———. *Peter Skene Ogden's Snake Country Journal, 1826–27*. Edited by E. E. Rich, K. G. Davies, and Glyndwr Williams. London: Hudson's Bay Record Society, 1961.

———. *Peter Skene Ogden's Snake Country Journals, 1827–28 and 1828–29*. Edited by Glyndwr Williams, David E. Miller, and David H. Miller. London: Hudson's Bay Record Society, 1971.

———. *Traits of American-Indian Life and Character*. London: Smith, Elder, 1853.

Palliser, John. *Exploration — British North America. Further Papers Relative to the Exploration by the Expedition under Captain Palliser of That Portion of British North America Which Lies between the Northern Branch of the River Saskatchewan and the Frontier of the United States; and between the Red River and the Rocky Mountains, and Thence to the Pacific Ocean*. London: G. E. Eyre & W. Spottiswoode, 1860.

———. *Exploration — British North America. The Journals, Detailed Reports, and Observations Relative to the Exploration, by Captain Palliser*. London: G. E. Eyre and W. Spottiswoode, 1863.

Partoll, Albert John, ed. "The Blackfoot Indian Peace Council: A Document of the Official Proceedings of the Treaty between the Blackfoot Nation and Other Indians and the United States." In *Sources of Northwest History*, No. 3, 3–11. Missoula, Mont.: State University Press, 1937.

Point, Nicolas. *Wilderness Kingdom: Indian Life in the Rocky Mountains, 1840-1847: The Journals and Paintings of Nicolas Point*. Edited by Joseph P. Donnelly and John Ewers. New York: Holt, Rinehart and Winston, 1967.

Radisson, Pierre-Esprit. *Pierre-Esprit Radisson: The Collected Writings*. Edited by Germaine Warkentin. Vol. 1, *The Voyages*. Montreal: McGill-Queen's University Press, 2012.

Rich, E. E., ed. *Cumberland House Journals and Inland Journal, 1775-82*. Vol. 2, *1779-82*. London: Hudson's Bay Record Society, 1951.

Robertson, Colin. *Colin Robertson's Correspondence Book, September 1817 to September 1822*. Edited by E. E. Rich. Toronto: Champlain Society, 1939.

Robinson, H. M. *The Great Fur Land*. New York: G. P. Putnam's Sons, 1879.

Rundle, Robert Terrill. *The Rundle Journals, 1840-1848*. Edited by Hugh Dempsey. Calgary: Historical Society of Alberta, 1977.

Saint-Pierre, Jacques Legardeur de. "Journal of Jacques Repentigny Legardeur St. Pierre of His Expedition for the Discovery of the Western Sea, 1750 to 1752." In *Report on Canadian Archives, 1886*, clviii–clxix. Ottawa: Maclean, Roger, 1886.

Schultz, James Willard. *My Life as an Indian: The Story of a Red Woman and White Man in the Lodges of the Blackfeet*. Boston: Houghton Mifflin, 1914.

Simpson, George. *An Overland Journey round the World: During the Years 1841 and 1842*. Philadelphia: Lea and Blanchard, 1847.

Southesk, James Carnegie. *Saskatchewan and the Rocky Mountains; a Diary and Narrative of Travel, Sport, and Adventure, during a Journey through the Hudson's Bay Company's Territories, in 1859 and 1860*. Edinburgh: Edmonston and Douglas, 1875.

Stevens, Isaac. *Campaigns of the Rio Grande and of Mexico: With Notices of the Recent Work of Major Ripley*. New York: D. Appleton, 1851.

Stewart, Wallace, ed. *Documents Relating to the North West Company*. Toronto: Champlain Society, 1934.

Stuart, Robert. *The Discovery of the Oregon Trail: Robert Stuart's Narratives of His Overland Trip Eastward from Astoria in 1812-13*. Edited by Philip Ashton Rollins. 1935. Reprint, Lincoln: University of Nebraska Press, 1995.

Thomas, Dr. "Journey to the Mandans, 1809: The Lost Narrative of Dr. Thomas." Edited by Donald Jackson. *Bulletin of the Missouri Historical Society* 20, no. 3 (April 1964): 179–92.

Thompson, David. *Columbia Journals*. Edited by Barbara Belyea. Montreal: McGill-Queen's University Press, 1994.

———. *David Thompson's Narrative of His Explorations in Western America, 1784-1812*. Edited by Joseph Tyrrell. Toronto: Champlain Society, 1916.

———. "Discoveries from the East Side of the Rocky Mountains to the Pacific Ocean." Edited by Joseph Tyrrell. *Canadian Historical Review* 15 (1934): 42–45.

———. "The Discovery of the Source of the Columbia River." Edited by T. C. Elliott. *Quarterly of the Oregon Historical Society* 26 (1925): 28–49.

———. *Journals Relating to Montana and Adjacent Regions, 1808-1812*. Edited by Catherine White. Missoula: Montana State University Press, 1950.

———. *Travels in Western North America, 1784-1812*. Edited by Victor G. Hopwood. Toronto: Macmillan of Canada, 1971.

———. *The Writings of David Thompson*. Edited by William E. Moreau. Vol. 1, *The Travels, 1850 Version*. Montreal: McGill-Queen's University Press, 2009.

———. *The Writings of David Thompson*. Edited by William E. Moreau. Vol. 2, *The Travels, 1848 Version*. Montreal: McGill-Queen's University Press, 2015.

Uhlenbeck-Melchior, Wilhelm. *Montana 1911: A Professor and His Wife among the Blackfeet*. Edited by Mary Eggermont-Molenaar. Calgary, Alta.: University of Calgary Press, 2005.

Umfreville, Edward. *The Present State of Hudson's Bay. Containing a Full Description of That Settlement, and the Adjacent Country; and Likewise of the Fur Trade, with Hints for Its Improvement*. London: Printed for C. Stalker, 1790.

Welch, James. *Fools Crow*. New York: Viking, 1986.

Wilkes, Charles. *Narrative of the United States Exploring Expedition, during the Years 1838, 1839, 1840, 1841, 1842*. Vol. 4. Philadelphia: C. Sherman, 1849.

Secondary Sources

Books, Articles, and Films

Albers, Patricia. "Symbiosis, Merger, and War: Contrasting Forms of Intertribal Relationship among Historic Plains Indians." In *The Political Economy of Northern Plains Indians*, edited by John Moore, 94–132. Norman: University of Oklahoma Press, 1993.

Ambrose, Stephen. *Undaunted Courage: Meriwether Lewis, Thomas Jefferson, and the Opening of the American West*. New York: Simon & Schuster, 1996.

Arima, Eugene. *Blackfeet and Palefaces: The Pikani and Rocky Mountain House*. Kemptville, Ore.: Golden Dog, 1995.

Aron, Stephen, and Jeremy Adelman. "From Borderlands to Borders: Empires, Nation-States, and the Peoples in Between in North American History." *American Historical Review* 104, no. 3 (June 1, 1999): 814–41.

Athearn, Robert. "Early Territorial Montana: A Problem in Colonial Administration." *Montana Magazine of History* 1, no. 3 (July 1951): 14–21.

Baltensperger, B. H. "Plains Booms and the Creation of the Great American Desert Myth." *Journal of Historical Geography* 18, no. 1 (January 1992): 59–73.

Bamforth, Douglas. *Ecology and Human Organization on the Great Plains*. New York: Plenum, 1988.

———. "Indigenous People, Indigenous Violence: Precontact Warfare on the North American Great Plains." *Man* 29, no. 1 (March 1994): 95–115.

Barbour, Barton H. *Fort Union and the Upper Missouri Fur Trade*. Norman: University of Oklahoma Press, 2001.

Barr, Juliana. "From Captives to Slaves: Commodifying Indian Women in the Borderlands." *Journal of American History* 92, no. 1 (June 2005): 19–46.

———. "Geographies of Power: Mapping Indian Borders in the 'Borderlands' of the Early Southwest." *William and Mary Quarterly* 68, no. 1 (2011): 5–46.

Basso, Keith. *Wisdom Sits in Places: Landscape and Language among the Western Apache*. Albuquerque: University of New Mexico Press, 1996.

Bastien, Betty. *Blackfoot Ways of Knowing: The Worldview of the Siksikaitsitapi.* Calgary, Alta.: University of Calgary Press, 2004.

Belich, James. *Replenishing the Earth: The Settler Revolution and the Rise of the Anglo World, 1783–1939.* New York: Oxford University Press, 2009.

Bernstein, David. *How the West Was Drawn: Mapping, Indians, and the Construction of the Trans-Mississippi West.* Lincoln: University of Nebraska Press, 2018.

Billington, Ray Allen. *Westward Expansion: A History of the American Frontier.* 4th ed. New York: Macmillan, 1974.

Binnema, Theodore. "Allegiances and Interests: Niitsitapi (Blackfoot) Trade, Diplomacy, and Warfare, 1806–1831." *Western Historical Quarterly* 37, no. 3 (Autumn 2006): 327–49.

———. *Common and Contested Ground: A Human and Environmental History of the Northwestern Plains.* Norman: University of Oklahoma Press, 2001.

———. "How Does a Map Mean?" In *From Rupert's Land to Canada,* edited by Gerhard Ens, Theodore Binnema, and Rod Macleod, 201–24. Edmonton: University of Alberta Press, 2001.

———. "Old Swan, Big Man and the Siksika Bands, 1794–1815." *Canadian Historical Review* 77, no. 1 (March 1996): 1–32.

———. "'With Tears, Shrieks, and Howlings of Despair': The Smallpox Epidemic of 1781–1782." In *Alberta Formed, Alberta Transformed,* edited by Michael Payne, Donald Wetherell, and Catherine Cavanaugh, vol. 1, 111–32. Edmonton: University of Alberta Press, 2006.

Binnema, Theodore, and William A. Dobak. "'Like the Greedy Wolf': The Blackfeet, the St. Louis Fur Trade, and War Fever, 1807–1831," *Journal of the Early Republic* 29, no. 3 (Fall 2009): 411–40.

A Blackfeet Encounter. Directed by Dennis Neary and Curly Bear Wagner. 2007. Lincoln, Neb.: VisionMaker Video, 2007. DVD.

The Blackfoot Gallery Committee. *The Story of the Blackfoot People: Niitsitapiisinni.* 2001. Reprint, Richmond Hill, Ont.: Firefly Books, 2013.

Blackhawk, Ned. *Violence over the Land: Indians and Empires in the Early American West.* Cambridge, Mass.: Harvard University Press, 2006.

Bobroff, Kenneth H. "Retelling Allotment: Indian Property Rights and the Myth of Common Ownership." *Vanderbilt Law Review* 54 (2001): 1559–623.

Bohr, Roland. *Gifts from the Thunder Beings: Indigenous Archery and European Firearms in the Northern Plains and Central Subarctic, 1670–1870.* Lincoln: University of Nebraska Press, 2014.

Bothwell, Robert. *The Penguin History of Canada.* Toronto: Penguin Canada, 2006.

Bouchet-Bert, Luc. "From Spiritual and Biographic to Boundary-Marking Deterrent Art: A Reinterpretation of Writing-on-Stone." *Plains Anthropologist* 44, no. 167 (February 1999): 27–46.

Bradley, James. "Affairs at Fort Benton from 1831 to 1869." In *Contributions to the Historical Society of Montana,* vol. 3, 201–87. Helena, Mont.: State Publishing Company, 1900.

———. "Blackfoot War with the Whites." In *Contributions to the Historical Society of Montana,* vol. 9, 252–55. Helena, Mont.: Rocky Mountain, 1923.

———. "Bradley Manuscript, Book F." In *Contributions to the Historical Society of Montana*, vol. 8, 197–250. Helena: Montana Historical and Miscellaneous Library, 1917.

———. "Bradley Manuscript, Book II." In *Contributions to the Historical Society of Montana*, vol. 8, 127–96. Helena: Montana Historical and Miscellaneous Library, 1917.

———. "Characteristics, Habits and Customs of the Blackfeet Indians." In *Contributions to the Historical Society of Montana*, vol. 9, 255–287. Helena, Mont.: Rocky Mountain, 1923.

———. "History of the Sioux." In *Contributions to the Historical Society of Montana*, vol. 9, 29–143. Helena, Mont.: Rocky Mountain, 1923.

———. "The Oregon Trail: Capture of an Emigrant Train by the Piegan Chief, Little Dog." In *Contributions to the Historical Society of Montana*, vol. 9, 335–40. Helena, Mont.: Rocky Mountain, 1923.

Brink, Jack. *Imagining Head-Smashed-In: Aboriginal Buffalo Hunting on the Northern Plains*. Athabasca, Alta.: Athabasca University Press, 2008.

Brink, John W., and Maureen Rollans. "Thoughts on the Structure and Function of Drive Lane Systems at Communal Buffalo Jumps." In *Hunters of the Recent Past*, edited by Leslie B. Davis and Brian O. K. Reeves, 152–167. London: Unwin Hyman, 1990.

Brooks, James. *Captives and Cousins: Slavery, Kinship, and Community in the Southwest Borderlands*. Chapel Hill: University of North Carolina Press, 2002.

Brunton, Bill. "Kootenai." In *Plateau*, edited by Deward Walker, Jr., 223–37. Vol. 12 of *Handbook of North American Indians*. Washington, D.C.: Smithsonian Institution Press, 1998.

Bryan, Liz. *The Buffalo People: Pre-Contact Archaeology on the Canadian Plains*. Surrey, B.C.: Heritage House, 1991.

Bullchild, Percy. *The Sun Came Down*. San Francisco: Harper & Row, 1985.

Calf Robe, Ben. *Siksiká: A Blackfoot Legacy*. Invermere, B.C.: Good Medicine Books, 1979.

Calloway, Colin G. *One Vast Winter Count: The Native American West before Lewis and Clark*. Lincoln: University of Nebraska Press, 2003.

———. "Snake Frontiers: The Eastern Shoshones in the Eighteenth Century." *Annals of Wyoming* 63, no. 1 (Winter 1991): 85–92.

Carter, Sarah. *The Importance of Being Monogamous: Marriage and Nation Building in Western Canada to 1915*. Edmonton, Alta.: Athabasca University Press, 2008.

———. *Lost Harvests: Prairie Indian Reserve Farmers and Government Policy*. Montreal: McGill–Queen's University Press, 1990.

Cebula, Larry. *Plateau Indians and the Quest for Spiritual Power, 1700–1850*. Lincoln: University of Nebraska Press, 2003.

Chambers, Cynthia, and Narcisse Blood. "Love Thy Neighbour: Repatriating Precarious Blackfoot Sites." *International Journal of Canadian Studies* 39–40 (2009): 254–55.

Chittenden, Hiram. *The American Fur Trade of the Far West; a History of the Pioneer Trading Posts and Early Fur Companies of the Missouri Valley and the Rocky Mountains and the Overland Commerce with Santa Fe*. 3 vols. New York: F. P. Harper, 1902.

————. *Early Steamboat Navigation on the Missouri River.* 2 vols. New York: F. P. Harper, 1903.

Clarke, Helen. "Sketch of Malcolm Clarke." In *Contributions to the Historical Society of Montana,* vol. 2, 255–68. Helena, Mont.: Rocky Mountain, 1896.

Clayton, James. "The Growth and Economic Significance of the American Fur Trade, 1790–1890." *Minnesota History* 40, no. 4 (December 1, 1966): 210–20.

Coleman, Jon. *Here Lies Hugh Glass: A Mountain Man, a Bear, and the Rise of the American Nation.* New York: Hill and Wang, 2012.

Colpitts, George. "Peace, War, and Climate Change on the Northern Plains: Bison Hunting in the Neutral Hills during the Mild Winters of 1830–34." *Canadian Journal of History* 50, no. 3 (2015): 420–41.

————. *Pemmican Empire: Food, Trade, and the Last Bison Hunts in the North American Plains, 1780–1882.* New York: Cambridge University Press, 2015.

————. "Provisioning the HBC: Market Economies in the British Buffalo Commons in the Early Nineteenth Century." *Western Historical Quarterly* 43, no. 2 (Summer 2012): 179–203.

Conaty, Gerald. "Economic Models and Blackfoot Ideology." *American Ethnologist* 22, no. 2 (May 1995): 403–9.

Crowshoe, Joe. *Weasel Tail: Stories Told by Joe Crowshoe, Sr. (Áápohsoy'yiis), a Peigan-Blackfoot Elder.* Edmonton, Alta.: NeWest, 2008.

Curtis, Edward S. *The North American Indian: Being a Series of Volumes Picturing and Describing the Indians of the United States, and Alaska.* Vol. 6. Seattle: E. S. Curtis, 1907.

Darnell, Regna. "Plains Cree." In *Plains,* edited by Raymond J. DeMallie, pt. 1, 638–51. Vol. 13 of *Handbook of North American Indians.* Washington, D.C.: Smithsonian Institution Press, 2001.

Daschuk, James. *Clearing the Plains: Disease, Politics of Starvation, and the Loss of Aboriginal Life.* Regina, Sask.: University of Regina Press, 2013.

DeLay, Brian. *War of a Thousand Deserts: Indian Raids and the U.S.-Mexican War.* New Haven, Conn.: Yale University Press, 2008.

DeMallie, Raymond J., and David Reed Miller. "Assiniboine." In *Plains,* edited by Raymond J. DeMallie, pt. 1, 572–95. Vol. 13 of *Handbook of North American Indians.* Washington, D.C.: Smithsonian Institution Press, 2001.

DeMarce, Roxanne, ed. *Blackfeet Heritage, 1907–1908: Blackfeet Indian Reservation, Browning, Montana.* Browning, Mont.: Blackfeet Heritage Program, 1980.

Dempsey, Hugh. *The Amazing Death of Calf Shirt and Other Blackfoot Stories: Three Hundred Years of Blackfoot History.* Norman: University of Oklahoma Press, 1996.

————. "Blackfoot." In *Plains,* edited by Raymond J. DeMallie, pt. 1, 604–28. Vol. 13 of *Handbook of North American Indians.* Washington, D.C.: Smithsonian Institution Press, 2001.

————. *Crowfoot, Chief of the Blackfeet.* Norman: University of Oklahoma Press, 1972.

————. *Firewater: The Impact of the Whisky Trade on the Blackfoot Nation.* Calgary, Alta.: Fifth House, 2002.

————. *The Great Blackfoot Treaties.* Victoria, B.C.: Heritage House, 2015.

———. *A History of Rocky Mountain House*. Ottawa: National Historic Sites Service, 1973.

———. *Red Crow, Warrior Chief*. Saskatoon, Sask.: Western Producer Prairie Books, 1980.

———. "Sarcee." In *Plains*, edited by Raymond J. DeMallie, pt. 1, 629–37. Vol. 13 of *Handbook of North American Indians*. Washington, D.C.: Smithsonian Institution Press, 2001.

Denig, Edwin. *Five Indian Tribes of the Upper Missouri: Sioux, Arickaras, Assiniboines, Crees, Crows*. Edited by John Ewers. Norman: University of Oklahoma Press, 1961.

De Voto, Bernard. *The Course of Empire*. Boston: Houghton Mifflin, 1952.

Dixon, Joseph Kossuth. *The Vanishing Race: The Last Great Indian Council*. Rev. ed. Garden City, N.Y.: Doubleday, Page, 1914.

Dobak, William. "Killing the Canadian Buffalo, 1821–1881." *Western Historical Quarterly* 27, no. 1 (April 1, 1996): 33–52.

Dolin, Eric Jay. *Fur, Fortune, and Empire: The Epic History of the Fur Trade in America*. New York: W. W. Norton, 2010.

Duke, P. G. *Points in Time: Structure and Event in a Late Northern Plains Hunting Society*. Niwot: University Press of Colorado, 1991.

DuVal, Kathleen. *The Native Ground: Indians and Colonists in the Heart of the Continent*. Philadelphia: University of Pennsylvania Press, 2006.

Eckstrom, Mikal Brotnov, and Margaret D. Jacobs. "Teaching American History as Settler Colonialism." In *Why You Can't Teach United States History without American Indians*, edited by Susan Sleeper-Smith et al., 259–72. Chapel Hill: University of North Carolina Press, 2015.

Ege, Robert J. *Tell Baker to Strike Them Hard!: Incident on the Marias, 23 Jan. 1870*. Bellevue, Neb.: Old Army Press, 1970.

Elliott, T. C. "The Strange Case of David Thompson and Jeremy Pinch." *Oregon Historical Quarterly* 40, no. 2 (June 1, 1939): 188–99.

Ens, Gerhard. "The Border, the Buffalo, and the Métis of Montana." In *The Borderlands of the American and Canadian Wests: Essays on the Regional History of the Forty-Ninth Parallel*, edited by Sterling Evans, 139–54. Lincoln: University of Nebraska Press, 2006.

———. "Dissenting Perspectives of the Whiskey Trade of Whoop-Up Country." In *Last Blast: The Fur Trade in Whoop-Up Country*, edited by Gordon Tolton et al., 117–28. Lethbridge, Alta.: Fort Whoop-Up Interpretive Society, 2013.

———. "Fatal Quarrels and Fur Trade Rivalries: A Year of Living Dangerously on the North Saskatchewan, 1806–1807." In *Alberta Formed, Alberta Transformed*, edited by Michael Payne, Donald G. Wetherell, and Catherine Cavanaugh, vol. 1, 133–60. Edmonton: University of Alberta Press, 2006.

Ewers, John. *The Blackfeet: Raiders on the Northwestern Plains*. Norman: University of Oklahoma Press, 1958.

———. *Gustavus Sohon's Portraits of Flathead and Pend d'Oreille Indians, 1854*. Washington, D.C.: Smithsonian Institution Press, 1948.

———. *The Horse in Blackfoot Indian Culture, with Comparative Material from Other Western Tribes*. Washington, D.C.: Government Printing Office, 1955.

————. *Indian Life on the Upper Missouri*. Norman: University of Oklahoma Press, 1968.

Fagan, Brian. *Ancient North America: The Archaeology of a Continent*. New York: Thames & Hudson, 2005.

Faragher, John Mack. "Commentary: Settler Colonial Studies and the North American Frontier." *Settler Colonial Studies* 4, no. 2 (2014): 181–91.

————. *Eternity Street: Violence and Justice in Frontier Los Angeles*. New York: W. W. Norton and Company, 2016.

————. *Women and Men on the Overland Trail*. New Haven, Conn.: Yale University Press, 1979.

Farr, William. "Going to Buffalo: Indian Hunting Migrations across the Rocky Mountains: Part 1, Making Meat and Taking Robes." *Montana: The Magazine of Western History* 53, no. 4 (December 2003): 2–21.

————. "Going to Buffalo: Indian Hunting Migrations across the Rocky Mountains: Part 2, Civilian Permits, Army Escorts." *Montana: The Magazine of Western History* 54, no. 1 (April 1, 2004): 26–43.

————. "'When We Were First Paid': The Blackfoot Treaty, The Western Tribes, and the Creation of the Common Hunting Ground, 1855." *Great Plains Quarterly* 21, no. 2 (Spring 2001): 131–54.

Fenn, Elizabeth. *Encounters at the Heart of the World: A History of the Mandan People*. New York: Hill and Wang, 2014.

————. *Pox Americana: The Great Smallpox Epidemic of 1775–82*. New York: Hill and Wang, 2001.

Ferguson, Brian, and Neil Whitehead, eds. *War in the Tribal Zone: Expanding States and Indigenous Warfare*. 2nd ed. Santa Fe, N. Mex.: School of American Research Press, 2000.

Flores, Dan. "Bison Ecology and Bison Diplomacy: The Southern Plains from 1800 to 1850." *Journal of American History* 78, no. 2 (September 1991): 465–85.

Foster, Michael. "Language and the Culture History of North America." In *Languages*, edited by Ives Goddard, 64–110. Vol. 17 of *Handbook of North American Indians*. Washington, D.C.: Smithsonian Institution Press, 1996.

Fowler, Loretta. *Shared Symbols, Contested Meanings: Gros Ventre Culture and History, 1778–1984*. Ithaca, N.Y.: Cornell University Press, 1987.

Fowler, Loretta, and Regina Flannery. "Gros Ventre." In *Plains*, edited by Raymond J. DeMallie, pt. 2, 677–94. Vol. 13 of *Handbook of North American Indians*. Washington, D.C.: Smithsonian Institution Press, 2001.

Frantz, Donald G., and Norma Jean Russell. *Blackfoot Dictionary of Stems, Roots, and Affixes*. 3rd ed. Toronto: University of Toronto Press, 2017.

Friesen, Gerald. *The Canadian Prairies: A History*. Lincoln: University of Nebraska Press, 1984.

Gallay, Alan. *The Indian Slave Trade: The Rise of the English Empire in the American South, 1670–1717*. New Haven, Conn.: Yale University Press, 2002.

Gitlin, Jay. *The Bourgeois Frontier: French Towns, French Traders, & American Expansion*. New Haven, Conn.: Yale University Press, 2010.

Goetzmann, William. *Exploration and Empire: The Explorer and the Scientist in the Winning of the American West*. New York: Alfred A. Knopf, 1966.

Grabowski, Jan, and Nicole St-Onge. "Montreal Iroquois Engagés in the Western Fur Trade, 1800–1821." In *From Rupert's Land to Canada*, edited by Theodore Binnema, Gerhard Ens, and R. C. Macleod, 23–58. Edmonton: University of Alberta Press, 2001.

Graybill, Andrew. *Policing the Great Plains: Rangers, Mounties, and the North American Frontier, 1875–1910*. Lincoln: University of Nebraska Press, 2007.

———. *The Red and the White: A Family Saga of the American West*. New York: W. W. Norton, 2013.

Greiser, Sally. "Late Prehistoric Cultures on the Montana Plains." In *Plains Indians, A.D. 500–1500: The Archaeological Past of Historic Groups*, edited by Karl Schlesier, 34–55. Norman: University of Oklahoma Press, 1994.

Grinnell, George. *Blackfoot Lodge Tales: The Story of a Prairie People*. New York: C. Scribner's Sons, 1892.

———. *The Story of the Indian*. New York: D. Appleton, 1895.

———. "A White Blackfoot." In *We Seized Our Rifles: Recollections of the Montana Frontier*, edited by Eugene Lee Silliman, 70–73. Missoula, Mont.: Mountain Press, 1982.

Hale, Horatio. "Ethnology of the Blackfoot Tribes." *Popular Science Monthly* 29 (June 1886): 204–12.

Hall, Ryan. "Before the Medicine Line: Blackfoot Trade Strategy and the Emergence of the Northwest Plains Borderlands, 1818–1846." *Pacific Historical Review* 86, no. 3 (August 2017): 381–406.

Hämäläinen, Pekka. *The Comanche Empire*. New Haven, Conn.: Yale University Press, 2008.

———. "The Rise and Fall of Plains Indian Horse Cultures." *Journal of American History* 90, no. 3 (December 1, 2003): 833–62.

Hämäläinen, Pekka, and Samuel Truett. "On Borderlands." *Journal of American History* 98, no. 2 (September 2011): 338–61.

Hansen, Jennifer. "A Tanner's View of the Bison Hunt: Global Tanning and Industrial Leather." In *Bison and People on the North American Plains: A Deep Environmental History*, edited by Geoff Cunfer and Bill Waiser, 227–44. College Station: Texas A&M University Press, 2016.

Hanson, James. "Laced Coats and Leather Jackets: The Great Plains Intercultural Clothing Exchange." In *Plains Indian Studies: A Collection of Essays in Honor of John C. Ewers and Waldo R. Wedel*, edited by Douglas Ubelaker and Viola Herman, 105–17. Washington, D.C.: Smithsonian Institution Press, 1982.

Harris, Burton. *John Colter: His Years in the Rockies*. New York: Scribner, 1952.

Harrod, Howard L. *Mission among the Blackfeet*. Norman: University of Oklahoma Press, 1971.

Hayden, F. V. *Contributions to the Ethnography and Philology of the Indian Tribes of the Missouri Valley*. 2 vols. Philadelphia: C. Sherman & Son, Printers, 1862.

Hellson, John C., and Morgan Gadd. *Ethnobotany of the Blackfoot Indians*. Ottawa: National Museums of Canada, 1974.

Henderson, Rodger. "The Piikuni and the U.S. Army's Piegan Expedition: Competing Narratives of the 1870 Massacre on the Marias River." *Montana: The Magazine of Western History* 68, no. 1 (Spring 2018): 48–70.

Hill, Edward. *The Office of Indian Affairs, 1824–1880: Historical Sketches*. New York: Clearwater, 1974.

Hine, Robert V., and John Mack Faragher. *The American West: A New Interpretive History*. New Haven, Conn.: Yale University Press, 2000.

Hodge, Adam R. "'In Want of Nourishment for to Keep Them Alive': Climate Fluctuations, Bison Scarcity, and the Smallpox Epidemic of 1780–82 on the Northern Great Plains." *Environmental History* 17, no. 2 (April 2012): 365–403.

Hogue, Michel. "Disputing the Medicine Line: The Plains Crees and the Canadian-American Border, 1876–1885." *Montana: The Magazine of Western History* 52, no. 4 (Winter 2002): 2–17.

———. *Metis and the Medicine Line: Creating a Border and Dividing a People*. Chapel Hill: University of North Carolina Press, 2015.

Howard, Joseph Kinsey. *Montana: High, Wide, and Handsome*. New Haven, Conn.: Yale University Press, 1943.

Howe, Daniel Walker. *What Hath God Wrought: The Transformation of America, 1815–1848*. New York: Oxford University Press, 2007.

Hoxie, Frederick. *Parading through History: The Making of the Crow Nation in America, 1805–1935*. New York: Cambridge University Press, 1995.

Hungry Wolf, Adolf. *The Blackfoot Papers, Volume One: Pikunni History and Culture*. Skookumchuck, B.C.: The Good Medicine Cultural Foundation, 2006.

Hungry Wolf, Beverly. *The Ways of My Grandmothers*. New York: William Morrow and Company, 1980.

Hurtado, Albert. "When Strangers Met: Sex and Gender on Three Frontiers." *Frontiers: A Journal of Women's Studies* 17, no. 3 (1996): 52–75.

Hyde, Anne. *Empires, Nations, and Families: A History of the North American West, 1800–1860*. Lincoln: University of Nebraska Press, 2011.

Hyde, George. *Indians of the High Plains: From the Prehistoric Period to the Coming of Europeans*. Norman: University of Oklahoma Press, 1959.

Innes, Robert. *Elder Brother and the Law of the People: Contemporary Kinship and Cowessess First Nation*. Winnipeg: University of Manitoba Press, 2013.

Innis, Harold Adams. *The Fur Trade in Canada: An Introduction to Canadian Economic History*. Rev. ed. Toronto: University of Toronto Press, 1999.

Isenberg, Andrew. *The Destruction of the Bison: An Environmental History, 1750–1920*. New York: Cambridge University Press, 2000.

Jablow, Joseph. *The Cheyenne in Plains Indian Trade Relations, 1795–1840*. New York: J. J. Augustin, 1951.

Jackson, John C. *By Honor and Right: How One Man Boldly Defined the Destiny of a Nation*. Amherst, N.Y.: Prometheus Books, 2010.

Johnson, Benjamin, and Andrew Graybill. "Borders and Their Historians in North America." In *Bridging National Borders in North America*, edited by Johnson and Graybill, 1–29. Durham, N.C.: Duke University Press, 2010.

Johnson, Walter. "List of Officers of the Territory of Montana to 1876." In *Contributions to the Historical Society of Montana*, vol. 1, 326–33. Helena, Mont.: Rocky Mountain, 1876.

————. "On Agency." *Journal of Social History* 37, no. 1 (Autumn 2003): 113–24.

Johnston, Alexander. *The Battle at Belly River: Stories of the Last Great Indian Battle*. Lethbridge: Historical Society of Alberta, 1966.

Josephy, Alvin. *The Nez Perce Indians and the Opening of the Northwest*. New Haven, Conn.: Yale University Press, 1965.

Judy, Mark. "Powder Keg on the Upper Missouri: Sources of Blackfeet Hostility, 1730–1810." *American Indian Quarterly* 11, no. 2 (Spring 1987): 127–44.

Kainayssini Imanistaisiwa: The People Go On. Directed by Loretta Sarah Todd. 2003. Ottawa: National Film Board of Canada, 2003. DVD.

Kehoe, Alice. "Blackfoot Persons." In *Women and Power in Native North America*, edited by Laura F. Klein and Lillian A. Ackerman, 113–25. Norman: University of Oklahoma Press, 1995.

————. "How the Ancient Peigans Lived." *Research in Economic Anthropology* 14 (1993): 87–103.

Kehoe, Alice, and Thomas Kehoe. "A Probable Late Blackfoot Clay Vessel." *The Plains Anthropologist* 6, no. 11 (February 1, 1961): 43–45.

Kennedy, Margaret A. *The Whiskey Trade of the Northwestern Plains: A Multidisciplinary Study*. New York: Peter Lang, 1997.

Krech, Shepard, ed. *Indians, Animals, and the Fur Trade: A Critique of "Keepers of the Game"*. Athens: University of Georgia Press, 1981.

LaDow, Beth. *The Medicine Line: Life and Death on a North American Borderland*. New York: Routledge, 2001.

Lamar, Howard. *Dakota Territory, 1861–1889: A Study of Frontier Politics*. New Haven, Conn.: Yale University Press, 1956.

Landals, Alison. "Horse Heaven: Change in Late Precontact to Contact Period Landscape Use in Southern Alberta." In *Archaeology on the Edge: New Perspectives on the Northwest Plains*, edited by Brian Kooyman and Jane H. Kelley, 231–62. Calgary, Alta.: University of Calgary Press, 2004.

Lansing, Michael. "Plains Indian Women and Interracial Marriage in the Upper Missouri Trade, 1804–1868." *Western Historical Quarterly* 31, no. 4 (Winter 2000): 413–33.

LaPier, Rosalyn. *Invisible Reality: Storytellers, Storytakers, and the Supernatural World of the Blackfeet*. Lincoln: University of Nebraska Press, 2017.

Lass, William. "The History and Significance of the Northwest Fur Company, 1865–1869." *North Dakota History* 61, no. 3 (Summer 1994): 21–40.

————. "The Northern Boundary of the Louisiana Purchase." *Great Plains Quarterly* 35, no. 1 (2015): 27–50.

Lecompte, Janet. "The Chouteaus and the St. Louis Fur Trade." In *A Guide to the Microfilm Edition of the Papers of the St. Louis Fur Trade*, edited by William Swagerty, xiii–xxii. Bethesda, Md.: University Publications of America, 1991.

————. "Pierre Chouteau, Junior." In *The Mountain Men and the Fur Trade of the Far West*, edited by LeRoy Hafen, vol. 9, 91–123. Glendale, Calif.: A. H. Clark, 1972.

Lee, Robert. "Accounting for Conquest: The Price of the Louisiana Purchase of Indian Country." *Journal of American History* 103, no. 4 (March 1, 2017): 921–42.

Lewis, David Rich, ed. "The WHA at Fifty: Essays on the State of Western History Scholarship." Special Issue, *The Western Historical Quarterly* 42, no. 3 (Autumn 2011): 287–423.

Mackie, Richard. *Trading beyond the Mountains: The British Fur Trade on the Pacific, 1793–1843*. Vancouver: University of British Columbia Press, 1997.

Maclean, John. "Blackfoot Mythology." *Journal of American Folklore* 6, no. 22 (1893): 165–72.

MacLeod, J. E. A. "Piegan Post and the Blackfoot Trade." *Canadian Historical Review* 24, no. 3 (September 1943): 273–79.

Majors, Harry. "John McClellan in the Montana Rockies 1807: The First Americans after Lewis and Clark." *Northwest Discovery* 2, no. 9 (November–December 1981): 555–630.

Malone, Michael, Richard Roeder, and William Lang. *Montana: A History of Two Centuries*. Rev. ed. Seattle: University of Washington Press, 1991.

Malouf, Carling. "Flathead and Pend d'Oreille." In *Plateau*, edited by Deward Walker, Jr., 297–312. Vol. 12 of *Handbook of North American Indians*. Washington, D.C.: Smithsonian Institution Press, 1998.

Mandelbaum, David G. *The Plains Cree: An Ethnographic, Historical, and Comparative Study*. 1940. Reprint, Regina, Sask.: Canadian Plains Research Center, 1979.

Marchildon, Gregory. *History of the Prairie West Series: Business and Industry*. Regina, Sask.: University of Regina Press, 2012.

Martin, Calvin. *Keepers of the Game: Indian-Animal Relationships and the Fur Trade*. Berkeley: University of California Press, 1978.

Mattison, Ray. "Kenneth McKenzie." In *The Mountain Men and the Fur Trade of the Far West*, edited by LeRoy Hafen, vol. 2, 217–24. Glendale, Calif.: A. H. Clark, 1965.

McClintock, Walter. *The Old North Trail: or, Life, Legends and Religion of the Blackfeet Indians*. London: Macmillan, 1910.

McDonnell, Michael. *Masters of Empire: Great Lakes Indians and the Making of America*. New York: Hill and Wang, 2015.

McManus, Sheila. *The Line Which Separates: Race, Gender, and the Making of the Alberta-Montana Borderlands*. Edmonton: University of Alberta Press, 2005.

McMillan, Alan D., and Eldon Yellowhorn. *First Peoples in Canada*. Vancouver: Douglas & McIntyre, 2004.

Merk, Frederick. *Manifest Destiny and Mission in American History: A Reinterpretation*. New York: Alfred A. Knopf, 1963.

Merrell, James. *The Indians' New World: Catawbas and Their Neighbors from European Contact through the Era of Removal*. Chapel Hill: University of North Carolina Press, 1989.

Meyer, David, and Paul C. Thistle. "Saskatchewan River Rendezvous Centers and Trading Posts: Continuity in a Cree Social Geography." *Ethnohistory* 42, no. 3 (Summer 1995): 403–44.

Middleton, Samuel Henry. *Kainai Chieftainship; History, Evolution and Culture of the Blood Indians [and] Origin of the Sun-Dance, with a Foreword by Viscount Alexander of Tunis*. Lethbridge, Alta.: Lethbridge Herald, 1952.

Miller, J. R. *Compact, Contract, Covenant: Aboriginal Treaty-Making in Canada.* Toronto: University of Toronto Press, 2009.

Milloy, John S. *The Plains Cree: Trade, Diplomacy and War, 1790 to 1870.* Winnipeg: University of Manitoba Press, 1988.

Milner, Clyde A., II, and Carol O'Connor. *As Big as the West: The Pioneer Life of Granville Stuart.* New York: Oxford University Press, 2008.

Moberly, Henry John. *When Fur Was King.* Toronto: J. M. Dent & Sons, 1929.

Morgan, Dale. *Jedediah Smith and the Opening of the West.* Lincoln: University of Nebraska Press, 1964.

———, ed. *The West of William H. Ashley: The International Struggle for the Fur Trade of the Missouri, the Rocky Mountains, and the Columbia, with Explorations beyond the Continental Divide, Recorded in the Diaries and Letters of William H. Ashley and His Contemporaries.* Denver: Old West, 1964.

Morris, Larry. "The Mysterious Charles Courtin and the Early Missouri Fur Trade." *Missouri Historical Review* 104, no. 1 (October 2009): 21–39.

Mountain Horse, Mike. *My People, the Bloods.* Calgary, Alta.: Glenbow-Alberta Institute, 1979.

Murphy, Robert, and Yolanda Murphy. "Northern Shoshone and Bannock." In *Great Basin,* edited by Warren L. d'Azevedo, 284–307. Vol. 11 of *Handbook of North American Indians.* Washington, D.C.: Smithsonian Institution Press, 1986.

Nichols, Roger. "The Arikara Indians and the Missouri River Trade: A Quest for Survival." *Great Plains Quarterly* 2, no. 2 (Spring 1982): 77–93.

Nicks, John. "Thompson, David (1770–1857)." *Dictionary of Canadian Biography.* Vol. 8. Toronto, Ont.: University of Toronto, 1985. Accessed June 23, 2018. http://www .biographi.ca/en/bio/thompson_david_1770_1857_8E.html.

Nicks, Trudy. "The Iroquois and the Fur Trade in Western Canada." In *Old Trails and New Directions: Papers of the Third North American Fur Trade Conference,* edited by Carol M. Judd and Arthur J. Ray, 85–101. Toronto: University of Toronto Press, 1980.

Nugent, David. "Property Relations, Production Relations, and Inequality: Anthropology, Political Economy, and the Blackfeet." *American Ethnologist* 20, no. 2 (May 1993): 336–62.

Nugent, Walter. *Habits of Empire: A History of American Expansion.* New York: Alfred A. Knopf, 2008.

Nute, Grace Lee. "Chouart des Groseilliers, Médard." *Dictionary of Canadian Biography.* Vol. 1. Rev ed. Toronto, Ont.: University of Toronto, 2016. Accessed October 25, 2016. http://www.biographi.ca/en/bio/chouart_des_groseilliers _medard_1E.html.

Oetelaar, Gerald. "The Archaeological Imprint of Oral Traditions on the Landscape of Northern Plains Hunter-Gatherers." In *The Oxford Handbook of North American Archaeology,* edited by Timothy R. Pauketat, 336–46. New York: Oxford University Press, 2012.

Oetelaar, Gerald, and D. Joy Oetelaar. "People, Places and Paths: The Cypress Hills and *Niitsitapi* Landscape of Southern Alberta." *Plains Anthropologist* 51, no. 199 (August 2006): 375–97.

―――. "The Structured World of the Niitsitapi: The Landscape as Historical Archive among Hunter-Gatherers of the Northern Plains." In *Structured Worlds: The Archaeology of Hunter-Gatherer Thought and Action*, edited by Aubrey Cannon, 64–94. New York: Routledge, 2011.

Oglesby, Richard Edward. *Manuel Lisa and the Opening of the Missouri Fur Trade*. Norman: University of Oklahoma Press, 1963.

Overholser, Joel. *Fort Benton: World's Innermost Port*. Fort Benton, Mont.: J. Overholser with Falcon Press, 1987.

Owram, Doug. *Promise of Eden: The Canadian Expansionist Movement and the Idea of the West, 1856–1900*. Toronto: University of Toronto Press, 1980.

Palladino, L. B. *Indian and White in the Northwest: or, A History of Catholicity in Montana*. Baltimore: J. Murphy, 1894.

Parks, Douglas. "Enigmatic Groups." In *Plains*, edited by Raymond J. DeMallie, pt. 2, 965–73. Vol. 13 of *Handbook of North American Indians*. Washington, D.C.: Smithsonian Institution Press, 2001.

Peck, Trevor, and J. Rod Vickers. "Buffalo and Dogs: The Prehistorical Lifeways of Aboriginal People on the Alberta Plains, 1004–1005." In *Alberta Formed, Alberta Transformed*, edited by Michael Payne, Donald Wetherell, and Catherine Cavanaugh, vol. 1, 55–86. Edmonton: University of Alberta Press, 2006.

Peers, Laura, and Alison K. Brown. *Visiting with the Ancestors: Blackfoot Shirts in Museum Spaces*. Edmonton, Alta.: Athabasca University Press, 2015.

Peterson, Jacqueline, with Laura Peers. *Sacred Encounters: Father De Smet and the Indians of the Rocky Mountains*. Norman: University of Oklahoma Press, 1993.

Podruchny, Carolyn. *Making the Voyageur World: Travelers and Traders in the North American Fur Trade*. Toronto: University of Toronto Press, 2006.

Podruchny, Carolyn, and Bethel Saler. "Glass Curtains and Storied Landscapes: The Fur Trade, National Boundaries, and Historians." In *Bridging National Borders in North America: Transnational and Comparative Histories*, edited by Benjamin Johnson and Andrew Graybill, 275–302. Durham, N.C.: Duke University Press, 2010.

Prucha, Francis Paul. *The Great Father: The United States Government and the American Indians*. Abridged ed. Lincoln: University of Nebraska Press, 1984.

Pyszczyk, Heinz W. "Historic Period Metal Projectile Points and Arrows, Alberta, Canada: A Theory for Aboriginal Arrow Design on the Great Plains." *Plains Anthropologist* 44, no. 168 (May 1, 1999): 163–87.

―――. "The Use of Fur Trade Goods by the Plains Indians, Central and Southern Alberta, Canada." *Canadian Journal of Archaeology* 21, no. 1 (January 1, 1997): 45–84.

Raczka, Paul. "Posted: No Trespassing: The Blackfoot and the American Fur Trappers." In *Selected Papers of the 2010 Fur Trade Symposium at the Three Forks*, edited by Jim Hardee, 140–48. Three Forks, Mont.: Three Forks Area Historical Society, 2010.

―――. "Traditions of Northern Plains Raiders in New Mexico." In *The Changing Ways of Southwestern Indians: A Historic Perspective*, edited by Albert Schroeder, 47–54. Glorieta, N. Mex.: Rio Grande Press, 1973.

―――. *Winter Count: A History of the Blackfoot People*. Brocket, Alta.: Oldman River Cultural Centre, 1979.

Ray, Arthur. *Indians in the Fur Trade: Their Role as Trappers, Hunters, and Middlemen in the Lands Southwest of Hudson Bay, 1660–1870*. Toronto: University of Toronto Press, 1974.

Ray, Arthur, and Donald B. Freeman. *"Give Us Good Measure": An Economic Analysis of Relations between the Indians and the Hudson's Bay Company before 1763*. Toronto: University of Toronto Press, 1978.

Reeves, Brian O. K. "Communal Bison Hunters of the Northern Plains." In *Hunters of the Recent Past*, edited by Leslie B. Davis and Brian O. K. Reeves, 168–94. London: Unwin Hyman, 1990.

Rensink, Brenden. *Native but Foreign: Indigenous Immigrants and Refugees in the North American Borderlands*. College Station: Texas A&M University Press, 2018.

Reséndez, Andrés. *The Other Slavery: The Uncovered Story of Indian Enslavement in America*. Boston: Houghton Mifflin Harcourt, 2016.

Rich, E. E. *The Fur Trade and the Northwest to 1857*. Toronto: McClelland and Steward, 1967.

Richards, Kent. *Isaac I. Stevens: Young Man in a Hurry*. Provo, Utah: Brigham Young University Press, 1979.

Richter, Daniel. *Facing East from Indian Country: A Native History of Early America*. Cambridge, Mass.: Harvard University Press, 2003.

———. *The Ordeal of the Longhouse: The Peoples of the Iroquois League in the Era of European Colonization*. Chapel Hill: University of North Carolina Press, 1992.

Rides at the Door, Darnell Davis. *Náápi Stories*. Browning, Mont.: Blackfeet Heritage Program, 1979.

Ronda, James. *Astoria and Empire*. Lincoln: University of Nebraska Press, 1990.

———. *Lewis and Clark among the Indians*. Lincoln: University of Nebraska Press, 1984.

Rushforth, Brett. *Bonds of Alliance: Indigenous and Atlantic Slaveries in New France*. Chapel Hill: University of North Carolina Press, 2012.

Russell, Dale. *Eighteenth-Century Western Cree and Their Neighbours*. Hull, Que.: Canadian Museum of Civilization, 1991.

Rzeczkowski, Frank. *Uniting the Tribes: The Rise and Fall of Pan-Indian Community on the Crow Reservation*. Lawrence: University Press of Kansas, 2012.

Sahlins, Marshall. *Stone Age Economics*. New York: Aldine, 1972.

Saunt, Claudio. "Go West: Mapping Early American Historiography." *William and Mary Quarterly* 65, no. 4 (2008): 745–78.

———. *West of the Revolution: An Uncommon History of 1776*. New York: W. W. Norton, 2014.

Schlesier, Karl. *The Wolves of Heaven: Cheyenne Shamanism, Ceremonies, and Prehistoric Origins*. Norman: University of Oklahoma Press, 1987.

Schultz, James Willard. *Signposts of Adventure: Glacier National Park as the Indians Know It*. Boston: Houghton Mifflin, 1926.

Secoy, Frank. *Changing Military Patterns on the Great Plains*. Locust Valley, N.Y.: J. J. Augustin, 1953.

Sharp, Paul. *Whoop-Up Country: The Canadian-American West, 1865–1885*. Minneapolis: University of Minnesota Press, 1955.

Shimkin, Demitri B. "Eastern Shoshone." In *Great Basin*, edited by Warren L. d'Azevedo, 308–35. Vol. 11 of *Handbook of North American Indians*. Washington, D.C.: Smithsonian Institution Press, 1986.

Shoemaker, Nancy. "A Typology of Colonialism." *Perspectives on History* 53, no. 7 (October 2015): 29–30.

Shurkin, Joel N. *The Invisible Fire: The Story of Mankind's Victory over the Ancient Scourge of Smallpox*. New York: G. P. Putnam's Sons, 1979.

Siebelt, Dagmar. *Die Winter Counts Der Blackfoot*. Münster, Germany: Lit-Verlag, 2005.

Silverman, David J. *Thundersticks: Firearms and the Violent Transformation of Native America*. Cambridge, Mass.: Harvard University Press, 2016.

Smith, Linda Tuhiwai. *Decolonizing Methodologies: Research and Indigenous Peoples*. New York: Zed Books, 1999.

Smyth, David. "Jacques Berger, Fur Trader." *The Beaver* 63 (June–July 1987): 39–50.

Smythe, Terry. *Thematic Study of the Fur Trade in the Canadian West, 1670–1870*. Ottawa: Historic Sites and Monuments Board of Canada, 1968.

Spector, Jane. *What This Awl Means: Feminist Archaeology at a Wahpeton Dakota Village*. St. Paul: Minnesota Historical Society Press, 1993.

Stevens, Hazard. *The Life of Isaac Ingalls Stevens*. 2 vols. Boston & New York: Houghton, Mifflin, 1900.

Sunder, John E. *The Fur Trade on the Upper Missouri, 1840–1865*. Norman: University of Oklahoma Press, 1965.

Swagerty, William R. "History of the United States Plains until 1850." In *Plains*, edited by Raymond J. DeMallie, pt. 1, 256–79. Vol. 13 of *Handbook of North American Indians*. Washington, D.C.: Smithsonian Institution Press, 2001.

———. "Indian Trade in the Trans-Mississippi West to 1870." In *History of Indian-White Relations*, edited by Wilcomb E. Washburn, 351–74. Vol. 4 of *Handbook of North American Indians*. Washington, D.C.: Smithsonian Institution Press, 1988.

Taylor, Alan. *American Colonies*. New York: Viking, 2001.

———. *The Divided Ground: Indians, Settlers and the Northern Borderland of the American Revolution*. New York: Alfred A. Knopf, 2006.

Taylor, Allan R. "Nonspeech Communication Systems." In *Languages*, edited by Ives Goddard, 275–89. Vol. 17 of *Handbook of North American Indians*. Washington, D.C.: Smithsonian Institution Press, 1996.

Taylor, John. "Two Views on the Meaning of Treaties Six and Seven." In *The Spirit of the Alberta Indian Treaties*, edited by Richard Price, 9–46. 3rd ed. Edmonton: University of Alberta Press, 1999.

Teit, James. "Salishan Tribes of the Western Plateau." *Annual Report of the Bureau of American Ethnology to the Secretary of the Smithsonian Institution* 45 (1927–28): 23–396.

Thistle, Paul. *Indian-European Trade Relations in the Lower Saskatchewan River Region to 1840*. Winnipeg: University of Manitoba Press, 1986.

Tough, Frank J. "Aboriginal Rights versus the Deed of Surrender: The Legal Rights of Native Peoples and Canada's Acquisition of the Hudson's Bay Company Territory." *Prairie Forum* 17, no. 2 (Fall 1992): 225–50.

Tovías, Blanca. "Diplomacy and Contestation before and after the 1870 Massacre of Amskapi Pikuni." *Ethnohistory* 60, no. 2 (March 20, 2013): 269–93.

Trachtenberg, Alan. *The Incorporation of America: Culture and Society in the Gilded Age.* Rev. ed. New York: Hill and Wang, 2007.

Treaty 7 Elders and Tribal Council, Walter Hildebrandt, Dorothy First Rider, and Sarah Carter. *The True Spirit and Original Intent of Treaty 7.* Montreal: McGill-Queen's University Press, 1996.

Trimble, Michael. *An Ethnohistorical Interpretation of the Spread of Smallpox on the Northern Plains Utilizing Concepts of Disease Ecology.* Lincoln, Neb.: J & L Reprint Company, 1979.

Turner, Frederick Jackson. *Rereading Frederick Jackson Turner: "The Significance of the Frontier in American History" and Other Essays.* Edited by John Mack Faragher. New York: Henry Holt, 1994.

Turney-High, Harry Holbert. *Ethnography of the Kutenai.* Menasha, Wisc.: American Anthropological Association, 1941.

Unrau, William. *White Man's Wicked Water: The Alcohol Trade and Prohibition in Indian Country, 1802–1892.* Lawrence: University Press of Kansas, 1996.

Unruh, John. *The Plains Across: The Overland Emigrants and the Trans-Mississippi West, 1840–1860.* Urbana: University of Illinois Press, 1979.

Utley, Robert. *The Indian Frontier of the American West, 1846–1890.* Albuquerque: University of New Mexico Press, 1984.

———. *A Life Wild and Perilous: Mountain Men and the Paths to the Pacific.* New York: Henry Holt, 1997.

Van Cleve, Charlotte Ouisconsin. "A Sketch of the Early Life of Malcolm Clarke." In *Contributions to the Historical Society of Montana,* vol. 1, 90–98. Helena, Mont.: Rocky Mountain, 1876.

Van Kirk, Sylvia. *Many Tender Ties: Women in Fur-Trade Society, 1670–1870.* Norman: University of Oklahoma Press, 1980.

Verbicky-Todd, Eleanor. *Communal Buffalo Hunting among the Plains Indians: An Ethnographic and Historic Review.* Occasional Paper No. 24, Archeological Survey of Alberta. Edmonton: Alberta Culture Historical Resources Division, 1984.

Vickers, J. Rod. "Cultures of the Northwestern Plains: From the Boreal Forest Edge to Milk River." In *Plains Indians, A.D. 500–1500: The Archaeological Past of Historic Groups,* edited by Karl H. Schlesier, 3–33. Norman: University of Oklahoma Press, 1994.

Vickers, J. Rod, and Trevor Peck. "Identifying the Prehistoric Blackfoot: Approaches to Nitsitapii (Blackfoot) Culture History." In *Painting the Past with a Broad Brush: Papers in Honour of James Valliere Wright,* edited by David L. Keenlyside and Jean-Luc Pilon, 473–97. Gatineau, Que.: Canadian Museum of Civilization, 2009.

Voget, Fred. "Crow." In *Plains,* edited by Raymond J. DeMallie, pt. 2, 695–717. Vol. 13 of *Handbook of North American Indians.* Washington, D.C.: Smithsonian Institution Press, 2001.

Walker, Deward, Jr. "Nez Perce." In *Plateau*, edited by Walker, Jr., 420–38. Vol. 12 of *Handbook of North American Indians*. Washington, D.C.: Smithsonian Institution Press, 1998.

Wallace, Anthony F. C. *The Death and Rebirth of the Seneca*. New York: Alfred A. Knopf, 1970.

Webb, Walter Prescott. *The Great Plains*. Boston: Gin and Company, 1931.

The West, Episode One: The People. Directed by Stephen Ives. 1996. Alexandria, Va.: PBS Video, 2003. DVD.

West, Elliott. *The Contested Plains: Indians, Goldseekers, and the Rush to Colorado*. Lawrence: University Press of Kansas, 1998.

———. *The Last Indian War: The Nez Perce Story*. New York: Oxford University Press, 2009.

———. *The Way to the West: Essays on the Central Plains*. Albuquerque: University of New Mexico Press, 1995.

Wheeler, Olin, ed. *The Trail of Lewis and Clark, 1804–1904: A Story of the Great Exploration across the Continent in 1804–6*. 2 vols. New York: G. P. Putnam's Sons, 1904.

White, Bruce M. "'Give Us a Little Milk': The Social and Cultural Meanings of Gift Giving in the Lake Superior Fur Trade." *Minnesota History* 48 (1982): 2–12.

White, Catherine. "Saleesh House: The First Trading Post among the Flathead." *Pacific Northwest Quarterly* 33, no. 3 (July 1, 1942): 251–63.

White, Elizabeth L. "Worlds in Collision: Jesuit Missionaries and Salish Indians on the Columbia Plateau, 1841–1850." *Oregon Historical Quarterly* 97, no. 1 (1996): 26–45.

White, Richard. *"It's Your Misfortune and None of My Own": A New History of the American West*. Norman: University of Oklahoma Press, 1991.

———. *The Middle Ground: Indians, Empires, and Republics in the Great Lakes Region, 1650–1815*. New York: Cambridge University Press, 1991.

———. *The Roots of Dependency: Subsistence, Environment, and Social Change among the Choctaws, Pawnees, and Navajos*. Lincoln: University of Nebraska Press, 1983.

———. *Western History*. Washington, D.C.: American Historical Association, 1997.

———. "The Winning of the West: The Expansion of the Western Sioux in the Eighteenth and Nineteenth Centuries." *Journal of American History* 65, no. 2 (September 1978): 319–43.

Williams, Glyndwr. "Ogden, Peter Skene." In *Dictionary of Canadian Biography*. Vol. 8. Toronto, Ont.: University of Toronto, 1985. Accessed May 12, 2014. http://www .biographi.ca/en/bio/ogden_peter_skene_8E.html.

Wilson, Edward F. "Report on the Blackfoot Tribes." In *Report of the Fifty-Seventh Meeting of the British Association for the Advancement of Science*, 183–200. London: John Murray, 1888.

Wilson, Jon E. "Agency, Narrative, and Resistance." In *The British Empire: Themes and Perspectives*, edited by Helen Gilbert and Chris Tiffin, 245–68. Malden, Mass.: Blackwell, 2008.

Wischmann, Lesley. *Frontier Diplomats: The Life and Times of Alexander Culbertson and Natoyist-Siksina'*. Spokane, Wash.: Arthur H. Clark, 2000.

Wise, Michael. *Producing Predators: Wolves, Work, and Conquest in the Northern Rockies*. Lincoln: University of Nebraska Press, 2016.

Wishart, David. *The Fur Trade of the American West, 1807–1840: A Geographical Synthesis*. Lincoln: University of Nebraska Press, 1979.

———. *Great Plains Indians*. Lincoln: University of Nebraska Press, 2016.

Wissler, Clark. "Ceremonial Bundles of the Blackfoot Indians." *Anthropological Papers of the American Museum of Natural History* 7, pt. 2 (1912): 69–288.

———. "Material Culture of the Blackfoot Indians." *Anthropological Papers of the American Museum of Natural History* 5 (1910): 1–175.

———. "Population Changes among the Northern Plains Indians." *Yale University Publications in Anthropology*, 1 (1936): 1–20.

———. "The Social Life of the Blackfoot Indians." *Anthropological Papers of the American Museum of Natural History* 7 (1911): 1–64.

Wissler, Clark, and D. C. Duvall. *Mythology of the Blackfoot Indians*. 1908. Reprint, Lincoln: University of Nebraska Press, 1995.

Witgen, Michael. *An Infinity of Nations: How the Native New World Shaped Early North America*. Philadelphia: University of Pennsylvania Press, 2012.

Wood, Gordon S. *Empire of Liberty: A History of the Early Republic, 1789–1815*. New York: Oxford University Press, 2009.

Wylie, Paul R. *Blood on the Marias: The Baker Massacre*. Norman: University of Oklahoma Press, 2016.

———. *The Irish General: Thomas Francis Meagher*. Norman: University of Oklahoma Press, 2007.

Yanicki, Gabriel M. *Old Man's Playing Ground: Gaming and Trade on the Plains/Plateau Frontier*. Ottawa: Canadian Museum of History and University of Ottawa Press, 2014.

Yellowhorn, Eldon. "The Never-Ending Journey of Anthony Henday," In *Alberta Formed, Alberta Transformed*, edited by Michael Payne, Donald Wetherell, and Catherine Cavanaugh, vol. 1, 87–110. Edmonton: University of Alberta Press, 2006.

Theses and Dissertations

Anderson, Kurt. "Illusions of Independence: The Teton Sioux and the American Fur Trade, 1804–1854." Ph.D. diss., Oklahoma State University, 2011.

Fox, Paulette. "Using Geographic Information Systems to Link Ecological Databases with Blackfoot Traditional Environmental Knowledge." M.S. thesis, University of Calgary, 2005.

Kennedy, Margaret. "A Whiskey Trade Frontier on the Northwestern Plains." Ph.D. diss., University of Calgary, 1991.

Hall, Ryan. "Blackfoot Country: The Indigenous Borderlands of the North American Fur Trade, 1782–1870." Ph.D. diss., Yale University, 2015.

Keyes, Sarah. "Beyond the Plains: Migration to the Pacific and the Reconfiguration of America, 1820s–1900s." Ph.D. diss., University of Southern California, 2012.

Klein, Alan Michael. "Adaptive Strategies and Process on the Plains: The Nineteenth-Century Cultural Sink." Ph.D. diss., State University of New York at Buffalo, 1977.

Morgan, R. Grace. "Beaver Ecology/Beaver Mythology." Ph.D. diss., University of Alberta, 1991.

Robert, Sheila. "The Negotiation and Implementation of Treaty 7, through 1880." M.A. thesis, University of Lethbridge, 2007.

Smyth, David. "The Niitsitapi Trade: Euroamericans and the Blackfoot-Speaking Peoples, to the Mid-1830s." Ph.D. diss., Carleton University, 2001.

Index

Page numbers in italics refer to illustrations and maps

moving camp, 32, 184–85n11
Mullan, John, 145
Mullan Road, 148
murders, 152
museums, 179
Musselshell River, 154

Náápi, 13–14, 17
náápiikoan, 4, 40
Nakoda. *See* Assiniboines
Natoyist-Siksina'. *See* Medicine Snake
   Woman
Navajos, 152
Nehiyaw. *See* Crees
Ne-tus-che-o. *See* Owl Child, Pete
neutral grounds, 72, 127, 136–38
Nevada City, 148
New Mexico, 31
newspapers, 151
Nez Percés, 24, 31, 58, 84–85, 99, 100,
   114, 121, 125, 134–36, 139
niitsáápiikoan, 40
Niitsitapi. *See* Blackfoot
Nimiipuu. *See* Nez Percés
North American history, 6
North Saskatchewan River, 16,
   45–46, 71–73, 86, 91, *105. See also*
   Saskatchewan River
North West Company (NWC), 46, 71,
   84–87, 91–92, 98, 150
northwest passage, 76
Numbered Treaties, 176
NWC. *See* North West Company (NWC)

Office of Indian Affairs, 131, 141,
   145–48, 153–54, 161
Office of the Superintendent of Indian
   Trade, 94
Ogden, Peter Skene, 89, 98–100
Okotoks, 18
Old Man. *See* Náápi
Old Person, Earl, 172
Old Sun, 112–13, 125, 158, 172, 176
Old Swan, 54–55, 73
Old Woman. *See* Kipitáaakii

Old Women's Society, 108
Oman, Mitchell, 45
Opened season, 21, 37
Ophir, 152, 157
Oregon Territory, 120
Oregon Trail, 83, 122
Osage, 114
Owen, John, 122, 141
Owl Child, Pete, 162–64, 167, 217n43

Pacific Fur Company (PFC), 83, 86
Parker, Ely, 164
parklands, 16
Paskoyac, 40
peace agreements, 1, 66, 73, 100–102,
   113, 129, 137–41, 177, 211n39
Peace Policy, 161
pemmican, 19, 49, 104, 123
Pend d'Oreilles, 23–24, 31, 34, 58, 71,
   84–85, 126, 134–35, 137, 139, 154
personal ties, with traders, 53
PFC. *See* Pacific Fur Company (PFC)
Piapot, 169–70
Picotte, Honoré, 113
Piegan Post, 103–4
Pierce, Franklin, 132
Pierre Chouteau, Jr., & Company. *See*
   Chouteau and Company
Piikani Nation reserve, 179
Piikanis: horse raids by, 56; origin of
   name, 15; rupture with Kainais, 103;
   territory of, 17
Pilcher, Joshua, 95
Pine Island Fort, 47, *47*, 55
Pink, William, 48
pisskans, 19–20
Plains sign language, 26, 66
plants, edible, 19
Platte River, 77
play-off system, 114
Point, Nicholas, 121, 122
poisons, wolf, 177
political resiliency, 7–8
Polk, James, 131
ponokáómitaa, 30

Two Medicine River, 65, 68, 200n37
Two Suns, 111

Umfreville, Edward, 35
United States: Alaska purchase, 168;
    annexation of territories, 168;
    assimilation to culture of, 133, 146;
    Blackfoot territory reduced in, 174;
    erosion of trust in, 147; expansion of,
    75–76, 91, 94–95, 100, 119–20,
    130–34, 142, 168; expulsion from
    Blackfoot territory, 79–82; history of,
    7; peace with Blackfoot, 90–91;
    relations with Blackfoot, 150–51;
    trappers, 78–79
Upham, Hiram, 156
Upper Missouri Outfit, AFC, 101
Upper Missouri River, 107–8. See also
    Missouri River
Upson, Gad, 148, 151, 153, 154, 156
U.S. See United States
used goods, trade in, 28
Utes, 35

vaccines, 108
Vaughan, Alfred, 141, 146, 150, 159
violence: alcohol and, 173; avoidance of,
    107–8; bands affected by, 70; chiefs
    and, 70; colonial expansion restricted
    by, 68; difficult times and, 27;
    domestic, 70; fur trade motivating,
    124; against government institutions,
    155; horse raids and, 34–35, 69;
    increase in, 4; perpetuation of, 69;
    between trading companies, 92.
    See also war
Violence over the Land (Blackhawk),
    201n38
Virginia City, 148

wagon trains, 122, 130
Walking Forward, 172
war: between British and French, 41–43;
    before European contact, 26; guns
    used in, 42; horse raids and, 69;
    horses used in, 33–34; Indian wars,
    152–53; songs, 69–70. See also
    violence
war chiefs, 22–23
War Department, U.S., 161
Washington, George, 41
Water world, 18–19
Western Department, AFC, 106
Wheeler, William, 164
whiskey. See alcohol
white bison robes, 141
White Buffalo Robe, 91
White Dog, 70
White Man's Horse, 129
White Striped Dog, 172
Wilkinson, James, 77
winter counts, 44, 85, 113, 119,
    127, 151
Wolf Calf, 67
wolf pelts, 48, 71, 75
wolf songs, 70
women: connections with traders,
    53–54; Manly-Hearted Women, 22;
    relations maintained by, 111; role in
    fur trade, 29; use of horses, 32;
    violence against, 70
Wright, George, 157

Yellowstone (steamboat), 144
Yellowstone River, 97, 154
Yellow Sun, 48
York Factory, 28–29, 39, 42, 45, 47
Young Man, 26, 30, 34, 42–43, 57, 59,
    72, 186n19, 189n8, 195n7